Economic Life in the Modern Age

Economic Life in the Modern Age

Werner Sombart

Nico Stehr & Reiner Grundmann
editors

Transaction Publishers
New Brunswick (U.S.A.) and London (U.K.)

This book is printed on acid-free paper that meets the American National Standard for Permanence of Paper for Printed Library Materials.

Library of Congress Catalog Number: 00-054381
ISBN: 0-7658-0030-6
Printed in the United States of America

Library of Congress Cataloging-in-Publication Data

Sombart, Werner, 1863-1941
Economic life in the modern age/Werner Sombart; Nico Stehr and Reiner Grundmann, editors.
p. cm.
Includes bibliographical references and index.
ISBN 0-7658-0030-6 (alk. paper)
1. Sombart, Werner, 1863-1941. 2. Economists—Germany—Biography. 3. Economic history—20th century. 4. Social history—20th century. 5. Capitalism—History—20th century. 6. Economics—History—20th century. I. Stehr, Nico. II. Grundmann, Reiner. III. Title

HB107.S75 A25 2001
330'.09'04--dc21 00-054381

Contents

Acknowledgements

We are grateful to the translators Gordon Gamlin and Paul Malone. We like to thank Robin Taylor for her competent and cheerful assistance in seeing the manuscript through production. Michal Bodemann, Volker Meja, Alan Sica, and Günter Büschges have commented on our introduction; their constructive suggestions and criticisms have improved the introduction. Our most important debt is to Volker Meja whose generous help in the initial stages of the conception of this volume was especially valuable. The book would not exist without his contribution.

Support to Nico Stehr from the Social Sciences and Humanities Research Council, Ottawa, Canada, is gratefully acknowledged.

Editorial Note

We have, in some places, tacitly corrected the style and conceptual errors found in previous editions of Sombart's translated work. However, in order to maintain the historical context and flavor, we have kept these alterations to a minimum. American spelling was adapted throughout the text. We left all the original comments by the editors and translators of earlier editions within footnotes (marked by *, †, —Ed. or —Trans.). We added our own marginal comments within footnotes marked #. Sombart's own notes are printed in endnotes.

Sources

I. The Nature of the Economic Market System

1. "Capitalism," in *Encyclopedia of the Social Sciences*, Edwin R. Seligman, Alvin Johnson (eds), vol. 3. New York: The Macmillan Company, 1930. 195-208.

II. The Diversity of Economic Actors and Motives

2. "The Origins of the Capitalist Spirit," in Sombart, *The Quintessence of Capitalism*. New York: Howard Fertig, 1967. 193-221.
3. "The Proletariat," (Originally published as "The Industrial Group") in *International Congress of Arts and Science*, Howard J. Rogers (ed.), vol. 7. London and New York: University Alliance, 1904. 791–799
4. "The Bourgeois—Past and Present," in Sombart, *The Quintessence of Capitalism*, translated by Mortimer Epstein. New York: Howard Fertig, 1967. 153–189.
5. "The Significance of the Jewish Religion in Economic Life," in Sombart, *The Jews and Modern Capitalism*, translated by Mortimer Epstein. New York: Collier Books, 1962. 187–237.

III. The Culture of Economic Phenomena and the Economy of Cultural Processes

6. "The City," in Sombart, *Luxury and Capitalism*, translated by W.R. Dittmar. Ann Arbor: The University of Michigan Press, 1967. 21–38.
7. "The Secularization of Love," in Sombart, *Luxury and Capitalism*. Ann Arbor: The University of Michigan Press, 1967. 42–57.
8. "Travel in Germany in 1800" (translation of "Eine Reise durch Deutschland vor hundert Jahren"), in Sombart, *Die deutsche Volkswirtschaft im neunzehnten Jahrhundert*. Berlin: Georg Bondi, 1912. 1–20.
9. "The Emergence of Fashion" (translation of "Wirtschaft und Mode," 1902). Reprinted in Silvia Bovenschen (ed.) *Die Listen der Mode*. Frankfurt: Suhrkamp, 1986. 81–104.

IV. The Interaction of Economy, Technology and Politics

10. "The Influence of Technical Inventions," in Sombart, *The Quintessence of Capitalism*. New York: Howard Fertig, 1967. 319–341.
11. "The Economic Life of the Future" (translation of "Das Wirtschaftsleben der Zukunft"), in Sombart, *Der moderne Kapitalismus*, vols. 3, 2. Munich and Leipzig: Duncker & Humblot, 1927. 1008–1022.
12. "Why is there no Socialism in the United States?" in Sombart, *Why is there no Socialism in the United States?*, translated by Patricia M. Hocking and C.T. Husbands. London and Basingstoke: The Macmillan Company, 1976. 3–24.
13. "Socialism and the Social Movement," in Sombart, *Socialism and the Social Movement*. London: J.M. Dent, 1909. 1–15, 279–287.

Introduction

Werner Sombart

Nico Stehr and Reiner Grundmann

During the first part of this century, Werner Sombart may well have been the most influential, most widely known, but also most controversial social scientist in Germany. In the words of rather divided voices in the United States during the same year, Sombart is the "nestor of German social sciences" (Neumann, 1939: 407) and one of the "most eminent living Nazified professors of social science" (Fosdick, 1939: 430). These divergent views show that the scholarly assessment and intellectual relation to Sombart inside and outside of Germany is strained, divided, and ambivalent.

Today he is among the least known social scientists, even though he left an enormous opus that spans disciplinary boundaries and was always somehow responsive to contemporary societal and political developments and personal troubles. Sombart is perhaps best known for his essay "Why is there no Socialism in the United States?" (Sombart, [1906] 1976; in this volume). Until this day, political scientists, historians, and labor specialists refer to the "Sombart question" when addressing the exceptional character of the American labor movement (e.g., Dubofsky, 1994: xvi; Lipset and Marks, 2000).

Nonetheless, Sombart presents us with a significant intellectual puzzle in the genealogy of modern social theorists: Why did he lose his status as one of the most influential scholars and intellectuals of the twentieth century? Why is his work almost forgotten today? After all, major social theorists rarely completely lose the stature they achieve during their lifetime. While Weber's thesis about the influence of Protestantism on the development of capitalism is widely known, even beyond sociological circles, few sociologists today know that Sombart had an alternative explanation. While many lay people not only know of a "Weber thesis" on the development of capitalism but also know what it says, few sociologists know of a "Sombart thesis," let alone what it says.

One might think that Sombart's initial unabashed support for the Nazi government ruined his post-war reputation. This simple logic is refuted by the post-war glory of another eminent German academic who became involved with fascism, Martin Heidegger. In order to examine the questions from above, we shall compare Sombart's fate to those of Weber and Heidegger.

Today, Werner Sombart inspires remarkably little empirical research on contemporary socio-economic and socio-political issues, and not much more on theoretical controversies. To be sure, a recent edition of "Sombart scholars" tries to affirm the importance of his work (Backhaus, 1996). There has been a vigorous debate about his Judaism thesis (Abraham, 1988; Mendes-Flohr, 1976; Mosse, 1979, 1987; Oelsner, 1962; Davis, 1999) and he still serves as source of inspiration for topics related to consumption and luxury in capitalism (Campbell, 1987; de Grazia, 1996; Mukerji, 1993; Roberts, 1998). Commentators seem to agree that only the latter is still a valid contribution. Overall, today Sombart, even in Germany, seems to have become only an object of passing historical interest where by necessity he is enumerated together with other (and what are evidently seen as more prominent) founding figures of sociology or other German thinkers of the Weimar period (e.g., Herf, 1984; Käsler, 1984; König, 1987a,b; Krause, 1962, 1969; Kruse, 1990; Lenger, 1994; Lübbe, 1974; Mitzman, 1973, 1985; Ringer, 1969; Röpke, 1945; Sieferle, 1995; Sontheimer, [1962] 1978).

During his lifetime, the situation was rather different.[1] He was held in high esteem by the grand old men of German sociology, above all Ferdinand Tönnies and Max Weber (with whom he was friends).

Sombart carried considerable weight in professional matters. Core sociology journals published countless major reviews of his books (see Appel, 1987). Everett C. Hughes, for example, described Sombart's volumes of *Der Moderne Kapitalismus* as a brilliant series. Against the critiques, he stresses the "keen and illuminating descriptions of economic processes sufficiently engaging to push contradictions into the dark nether regions of the subconscious" (Hughes, 1927/28: 501). W.H. Dawson, in a review of *Der proletarische Sozialismus*, calls the book a "clever, indeed brilliant, piece of dialectic, however one may judge the writer's arguments and conclusions." He also praises Sombart's style, which is concise and flowing, often vivacious and incisive, sometimes a little unorthodox, "but certainly never dull." This stands in "strong contrast to the typical German heavyweight *Gelehrte's* stolid and massive phraseology" (Dawson, 1927/28: 364). In 1930, Robert E. Park wrote a seven-page review of Sombart's *Die drei Nationalökonomien* for the *American Journal of Sociology*, in which he reflects extensively about problems of the social sciences in general and *verstehende Soziologie* in particular, without ever touching upon the content of Sombart's book. At the very end of the review he spells out what he thinks about it (Park, 1930/31: 1076–7):

> Sombart has cited something like 350 authors in the course of this brilliant and scholarly work. Some of them he damns utterly. With most of them he disagrees. In view of the unique character of his own work it seems that the world might have understood his purpose, point of view, and method somewhat better if he had written his personal confessions rather than a treatise on the logic of the social sciences.

Joseph Schumpeter said that *Modern Capitalism* "shocked professional historians by its often unsubstantial brilliance. They failed to see in it anything that they would call real research—the material of the book is in fact wholly second-hand" (Schumpeter, 1954: 816 fn). He attested to the book's artistic quality but hastened to add that it followed a primitive analytic scheme. In an earlier review, Schumpeter (1927: 349–50) acknowledged "the right of existence of this work is out of question. It most certainly does not belong to that limbo populated with the creations unfit for life which, unfortunately, we have to count among the costs of production of our work." He called the work "pioneering"—and compared Sombart with Marx. However, he also concluded that Marx was systematic and analytic, Sombart sketchy and impressionistic. In both reviews, Schumpeter recognizes the enormous amount of detailed evidence and the ambitious attempt to bring together many different disciplinary strands. However, and more importantly in our view, he dismisses Sombart's methodology as outdated: "Sombart's 'methodological' pronouncements followed fashions too closely to be interesting. At first he was duly contemptuous of those who 'drilled Robinson Crusoe'....When the wind changed he was anxious to be recognized as a theorist and took credit for having used, in spots, the 'deductive method'" (Schumpeter, 1954: 818).[2]

Ludwig von Mises, another noted economist, had nothing positive to say either. Although his judgment is tainted by his unfortunate experience with the German academic scene in the pre-Nazi period, he was especially outspoken about members of the historical school, which he accused of being

> always ready to turn with the wind. In 1918 most of them sympathized with the Social-Democrats; in 1933 they joined the Nazis. If Bolshevism had come to power, they would have become communists. Werner Sombart was the great master of this set. He was known as a pioneer in economic history, economic theory, and sociology. And he enjoyed a reputation as an independent man, because he had once aroused Kaiser Wilhelm's anger. Professor Sombart really deserved the recognition of his colleagues because to the greatest degree he combined in his person all their shortcomings. He never knew any ambition other than to draw attention to himself and to make money. His imposing work on modern capitalism is a historical monstrosity. He was always seeking public applause.

However, after this rant he adds: "And yet, it was more stimulating to talk to Sombart than to most other professors. At least he was not stupid and obtuse" (von Mises, 1978: 102–3).

It seems as if every commentator, whether for or against Sombart's intellectual accomplishment, is enthused by his writing style and his mastery of a vast array of historical material. If there is one word that comes up most often during his lifetime of assessment by peers, it is "brilliant."

Biography

Werner Sombart was born on January 19, 1863, in a small community in Prussia, the small city of Ermsleben near Merseburg with a population of about 3000 mostly Protestant inhabitants, and he died in Berlin on May 18, 1941. He was born into a liberal bourgeois family shaped, to some extent, by Calvinist traditions and beliefs. His father, Anton Ludwig Sombart (born 1816), was a self-made man who left a fortune to his four children at his death in 1898. Anton Sombart rose from surveyor to mayor of Ermsleben to successful businessman and politician. Only three years after his appointment as mayor, he started a new and successful career as an entrepreneur in the sugar industry, although he abandoned these business activities to move to Berlin in 1875, investing his money in a large Prussian farm. Anton Sombart was politically active and influential before and after he moved to Berlin; for example, he was a member of the Prussian and the German Parliament for the national liberal party and the *Verein für Sozialpolitik.*

Sombart obtained his doctoral degree under Gustav Schmoller in Berlin in 1888 with a brilliant dissertation on the Roman Campagna. Two years later, at the recommendation of Schmoller, but against the opposition of the faculty, he was appointed Associate Professor at Breslau. In 1896, he was elected to the Breslau city council. From 1906 on, Sombart taught at the newly founded *Handelshochschule* in Berlin where he became an even better known, well-to-do, and popular professor, public speaker, frequent contributor to journals, and generally influential figure. It was not until the end of the First World War when Sombart was in his mid-fifties that he became Full Professor in Berlin where he succeeded one of his teachers, Adolph Wagner, again despite formidable opposition. Arguably, political reasons—he was close to the socialists—as well as reactions to Sombart's personal lifestyle are mainly responsible for the slow advance in his career. Max Weber twice tried to get him appointed as his successor, first in Freiburg, later in Heidelberg (cf. Käsler, 1984: 426; Lenger, 1994: 115–18, 176).

In Berlin, he joined the circles of many of the most prominent artists, writers, and painters of the day. Some of the keys to Sombart's partly opportunistic ideas, which are at times at odds with each other, can be found in his personality, especially his urge to incessantly present himself in public and in private as a super-intellectual, scholar, politician, expert, and lover. Sombart was a star on the lecture circuit. His intense views of the shortcomings of modernity not only resonated with intellectual currents of the day but also appeared to have been a popular topic on which he lectured successfully to large audiences in many German cities and abroad. These well-paid lectures on "Culture and Individual," and later talks on Jews and the economy as well as the future of Jews, were arranged by agencies, and are reminiscent of the lecture tours and appearances of well-known politicians, media stars, and other celebrities today (cf. Lenger, 1994: 180–1).

This is not the place to engage in psychological speculations about Sombart. However, it seems plausible that his ambition to convince large audiences and his desire to play the role of a *prima donna* made him vulnerable in many directions. Above all, his drive towards recognition at any cost might explain his numerous *volte-faces.* He changed the circles from which he expected recognition several times during his career. As we have seen already, many observers remarked that he turned with the wind. However, as we shall see, he did sail against the wind in the first part of his career when he was stuck in Breslau and could not obtain a university chair. And is it plausible—as von Mises suggests—that Sombart would have turned communist if in Germany the Communist Party would have gained power in the 1930s, especially after he had converted from Marxism to a German nationalism? Is it not more likely that a certain mind-set dominated Weimar Germany that largely explains the adherence of many intellectuals and academics to the Nazi regime? We examine this question at length below.

In 1904 Sombart became an editor of the *Archiv für Sozialwissenschaft und Sozialpolitik,* along with Max Weber and Edgar Jaffé. Until its closure in 1933, the *Archiv* was the most influential German social science journal of the time.

Jaffé had bought the *Archiv* in 1903 from the previous editor Heinrich Braun, with whom Sombart had already collaborated. Sombart was quite active in the editorial work, and as an author, for the *Archiv*, at least during the first few years of his tenure as editor. The new editors promised continuity and published the journal along the established lines, which included an uncompromising commitment to capitalism as an irreversible outcome of the historical process that had to be accepted. However, the *Geleitwort* of the new editors also reflects a commitment to the analysis of the cultural significance of contemporary economic developments as well as the interdependence between race and economic processes.[3]

If one were to summarize his intellectual development, one could say that he radically changed his mind about two crucial issues: Marxism and Germany. He started out as a Marxist and an ardent fighter for the cause of the Socialist movement (cf. Sombart's essays "Capitalism," "The Proletariat," and "Socialism and the Social Movement," in this volume). This earned him the recognition of Friedrich Engels, who, in the supplement to the third volume of *Capital*, says that Sombart "gives an outline of the Marxian system which, taken all in all, is excellent. It is the first time that a German university professor succeeds on the whole in seeing in Marx's writings what Marx really says" (Engels, [1895] 1977: 893–4). In this period, Sombart did not try to reject or transcend Marx (e.g., Sombart, 1896: 72).[4] Instead, he attempted to complete the Marxian perspective by adding a socio-psychological and socio-cultural dimension to the analysis of the genesis and the nature of capitalism: "We want a psychological foundation of social events and Marx did not bother about it." The nature of the intentions of individual economic subject is a primary concern to Sombart (see also Sombart, 1902a: xviii).

After the turn of the century, Sombart became a fervent anti-Marxist, with some anti-Semitic overtones. His relation to Germany was marked by an equal shift of valuation: In his early writings, Sombart had many reservations about his country, but around 1910 he turned into a strident nationalist. His intellectual development can also be followed through different editions of the same book, *Sozialismus und soziale Bewegung* (cf. Epstein, 1941: 525). It first appeared in 1896 and was based on lectures delivered at Zürich; the English translation in 1909 (Sombart, [1896] 1909) was based on the sixth German edition (the book was translated into 24 languages). While the first nine editions were sympathetic to the Socialist movement, the tenth edition in 1924 revealed Sombart as a critic of Marx and Socialism. This edition had the title *Der proletarische Sozialismus (Marxismus)* (Sombart, 1924a, 1924b). In 1934 when the final edition of the book appeared, it was entitled *German Socialism* (*Deutscher Sozialismus*; Sombart, 1934b); Sombart did not mince words, explicitly favoring the rule of the Nazis and the ideology of the Nazi party. He dedicated the book to, and as written in the spirit of, "everything for Germany" (*Alles für Deutschland*). In his introduction, Sombart (1934b: xii) identifies his (scientific) task as that of a superior handmaiden for the existing political system. The specific purpose of the treatise is to provide a coherent analysis of contemporary social issues from the platform of national socialism (ibid.). Moreover, the function of a responsible science, as Sombart underlines in the same context, is not to discharge warm comfort but to enlighten. But Sombart's rhetoric of clarity, logic, and soberness almost always immediately comes into conflict with, and falls victim to, its opposite. He even vaguely speculates about a new and successful war that could significantly alter the composition of the German population and its boundaries, as well as the possibility that Germany will become a colony of its enemies.

The core of Sombart's book has been identified in the words: "For us there is only one aim—Germany. For the sake of Germany's greatness, power and glory, we will gladly sacrifice every 'theory,' and every 'principle,' whether it bears a liberal or any other stamp" (quoted by Fosdick, 1939: 429). Princeton University Press published an English translation of this book under the title *A New Social Philosophy* in 1937.

Going into more detail, we argue that Sombart's turn away from socialism was first accompanied with a similar turn against Germany (around 1903), to be followed by a return to Germany and taking issue with the Jews.[5] His disappointment with socialism was a consequence of his high and unfulfilled hopes in the proletariat's capacity to develop a community spirit in the course of class struggle (cf. "The Proletariat" in this volume). First cracks in this faith become visible around 1900 ("is the proletarian movement qualified to lead our capitalistic urban life to higher forms?"),[6] giving way to utter disillusionment in 1906. In this year Sombart published *Das Proletariat* (1906: 9–15) where he tries to sum up the characteristics of the proletarian by enumerating what such an individual is not (or, more precisely, is no longer): "like all city people, he [the proletarian] distinguishes himself from the earthbound, rooted, child of the land through the predominance of the understanding over the feeling and instinctual faculties....He is remote from nature and fantasy, rather he is abstract, rational and utilitarian" (quoted in Mendes-Flohr, 1976: 91). With the spiritual death of the working class, Sombart lost all hope for reconciling industrial civilization with *Volksgemeinschaft.* His consequent estrangement from industrial Germany is well documented in his book *Die deutsche Volkswirtschaft im Neunzehnten Jahrhundert,* published in 1903. There he points to the alleged link between the national character of the German people and the spirit of capitalism. "*Deutschtum* is responsible for the rise of capitalism. This conclusion left Sombart bitter and estranged from his people" (ibid.). While retaining his hostility towards capitalism, he would, however, slowly develop a 'strategy' of reconciliation with *Deutschtum*, Mendes-Flohr observed. Sombart achieves this by distinguishing between two types of capitalists: entrepreneurs and traders. This first appears in an article (1909), then in *Der Bourgeois* (1913a). The entrepreneur "has quick perception, sharp judgment on men and conditions, a keen sense of what is essential and a good memory" (see "The Bourgeois—Past and Present" in this volume). It would be a mistake to take this sort of person for a decadent man, Sombart tells us. Contrast this with the trader whose "intellectual and emotional world is directed to the money value of conditions and dealings, who therefore calculates everything in terms of money" (quoted in Mendes-Flohr, 1976: 92). Sombart identified this role as occupied by the "Jewish species."

Sombart constantly dwelled upon the topic of racial categories. It was thus no surprise that he welcomed the Nazis' rise to power, whose chief ideologue he thought himself to be—a feeling that was not reciprocated. In addition, one must conclude, he was naïve at that, given that Sombart, even in his most Nazified book (Sombart, [1934] 1937), repeatedly mentions Marx as intellectual authority. Even after he had turned away from Marxism, Sombart characterizes his relationship to Marx in the following way (Sombart, [1925] 1927: xviii):

> However bluntly I reject the *Weltanschauung* of the man...I admire him unreservedly as a theorist and historian of capitalism...and it was his great talent to know how to approach it. In his genial problematic he gave economic science a path of fruitful research for a century. All social economists who did not take up this problematic were doomed to sterility.[7]

Every Nazi must have been bewildered by the idea that Germany should be a product of Jewish activity and that Marx was a hero. Given these oddities, from a Nazi's viewpoint, it probably did not matter much that Sombart professed to believe in the principle of leadership with the *Führer* receiving his directions only from God (Sombart, [1934] 1937: 194).

Main Works

Der moderne Kapitalismus, first published in two volumes in 1902 and re-issued from 1916 to 1928 in a much-enlarged second edition (e.g., Sombart, [1916] 1921a, 1928), was Sombart's most important scholarly work. In this book, he first introduces the concept of capitalism into the academic discourse (Robbins, 1999). At least some of his contemporary social scientists praised the work as a classical and therefore definitive analysis of the origins and the nature of capitalism (e.g., Alfred Weber, [1935] 1950: 375).

Sombart (1902a: ix–xxxiv) uses his introduction to *Der moderne Kapitalismus* to advance a kind of methodological and epistemological manifesto for a modern social science. Feeling uneasy with the "historical school" in economics from which he started, he came to differ from the older generation, e.g., his teacher Schmoller, in that he aimed for explanations based on ultimate causes. For Sombart, historical appearances built up to a social system that can be grasped by theory (and here he mentions explicitly the theory of Marx, see Sombart, 1902a: xxix). However, he still considers himself a member of the historical school. Talcott Parsons essentially shares this judgment, since Sombart did not follow the intellectual agenda of Marx's base-superstructure theorem in which productive forces are the most basic layer in society, upon which relations of production are erected and are, in turn, overlaid with an ideological sphere.[8] In Marx, the primacy is with the former two, in Sombart, with the last—he gives definite priority to the spirit. Parsons is thus right to say that Sombart has "assimilated the main content of Marx into the framework of historicoidealistic [sic] thought" (Parsons, [1937] 1949: 495).

Technology

Sombart addressed the question of the role of *technology* in society repeatedly and at length, and for the most part, he subscribes to a rather conventional conception of technology that sees technological artifacts as instruments or means of social action. In fact, Sombart refers to technology, narrowly, as the production of instruments, particularly in the productive sphere ([1910] 1911: 64; 1913a: 413), or, somewhat more broadly, as a means toward the realization of a specific goal (e.g., [1910] 1911: 63–4). At this time, Sombart's discussion of the function of technology is almost always descriptive; perhaps his discussion is even a bit impatient because the ubiquitous influence of technology on most social and economic activities is quite obvious. Sombart (e.g., ibid., 76–8) rejects a materialist interpretation of history that asserts that the economy is a function of technology and culture a function of the economy. He opposes such a narrow conception because there is neither the absolute necessity that a specific technology is in fact always realized nor that a particular technology results in a certain and only a certain form of economic organization; for example, a technology specific to a capitalist economy does not exist.[9] Similarly, direct links between technology and culture are multiple and extremely varied. In other words, there is at this juncture not a single assessment of the societal role of technology that would justify the conclusion that Sombart views technology from the perspective of an engaged cultural critic implicating, as it were, technology in the demise of traditional social and cultural relations and values.[10]

In a rare and uncharacteristic moment of a self-deprecation, Sombart ([1910] 1911: 63; 1912a: 305) comments that his performance during the Meetings of the German Sociological Association must have been dismal since his lecture was not understood, as the discussion demonstrated to him, and was likely incomprehensible because it was poorly formulated. He feels compelled to re-assign the topic to himself and publishes another essay on "Technology and Culture" in 1912 in the *Archiv*.

The *Archiv* essay repeats the position outlined in his lecture in 1910, though he attempts to provide some additional illustrative material, in particular, on his initially terse comments on the impact of technology on music. He devotes some six pages of the essay to a discussion of the relation of technology to the various aspect of modern music life. In this context, some of his remarks can be read as disparaging, particularly about the "destructive" force of technological progress in the last century, about the city as wasteland, or that modern haste and noise prompt a kind of music that itself is tough, cold, and without life. Whether such observations are cultural critique (cf. Lenger, 1994: 163), or whether they also are productive questions for a sociology of music (in the sense that music reflects its time and place), is indeed a matter of perspective. In any event, Sombart offers, in these oral and written publications intended for a "scientific" audience, an effort towards a balanced assessment of the social and intellectual consequences of technology. After all, it is here too that Sombart (1912a: 347) talks, and not ironically as far as we can tell, about the immensely beneficial consequences of technology, for example, with respect to democratization processes in modern society.

"*Methodenstreit*"

Several founding figures of German sociology attempted to reconcile historical-empirical and theoretical tasks (Kruse, 1990). Besides Sombart, the outstanding figures were Max and Alfred Weber and Franz Oppenheimer. Ultimately, Max Weber's approach based on "ideal types" became widely known, if not dominant.[11]

Going beyond the historicists' agenda and trying to explicate his method, Sombart suggests that the nature of the modern economy, that is, the extent to which it is increasingly driven by individual decisions and market forces rather than imposed regulations, demands a causal rather a teleological perspective. Although claiming that social science should not follow a teleological perspective, he does not always obey this methodological rule. As his essay on the Jews (in this volume) makes clear, he uses functionalist arguments:

> Such then was one result of the family life current among Jews and introduced by them. The man contributed to it the best that was in him, and in return he drew from it invigorating strength, courage, and an inducement to maintain and to expand his position in life. Family life of this kind generated centers for masculine energy large enough to set in motion such a mighty economic system as capitalism. For this system calls for great energy, and we can scarcely imagine it being produced except through the agency of psychological influences which appeal not only to the social instincts but also to the family ideal.

Likewise, in his piece on the United States he states: "One can truly say that if one wanted to construct the ideal country for the development of capitalism on the lines required by this economic system, such a country could take on the dimensions and particular characteristics only of the United States" (see "Why is there no Socialism in the United States?" in this volume).

Sombart stipulates that causal social relations are limited in terms of time and place (i.e., every distinctive economic period requires its own theoretical elaboration). From this it follows that they can only be established as restricted regularities not to be confused with universal law-like natural processes. He therefore claims that the nature of the contemporary subject matter leaves no choice to the observer.[12] In addition, the "final" cause of social regularities has to be found in webs of motives espoused by living human beings within specific contexts. Given the complexity (*Mannigfaltigkeit*) of social existence, the observer must concentrate on those motives that are central and not marginal.[13] According to Sombart, it would be foolish to reduce the complex motives that drive economic activity to the acquisitive motive. Instead, various motives as principles of economic activity assert themselves in different periods. Motives correspond to a certain economic order and generate in combination an economic system. In addition to various motives of individual and corporate actors, Sombart (1902a: xxiv–xxv) identifies "objective" conditions as sources of economic action that include and extend to natural or absolute conditions. Among the latter, Sombart counts the environment, race, and technical skills.

Sombart insists that the distinction between economic system (*Wirtschaft*) and economic organization (*Betrieb*) is basic to his discussion of the origins and the nature of modern capitalism (1902a: 3–8). In as much as this book was originally on "Capitalism and craftsmanship," the distinction is indeed important. Economic motives are realized within the confines of producing organizations. Producing organizations manage communal work. Thus, work takes place within the boundaries of economic enterprises and business organizations. However, enterprises and business organizations do not always stand in a symmetric relation to economic systems since certain organizational forms may promote different economic principles while different economic motives may be realized within different organizational settings. More specifically, craft-based enterprises may still exist in capitalist systems. In fact, Sombart devotes a long chapter to an analysis of the decline (but not the disappearance) in the sense of a loss of independence and autonomy of craft-based organizations in nineteenth-century Germany. Craft based enterprises that converted to the capitalist spirit were able to survive as more independent business organizations.

Noo-sociology

One of the peculiar notions in Sombart's writing that has found few, if any, followers is his notion of a *noo-sociology* and therefore a noological approach to social phenomena. In an introduction to what might well be considered one of the first "readers" (of classical theoretical texts) within German sociology, Sombart (1923: 13) defines the methodological basis for a noological approach within sociology as a variant of the method of understanding directed more specifically toward an understanding of spiritual phenomena (*Geist-verstehen*). Such an approach not only differs from attempts to comprehend phenomena connected to the "soul" but from any Newtonian "naturalistic-psychological" sociology. It is worth noting that Sombart (1923: 11) calls the latter "western" and the former, the noological approach, "German" sociology.

A noological sociology is based on the premise that all society is spirit (*Geist*) and all spirit, society.[14] Its fields of investigation are forms and cycles of civilization. Its methods, therefore, cannot be those of the natural sciences. It is committed to emergent social phenomena that must be understood and placed in restrictive socio-historical and institutional contexts, for example, religion, the state, the church, the economy, etc. In line with Max Weber's methodological prescriptions, Sombart's noological sociology does not recognize general concepts as useful and employ them, nor does it aim to produce general laws. It endorses and attempts to understand the uniqueness of historical phenomena. As a "theory of understanding," it has to avoid the Scylla of metaphysics and the Charybdis of naturalism, as Neumann (1939: 408) aptly put it.

In the introduction to *Vom Menschen*: *Versuch einer geisteswissenschaftlichen Anthropologie* (*About Man*: *Toward a Humanistic Anthropology*),[15] published just three years before his death, Sombart characterizes his last book as an effort to disclose not so much, as one might say today, the social construction of society (in the sense of human history and culture) but the natural foundations of the existence of man. Another way of characterizing Sombart's basic point of departure in this treatise would be to say that his "philosophical anthropology" is written from the perspective of nature or the natural environment rather than human existence, as is the case for the better known contributions to philosophical anthropology by Helmut Plessner and Arnold Gehlen.[16] Or, as Sombart (1938b: xix) puts it, his subject is a discussion of human being (*Sein des Menschen*) rather than human creation (*Tun*), while disregarding, as he emphasizes, the conventional intellectual division of labor in science. Sombart anticipates to address the latter, an analysis of the human action, in a later study. The "final" foundations and conditions for human culture and history are the human being itself and its natural environment. Clearly then, an anthropological examination of the "substructure" of human existence requires urgently and foremost not a natural scientific but a humanistic (*geisteswissenschaftliche*) analysis of the interaction between physical milieu and human being. Indeed Sombart's *Vom Menschen* tries to provide such a theoretical framework. It is questionable whether such an effort leads toward a new science, a basic science inspiring all branches of the human sciences, as Sombart would have liked.

Race

In his book *Vom Menschen*, written under the Nazi Regime and published in 1938, Sombart offers a number of explicit comments about the usefulness of the concept of "race" in the kind of social science he advocates. One has to distinguish between epistemological and methodological comments and Sombart's substantive use of the notion of race in this book.

Undoubtedly, Sombart's programmatic statement on anthropological approaches, based on the idea of the ubiquity and the uniqueness of the spirit in humans that continually affirms the independent importance (*Eigenständigkeit*) of motives in human action, can be read as a polemic and critique of the vague and therefore unscientific notion of *Volk*: "One has to realize that there are two different lessons about people: one is to tell fairy tales about the people, or to write novels about it, the other to put the people into a scientific system. If you do not make this distinction, you are guilty of an untruthful mixing" (Sombart, 1938b: 163, our translation). On the other hand, in 1935 Sombart does not indicate any difficulties with the term *Volk* and *Volksgeist* (in a treatise surely not accidentally pulled from his *Deutscher Sozialismus* as a separate booklet and entitled *Was ist deutsch*?). After detailing, in the manner of conventional empirical social research, some of the attributes of contemporary German society, he quickly moves onto the royal road of metaphysics and into the heavens of bright ideas, as he calls it. It is in this superior environment that Sombart—although he does not rage against all that is "foreign"—employs strong language to encourage his audience to stamp out all that is diseased and inferior (*gemein*) from the German spirit (Sombart, 1935: 38).

However, for events in this instance and particularly in the case of his stance toward the notion of race, matters are more complicated. It would appear that Sombart at times fails to heed his own warnings about the disastrous pitfalls of racist observations and terminology; he attributes "weak" or "strong" type of conduct to a collectivity in the most undifferentiated manner. In the process, he comes close to endorsing what he emphatically rejects elsewhere, namely the idea that racial or "völkische" attributes are real constraints of human action and even allow for a ranking of collectivities. Such ranking, of course, amounts to a reification of the notion of "Volk" which Sombart vehemently rejects elsewhere as unscientific: "Strong peoples are more affected by the milieu than weak peoples. Thus strong peoples (German tribes!) decay more quickly in a hostile environment than weak ones, but in a friendly environment are culturally more productive than weak ones: think of the transformation of North America" (Sombart, 1938b: 401, our translation).

Sombart stipulates that the crucial usage of the term "race," despite the infinite range of differences among individuals that are human cognitive and cultural manifestations, may be traced to and based on bodily or biological features (cf. Sombart, 1938b: 346). He calls such a notion an abstract working hypothesis, a regulative idea in the human sciences similar to the notion of a geographic, economic, or erotic hypothesis invoked as means of understanding certain manifestations of human conduct. And, Sombart adds affirmatively, the race concept, if understood as a working hypothesis may indeed serve significant purposes in the humanities in general and in a humanistic anthropology in particular, and he fails to see why any serious scholar would refuse to employ the race hypothesis in the sense specified.

However, he explicates the methodological status of the race hypothesis in greater detail and suggests for example that it should always be a hypothesis of last resort after all other attempts to understand have been exhausted. He hints also that the race hypothesis cannot, in the final analysis, offer any genuine understanding. Instead, such accounts if invoked must admit that they confront mysterious phenomena, because as Sombart emphasizes as one of the basic epistemological premises of the social sciences, the development of the individual must be seen to be the outcome of "freedom" and not "necessity" (Sombart, 1938b: 381).

Sombart differentiates further and argues that the race working hypothesis offers different insights depending on the following three conditions: If (1) the peoples examined are particularly "primitive"; (2) phenomena of mass behavior are involved, and (3) the conduct in question is close to material phenomena, then the race hypothesis acquires greater validity.

According to Sombart (1938b: 347), objection against the usage of the term race in social sciences arises once the concept refers to a personalized corporate actor that performs specific roles and functions: "Acting, creating, vital collectivities are always crowds, tribes, peoples." Although Sombart consistently rejects the use of the notion of race or *Volk* as the master concept and as the sole explanatory attribute in philosophical anthropology as well as the idea of a natural racial hierarchy as *unscientific*, nonetheless, he frequently refers to the concept of *race* in an affirmative as well as ambivalent manner. What is more, in the context of a polemic against abandoning the notion of race in the human sciences altogether, he confidently enumerates the knowledge gains when employing the concept of "race." To be sure, he unambiguously designates all attempts to establish a causal connection between biological and cultural attributes and/or a structure of inequality based on racial attributes as mere opinion and therefore unscientific. But surprisingly, he concludes: "The more the racial concept is abused the more we should try to bring out its healthy kernel and thus justify its existence, and, what is more, its fruitfulness in the research context of the social sciences and humanities" (Sombart, 1938b: 348–9).

Sombart thereby advocates a dangerous path for social science. Although he points out several qualifications that scholars should observe when employing the race concept, they are put into question by the reductionist drive inherent in such notions as race and racially based conduct. In that sense, Sombart's efforts were futile and provided only limited legitimization for some scholars to endorse the virtue of the race hypothesis. Even more important is Sombart's precise use of the race hypothesis elsewhere in the same book. It could easily be seen to undermine, even contradict, his cautious advice about the limited scholarly virtues of the working hypothesis in attempts to arrive at an understanding of specific features of human conduct.

References to, comments, and observations about race and racial attributes abound in Sombart's earlier writings. In the context of these writings, he is apparently much less cautious, aware that his exposition in fact amounts to a promulgation of a racist ideology. For example, his comments describing followers of socialism, and about racially mixed individuals who are invariably, that is, naturally endowed with imbalanced personalities, are undoubtedly of such dubious quality (Sombart, 1924a: 76).

Sombart: A Reactionary Modernist?

Jeffrey Herf (1984) characterizes Sombart, along with Ernst Jünger, Oswald Spengler, Hans Freyer, Carl Schmitt, and Martin Heidegger, as one of the main intellectual architects of what he terms "reactionary modernism."[17] The term, an ideal type, is designed to capture the paradoxes of embracing in conservative thought both the manifestations of technological advance and a romanticized version of pastoral life, while using a core of emotionally appealing metaphors and codes to reject most other features of the enlightenment or modernity, especially its main cultural achievements and political institutions.[18] Reactionary modernism joins backward- and forward-looking elements, namely progressive technology and regressive culture. The reactionary modernists were "nationalists who turned the romantic anti-capitalism of the German Right away from backward-looking pastoralism, pointing instead to the outlines of a beautifully new order replacing the formless chaos due to capitalism in a united, technologically advanced nation" (Herf, 1984: 2).

In Germany, reactionary modernism was based on support for industrial development and rejection of liberal democracy, and it became a major ideological platform of the Nazi regime. With regards to Sombart, the question requiring re-examination is of course whether he fits Herf's description of reactionary modernists and therefore the ideological *Wegbereiter* of the Nazis, or whether Sombart in the end aligns himself more closely with those conservative and fundamentalist reactions to the Enlightenment that rejected the forces of modernization *tout court.*[19]

Consider the following quote from "Travel in Germany" (see "Travel in Germany in 1800" in this volume):

> The old German culture as it was still basically maintained in the beginning of the nineteenth century had actually derived from this ideal of a forest; the murmuring brook, the rustling oak tree are synonymous of the German soul, which in those very days when our imagination travels through the German countryside created the romantic notion of the magic "blue flower." The sensitive, the fragile, the feelings of dread, the deep sentimental disposition and whatever else differentiates the Germans from all other nations: Its primary cause lies in the forest, in the untended wild grown forest, where the birds sang in the bushes during springtime, where fog moved across clearings in the fall. But also the material culture of the Nordic countries is rooted in the forest before iron and other inorganic matter created a new culture.

Reactionary modernists such as Ernst Jünger[20] or Gottfried Benn embrace both technological progress and certain modernist aesthetic tendencies while rejecting reason and its institutional accomplishments and safeguards in political and social affairs more or less wholesale.[21] However, Sombart leaves little room for ambivalence and interpretation. He becomes a proponent of the natural and mythic precapitalist conditions of life and an ardent foe of the artificial form of life of capitalism and the conditions for its possibility, including modern technology. The rural conditions of a natural, living *Gemeinschaft* constitute much more desirable conditions of social existence than those of the artificial *Gesellschaft.*[22] The relatively objective conceptual apparatus concerned with the origins of capitalism becomes *Zivilisationskritik* and is driven by anti-capitalism and anti-modernism rhetoric. The relatively detached analysis of capitalism is followed by an emotional lament over capitalism.

Stefan Breuer has argued that one can identify a "German" line in sociology. His main criterion for setting up this category is the Germans' romantic criticism of capitalist rationality, the utility principle, and the lament over the breaking up of community bonds. Main figures like Tönnies, Scheler, Sombart, and even Simmel belong to this group while Max Weber stands apart. Unlike them, Weber did not welcome the First World War as a chance for redemption from fragmentation and alienation by means of German heroism, and what seems even more important, he defended liberal democracy and its institutions (Breuer, 1996: 241; Liebersohn, 1988).

In what follows, we illustrate some characteristic traits of Sombart's anti-modernist thought. Among them are his rejection of quantification, of trading, and, correspondingly, his longing for a golden age that has passed.

Sombart against Quantification

The Louisiana Purchase Exposition in St. Louis in 1904 brought a number of prominent German social scientists to the United States. Sombart joined Max Weber, Ferdinand Tönnies, Ernst Troeltsch, Karl Lamprecht, and others in presenting lectures during the "Congress of Arts and Science" that accompanied the exhibition. Sombart's (1904) lecture during the Exhibition under the somewhat misleading title "The Industrial Group" tried to hastily sketch a portrait of the modern proletariat. Nonetheless, Sombart's acquaintance with the United States prompted him to assemble a wide range of information about the American working class that culminated in the famous study *Warum gibt es in den Vereinigten Staaten keinen Sozialismus?*[23] In this classic essay, Sombart (in this volume) writes:

> We therefore see in every American—beginning with the paperboy—restlessness, yearning, and compulsion to be way and beyond other people. Neither the enjoyment of life in comfort to the full nor the fine harmony of a personality at peace with itself can be the American's ideal in life; instead, this ideal is constant self-advancement. From this follow haste, restless striving, and ruthless competition in all areas, since, when all individuals are bent on success, each must aim to come ahead of the rest. Thus there begins what one might call a steeplechase, or a search for Good Fortune, as—in somewhat superficial manner—we are wont to express it. However, this steeplechase is different from all other races because the winning-post does not stay still but forever retreats farther ahead of the advancing runners.

The reason why there is no socialist movement in the United States is partly explained by the emotional link the workers have to their capitalist economy: "I believe that emotionally the American worker has a share in capitalism; I believe that he loves it."

In this essay, Sombart clearly expresses his disdain for quantification in modern life:

> The estimation of size in terms of numbers has been able to take root in man's heart only through the medium of money as employed by capitalism....The huge dimensions of the American continent have certainly encouraged this characteristic, but the feeling for numbers had first of all to be awaked before it was possible to transform geographical ideas into sizes comprehensible in numerical terms.

Sombart against Trading and Merchandising

Even more intriguing is Sombart's characterization of economic actors as either 'traders' or 'heroes.' Both are used as opposites and the choice of terms makes it clear from the outset where his (everyone's) sympathies lie:

> Trader and hero: they constitute the two great opposites, the two poles, as it were, of all human orientation....The trader approaches life with the question: what can you give me....The hero approaches life with the question: what can I give you? He wants to give many things away, to spend himself, to make sacrifices—without a return....The trader speaks only of "rights," the hero only of his duties. [The trader] regards the whole existence of man on earth as a sum of commercial transactions which everyone makes as favorably as possible for himself....The profit which is expected to result for the life of each individual is as much well-being as possible....Within this conception of life, material values will thus be given an important place....Economic and especially commercial activity will achieve honor and respect. Consequently, economic interest will...gradually subordinate the other aspects of life. Once the representatives of the economy have the upper hand in the country, they will easily transfer the attitudes of their profession to all sectors of life...until the trader's world view and practical commercialism finally join together in an inseparable unity, as is the case in England today (Sombart, *Händler und Helden, Patriotische Besinnungen* 1915, quoted after Ringer, 1969: 183–4).

As Hayek observed, "War is to Sombart the consummation of the heroic view of life, and the war against England is the war against the opposite ideal, the commercial ideal of individual freedom and English comfort" (Hayek, 1944: 159).

Sombart made the distinction between trader and hero under the spell of wartime patriotism and hatred. However, the conceptual basis of the distinction had been laid earlier. As noted above, it is basically the distinction between two types of capitalists: entrepreneurs and traders. In *The Quintessence of Capitalism* ([1913] 1915, the translation of *Der Bourgeois*), Sombart states (see "The Origins of the Capitalist Spirit" in this volume):

> What peoples may be described as under-inclined to capitalism? I should say the Celts and a few of the Germanic tribes, the Goths in particular. Wherever the Celtic element predominated capitalism made little headway....The capitalist spirit in Europe was cultivated by a number of races, each with different characteristics of its own, and that of these races the Trading peoples (Etruscans, Frisians, and Jews) may be divided off from those we have termed Heroic....The Scotch, the Jews, the Frisians, and Etruscans are trading peoples, the Celts and the Goths heroic people. Since the Jewish spirit is capitalistic, and the English are said to possess the capitalist spirit, they also possess the Jewish spirit.

In his *Deutscher Sozialismus* (1934b), he draws to a close: "What we have characterized as the spirit of this economic age...is in many respects a manifestation of the Jewish spirit...which dominates our entire era." To rid mankind of this spirit, "the institutional culture" must be so transformed that "it will no longer serve as a bulwark for the Jewish spirit" (quoted in Harris, 1942: 813).

Sombart's "Kulturkritik"

Sombart speculates whether there has ever been an optimum balance in the relation between the forces of the natural and human environment and the individual. He concludes that there have been such periods in human history, most recently the sixteenth, the seventeenth, and part of the eighteenth century in Western Europe. During this period "there existed the greatest number of autonomous and extraordinary personalities" (Sombart 1938b: 402). However, soon thereafter, with the quantitative growth of culture, a rapid decline set in and the intellectual environment began to suppress and level down individual expressions.

Sombart's *Kulturkritik* amounts to a celebration of, and peculiar longing for, pre-industrial and pre-modern forms of life incapable of transcending themselves and a kind of modern fundamentalism about the failings of modernity, in which its whole development right up to the present is seen as a sin against the immobile pre-modern order of society and nature.[24] A way forward appears to be almost impossible. Only the destruction, perhaps the self-annihilation of modern society, remains a possibility (see also Gorz, [1991] 1994). Sombart continually tries to expose the defects of industrial capitalism, functional specialization, urban concentration, and individualism that are bound to destroy themselves, its members, and its structures.

As indicated, the notion of reactionary modernism as developed by Jeffrey Herf stipulates a kind of conflation of otherwise oppositional forms, namely technology and culture. At this point, we will return to Sombart's extensive writings on technology to see if he is indeed a genuine representative of reactionary modernism or, more accurately, a proponent of anti-modernism.

His last and largely innocuous statement on the role of technology is in his book *Vom Menschen* (Sombart, 1938b). Aside from attempts to categorize and classify technologies and their historical development, Sombart follows the dominant convention of the day and describes technology as a means and not as an independent cultural realm, such as the economy, religion, and politics. In short, he really does not offer any significant novel insights into the place of technology nor does he directly conflate technology, culture, and national greatness (Sombart, 1938b: 82–8). On the contrary, Sombart (ibid: 339) reiterates his disdain for the objectivations of the human spirit in the form of technology claiming that they force modern human beings into a condition of new and mere primitivity and passivity. Technology robs humans of the last bit of initiative and turns them into automatons. He worries about the inherent logic of modern technology that is about to produce a uniform world, thereby anticipating current theories about the "McDonaldization of Society" (Ritzer, 1996).[25]

In his earlier discussions of the role of technology, for example, within the context of his efforts to trace the origins and the consequences of the capitalist economy, production and transportation technologies play of course a significant role. New technologies, enlarging the productive capacity and the means of transportation, encourage and enable the latent entrepreneurial spirit. Technology is one of the essential motors of capitalism and modernity (Breuer, 1996). Technological inventions mobilize entrepreneurial energies, and, as Sombart (1913a: 414) formulates it in his study of *Der Bourgeois*, technology thereby is a consequence and a cause of capitalism.

However, Merton questions Sombart's generalization that seventeenth-century technology and contemporary science were almost completely separated (Sombart [1916] 1921a: 466–7), in view of the interest shown by many scientists during the seventeenth century to turn their theoretical knowledge into practical concerns. Equally telling is the normative commitment and conviction of these scientists that the legitimacy of scientific activity derives from the practical benefits of their activity for society. Since industrial production was not sufficiently developed, Merton concludes that "the grain of truth in Sombart's thesis is reduced to the fact that these men of science were concerned not with advancing the development of industrial machinery for factory use but with innovations which implemented commerce, mining and military technique" (Merton, [1939] 1957: 609).

Sombart and Weber

When looking at the intriguing question of why Sombart fell from a highly visible and influential position into near oblivion, and why his colleague and erstwhile friend Max Weber rose to posthumous fame and became (besides Durkheim, and, perhaps, Marx and Simmel) *the* sociological classic, one could be tempted to suggest that one possible explanation is their different analyses of world religions, especially Judaism. Specifically, one might think that Sombart's latent (and at times manifest) anti-Semitism made him a less suitable figure for the post-war period than Weber.[26] There is much to recommend this interpretation. However, it needs some qualification.[27]

Werner Sombart and Max Weber were born within a year of one another, and each spent their youth and young adulthood in a Germany united by Bismarck in 1871, that is, in a country in which nationalistic, even chauvinistic and racist convictions were entirely credible orientations. Categories such as the nation state, imperialism, colonialism, or ambition to be a world power were common conceptions and not tainted and implicated as they are today in subsequent catastrophic political developments.[28] Scholars and intellectuals, let alone politicians, took such notions for granted and considered themselves champions of the causes connected with them.

During the emergence of the German nation state, Max Weber, despite the image he acquired to the contrary in much of the exegesis of his work in the post-WWII era, was just as ardent a nationalist and chauvinist as was Werner Sombart.[29] In addition, as we shall see, his analysis of the role of the Jews in historical development was equally problematic on a theoretical level (although far less on the political level).

The Role of the Jews

Sombart's work on Judaism was largely a response to Weber, as Sombart tells us (1911: V, as translated by Bodemann, 1997):

> I hit upon the Jewish question completely by accident when I had embarked upon a fundamental revision of my *Modern Capitalism*....Max Weber's analyses in relation to the interconnection between Puritanism and capitalism forced me to pursue the influence of religion on economic life more than I had done so far, and here I encountered the Jewish problem first. Because, as a careful examination of Weber's argumentation demonstrated, all those components of the Puritan dogma that appear to me to be of real significance for the elaboration of the capitalist spirit were borrowings from the sphere of ideas of the Jewish religion.

Commenting on Sombart's *The Jews and Modern Capitalism* ([1911] 1951), David Landes notes, "Sombart's book received far more attention than it deserved. It should have been dismissed out of hand as pseudo-scholarly hoax" (Landes, 1974: 22). And Paul Mendes-Flohr adds: "Indeed, the faults of his logic are so blatant, the tendentiousness of his presentation of the data so patent, that it is difficult to understand why his book was not summarily dismissed" (Mendes-Flohr, 1976: 94). Bert Hoselitz had written an introduction to the English edition of *The Jews and Modern Capitalism* where he called the book a "classic." Barth Landheer reviewed the book and replied to Hoselitz: "If the term 'classic' conveys excellence in regard to analytical powers as well as to formal expression, Sombart's work hardly merits a place in this category. It is a standard example of how 'facts' can be made to fit an idea" (Landheer, 1951: 587).

Sombart has some quite sinister statements in stock. Above all, he employs the popular stereotypes of the Jew as moneylender and usurer (see "The Significance of Jewish Religion in Economic Life" in this volume).[30]

> One of the causes to which the Jew owed his economic progress was...the fact that Israel was for generations a stranger and an alien. If we seek to account for this aloofness we shall find its roots in the ordinances of the Jewish religion, shall find that this religion always maintained and broadened the line of separation. As Leroy-Beaulieu, who has studied this aspect of Jewish history with great success, has so well said, "La loi leur donnait l'esprit de clan." The very fact that they had their Law forced the Jews to live apart from the Gentiles. For if they desired to observe the Law they needs must keep to themselves. The Jews created the Ghetto,

> which from the non-Jewish point of view was a concession and a privilege and not the result of enmity.

In "The Influence of Technical Inventions," (this volume) he wrote:

> One reason why the Jews were so eminently prepared for capitalism was that they had been money-lenders from the days of Solomon, while in the Middle Ages it was a calling which they practically monopolized.... Money-lending was one of the wellsprings of the capitalist spirit, much more so than trade, especially in an age when production was on a natural basis and quality a prime factor in it. And why? Money-lending knows nothing of quality; its all-embracing concern is with quantities only.

Oelsner has claimed that, apart from Sombart, Wilhelm Roscher and Max Weber followed the same path in stereotyping the Jews as the commercial people par excellence. According to Roscher, the Western world owed three "economic advances to the Jews: the taking of interest on principal; the *bona fide* protection of merchants who unwillingly purchased stolen goods...and finally the bill of exchange as a 'world historical innovation'" (Oelsner, 1962: 202)—none of which stand up to scrutiny (ibid., 194):

> Roscher was the first of the leading economists to assign a definite economic preoccupation to the Jews, radically different from that of other groups, and which could be cast anew into sociological formulae. The notion of a historically determined Jewish occupation was epitomized by Max Weber in his concept of the Jewish pariah people—a position they supposedly assumed in the post-exile period.

It is true that Weber wholeheartedly agreed with Sombart's theory that the Jews played a conspicuous role in the evolution of the modern capitalistic system. He lists several distinctive economic achievements of the Jews from the Middle Ages to modern times:

> ...moneylending, from pawnbroking to the financing of great states; certain types of commodity business, particularly retailing, peddling and produce trade of a distinctively rural type; certain branches of wholesale business; and trading in securities, above all the brokerage of stocks (Weber, 1968: 612).

While Weber argues that many of these were not Jewish inventions, he nonetheless stresses that "one finds Jews involved in just these activities"—activities that were "absent from the new and distinctive forms of modern capitalism, the rational organization of labor, especially production in an industrial enterprise of the factory type" (ibid., 614). Weber sees the reason for this in the peculiar character of the Jews as a pariah people prohibited from agriculture, industry, and manual labor by their religion. This transformed them into an urban commercial "guest" people, especially prone to money trade. In addition, their religious ethic let them "retain a double standard of morals which is characteristic of primordial economic practice in all communities: what is prohibited in relation to one's brothers is permitted in relation to strangers" (ibid.).

Weber thus saw an ancient tribal dualism of in-group and out-group ethics in operation. However, he disagreed with Sombart on the role of Judaism for capitalist development. He saw Puritanism rather than Judaism as the prime cause for the modern 'spirit of capitalism' (Weber, 1905a, 1905b). Based on his in-group out-group model, Weber thought that the Jews limited themselves in their exchange relations and did not participate fully in social intercourse. This was a drawback for the process of modernization of German society. As Abraham argued, it is their religion that "directs them to single out for especially 'rationalistic' evaluation their relations with Gentiles, so long as their religious motivation remains viable" (Abraham, 1988: 359). As a consequence, Weber views the Jews alongside other *staendische* interests and groups as an obstacle to a fully developed modern class society. Although Weber identified himself with liberalism in Germany, enthusiasm for German nationalism in his day (which he also shared) excluded consideration of equal rights for religious minorities—Catholics and Jews (Abraham, 1988: 374). Oelsner (1962: 210-11) even claims that

> Weber denied the existence of a Jewish working class as well as manufacturers, in Eastern Europe or in the countries of emigration, and he minimized the part played by Jews in industrial capitalist organization. All this fitted into his concept of pariah capitalism as contrasted to Puritan 'work capitalism."

Both Sombart and Weber agreed that there was a "spirit of capitalism" based on a particular rationalism that came to fruition in the United States and England. France and the Latin peoples stand on the other side of 'spontaneity' and naïve enjoyment of life (Abraham, 1988: 363).[31]

As Oelsner shows in great detail, three basic claims of Weber, Sombart, and others turn out to be myths: first, that the Jews were moneylenders since early medieval times, second, that their religion prescribed taking higher interest from strangers than from their fellows, and third, that Jews did not possess land or were not parts of the guilds. Moses Hoffmann was one of the first to make that information available "in any Western language…[but] despite the evidence furnished by Hoffmann himself he followed in many points the bias indicated by the title ['The money trade of the German Jews'[32]]" (Oelsner, 1962: 201). Based on Jewish religious sources and historical research, among which Hoffmann's book figures prominently, Oelsner (ibid., 197) concludes:

> All this was entirely unknown to Weber. His generalization on the double morality of in-group out-group ethics epitomized in Jewish moneylending which he considered to be a one-way street, only directed toward the Gentile—pariah capitalism pure and simple—is based on scanty knowledge of the facts, and must therefore be rejected.[33] If there was an in-group out-group ethics it had its roots in the mutually exclusive creeds of the great denominations, Jewish, Islam, and Christian, each considering the other as strangers, disbeliever, and infidels.

Why, then, this common confusion about the Jews' role in economic history? Why the benevolent attitude of many Jewish scholars towards Sombart's analysis of Judaism? Regarding the first question, Oelsner offers the following explanation: "The drama of the Jews' fate, together with their minority position, 'inflated their importance in the popular and scholastic imagination'" (Oelsner 1962: 212, quoting Samuelson). We postpone the answer to the second question until after the next section ("Sombart and the Problem of Facts and Values").

It thus appears that all differences about the religious origins of capitalism notwithstanding, both Weber and Sombart shared the same view regarding the Jews as a self-segregating tribe with a special inclination towards trading and money-lending.[34] However, Weber was not an anti-Semite. He was in favor of Jews being employed in universities and supported actions in this respect. Abraham (1988: 376–7) claims that Weber's view on the integration of Jews into German society was much closer to the socialists' position than Sombart's was. While this may be correct, the portrayal of the socialist movement is problematic. It certainly was not free from anti-Semitism. Marx stated in the *Jewish Question* that "the social emancipation of the Jews is the emancipation of society from Judaism" (Marx [1843] 1975: 174) and almost all German and French socialists decried Jewry for its putative predominance in trade and finance (cf. Mendes-Flohr, 1976: 95 and the literature quoted in fn. 57). Ironically, the liberal professor of history, Jakob Fries, had introduced the argument, later taken up by Marx and others. While urging Jewish civic parity, Fries said that "to improve the civic position of the Jews means to wipe out Jewry, to destroy the society of mendacious hucksters and merchants" (quoted in Mendes-Flohr, 1976: 94–5).[35] For Sombart, in "moneylending all elements of workmanship, of labor in the sweat of one's brow were abandoned for the opportunity of making money without such efforts" (Oelsner, 1962: 202). The Jew is "whether by nature or through the course of historical development...the incarnation of the capitalist commercial spirit" (Sombart, 1902a: 349, as quoted by Oelsner 1962: 186).[36] In Sombart's essay on the Jews we read (in this volume):

> Before capitalism could develop the natural man had to be changed out of all recognition, and a rationalistically minded mechanism introduced in his stead. There had to be a transvaluation of all economic values. And what was the result? The *homo capitalisticus*, who is closely related to the *homo Judoeus*, both belonging to the same species, *homines rationalistici artificiales*.

If there is no significant difference between Sombart and Weber as regards their judgment of Judaism, what can then account for their different post-war reception by the social science community? First, and obviously, Weber did not live long enough to be involved with the darkest chapter of German history. It may well be that his early death secured him the place in the pantheon of science. But this seems to be a faint possibility; for all we know, Weber was not a reactionary modernist, nor an anti-Semite. He was strongly in favor of liberal democracy and did not express longings for a "paradise lost." Apart from these important differences, there are two more. The first concerns the attribution of blame, the second the issue of race.

Briefly put, although both authors had reservations about capitalist rationality, Sombart was much more expressed about it.[37] Where Weber would reflect about the "iron cage" of modern society, the domination of bureaucracies and the reign of utilitarianism,[38] Sombart was not only espousing a golden age but also trying to identify the guilty party for ruining it. His obsession with the question of "who dunnit?" led him to identify the Germans in his earlier work. After his nationalist turn around 1910, he put the blame on the Jews, and there it remained. Sombart thus arrived at a clear-cut worldview that separated good and bad: those who earn their living in an honest and productive way and those who do so by dubious methods. This anti-Semitic juxtaposition between industrial capitalism and money capitalism was also expressed by the fascist movement in Weimar Germany, and lay at the basis of the extermination program of the Nazi rulers after their rise to power. In identifying the Puritan spirit as the main cause of capitalism, Weber assigned only a minor world historical view to the Jews. In addition, he did not link the analysis of causes of capitalism to the attribution of guilt. That Calvinism had "invented" capitalism does not lead Weber to condemn people of this creed. How could he, being himself deeply imbued in Protestantism?[39]

The last difference concerns race as a category in their thought. While Weber did not engage in this discourse, Sombart never ceased to be interested in it. Weber and Sombart, in their partly converging theoretical attempt to account for the origins of capitalism, concur that the uniquely European capitalist spirit cannot be explained by reference to singular characteristic of European races (cf. Sombart, 1902a: 379; Weber, 1905a: 23, Note 1) but must make use of mental categories. Yet, Sombart's affirmation of a socio-cultural account and his opposition to a "racial" explanation remains characteristically ambivalent. In briefly assessing in the same context the role of the Jews in the genesis of capitalism, Sombart (1902a: 390) remarks "One can be sure that the Jews have had a significant share in the genesis of capitalism. This follows from, among other things, their racial disposition." In later publications, the same ambivalence becomes even more pronounced. Here Sombart goes a step further (e.g., 1903: 128–31) in liberally mixing what should be conceptualized as socio-cultural attributes of ethnic groups but what he presents as alleged racial traits.[40] At the same time, Sombart assigns much more room to the discussion of the role of Jews in these publications, prompting Weber ([1920] 1988: 181) to cancel his initial explicit and general agreement with Sombart on this matter.

Summing up our argument, it appears that Weber and Sombart

largely agreed about the role of the Jews in economic history as being traders and moneylenders. They disagreed about the Jews' role in the development of capitalism, and about the role of race. While Sombart was beset with issues of race, Weber was not. Most importantly, Sombart seems to mix these contested issues with ethical and moral aspects. His analysis of causes of capitalism is thus joined by a discussion about the attribution of blame. Likewise, his discussion about the course of civilization is interspersed with arguments about "superior" and "inferior," "mixed" and "pure" races. Again, for Weber this was largely a non-issue. This leads us to the problem of scientific objectivity, or the fact-value distinction.

Sombart and the Problem of Facts and Values

After the foregoing discussion, it is surprising to learn that Sombart emphatically states that he refrains from any value judgment. In his introduction to *Die Juden und das Wirtschaftsleben* (not included in the English translation), he insists that the book is purely scientific, states only the facts and withholds any value judgment (Sombart, 1911: xi). Moreover, in his book *Vom Menschen*, he states with considerable seriousness that his study of the conditions for the possibility of human existence is a purely scientific one and refrains from any value judgments whatsoever, and is strictly immune to the kinds of political and cultural judgments found in "metaphysical" anthropology.[41] Although he had affirmed only weeks and months before the political utility of economics under and for National Socialism (Sombart, 1934a), beginning sometime in 1934, Sombart made pronouncements in a dispute about the practical-political role of economics in which abruptly and without realizing his inconsistency he praises again the virtues of a value-free social science.

What is more, he even makes rather blatant value judgments that have become the hallmark of his thought. For example, Sombart (1938b: 148) declares as self-evident that the mass of people are aesthetically inferior, that is, the mass are "gemein, gewöhnlich, ordinär, banal, trivial," or he proclaims self-assuredly that those who are descendants of racially mixed parentage are generally more ugly in appearance that those from racially pure backgrounds. He repeats the assertion that among the contemporary sins of mankind is the willful destruction of the naturalness of human beings "as any cultured person has to accept as self-evident" (Sombart, 1938b: 22) or that modern technology destroys the fabric of social existence and degrades man to the level of a monkey (ibid: 339).

We can now return to the question that was left open: Why did many scholars—Jewish and non-Jewish alike—appreciate Sombart's analysis?[42] We suggest that there is a misunderstanding going on which is explained by the confusion created by mixing facts and values in the Jewish-capitalist connection. We can unravel this confusion by distinguishing between a positive and negative judgment of capitalism on the one hand and an analysis of the Jews in economic history as either central or not important on the other. Combining these two dimensions results in four possibilities: first, those who regard capitalism in a negative light and the Jews' role as important (Sombart).[43] Second, those who regard capitalism in a positive light and the Jews' role as important (some Jewish scholars). Third, those who regard capitalism as probably bad but inevitable but see the role of the Jews as not important. (For the sake of the argument, let us put Weber in this category, even though there is room for speculation. This is why we write "probably bad.") Finally, those who regard capitalism as good and the role of the Jews as not important (mainstream economics?).[44] Jews like Mosse are proud of the achievements of Jews in economic history; therefore they applaud Sombart in his attempt to prove their beneficial role for the emergence and development of capitalism. It is telling that Mosse concludes his book with a quote from Sombart that emphasizes the beneficial consequences of the Jews for the German economic development.

Sombart and Heidegger

Not surprisingly, Sombart unequivocally expresses his admiration and hopes for the Nazi-regime early in its rule (cf. Lenger, 1994: 358). Any distance and disappointment toward the Nazi regime that Sombart may have expressed derives purely from the regime's failure to directly engage him in its policy decisions and implementation.[45] The case of Heidegger and the case of Sombart appear to intersect and converge for the same reasons. Any distance they express in words and maybe even deeds does not articulate any alienation from the ideology of the regime but frustration with those officials who did not sufficiently honor and engage its strong intellectual forerunners and proponents, for example, as highly competent experts in the practice of the regime. Sombart's advice in economic policy matters was not sought by the government. Sombart listed his books and articles, beginning with his 1911 treatise on the Jews, as evidence that his anticipatory ideas were not then properly recognized.[46] But his frustration did not translate into a critique of the regime, or result in a protest against the removal of his successor Emil Lederer or one-time colleague Karl Mannheim from their chairs in April 1933 (cf. Kettler, Meja, and Stehr, 1984). On the contrary, he accepted and even furthered the latter, for example, by expelling Lederer from the leadership of the *Verein für Sozialpolitik*. Similarly, Sombart did his utmost to accomplish much the same for the German Sociological Association (cf. Lenger, 1994: 358–64) and remained a repeatedly honored scholar during the Nazi regime.

His most recent biographer, the young German historian Friedrich Lenger (1994: 377, 379),[47] attempts to systematically relativize and minimize the significance of certain of Sombart's public pronouncements during the Nazi era in favor of the Nazi regime and its ideology.[48] In one case, he pronounces that Sombart's signature in 1934 on an *Ergebenheitsadresse* cannot have been affixed to the document praising Hitler with much conviction, while in another instance he dismisses Sombart's applause for the institution of the *Führerprinzip* in German politics as mere lip service. Moreover, Lenger (1994: 381–383) considers Sombart's last book *Vom Menschen* to represent a decisive and unabashed criticism of the contemporary racism and the mythology of the notion of *Volk*.

It is in a way surprising to see how much effort is invested in interpretations of Sombart's work designed to show that he really was not, did not mean to be, or somehow became an accidental proponent of racist and national-socialist ideology (cf. Lenger, 1994; Sapori, 1955). One of the common apologetic strategies among interpreters of Sombart's work, attitudes, and behavior during the Nazi era, especially among European intellectuals and scholars, is to garner arguments and evidence from different, as some might however see it, distinct phases of his writings to balance or offset ideas uttered at another time, namely during the Nazi period (e.g. Allodi, 1989: 478).

Why did Sombart not have a comeback like Heidegger did after WWII? Sombart pales into insignificance when compared with Heidegger's posthumous success. Such a comparison seems obvious since both actively served the fascist rulers in Hitler's Germany. Both had certain intellectual affinities to the ideological basis of the new regime, which they eagerly welcomed. But only Heidegger enjoyed a considerable post-war success.[49] This can easily be quantified by looking at citation figures, which show a characteristic difference in regards to historical periods.[50] While Sombart enjoyed his greatest success with his writings published before the two World Wars (those of the period 1887–1945 were cited about 300 times, twice as much as those published after WWII), Heidegger's success was primarily based on the English translation of *Sein und Zeit* (*Being and Time*), which appeared in 1962. He scores around 150 citations with publications that appeared before 1945, but more than 2000 citations after WWII.[51] To be sure, Sombart's writings, apart from his main work, *Der moderne Kapitalismus* (which has never been translated in its entirety into English), have been re-issued after 1945, just as Heidegger's have been. *The Quintessence of Capitalism* was published by Howard Fertig in 1967,[52] *The Jews and Modern Capitalism* by Collier in 1962,[53] *Why is there no Socialism in the United States?* by Macmillan in 1976,[54] and *Luxury and Capitalism* by the University of Michigan Press in 1967.[55] While there was a market for his writings after the war, the reception was far less enthusiastic than in Heidegger's case.

How do we account for the difference between the reception of both authors? First of all, we must exclude several hypotheses. Heidegger did not "convert" after the war to an "anti-fascist"; as is well-known, he refused to make a self-critical remark regarding his fascist past.[56] The late Sombart, for his part, did distance himself to some degree from the racist Nazi ideology in his last book, *Vom Menschen*. Unlike Heidegger, Sombart did not live through WWII, so how he would have reacted to expectations posed on him to "renounce" remains open to speculation. In regards to anti-Semitic tendencies in their writings, we have seen that Sombart was ready to blame the Jews for the rise of capitalism and the destruction of the pre-modern social forms he cherished. While not particularly known for statements about Jews, Heidegger's silence regarding their extermination can be regarded as his greatest failure (Lyotard, 1990). In sum, it seems impossible to explain the differing post-war success of both authors by claiming that one was politically or morally better (or worse) than the other.

We get somewhat closer to an explanation of the difference if we look at the intellectual climate of the post-WWII period and the conditions that determined their contrasting receptions. Heidegger became fashionable in two related but distinct waves: existentialism and post-modernism. Anti-fascists like Sartre made ample reference to his work, as did later post-modernists and deconstructivists like Derrida. Heidegger seems to provide a link between Greek philosophy, Nietzsche, and the twentieth century that many were keen to explore. Above all the renaissance of Nietzsche has probably contributed considerably to Heidegger's success until this day.[57] If Sombart, in turn, can be characterized as the mouthpiece of one classical figure, that figure was, of course, Marx. However, at all times, and particularly after the war, there were many Marxisms on offer—and Sombart's version was just one among very many, and one might even say it was not a very original or visible one. Last, but not least, Parsons' role in post-war sociology must be taken into account. He was the propagandist (and, of course, the translator) of Max Weber, not of Sombart. By introducing Weber to Anglo-Saxon sociology, Parsons laid the foundation to his worldwide reception.

What Remains?

After so much criticism, we would like to draw attention to those parts of Sombart's oeuvre that have survived the test of the time, at least in part. After all, we think there is more that justifies interest in his writings apart from his sinister statements about race, Judaism, and capitalism.

We refer to two of what we consider very promising intellectual developments within the social sciences that could well lead to a significant re-evaluation of the value of Sombart's contribution. Both developments are related to, perhaps are even a backlash against, the apparently incessant specialization within science. However, realization is growing that this increasing differentiation of modes of discourse within social science (let alone between social science and natural science) has, apart from its undoubtable benefits, also incurred significant intellectual and practical costs.

Following these growing sentiments within the social sciences, Sombart's contributions to the analysis of the modern economy, and what he considered his reflections in the field of the cultural sciences (both documented in our collection), may prove to be at least a part of a road back to renewed and invigorated debate with his broadly based reflections on the nature of modern society in general, and the modern economy in particular.

More concretely, and first, *sociological discourse* in the past few decades has been increasingly separated from *economic discourse*. Economics has rarely competed with sociological knowledge.[58] In the process, as Robert Heilbronner is quick to note, it has squeezed out the term 'capitalism'; the word no longer appears in popular introductory economics textbooks (cp. *New York Times*, 23 January 1999).

Such distancing from each other could be conceived as only a matter of the increasing differentiation in as well as scientification of social science discourse. Economics lost interest in the analysis of social institutions while sociology conceded the study of socio-economic phenomena to economics (cf. Granovetter, 1990; Swedberg, 1987).[59] Economic analysis and sociology have both largely lost interest in the study of the societal and socio-economic impact of science and technology.[60] And, against Sombart, economists and sociologists claim, independently of each other but committed to the same philosophical and methodological principles, that they have made considerable strides in advancing the cause of positive social science.

In light of current socio-economic and political conditions, however, it is less certain that such a state of affairs represents a proper cognitive priority and intellectual division of labour. The sociological contribution to the analysis of economic relations should not be merely peripheral, nor should the treatment of scientific and technical change be considered exogenous to economic analysis (cf. Dosi et al., 1988). As well, a number of voices have demanded a rapprochement or unification of the social sciences. This is, however, hardly possible on the cognitive territory, or under the intellectual auspices of *one* of the social science disciplines.[61] A "unity" of the social sciences under these conditions amounts merely to a perpetuation of the status quo and not interdisciplinarity.

Second, Werner Sombart's self-conception was consistently that of a contributor to development of cultural science (*Kulturwissenschaften*). His idea of cultural science was expansive and comprehensive indeed.[62] Using more contemporary terms, Sombart's self-conception encompasses much of the social sciences and some fields that can be included in the humanities. However, he insists that his contributions, including those on the modern economy represented in this volume, ought to be seen as reflections constitutive of the cultural sciences (cp. Sombart, [1931] 1959: 258; 1938c). In the meantime, of course, interest in cultural studies from diverse disciplinary perspectives has grown considerably. One might anticipate that Sombart's distinctive approach and contribution to cultural science will be recognized before long as an intellectual precursor of cultural analysis and cultural studies.

His work on culture, consumption, and luxury is still regarded as "classic" (Roberts, 1998: 822). Several authors in the field of cultural history turn to his work for inspiration. For example, de Grazia refers to Veblen and Sombart in her discussion of the role of women in capitalist consumption; she describes both as "eccentric and idiosyncratic." In examining Veblen's *Theory of the Leisure Class* (published 1899) and Sombart's *Luxury and Capitalism* (1913), she, surprisingly, finds Sombart's approach far more convincing than Veblen's, even though Veblen was a "deeply committed feminist"—a trait which cannot be attributed to Sombart. "What prejudices Veblen's analysis is not antifeminism but his idolization of the sphere of production...[he] saw the fullness of life only in fulfilling the work instinct"; Sombart's analysis, in contrast, is "seductive in its recognition of sensuous pleasures, and particularly that these have operated historically to refine and multiply the taste for consumer goods" (de Grazia, 1996: 21). Likewise, Colin Campbell stated that he did not find much that was valuable in the social science literature on consumer behavior (1987: 6–7). This field had been left almost exclusively to economists who treat consumer behavior in an ahistorical framework of assumptions and consider it to be basically the same for all peoples at all times. "Of the classical writers only Sombart has clearly elucidated what Trilling has called the 'pleasure-sensuality-luxury complex,' and perceived that 'at base' a 'love of luxury' might derive from 'purely sensuous pleasures,' with Scitovsky the only contemporary economist to attempt to pursue this line of thought" (Campbell, 1987: 59).

In his *Civilization and Capitalism*, Fernand Braudel discusses the role of luxury consumption in the emergence of modern capitalism. Marcel Mauss and Bachelard agreed that luxury was the great stimulus for capitalist development and accumulation. While Braudel seems to agree with this general statement, he casts some doubt on the more specific proposition that therefore the princely courts laid the foundations of early modern capitalism. He attributes this view to Sombart who advanced it "most forcefully." Instead, Braudel argues, before the innovations of the nineteenth century, "the many forms of luxury were not so much an element of growth as a sign of an economy failing to engange with anything" and that a "*certain* kind of luxury was...a phenomenon or sign of sickness peculiar to the ancient regime..." (Braudel, 1992: 186). Braudel thus dismissed out of hand Sombart's suggestion that there is a close connection between the insatiable patterns of consumption in early modern court life and the growth of capitalist production.

Chandra Mukerji defends Sombart against Braudel's criticism. She states: "What Sombart recognizes quite correctly is that the court cultural system was deeply embedded in capitalist economic development" (1993: 439). She then examines business culture's development in the early modern period. The demand for luxury was not so much connected to a pursuit of comfort, but with social ambition and mobility, a point also made by Norbert Elias (1983), who argued that the highly complex and expensive culture of consumption within the court was not only there to "distract a bored aristocracy, but a central means by which Louis XIV controlled the French aristocracy" (Mukerji, 1993: 440). Aristocrats became especially passionate about assembling rare objects from round the world. The display of these objects, plants, and animals prefigures Veblen's conspicuous consumption, although Veblen would (quite wrongly, in Mukerji's view) stress the point that this was wasteful consumption. According to Mukerji (1993: 442), conspicuous consumption "was a way to mark ranks where social stratification was unclear...social instability of the seventeenth century was reproduced within court society and helped to promote the extensive use of material culture for making social claims. In this society, knowing who to imitate in patterns of consumption and how to use prescribed fashions showed political shrewdness and made social life possible."[63] In Sombart's words: "It is the court society which shapes the habits and manners of all good society: 'Paris apes the court,' says La Bruyère. Court society in turn is molded by the acknowledged favourite of the prince, who thus puts his stamp on all strata of society. The court favourite is above all the model which is copied by the ambitious woman of the town, the *grande cocotte*. At the outset, the latter almost becomes a competitor of her sister at court" ("The Secularization of Love," this volume; Sombart, [1913] 1967a: 56).

In summarizing Sombart's contribution, we can say that, despite his daft statements on race and nation, he had a sense for fine cultural distinctions and broad historical developments. If one looks today at his essay about "The Economic Life of the Future" (this volume; Sombart, 1927), one is amazed how close some of his predictions are to reality, especially his vision that an Asian version of capitalism might emerge and his assertion that there is little difference between a stabilized and regulated capitalism and a mechanized and streamlined socialism. But perhaps most of all, his style is outstanding. George Bernard Shaw's remark (1946):

> He who has something to assert will go as far in power of style as its momentousness and his conviction will carry him. Disprove his assertion after it is made, yet his style remains....All the assertions get disproved sooner or later; and so we find the world full of a magnificent debris of artistic fossils, with the matter-of-fact credibility gone clean out of them, but the form still splendid.

C. Wright Mills used these words to describe the heritage of Veblen. They seem to fit Sombart equally well, as does Mills' comment that in "his case we cannot say that *all* 'the matter-of-fact credibility' in his works has 'gone clean out of them'" (Mills, 1970: vii, our emphasis).

Notes

1. The celebrity status he had achieved can be fathomed from the obituary the *New York Times* published two days after his death (20 May 1941) and their editorial on Sombart published on 22 May 1941.
2. But see how Lenger (1994: 344) tries to "explain away" this criticism by stating that Schumpeter basically was in praise of Sombart.

3. Lenger (1994: 143) points out that Sombart was likely the main author of the *Geleitwort* since it bears many resemblances with an essay on social science journals published by him in 1897.
4. In his book *History and Class Consciousness,* Georg Lukács ([1922] 1971: 227) offers a forced sociology of knowledge account for Sombart's intellectual affinity to Marxism. Lukács suggests that, in societies such as Germany in which capitalism was relatively late in developing, economic theories did not have a purely bourgeois base, as they did in the era of classical economics. In countries where the growth of capitalism was delayed, "there was a direct need for theoretical backing it turned out that the theory that did emerge bore a strong 'Marxist' character."; Lukács uses Sombart's theories as a case in point for the German situation.
5. We follow the line of argument provided by Mitzman (1973) and Mendes-Flohr (1976).
6. Cited in Mendes-Flohr (1976: 91).
7. Werner Sombart (1927: xviii) "Der moderne Kapitalismus: Das Wirtschaftsleben im Zeitalter des Hochkapitalismus," translated by Keith Tribe in Hennis ([1987] 1988: 209).
8. The canonical quote from Marx is as follows (Marx, [1859] 1987: 263): "In the social production of their life, men enter into definite relations that are indispensable and independent of their will, relations of production which correspond to a definite stage of development of their material productive forces. The sum total of these relations of production constitutes the economic structure of society, the real basis, on which rises a legal and political superstructure, and to which correspond definite forms of social consciousness. The mode of production of material life conditions the social, political and intellectual life process in general. It is not the consciousness of men that determines their being, but, on the contrary, their social being that determines their consciousness."
9. Contrast this with Marx who wrote in *The Poverty of Philosophy:* "Social relations are closely bound up with productive forces. In acquiring new productive forces men change their mode of production; and in changing their mode of production, in changing their way of earning their living, they change all their social relations. The hand-mill gives you society with the feudal lord; the steam-mill, society with the industrial capitalist" (Marx [1847] 1976: 166). For a discussion of this technological determinism, see Cohen (1978), Grundmann (1991), and Smith and Marx (1994).
10. As a matter of fact, in his presentation on "technology and culture" to the first meeting of the German Sociological Association, Sombart ([1910] 1911: 82) notes that his audience may have been disappointed of his lecture because, contrary to expectations, he totally refrained from passing judgment about the "cultural value" (*Kulturwert*) of technology. However, such a passive stance, he stresses, is only consistent with a scientific attitude toward his subject matter, because science lacks any objective measures to engineer such judgments.
11. One may speculate if this was primarily due to his use of a simple concept that could be understood and remembered easily. In any case, commentators have suggested that Sombart was trying to solve the theory/history problem in the same way as Weber did (Kruse, 1990: 155; Lenger, 1994; Parsons [1937] 1949: 496).
12. Here he seems to differ from Weber, who had forcefully criticized Windelband's and Rickert's division of reality into two separate realms, which they imagined to

be ontologically different (i.e., nature and society) and therefore required different methods (nomological and ideographic). This does not mean that for Weber society could be described with the positivistic approaches developed by the natural sciences because the sociologist has to *understand* the motives and intentions of the acting subjects (hence Weber's term *verstehende Soziologie*).

13. It is here that Weber's formula of the *ideal type* comes to mind.
14. Cf. Luhmann's (1996) definition of society: all society is communication and all communication is society.
15. We have translated Sombart's title "Versuch einer geisteswissenschafltichen Anthropologie" not as "Toward a philosophical anthropology" because Sombart explicitly rejects the adjective "philosophical anthropology" as characteristic of his work. Sombart wants to fashion a "scientific" and not a "metaphysical" anthropology. At least, he is of the opinion that what was known at the time as philosophical anthropology does not qualify as a version of a scientific anthropology (cf. Sombart, 1938a: XIVX–XXIII).
16. It is perhaps also for this reason that the writings of Sombart, Plessner, and Gehlen display mutual ignorance. In the context of the development *and* reception of philosophical anthropology especially as associated with the work of Helmut Plessner and Arnold Gehlen, Sombart's efforts play, to our knowledge, little if any role (perhaps justifiably so). Neither Gehlen in *Der Mensch* (first published 1940) nor Plessner in *Die Stufen des Organischen und der Mensch* (first published 1928) refer to Sombart. Similarly, Sombart fails to mention Plessner or Gehlen. Because his anthropological approach wants to be neutral with respect to any evaluative judgments, and refrains from contributing to a metaphysical anthropology, reference to that literature can be omitted, according to Sombart (1938a: xx–xxi).
17. Cf. Ringer (1969), Röpke (1945), Sontheimer ([1962] 1978), Stern (1961) for earlier treatments of reactionary German intellectuals.
18. The writer Hugo von Hofmannsthal coined the term "conservative revolution" in 1927. This was to capture the paradox prevalent within a movement whose followers "sought to destroy the despised present in order to recapture an idealized past in an imaginary future," as Stern (1961: xvi) put it.
19. Röpke (1945: 71) calls these authors (including Sombart) "perfumed fascists" who greatly helped to make nazi-ism acceptable to the German bourgeoisie and the academic youth. Harris listed the following parallels between the program of the NSDAP and Sombart: "(1) the repudiation of nineteenth century liberalism and its 'atomistic' or individualistic conception of society; (2) the idealization of the Middle Ages; (3) the proposal to reconstruct society on the model of estates; and (4) folk nationalism and its corollary, pan-Germanism" (Harris, 1942: 815–16).
20. Compare Siegfried Kracauer's ([1932] 1990) review of Ernst Jünger's *Der Arbeiter, Herrschaft und Gestalt* (1932) in which he refers to the strong affinity in views between Sombart's characterization and assessment of bourgeois thought and Jünger's anti-bourgeois stance.
21. Cf. also the Italian futurists for a similar view, cf. Hinz (1985; we are indebted to Pierre Lafranchi for this suggestion).
22. The development of Sombart's thinking is significantly influenced by his clear and repeated commitment to his contemporary Ferdinand Tönnies (1855–1936), especially Tönnies' dichotomy *Gemeinschaft und Gesellschaft* (first published in

1887; see also König, 1987b: 265–7). Excerpts from this book are included in Sombart's *Soziologie* (published by Sombart in 1923; cf. also Sombart, 1903: 89, 397).

23. According to Marianne Weber, Max was quite distressed by his German "fellow-travellers" who did not enjoy America as much as he did ([1926] 1975: 281–2).
24. Sombart's critique resonates with the distance and disdain of many German intellectuals at the time. Both Sombart and Adorno express very similar sentiments about the 'barbarian' New York City (cf. Lenger, 1994: 147–8; Adorno's letter to Walter Benjamin, cf. Adorno and Benjamin, 1994: 410).
25. "One type of table, one type of house, one type of shoe, one type of dance, one type of song, one type of meal on the whole civilized earth is where we are heading to, due to modern technology. And mankind will be modeled after this uniformity in which every tribal and *völkisch* specificity will be extinguished" ("Ein Stuhl, ein Haus, ein Schuh, ein Tanz, ein Sang, ein Essen auf der ganzen zivilisierten Erde und eine dieser Gleichförmigkeit der Kulturgüter angepaßte Menschheit, in der alle stammliche und alle völkische Eigenart ausgelöscht ist, ist doch wohl das Ziel, dem wir zustreben: dank der modern Technik"; Sombart, 1938a: 367, our translation).
26. Cf. Fetscher: "It is perhaps no coincidence that Sombart became a Nazi later on while Weber was among those few Germans who were in favor of democracy even before 1914..." (Fetscher, 1962: 11).
27. Irving Horowitz argues that both Weber and Sombart did not include a political element into their analysis of Judaism and therefore could not explain real world events of the twentieth century: "That is why Sombart in particular fell into disrepute. His analysis did not explain the political inspiration for German anti-Semitism nor the blockage of its Jews to the political process" (Horowitz, 1986: 22). This may be true but does not account for the different fate of Weber.
28. Mitzman (1985: 11) offers the observation that the fathers of Werner Sombart, Max Weber, and Robert Michels all had been "powerful figures in the creation of the new Germany, had joined their fortunes to those of the Bismarckian state, and it was precisely this merging of the bourgeois spirit with the spirit of the state that made it impossible for these three sons of the German bourgeoisie to maintain their generational hostility in the heretofore traditional manner of bourgeois radicalism: as an attack from rational grounds on the irrationality of state and society."
29. The relevant documents in the case of Max Weber, previously in parts at least somewhat difficult to access, are now part of his *Collected Works* (cf. Weber, 1993). Mitzman is convinced that it is not by chance that Werner Sombart, Max Weber, and Robert Michels "after an initial flirtation—of greater or lesser duration and intensity—with socialism, became, in later stages of their development, either ideological predecessors or apologists of fascism" (Mitzman, 1985: 145–6). (Cf. the debate between Klingemann, 1997, and Käsler, 1997.)
30. "Despite its scholarly presentation, *The Jews and Modern Capitalism* is clearly an ideological exercise, preparatory to the Germanophilia that would distinguish Sombart's later work....By demonstrating that fundamentally 'Puritanism is Judaism', Sombart argues that Weber should have localised the spirit of capitalism in Judaism" (Mendes-Flohr, 1976: 88, 87).
31. Therefore, "his slap against Sombart becomes an odd farce," as Oelsner remarks (1962: 210–11).

32. "Der Geldhandel der deutschen Juden im Mittelalter," *Staats- und Sozialwissenschaftliche Untersuchungen*, Heft 152, 1910. It is curious that Hoffman wrote a favorable review of Sombart's book *Die Juden und das Wirtschaftsleben* where he states that "Sombart is by no means an anti-Semite and has the best intentions... His book will not only be the book of the season but the standard work on Jews and Judaism" (quoted in Mendes-Flohr 1976: 88 fn 6, our translation).
33. However, Weber also says that some of these techniques of trading and money-lending were invented in the Orient (probably Babylonia) and only introduced by the Jews to the Occident (Weber 1968: 613).
34. Consider the following quote from Weber's discussion of the economic ethos in Judaism ([1922] 1968: 1202): "The specifically urban, yet inassimilable and international character of Judaism, which was the same in ancient and in later times, has two causes." The "causes" Weber mentions are the persistence of messianic hopes despite the destruction of the hierocracy and ritual motives.
35. Fishman (1989) mentions also the influence of Moses Hess, although neither Fries nor Hess are mentioned in Marx's text.
36. "Had not Karl Marx himself—gleefully quoted by Sombart—argued the virtual identity of the terms 'Jew' and 'capitalist'?" remarks Mosse (1987: 398).
37. Turner (1992: 240) claims that Weber's personal sense of tragedy was "part of a general *Kulturpessimismus* in German intellectual life which had its roots in Schopenhauer, Nietzsche and Simmel." There are reasons to cast doubt on this reading, cf. Breuer (1996).
38. At times, Weber would also criticize Protestant recklessness and intolerance and praise Confucian grace and dignity (cf. Breuer, 1996: 240).
39. One may still agree with Horowitz (1986: 20) who states that classical sociological positions in Germany reveal an "unabashed archaic quality. They present a simplistic approach to cultural survival by reducing such issues to psychic properties and cultural propensities." What is more, the fate of the Jews is not to be understood in economic, but in political terms: it is the role of the state that determined their degree of participation in the economy and their survivability in totalitarian systems, "whatever their economics"—Jews suffered in capitalist Nazi Germany as in the socialist Soviet Union.
40. He mentions dominance of will-power, egotism, and abstract mentality in the Jewish race (Sombart, 1913, quoted in Mosse, 1987: 14).
41. What follows is that Sombart's (e.g., 1938a: 24, 26) repeated and affirmative use of the notion of a human "soul" does not in his eyes represent a metaphysical entity.
42. There are many examples from different times: Mendes-Flohr (1976: 87 fn 6) mentions Mendelssohn and an article by Mosse, written in 1964. Meanwhile, Mosse has published a large monograph (1987) where he quotes Sombart about the functional role of the Jews for the development of capitalism: if the Jew did not exist, he would have to be invented. Mosse comments: "But the Jew (luckily for the German economy) did not have to be invented. He was already to be found in Germany in numbers at the dawn of the age of early industrialization able and ready" (Mosse, 1987: 27).
43. In his book *Deutscher Sozialismus* (translated as *A New Social Philosophy*), he leaves no doubt that capitalism is the work of the devil: "Only he who believes in the power of the devil can understand what has taken place in western Europe and

America in the last hundred and fifty years. For what we have experienced can be explained only as the work of the devil" (Sombart, [1934] 1937: 5).

44. It should be noted that this typology does not map the whole spectrum of positions. There are, after all, scholars who aim at deconstructing the stereotypes about Jewishness (Oelsner, Mendes-Flohr) since they consider the demagogic political use to which these stereotypes can (and have been) put.
45. Werner Sombart's son, Nicolaus Sombart ([1984] 1998: 11–48) has published his memoirs about his youth in Berlin covering the decade between 1933–1943 in which he adduces a number of other socio-psychological and socio-political motives for such distancing by his father from the Nazi regime.
46. See Werner Sombart's letter to Johannes Plenge dated 24 September 1993 (Plenge papers, Library, Universität Bielefeld).
47. Lenger tends to present and argue his case primarily from the perspective of the archival material he employs and utilizes in such an extensive manner for the first time by an intellectual historian. However, by making his evaluations from the platform and the perspective of the written archival material, Lenger tends to overlook tensions and contradictions found in Sombart's published texts. He tends to look for confirmation for his archival discoveries in the texts rather than vice versa. This also leads him to overlook important critical, secondary interpretations of the work on Sombart, like Mendes-Flohr and Oelsner. The disciplinary perspective Lenger employs has of course advantages as well.
48. Lenger's Sombart biography has received a number of very favorable reviews in the German press and the author was awarded a prestigious award from the German Historical Society in 1994. However, the political scientist Kurt Sontheimer (1994) wrote a stinging rebuke of Lenger's relativizing interpretations of Sombart's action during the Nazi regime and his preparatory ideology and affinity to the Nazi propaganda.
49. There is a slight difference in their respective behavior towards colleagues threatened by the regime. While Sombart did nothing to support them (as mentioned earlier), Heidegger tried to protect two colleagues from expulsion from the university in 1934 (Ott, [1988] 1994: 207).
50. Figures according to the database collected in the *Social Science Citation Index*.
51. Figures are even higher if one looks at the database *Arts and Humanities*.
52. First German edition: *Der Bourgeois*, München, 1913, reprinted in Berlin, 1987.
53. First German edition: *Die Juden und das Wirtschaftsleben*, Leipzig, 1911.
54. First German edition: *Warum gibt es in den Vereinigten Staaten keinen Sozialismus?*, Tübingen, 1906.
55. First German edition, 1913; second edition, 1922 (German reprint as *Liebe, Luxus und Kapitalismus*, Berlin, 1983.)
56. More precisely, while his whole later work can be seen as an attempt to digest the Nazi involvement on a theoretical level (some would say to rationalize it)—and therefore he did say something—he remained silent in respect to the Holocaust (cf. Singer, 1993).
57. Co-citation analysis reveals that authors citing Nietzsche were also heavily citing Freud, Foucault, Heidegger, Habermas, Derrida, Weber and Marx—but not Sombart.
58. In the course of the persistent intellectual differentiation of sociological and economic knowledge, flashes of mutual signs of recognition and attention across the entrenched disciplinary boundaries can be characterized, at best, by shared ex-

pressions of irritation and disbelief. For example, sociologists have expressed quite pronounced amazement about the restrictive assumptions in economic models of the rational basis of social conduct. Conversely, economist have been exasperated by such critiques and have proceeded to extend their analysis to issues considered by sociologists to be squarely located within the domain of sociological inquiry.

59. For example, as Christopher Freeman and his colleagues resolutely stress, "The development of industrialized economies cannot be reduced to statistics of the growth of GNP, of industrial production, of capital stock, investment, employment etc., valuable though these statistics undoubtedly are. Underlying these statistical aggregates are the growth of entirely new industries and technologies and are the decline of old ones and many social and institutional changes in the structure of industry and government" (Freeman et al., 1982: ix).
60. With some notable exceptions, of course. See Bijker et al. (1987); Dasgupta and David (1994); Stephan (1996); Latour and Woolgar (1986); of course, authors in the tradition of historical materialism never lost interest in the topic.
61. Hirshleifer's observations are exemplary of this type of perspective and the typical (discipline-bound) intellectual conditions under which such unity is to be achieved: "*There is only one social science.* What gives economics its imperialist invasive power is that *our* [emphasis added] analytical categories—scarcity, cost, preferences, opportunities, etc.—are truly universal categories. Even more important is our structured organization of these concepts into the distinct yet intertwined processes of optimization on the individual decision level and equilibrium on the social level of analysis (Hirshleifer, 1985: 53)." Sombart is not immune to discipline-bound visions of interdisciplinarity when he argues, for instance, that sociology is the science of social conduct and since economic conduct is social conduct then economics must be sociology (cp. Sombart, [1931] 1959: 659).
62. We cite for illustrative purposes one of Sombart's repeated definitions, that of the "nature" of cultural analysis: "Aufgabe aller Kulturwissenschaften ist es nun, Mittel und Wege zu finden, die von ihnen bearbeiteten Kulturerscheinungen in ihrer geschichtlichen Besonderheit zu erfassen. Es gilt, ein bestimmtes Kulturgebiet dadurch gleichsam wissenschaftsreif zu machen, daß man lernt, durch Heraushebung seiner historischen Konkretheit seine Stellung in der Geschichte zu bestimmen und es in seiner Eigenart von anderen Verwirklichungen derselben Kulturidee zu unterscheiden. Das erreicht man abermals mit Hilfe einer an den Tatbestand herangetragenen Idee, die aber in diesem Falle keine abgrenzende, sondern eine gestaltende Funktion auszuüben berufen ist (Sombart, [1931] 1959: 653)." In the case of linguistics such an idea may be the "inner form of language," in theology it is the idea of the dogma, in the arts it is the concept of style, and in economics according to Sombart it is the notion of an economic system such as capitalism.
63. Appadurai joins Mukerji in stating that a materialist consumer culture oriented around products and goods from all over the world was the "prerequisite for the technological revolution of industrial capitalism"—not its result (Appadurai, 1986: 37).

References

Abraham, Gary (1988) "Max Weber on 'Jewish rationalism' and the Jewish question," *Politics, Culture and Society* 1: 358–91.

Adorno, Theodor W., and Walter Benjamin (1994) *Briefwechsel 1928–1940*. Frankfurt am Main: Suhrkamp.

Allodi, Leonardo (1989) "Die Analyse des modernen Menschen bei Max Scheler und Werner Sombart," *Annali di Sociologia* 5: 458–93.

Appadurai, Arjun (1986) *The Social Life of Things. Commodities in Cultural Perspective*. Cambridge: Cambridge Univ. Press.

Appel, Michael (1987) "Der 'Moderne Kapitalismus' im Urteil zeitgenössischer Besprechungen," in Bernhard vom Brocke (ed.) *Sombarts 'Moderner Kapitalismus.' Materialien zur Kritik und Rezeption*. München: n. p. 67–85.

Appel, Michael (1992) *Werner Sombart. Historiker und Theoretiker des modernen Kapitalimus*. München: n. p.

Backhaus, Jürgen (1989) "Sombart's 'Modern Capitalism'," *Kyklos* 42: 599–611.

Backhaus, Jürgen (1996) *Werner Sombart (1863–1941): Social Scientist*. Marburg and der Lahn: Metropolis.

Bijker, Wiebe, Thomas P. Hughes, and Trevor Pinch, eds (1987) *The Social Construction of Technological Systems*. Cambridge, MA: MIT Press.

Bodemann, Y. Michal (1994) "Ethnos, Race and Nation. Werner Sombart, The Jews and Classical German Sociology," in Wsevolod W. Isajiw, *Multiculturalism in North America and Europe. Comparative Perspective on Interethnic Relations and Social Incorporation*. Toronto: Canadian Scholars' Press.

Braudel, Fernand (1992) *The Structures of Everyday Life*. New York: Harper & Row.

Breuer, Stefan (1996) "Von Tönnies zu Weber. Zur Frage einer 'deutschen Linie' in der Soziologie," *Berliner Journal für Soziologie* 6: 227–45.

Brocke, Bernhard vom (1987) *Sombart's 'Moderner Kapitalismus.' Materialien zur Kritik und Rezeption*. München: n. p.

Campbell, Colin (1987) *The Romantic Ethic and the Spirit of Modern Consumerism*. Oxford: Blackwell.

Cohen, Gerald A. (1978) *Karl Marx's Theory of History: A Defence*. Oxford: Clarendon.

Dasgupta, Partha, and Paul A. David (1994) "Toward a New Economics of Science," *Research Policy* 23: 487–521.

Davis, Natalie Zemon (1999) "Religion and Capitalism Once Again? Jewish Merchant Culture in the Seventeenth Century," in Sherry B. Ortner (ed.) *The Fate of "Culture": Geertz and Beyond*. Berkeley: Univ. of California Press. 56–85.

Dawson, W. H. (1927/28) "Review of Werner Sombart's 'Der proletarische Sozialismus'," *Economic History Review* 1: 363–5.

de Grazia, Victoria (1996) "Introduction," in Victoria de Grazia (ed.) *The Sex of Things. Gender and Consumption in Historical Perspective*. Berkeley: Univ. of California Press. 1–14.

Dosi, Giovanni, Christopher Freeman, Richard Nelson, Gerald Silverberg, and Luc Soete, eds (1988) *Technical Change and Economic Theory*. London: Pinter.

Dubofsky, Melvyn (1994) *The State and Labor in Modern America*. Chapel Hill: Univ. of North Carolina Press.

Elias, Norbert (1983) *The Court Society*. New York: Pantheon.

Engels, Friedrich ([1895] 1977) "Supplement to 'Capital Vol. 3'," *Capital, Volume 3*. London: Lawrence & Wishart.
Epstein, Mortimer (1941) "Werner Sombart's obituary," *Economic Journal* 51: 523–6.
Fetscher, Irving (1962) "Die industrielle Gesellschaft und die Ideologie der Nationalsozialisten," *Gesellschaft, Staat und Erziehung* 5: 16–23.
Fishman, Aryei (1989) "The religious kibbutz: A note on the theories of Marx, Sombart and Weber on Judaism and economic success," *Sociological Analysis* 50: 281–90.
Fosdick, Dorothy (1939) "Review of Werner Sombart's 'A New Social Philosophy'," *American Sociological Review* 4: 429–30.
Freeman, Christopher, John Clark, and Luc Soete (1982) *Unemployment and Technical Change. A Study of Long Waves and Economic Development*. Westport, CT: Greenwood Press.
Gehlen, Arnold (1940) *Der Mensch. Seine Natur und seine Stellung in der Welt*. Berlin: Junker & Dünnhaupt.
Gorz, André ([1991] 1994) *Capitalism, Socialism, Ecology*. London: Verso.
Granovetter, Mark (1990) "The old and the new economic sociology: A history and an agenda," in Roger Friedland and Alton F. Robertson (eds) *Beyond the Marketplace. Rethinking Economy and Society*. New York: Aldine de Gruyter. 89–112.
Grundmann, Reiner (1991) *Marxism and Ecology*. Oxford: Oxford Univ. Press.
Harris, Abram L. (1942) "Sombart and German (National) Socialism," *Journal of Political Economy* 50: 805–35.
Hayek, Friedrich A. (1944) *The Road to Serfdom*. Sydney: Dymock's Book Arcade.
Hennis, Wilhelm ([1987] 1988) *Max Weber. Essays in Reconstruction*. London: Allen & Unwin.
Herf, Jeffrey (1984) *Reactionary Modernism. Technology, Culture, and Politics in Weimar and the Third Reich*. Cambridge: Cambridge Univ. Press.
Hinz, Manfred (1985) *Die Zukunft der Katastrophe. Mythische und rationalistische Geschichtstheorie im italienischen Futurismus*. Berlin: de Gruyter.
Hirshleifer, Jack (1985) "The expanding domain of economics," *American Economic Review* 75: 53–66.
Hofmannsthal, Hugo von (1927) *Das Schrifttum als geistiger Raum der Nation*. München: Bremer Presse.
Horowitz, Irving L. (1986) "The Jews and modern communism: the Sombart thesis reconsidered," *Modern Judaism* 6: 13–25.
Hughes, Everett C. (1927/28) "Review of Werner Sombart's 'Wirtschaftsleben im Zeitalter des Hochkapitalismus: Zweiter Halbband: Der Hergang der hochkapitalistischen Wirtschaft. Das Gesamtswirtschaft'," *American Journal of Sociology* 33: 501.
Käsler, Dirk (1984) *Frühe Deutsche Soziologie 1909 bis 1934 und ihre Entstehungsmilieus*. Opladen: Westdeutscher Verlag.
Käsler, Dirk (1997) "Soziologie und Nationalsozialismus," in *Soziologie. Mitteilungsblatt der Deutschen Gesellschaft für Soziologie* 3: 20–32.
Kettler, David, Volker Meja, and Nico Stehr (1984) *Karl Mannheim*. London: Routledge.
Klingemann, Carsten (1997) "Der Oberförster jagt den Nazijäger. Rufmord als letztes Mittel der Vergangenheitsbewältigung," in *Soziologie. Mitteilungsblatt der Deutschen Gesellschaft für Soziologie* 3: 33–51.
Knight, Melvin M. (1934) "Review of Frederick L. Nussbaum's 'A History of the

Economic Institutions of Modern Europe: An Introduction to "Der moderne Kapitalismus" of Werner Sombart.'," *Journal of Political Economy* 42: 260–4.
König, René (1987a) "Zur Soziologie der Zwanziger Jahre oder Epilog zu zwei Revolutionen, die niemals stattgefunden haben, und was daraus für unsere Gegenwart resultiert", in René König *Soziologie in Deutschland.* Begründer/Verächter/Verfechter. München: Hanser. 230–57, 466–8.
König, René (1987b) "Die Soziologie in Berlin um 1930," in René König *Soziologie in Deutschland.* Begründer/Verächter/Verfechter. München: Hanser. 253–97, 469–73.
Kracauer, Siegfried ([1932] 1990) "Gestaltschau oder Politik? Eine Rezension von Ernst Jüngers 'Der Arbeiter, Herrschaft und Gestalt'," in Siegfried Kracauer *Schriften.* Vol. 5.3. Frankfurt am Main: Suhrkamp. 118–23.
Krause, Werner (1962) *Werner Sombarts Weg vom Kathedersozialismus zum Faschismus.* Berlin: Akademie Verlag.
Krause, Werner (1969) *Wirtschaftstheorie unter dem Hakenkreuz. Die bürgerliche politische Ökonomie in Deutschland während der faschistischen Herrschaft.* Berlin: Akademie Verlag.
Kruse, Werner (1990) "Von der historischen Nationalökonomie zur historischen Soziologie. Ein Paradigmawechsel in den deutsche Sozialwissenschaften um 1900," *Zeitschrift für Soziologie* 19: 149–65.
Landes, David S. (1974) "The Jewish merchant. Typology and stereotypology in Germany," *Leo Baeck Yearbook* 14: 11–23.
Landheer, Barth (1951) "Review of Werner Sombart's 'The Jews and Modern Capitalism'," *American Sociological Review* 16: 587–8.
Latour, Bruno, and Steve Woolgar (1986) *Laboratory Life. The Construction of Scientific Facts.* Princeton, NJ: Princeton Univ. Press.
Lenger, Friedrich (1994) *Werner Sombart 1963–1941. Eine Biographie.* München: C.H. Beck.
Liebersohn, Harry (1988) *Fate and Utopia in German Sociology, 1870–1923.* Cambridge, MA: MIT Press.
Lipset, Seymour Martin, and Gary Marks (2000) *It Didn't Happen Here. Why Socialism Failed in the United States.* New York: W.W. Norton & Co.
Loader, Colin, Jeffrey Waddous, and Rick Tilman (1991) "Thorstein Veblen, Werner Sombart and the periodization of history," *Journal of Economic Issues* 25: 421–429.
Luhmann, Niklas (1996) *Social Systems.* Stanford: Stanford Univ. Press.
Lukács. Georg ([1922] 1971) *History and Class Consciousness.* Studies in Marxist Dialectics. Cambridge, MA: MIT Press.
Lübbe, Herman (1974) *Politische Philosophie in Deutschland. Studien zu ihrer Geschichte.* München: n. p.
Lyotard, Jean-François (1990) *Heidegger and "the Jews."* Minneapolis, MN: Minnesota Univ. Press.
MacDonald, H. Malcolm (1938/39) "Review of Werner Sombart's 'A New Social Philosophy'," *Southwestern Social Sciences Quarterly* 19: 219.
Marx, Karl ([1843] 1975) "On the Jewish Question," in *Marx Engels Collected Works 3.* London: Lawrence & Wishart.
Marx, Karl ([1847] 1976) "The Poverty of Philosophy," in *Marx Engels Collected Works 6.* London: Lawrence & Wishart.
Marx, Karl ([1859] 1987) "A Contribution to the Critique of Political Economy," in

Marx Engels Collected Works 29. London: Lawrence & Wishart.
Mendes-Flohr, Paul R. (1976) "Werner Sombart's 'The Jews and Modern Capitalism' An analysis of its ideological premises," *Leo Baeck Yearbook* 21: 87–107.
Merton, Robert K. ([1939] 1957) "Science and economy of 17th century England," in Robert K. Merton, *Social Theory and Social Structure*. Revised and Enlarged Edition. New York: The Free Press. 607–27.
Mills, C. Wright (1970) "Introduction," in *Theory of the Leisure Class*. London: Allen & Unwin.
Mises, Ludwig von (1978) *Notes and Recollections*. Spring Mills: Libertarian Press.
Mitzman, Arthur (1973) *Sociology and Estrangement. Three Sociologists of Imperial Germany*. New York: Alfred A. Knopf.
Mitzman, Arthur (1985) *The Iron Cage. An Historical Interpretation of Max Weber. With a new Introduction*. New Brunswick, NJ: Transaction Books.
Mosse, Werner (1979) "Judaism, Jews and Capitalism. Weber, Sombart and Beyond," *Leo Baeck Yearbook* 24: 3–15.
Mosse, Werner (1987) *Jews in the German Economy*. Oxford: Clarendon.
Mukerji, Chandra (1993) "Reading and Writing with Nature: A Materialist Approach to French Formal Gardens," in John Brewer and Roy Porter (eds) *Consumption and the World of Goods*. London: Routledge. 439–61.
Neumann, Sigmund (1939) "Review of Sombart's 'Soziologie: Was sie ist und was sie sein sollte'," *American Sociological Review* 4: 407–9.
Oelsner, Toni (1962) "The place of the Jews in Economic History as Viewed by German Scholars," *Leo Baeck Yearbook* 7: 183–212.
Ott, Hugo ([1988] 1994) *Martin Heidegger. A Political Life*. London: Fontana.
Park, Robert E. (1930/31) "Review of Werner Sombart's 'Die drei Nationalökonomien'," *American Journal of Sociology* 36: 1071–7.
Parsons, Talcott ([1937] 1949) *The Structure of Social Action. A Study in Social Theory with Special Reference to a Group of Recent European Writers*. Glencoe, IL: Free Press.
Plessner, Helmut (1928) *Die Stufen des Organischen und der Mensch*.
Ringer, Fritz K. (1969) *The Decline of the German Mandarins. The German Academic Community 1890–1933*. Cambridge, MA: Harvard Univ. Press.
Ritzer, George (1996) *The McDonaldization of Society*. London: Pine Forge Press.
Robbins, Richard H. (1999) *Global Problems and the Culture of Capitalism*. N. p.: Allyn & Bacon.
Roberts, Mary Louise (1998) "Gender, Consumption, and Commodity Culture," *American Historical Review* 103(3): 817–44.
Rogin, Leo (1933) "Werner Sombart and the 'Natural Science Method' in Economics," *Journal of Political Economy* 41: 222–36.
Röpke, Wilhelm (1945) *Die deutsche Frage*. Erlenbach-Zürich: Eugen Rentsch Verlag.
Sapori, Armando (1955) "Werner Sombart," in *Studi di storia economica*. Firenze: Sansoni.
Schumpeter, Joseph Alois (1927) "Sombarts dritter Band," *Schmollers Jahrbuch für Gesetzgebung, Verwaltung und Volkswirtschaft im deutschen Reiche* 51: 349–69.
Schumpeter, Joseph Alois (1954) *History of Economic Analysis*. New York: Oxford Univ. Press.
Shaw, George Bernard (1946) *Man and Superman, a Comedy and a Philosophy*. Harmondsworth: Penguin.

Sieferle, Rolf-Peter (1995) *Die Konservative Revolution. Fünf biographische Skizzen.* Frankfurt am Main: Fischer Taschenbuch Verlag.

Singer, Brian (1993) "The 'Heidegger Affair': Philosophy, Politics, and the 'Political'," *Theory and Society* 22: 539–68.

Smith, Merritt Roe and Leo Marx, eds (1994) *Does Technology drive History? The Dilemma of Technological Determinism.* Cambridge, MA: MIT Press.

Sombart, Nicolaus ([1984] 1998) *Jugend in Berlin 1933–1943. Ein Bericht.* Frankfurt am Main: Fischer.

Sombart, Werner (1896) *Sozialismus und soziale Bewegung im 19. Jahrhundert.* Jena: n. p.

Sombart, Werner (1902a) *Der moderne Kapitalismus. Erster Band: Die Genesis des Kapitalismus.* Leipzig: Duncker & Humblot.

Sombart, Werner (1902b) "Einleitende Bemerkungen zu einer Theorie des modernen Kapitalismus." *Vierteljahresschrift für* wissenschaftliche Philisophie und Soziologie 26: 21–47.

Sombart, Werner (1903) *Die deutsche Volkswirtschaft im Neunzehnten Jahrhundert.* Berlin: Georg Bondi.

Sombart, Werner (1904) "The Proletariat, Originally published as 'The Industrial Group'," in Howard J. Rogers (ed.) *International Congress of Arts and Science Vol. 7*, London and New York: University Alliance. 791–9.

Sombart, Werner (1906a) *Das Proletariat.* Frankfurt am Main: Rütten and Loening.

Sombart, Werner (1906b) *Warum gibt es in den Vereinigten Staaten keinen Sozialismus?* Tübingen: J.C.B. Mohr (Paul Siebeck).

Sombart, Werner ([1896] 1909) *Socialism and the Social Movement.* (Translation of *Sozialismus und Soziale Bewegung im 19. Jahrhundert*). London: Dutton.

Sombart, Werner (1909) "Der kapitalistische Unternehmer," *Archiv für Sozialwissenschaft und Sozialpolitik* 29: 689–758.

Sombart, Werner ([1910] 1911) "Technik und Kultur," in *Verhandlungen des ersten Deutschen Soziologentages.* Tübingen: J.C.B. Mohr (Paul Siebeck). 63–83.

Sombart, Werner (1911) *Die Juden und das Wirtschaftsleben.* Leipzig: Duncker & Humblot.

Sombart, Werner (1912a) "Technik und Kultur," *Archiv für Sozialwissenschaft und Sozialpolitik* 33: 305–47.

Sombart, Werner (1912b) "Die Technik im Zeitalter des Frühkapitalismus." *Archiv für Sozialwissenschaft und Sozialpolitik* 34: 721–760.

Sombart, Werner (1912c) "Travel in Germany in 1800" in Werner Sombart *Die deutsche Volkswirtschaft im neunzehnten Jahrhundert.* Berlin: Georg Bondi. 1–20.

Sombart, Werner (1913a) *Der Bourgeois. Zur Geistesgeschichte des modernen Wirtschaftsmenschen.* München und Leipzig: Duncker & Humblot.

Sombart, Werner (1913b) *Die deutsche Volkswirtschaft im neunzehnten Jahrhundert. Dritte, durchgesehene und bis auf die Gegenwart weitergeführte Auflage.* Berlin: Georg Bondi.

Sombart, Werner ([1911] 1913) *The Jews and Modern Capitalism.* Mortimer Epstein (trans.). London: Unwin.

Sombart, Werner ([1913] 1915) *The Quintessence of Capitalism. A Study of the History and Psychology of Modern Business Man.* Mortimer Epstein (trans.). New York: Dutton.

Sombart, Werner ([1916] 1921a) *Der moderne Kapitalismus. Historisch-systematische Darstellung des gesamten Wirtschaftslebens von seinen Anfängen bis zur Gegen-*

wart. Erster Band: Einleitung-Die vorkapitalistsische Wirtschaft—Die historischen Grundlagen des modernen Kapitalismus. Zweiter Halbband. München und Leipzig: Duncker & Humblot.

Sombart, Werner ([1916] 1921b) *Der moderne Kapitalismus. Historisch-systematische Darstellung des gesamten Wirtschaftslebens von seinen Anfängen bis zur Gegenwart. Zweiter Band: Das europäischer Wirtschaftsleben im Zeitalter des Frükapitalismus vornehmlich im 16., 17. und 18. Jahrhundert. Erster Halbband.* München und Leipzig: Duncker & Humblot.

Sombart, Werner ([1912] 1922) *Luxus und Kapitalismus.* München und Leipzig: Duncker & Humblot.

Sombart, Werner (1923) *Soziologie.* Berlin: Pan-Verlag Rolf Heise.

Sombart, Werner (1924a) *Der proletarische Sozialismus ("Marxismus"). Erster Band: Die Lehre. Zehnte neubearbeutete Auflage der Schrift "Sozialismus und soziale Bewegung."* Jena: Gustav Fischer.

Sombart, Werner (1924b) *Der proletarische Sozialismus ("Marxismus"). Zweiter Band: Die Bewegung. Zehnte neubearbeutete Auflage der Schrift "Sozialismus und soziale Bewegung."* Jena: Gustav Fischer.

Sombart, Werner ([1925] 1927) *Die Ordnung des Wirtschaftslebens Zweite, verbesserte Auflage.* Berlin: Julius Springer.

Sombart, Werner (1927) "Das Wirtschaftsleben der Zukunft," in *Der moderne Kapitalismus*, Vol. 3.2. München and Leipzig: Duncker & Humblot. 1008–22.

Sombart, Werner (1928) *Der moderne Kapitalismus. Historisch-systematische Darstellung des gesamteuropäischen Wirtschaftslebens von seinen Anfängen bis zur Gegenwart. Dritter Band: Das Wirtschaftsleben im Zeitalter des Hochkapitalismus. Zweiter Halbband: Der Hergang der hochkapitalistischen Wirtschaft. Die Gesamtwirtschaft.* München und Leipzig: Duncker & Humblot.

Sombart, Werner (1930) *Die drei Nationalökonomien.* Geschichte und System der Lehr von der Wirtschaft. München and Leipzig: n. p.

Sombart, Werner (1934a) "Antrittsrede," in *Sitzungsberichte der Preußischen Akademie der Wissenschaften.* Berlin: n. p.

Sombart, Werner (1934b) *Deutscher Sozialismus.* Berlin: Buchholz & Weisswange.

Sombart, Werner (1934c) "Vom praktischen Nutzen theoretischen Wissens. Antwort an Wiskemann I and II." *Der Deutsche Volkswirt* 8 (10.8, 17.8): 2009ff, 2055ff.

Sombart., Werner (1935) *Was ist deutsch? Durchgesehender und durch Zusätze erweiterter Abdruck aus dem Buche "Deutscher Sozialismus."* Berlin: Buchholz & Weißwange.

Sombart, Werner ([1934] 1937) *A New Social Philosophy* (Translation of *Deutscher Sozialismus.*) Karl F. Geisser (trans. and ed.). Princeton, NJ: Princeton Univ. Press.

Sombart, Werner (1938a) "Beiträge zur Geschichte der wissenschaftlichen Anthropologie," in *Sitzungsberichte der Preußischen Akademie der Wissenschaften.* Philosophische-historische Klasse 1938. Berlin: n. p. 749–789.

Sombart, Werner (1938b) *Vom Menschen. Versuch einer geisteswissenschaftlichen Anthropologie.* Berlin: Buchholz & Weisswange.

Sombart, Werner (1938c) *Weltanschauung: Wissenschaft and Wirtschaft.* Berlin: Bucholz & Weibwange, Verlagsbuchhandlung.

Sombart, Werner ([1911] 1951) *The Jews and Modern Capitalism.* Mortimer Epstein (trans.). With an Introduction to the American Edition by Bert F. Hoselitz. Glencoe, IL.: Free Press.

Sombart, Werner ([1936] 1956) "Soziologie: Was sie ist und was sie sein sollte," in

Werner Sombart, *Noo-Soziologie*. Berlin: Duncker & Humblot. 95–123.
Sombart, Werner ([1931] 1959) "Wirtschaft," in Alfred Vierkandt (ed.) *Handwörterbuch der Soziologie*. Stuttgart: Enke. 652–9.
Sombart, Werner ([1911] 1962) "The Significance of the Jewish Religion in Economic Life," in Mortimer Epstein (trans.) Werner Sombart *The Jews and Modern Capitalism*. New York: Collier Books. 187–237.
Sombart, Werner ([1913] 1967a) "The Secularization of Love," in Werner Sombart, *Luxury and Capitalism*. Ann Arbor, MI: Univ. of Michigan Press. 42–57.
Sombart, Werner ([1913] 1967b) "The Bourgeois—Past and Present," in Mortimer Epstein (trans.) Werner Sombart *The Quintessence of Capitalism*. New York: Howard Fertig. 153–89.
Sombart, Werner ([1913] 1967c) "The Origins of the Capitalist Spirit," in Mortimer Epstein (trans.) Werner Sombart *The Quintessence of Capitalism*. New York: Howard Fertig. 193–221.
Sombart, Werner ([1913] 1967d) "The Influence of Technical Inventions," in Mortimer Epstein (trans.) Werner Sombart *The Quintessence of Capitalism*. New York: Howard Fertig. 319–41.
Sombart, Werner (1967) *Luxury and Capitalism*. Ann Arbor: Univ. of Michigan Press.
Sombart, Werner ([1906] 1969) *Warum gibt es in den Vereinigten Staaten Keinen Sozialismus*? Darmstadt: Wissenschaftliche Buchgesellschaft.
Sombart, Werner ([1906] 1976) "Why is there no Socialism in the United States?" in Patricia M. Hocking and Christopher T. Husbands (trans) Werner Sombart *Why is there no Socialism in the United States?* London and Basingstoke: Macmillan. 3-24.
Sombart, Werner ([1902] 1986) "Wirtschaft und Mode. Ein Beitrag zur Theorie der modernen Bedarfsgestaltung," in Silvia Bovenschen (ed.), *Die Listen der Mode*. Frankfurt am Main: n.□p. 80–105.
Sombart, Werner ([1913] 1987) *Der Bourgeois*. Berlin: Duncker & Humblot.
Sontheimer, Kurt ([1962] 1978) *Antidemokratisches Denken in der Weimarer Republik. Die politischen Ideen des deutschen Nationalismus zwischen 1918 und 1933*. München: Hanser.
Sontheimer, Kurt (1994) "Wider die Leisetreterei der Historiker," *Die Zeit* 45: 15–16.
Stephan, Paula E. (1996) "The Economics of Science," *Journal of Economic Literature* 34: 1199–235.
Stern, Fritz (1961) *The Politics of Cultural Despair. A Study in the Rise of the German Ideology*. Berkeley, CA: Univ. of California Press.
Swedberg, Richard (1987) "Economic sociology: Past and Present," *Current Sociology* 35: 1–221.
Turner, Bryan S. (1992) *Max Weber: From History to Modernity*. London: Routledge.
Veblen, Thorstein Bunde (1899) *The Theory of the Leisure Class*. New York, NY: Macmillan.
Weber, Alfred ([1935] 1950) *Kulturgeschichte als Kultursoziologie*. Frankfurt am Main: Büchergilde Gutenberg.
Weber, Marianne ([1926] 1975) *Max Weber: A Biography*. New York: Wiley.
Weber, Max (1905a) "Die protestantische Ethik und der 'Geist' des Kapitalismus. I: Das Problem," *Archiv für Sozialwissenschaft und Sozialpolitik* 20: 1–54.
Weber, Max (1905b) "Die protestantische Ethik und der 'Geist' des Kapitalismus. II: Die Berufsidee des asketischen Protestantismus," *Archiv für Sozialwissenschaft und Sozialpolitik* 21: 1–110.

Weber, Max ([1922] 1968) *Economy and Society. An Outline of Interpretive Sociology*. E. Fischoff et al. (trans), Günther Roth and Claus Wittich (eds). New York: Bedminster Press.
Weber, Max ([1920] 1988) *Gesammelte Aufsätze zur Religionssoziologie*, vol. 1. Tübingen: J.C.B. Mohr (Paul Siebeck).
Weber, Max (1993) *Max Weber Gesamtausgabe*, vol. 4, *Landarbeiterfragen, Nationalstaat und Volkswirtschaftspolitik, 1892–1899*. Tübingen: J.C.B. Mohr (Paul Siebeck).

I

The Nature of the Economic Market System

1

Capitalism

The Concept of Capitalism

The concept of capitalism and even more clearly the term itself may be traced primarily to the writings of socialist theoreticians. It has in fact remained one of the key concepts of socialism down to the present time. Nevertheless, it cannot be said that a clear-cut definition has ever been attempted. Even Karl Marx, who virtually discovered the phenomenon, defined only certain aspects of capitalism as the occasion required. When the term is used by socialists in any definite sense it has the character of a political byword with a strong ethical tinge.

Despite the fact that capitalism tends to become the sole subject matter of economics, neither the term nor the concept has as yet been universally recognized by representatives of academic economics. The older German economists and to a much greater extent the economists of other countries rejected entirely the concept of capitalism. In many cases the rejection was merely implicit; capitalism was not discussed at all except perhaps in connection with the history of economic doctrines, and when it was mentioned there was no indication that it was of particular importance. The term is not found in Gide, Cauwes, Marshall, Seligman, or Cassel, to mention only the best-known texts. In other treatises, such as those of Schmoller, Adolf Wagner, Richard Ehrenberg, and Philippovich, there is some discussion of capitalism but the concept is subsequently rejected. In the newer economics it is recognized as indispensable or at least useful, but the uncertainty as to its exact meaning is generally expressed by quotation marks about the word. Representatives of this school are little inclined to attempt the constructive development or more accurate analysis of the concept.

The works of Sombart are the first in which the concept of capitalism has been definitively recognized as fundamental to the system of economic thought. Here it is demonstrated that capitalism designates an economic system significantly characterized by the predominance of "capital," and it is argued that the word "capitalism," which by its very etymology suggests this feature of the economic system, must be retained as the appropriate term for it. The fact that this term has received a negative ethical emphasis in socialist literature should not qualify its use as a completely non-ethical designation for a definite economic system, particularly since there is apparently no better substitute.

Capitalism as a specific economic system cannot be understood without an analysis of the concept of economic system with a view to pointing out the function of this concept in economic science. Economic life is distinguished as a particular sphere of cultural life by the principle of "economy." This principle as a logical concept is removed from the realm of space and time, but "economy" in the sense of economic life is an existential complex with definite spatial and temporal aspects. All culture, and consequently all economy, is historical. As there is in the abstract no religion, no art, no language, no state, but merely a certain religion, a certain art, a certain language, a certain state, so there is no economy in the abstract, but a particularly constituted, historically distinguishable economic life.

The task of all the cultural sciences is to find ways and means by which to grasp cultural phenomena in their historical singularity. A certain field of culture is rendered scientifically mature when science learns to determine its place in history on the basis of its concrete historical manifestations and to distinguish it in its characteristic phases from other concrete manifestations of the same cultural principle. This is achieved by the introduction of a formative conception not derived from empirical observation, which makes possible the construction of systems. Thus linguistics utilizes the conception of inherent language form, the science of religion the conception of dogma, the science of art the conception of style.

Economic science likewise requires a constitutive conception in order to arrange its material in systems. The function of such a conception is to enable us to classify the fundamental characteristics of economic life of a particular time, to distinguish it from the economic organization of other periods and thus to delimit the major economic epochs in history. A conception which will make possible the systematization of economic phenomena must be derived directly from the notion of "economy," the essentials of which it must comprise, collate, and connect—and not merely in their abstract form, not merely as ideas, but in the concrete, as definite historical facts. These requirements are satisfied by the general conception of the economic system. By an economic system is understood a mode of satisfying and making provisions for material wants which can be comprehended as a unit and wherein each constituent element of the economic process displays some given characteristic. These constituent elements are the economic spirit or outlook—the sum total of the purposes, motives, and principles which determine men's behavior in economic life—the form of economic life or the objective system of regulations of economic relations, and the technology employed in economic processes. Defined more precisely, an economic system is a unitary mode of providing for material wants, animated by a definite spirit, regulated and organized according to a definite plan, and applying a definite technical knowledge.

It will be observed that the economic system is superior to all other systematizing conceptions hitherto employed, because they stressed merely single, prominent characteristics and made it possible to distinguish only single aspects of economic life, whereas the conception of the economic system is broad enough to comprehend every aspect. On the other hand, it is definite enough to encompass the historical concreteness of economic life and is thus far superior, for the purpose of framing a system, to purely formal ideas such as that of national economy (*Volkswirtschaft*). Finally, it is general enough to permit application to every conceivable economic institution, from the most primitive to the most highly developed.

The Spirit of the Capitalist System

The special character of capitalism will be brought out most clearly if we consider separately the characteristic forms which the three constituent elements—spirit, form, and technology—assume in the capitalist system.

The spirit, or the economic outlook, of capitalism is dominated by three ideas: acquisition, competition, and rationality.

The purpose of economic activity under capitalism is acquisition, and more specifically acquisition in terms of money. The idea of increasing the sum of money on hand is the exact opposite of the idea of earning a livelihood, which dominated all precapitalistic systems, particularly the feudal-handicraft economy. In pre-capitalistic systems, economic as well as all other thought and action was centered about the human being. Man's interests as producer or as consumer determined the conduct of individuals and of the community, the organization of the economic life of society as a whole, and the ordinary routine of business life in its concrete manifestations. Goods were produced and traded in order adequately to meet the consumers' needs and to provide an ample livelihood for producers and merchants; the standards for the expectations of both consumers and producers were fixed by long established usage. The category of qualitative use value was the determining principle of valuation. All social and individual norms affecting economic processes were grounded in human, personal values. On the other hand, in systems dominated by the idea of acquisition the aim of all economic activity is not referred back to the living person. An abstraction, the stock of material things, occupies the center of the economic stage; an increase of possessions is basic to all economic activity. The idea of such an economic system is expressed most perfectly in the endeavor to utilize that fund of exchange value which supplies the necessary substratum for production activities (capital).

While acquisition constitutes the purpose of economic activity, the attitudes displayed in the process of acquisition form the content of the idea of competition. These attitudes, which are logically inherent in acquisition, may be described as freedom of acquisition from regulation by norms imposed upon the individual from the outside, the lack of quantitative limits to acquisition, its superiority over all other aims, and its ruthlessness.

By reason of its freedom from regulation capitalism rests essentially on the individual's assertion of his natural power. Every economic agent may and should extend his sphere of action as far as the complete exercise of his powers will allow; in case of failure, however, he completely foregoes assistance. Economic activity is closely associated with personal risk, but the economic agent is free to strive for economic success in any way he chooses provided he does not violate the penal code.

There are no absolute limits to acquisition, and the system exercises a psychological compulsion to boundless extension. The fact that capitalistic enterprise has as its purpose a certain mode of utilizing a stock of goods signifies a complete divorce of the aims of capitalistic economy from the personality of the economic agent. The abstract, impersonal character of the aim indicates its limitlessness. Activity in the capitalistic system is no longer determined by the needs, quantitatively and qualitatively limited, of one person or of a group of persons. Profits, no matter how large, can never reach a level sufficiently high to satisfy the economic agent. The positive drive toward boundless acquisition is grounded in the conditions of management. It is empirically true, though not logically inevitable, that any enlargement of business reacts to its own advantage, at least quantitatively through an extension of its sphere of exploitation and sometimes also qualitatively through a reduction of costs. This provides the stimulus to the continuous expansion of a business, often contrary to the expressed wishes of its owners and managers. In this peculiar orientation of human activity upon an infinitely removed goal lies the reason for the dynamic potency of the capitalistic system, a potency which renders intelligible all its remarkable achievements.

Acquisition therefore becomes unconditional, absolute. Not only does it seize upon all phenomena within the economic realm, but it reaches over into other cultural fields and develops a tendency to proclaim the supremacy of business interests over all other values. Wherever acquisition is absolute the importance of everything else is predicated upon its serviceability to economic interests: a human being is regarded merely as labor power, nature as an instrument of production, life as one grand commercial transaction, heaven and earth as a large business concern in which everything that lives and moves is registered in a gigantic ledger in terms of its money value. Ideals oriented upon the value of the human personality loosen their hold upon man's mind; efforts for the increase of human welfare cease to have value. Perfection of the business mechanism appears as the only goal worth striving for; the means become an end. The vague notion of progress comes to include only such developments as advances in technology, reductions in costs, increase in the briskness of trade, growth of wealth. *Fiat quaestus et pereat mundus.*

Acquisition which is quantitatively and qualitatively absolute degenerates eventually into unscrupulousness and ruthlessness. Business draws practical conclusions from the revolutionary supremacy of its ideals and seeks, without consideration for any conflicting interests, to clear all obstacles to the limitless and unqualified exercise of acquisition. The intensity of the acquisitive drive attains a point at which all moral and temperamental inhibitions disappear and all conflicting drives become inhibited. The business man is "unscrupulous" in his choice of ways and means, because the selection is based exclusively on their serviceability in the achievement of the final goal, on their usefulness as instruments of acquisition.

When the direction of economic affairs is oriented solely upon acquisition it is inevitable that those modes of economic behavior should be adopted which seem most rational, most systematic, best adapted to the purpose in hand. In the old, precapitalistic economic organization, which is essentially traditionalistic and static, there sets in a process of rationalization representing a manifestation of the dynamic principle. Economic rationality is thus the third dominating idea of the capitalist system.

Economic rationality is manifested in several aspects of the capitalistic business management—its predilection for long-range planning, for the strict adaptation of means to ends, for exact calculation. The genuinely capitalistic enterprise is managed on the basis of a plan which extends as far as possible into the future, thus leading to the introduction, among other things, of roundabout methods of production. The execution of the plan is accomplished by means which are painstakingly examined with reference to maximum serviceability for the purposes in hand—a vivid contrast to the ill-considered employment of means in more traditionalistic economies. Underlying the planning and its execution are the evaluation and registration of all business facts in precise quantitative terms and the coordination of these records as a significant whole. This adherence to exact accounting is only natural in a situation where all economic acts are regulated in accordance with their pecuniary value and where management looks to maximized profits as its ultimate aim.

Rationalization permeates, of course, the entire scope of business and affects its technical as well as its commercial aspects. It introduces into the sphere of production the most "rational" methods and stimulates thereby the development of scientific technology. It creates rational factory management and leads to proper departmentalization and departmental coordination. The rationalization of the procedures of manual labor results in the employment of the individual worker most serviceably with respect to the ultimate capitalistic aim. On the commercial side rationalization affects the purchase of production equipment and materials, the sale of the ready product at the most suitable time or in the best market, the creation of new outlets, whether through clever salesmanship or through the development of new forms of retailing.

Economic rationality penetrates gradually into other cultural spheres, reaching even those which are only remotely connected with economic life. Under its influence, all untamed natural growth disappears and, where it proves disturbing, even the aesthetically-pleasing individual is mercilessly weeded out. The idea of strict adaptation of means to ends, one of the essential ideological props of capitalism, permeates the totality of culture and leads in the course of time to a purely utilitarian valuation of human beings, objects, and events.

While individual action under capitalism is informed by the idea of highest rationality, the capitalistic system as a whole remains irrational, because the other dominant capitalistic idea, that of acquisition, of the unrestricted assertion by the individual of his power, leaves the regulation of the total economic process to the uncoordinated discretion of individual economic agents. From this coexistence of well nigh perfect rationality and of the greatest irrationality originate the numerous strains and stresses which are peculiarly characteristic of the economic system of capitalism.

The Form of the Capitalist System

The objective, institutional order of capitalism is characteristically free. The dominance of economic individualism has its counterpart in the far-reaching independence of the individual economic agents. The restrictions which law and usage impose upon them affect only the most marginal of their activities; essentially restrictions are intended to forestall merely criminal dealings, leaving a wide area of discretion to the individual. "Economic freedom," an aspect of the philosophy of natural rights, assumes, when regarded as an element of the economic order, the form of a system of positive rights conferred upon the individual by law and morals; these positive rights constitute the substance of economic liberalism.

Capitalistic business is typically private, so that economic initiative is lodged with enterprises which are actuated by the quest for private gain. These enterprises, subject to little regulation from the outside, assume the full risk of failure but enjoy also the unrestricted chance of success. Their activity keeps the economic machinery of society in motion.

The structure of capitalist economy is aristocratic. The number of economic agents is small as compared with the total number of persons participating in economic life, with the result that a large majority is subject to the power of a few economic agents. In a regime of economic freedom the relation between the economic agent and the persons controlled by him takes appropriately the legal form of a free contract. The dominance of a minority is explained by the fact that because of the high standard of technical knowledge and organizational skill required under capitalism people of average abilities and fortunes are incapable of assuming the direction of production and can therefore no longer act as economic agents as they could under the handicraft system.

The capitalist system, based as it is upon highly developed occupational specialization and functional separation, is marked by a high degree of decentralization. The principles underlying the division of labor in capitalist industry differ from those which governed handicraft economy to the extent that the segregation of a certain range of activities into a distinct branch of industry is determined not by the outlook and limitations of a living personality but by purely material factors, the causal sequences of the technological processes. Organic articulation enforced by an active, creative person is superseded under capitalism by purposefully directed mechanistic separation and coordination. The degree of specialization depends ultimately upon the advantages which it may bring to the private economic agents in their pursuit of profits.

Capitalist economy rests upon an exchange basis, the links between its constituent elements being the connections and relations established in the market. All production is intended for the market, is characteristically limited to the production of saleable goods; all products enter into commercial traffic. Similarly all means of production emerge from exchange transactions, are purchased in the market. No less important is the fact that the connection between economic agents and the persons controlled by them is established by contract entered into in the market; labor is thus treated as a species of saleable goods. The relationship between wants and their satisfaction through production is established indirectly through the medium of price, which regulates the quantity and character of output. Since the guiding principle of capitalism is gain, there is production only if prices yield profit, if they offer to the individual enterprise the prospect of economic success. This system of satisfying wants is therefore flexible, unlike the systems found in economic organizations oriented directly upon the satisfaction of needs. Distribution of the results of production, involving as it does a conflict between various groups, particularly between the two great classes of recipients of surplus value and of wages, is likewise regulated through the mechanisms of pricing.

Finally, the organization of production under capitalism is not limited to any single form. Although large-scale production predominates, production on a small scale (e.g., domestic system) has also its place in the system.

The Technology of the Capitalist System

The technology of the capitalist system must satisfy certain conditions. To begin with, capitalist technology must insure a high degree of productivity. It cannot fall below a certain minimum, because capitalist organization of production, involving necessarily the differentiation between the work of organization and management on the one hand and that of technical execution on the other, would then be impossible. For example, as long as every hunter can manage to subsist on the yield of his daily hunt, there is no room for a capitalist organization of hunting under the leadership of an organizer who does no actual hunting himself. Moreover, this productivity must be as high as possible, because, other things being equal, an increase in productivity means a correspondingly greater profit to the capitalist enterprise. The compensation of the wage earners, which is limited to the amount needed for subsistence, can with increased productivity be produced in a shorter time, and a larger proportion of the total working time remains therefore for the production of profits. Again, an advance in technology, particularly in the technique of transportation, involves capitalist expansion whether through an extension of the markets or an intensive accumulation of stock. Capitalist expansion under these conditions is accompanied by an increase in total profits and, in view of the decline in the costs of production, by a rise in the profit rate.

The technology characteristic of the capitalist system must also lend itself most readily to improvement and perfection. For constant technical improvements are an important weapon in the hands of the capitalist entrepreneur, who seeks to eliminate his competitor and to extend his market by offering goods superior in quality or lower in price. Moreover, such improvements yield a considerable differential profit, since the entrepreneur can realize a profit larger than the average so long as his improvements do not become widely accessible, and thus tend to reduce the socially necessary production costs. It will be observed that the quest for differential profit is an important dynamic factor in capitalist society.

The scientific, mechanistic technology, which is based on the accomplishments of natural science and breaks through the limitations of an organic environment, meets the tests both of productivity and of perfectibility. In addition, the ideas underlying this technology are in precise correspondence with the spirit of the capitalist system. Thus the rationalistic spirit which permeates this technology merely testifies to the fact that the economic principles of capitalistic organization have been applied to its technical processes. The inorganic character of this technology finds its economic counterpart in the divorce of economic life from the personality of the individual, in the impersonality of all economic relationships. The depersonalization of commercial as well as technical management transforms them into satisfactory instrumentalities for the practise of a technology based on the depersonalization of human labor.

The Capitalistic Enterprise

Modern capitalism made its appearance with the development of the capitalistic enterprise. It represents the form through which an independent existence is granted to business as such. By the combination of all simultaneous and successive business transactions into a conceptual whole, an independent economic organism is created over and above the individuals who constitute it. This entity appears then as the agent in each of these transactions and leads, as it were, a life of its own, which often exceeds in length that of its human members. This integrated system of relationships treated as an entity in the sciences of law and accounting becomes independent of any particular owner; it sets itself tasks, chooses means for their realization, forces men into its path, and carries them off in its wake. It is an intellectual construct which acts as a material monster.

The capitalistic enterprise has its own aims or, more properly, it has a single, very definite goal, profit; for only this particular goal corresponds to its spiritual essence. While it is in a sense sheer tautology to say that profit is its only goal, for conceptually the capitalistic enterprise is nothing but an instrumentality for the purpose of profit making, it is nevertheless of great significance that in this economic construct the spirit of the capitalist system and the aims of the individual economic agents become merged. Since the aims of these individuals are essentially arbitrary because they are freely determined, it is merely a happy coincidence if the immanent spirit of capitalism, acquisition, appears also as the subjectively experienced motive for individual action in the form of a striving for profit. The motives of capitalistic entrepreneurs are by no means restricted to acquisitive drives; among them, the craving for acclaim, the impulsion to serve the common good, the urge to action. But as all these motives work out in the capitalistic enterprise, they become, by virtue of an inner necessity, subordinate to profit making. For on closer examination it appears that none of the strivings which actuate the entrepreneur has any chance of success unless the capitalistic enterprise itself is successful, unless it yields a surplus above cost. Whatever other desires the entrepreneur, whatever subjectively conceived purpose his work may serve, he must always, simply because he is a capitalistic entrepreneur, want his enterprise to flourish, and so concentrate his energies upon the making of profit. This transformation of the subjective purposes of the entrepreneur in the capitalistic enterprise objectifies the quest for profit. The fact that the capitalistic enterprise performs this function justifies the inclusion of the spirit of capitalism as a factor in the causal sequences of capitalist actuality. We do not depart from the realm of fact when we relate the spiritual essence of capitalist economy to its actual driving forces, the motives of the capitalistic entrepreneur, by showing that because of the objectification of the striving for profit these appear to be the necessary realization of this spirit. Marx aptly spoke of "the drive of capital for profit."

In addition to an aim distinct from the purposes of its owners the capitalistic enterprise has a separate intelligence: it is the *locus* of economic rationality which is quite independent of the personality of the owner or of the staff. At first, rational business methods, objectively adapted to make the business profitable, are developed only in the course of time as a crystallization of experience; but in the period of full capitalism we observe the characteristic activity of artificial and self-conscious creation of economic rationality. Rational business methods are steadily and systematically developed and improved by persons who devote all or part of their time to this pursuit, which may itself be directed toward profit making. Thousands upon thousands of people, ranging in occupation from professors of business disciplines to humble bookkeepers, from downtrodden computers to manufacturers of all sorts of office equipment, are engaged in a perpetual quest for ways and means of perfecting economic rationality. As a result of these manifold efforts there exists at present a highly developed and constantly improving system of procedures (supplemented by specifications regarding the physical equipment to be employed therein) designed to insure business efficiency. This system is important primarily because it exists independently of any specific concern and is applicable to any line of business. Such a ready made economic rationality can be bought by the entrepreneur and installed in his concern to regulate it for the future.

Finally, the capitalistic enterprise possesses also the bourgeois virtues of industry, thrift, and stability, which the entrepreneur in the early days of capitalism had to cultivate in his own person in order to achieve success. These have now been transferred to the business concern and it is possible for the entrepreneur himself to dispense with them.

The infusion of the capitalist spirit in material objects affects in a number of obvious ways the course of economic activity. In the first place, management becomes more intensive, business planning more definitive. The incorporation of human beings into a material system fixes a definite minimum of energy which must be put forth: just as the speed of the worker is determined by that of the machine, so the tempo of work of the office force, from president to errand boy, is set by an external factor, the routine of the enterprise. The knowledge at the disposal of the executive is also increased thereby; now it far surpasses his personal erudition. Yet he is no longer burdened with the problem of the perfect organization of his business, which formerly consumed a large proportion of his energy; he is relieved of much useless activity and is thereby freed for specifically entrepreneurial work. Secondly, objectification of the capitalist spirit helps also to extend its domain. Thus the spread of the capitalist ideology over the entire world and to all strata of the entrepreneurial class is easily explained by the fact that economic rationality can be readily transmitted. Finally, the same process contributes to the spreading uniformity of economic life. Since economic procedures are objectively selected for their maximum serviceability in the achievement of certain ends, the fact that the ultimate aim is the same wherever capitalism prevails explains the increase in similarity of these economic procedures along with the development of economic rationality.

The Capitalistic Entrepreneur

The Ideal Entrepreneur combines the traits of inventor, discoverer, conqueror, organizer, and merchant. He is an inventor not so much of technical innovations as of new forms of organization for production, transportation, and marketing. Moreover, the entrepreneur as inventor does not terminate his activity with the formulation of the invention; in utilizing it he improves and vitalizes it in countless ways. The discoveries of the entrepreneur are in the realm of new outlets for his products, whether these be new territories or new layers of demand in areas already exploited. The entrepreneur is a conqueror in that he overcomes all obstacles and is courageous enough to take great risks for the success of his enterprise.

In his capacity as organizer the entrepreneur unites many individuals in a common and effective endeavor and so manages human beings and inanimate objects that he wrests from them the maximum productivity of which they are capable. To achieve such results the organizer must in the first place be a keen judge of human potentialities; he must be capable of selecting from a great number of people those best adapted to his particular needs. He must also have mastered the art of shifting responsibility, in part, to subordinates and of advancing those who, with the expansion of the enterprise, will take over systematically various phases of his own job. In this connection the gradual crystallization of the less important functions of the executive and their assignment in the course of years to a directorate, as accomplished by Alfred Krupp, must be regarded as a particularly distinguished example of functional separation and delegation. Similar problems are encountered in the organization of factory personnel. After the services of a promising worker are secured, he must be systematically trained and then assigned to a task which will develop his maximum serviceability. The entrepreneur must attend to the proper organization of groups of persons set to work together and, if there are several such units, he must establish the best possible relations between them. It would be erroneous, however, to consider that business and factory involve merely the clever choice of technically most advantageous nuclei for grouping men and materials. Special geographical, ethnological, commercial, and other conditions must be taken into account in making such selections. The organization which is relatively best is practically more important than the absolutely perfect one.

The entrepreneur as merchant is not merely a specialist in the buying and selling of goods, for the term merchant is here employed to designate one who is charged with definite functions in the capitalistic system. There are professional traders who are indeed anything but merchants; and those who go out "in search of wealth" and of whom our historians tell such an edifying tale are in most cases no merchants at all. Trading or merchandising may imply a number of very different things. It may cover such activities as the equipping and arming of ships, the recruiting of warriors, the conquest and pillage of new lands, the loading of the booty on ships and the sale of it at home to the highest bidder at public auction. Or it may mean the purchase of an old suit of clothes after clever spying upon a gentleman in dire need of money who resisted previous offers to sell it, and its sale to a country yokel who is eventually persuaded by the eloquence of the seller. Trading may also mean security speculation. Obviously the specific differentia of the merchant vary from case to case. Thus in the precapitalistic period to trade on a grand scale, as did the "royal merchants" of the Italian and German commercial cities, one had to be above all an adventurer, combining the traits of discoverer and conqueror. Yet to be a merchant in our sense of the term—the functional rather than the occupational sense—is to conduct a lucrative business, to combine the activities of calculation and negotiation. The merchant is a shrewd, speculating calculator and a persuasive negotiator.

As a calculator the merchant must conduct profitable transactions, buy cheap and sell dear, whatever the object of purchase and sale. Thus, assuming a fully developed enterprise, he must purchase the material and personal factors of production at the lowest price; in the process of production proper he must be continually on the lookout for the most economical employment of these factors; later he must sell the finished product, or whatever else he may have to sell, on the most advantageous terms to the person who can pay most in the best of the seller's markets when demand is greatest. To master these tasks he must be able to "speculate" and to "calculate." To speculate, in this sense, is to draw correct conclusions applying to the individual case from the evaluation of the total market situation. It necessitates a correct economic diagnosis. It implies a survey of all facts bearing upon the market and the recognition of their true interrelations, an accurate estimate of the significance of individual events, a correct interpretation of certain symptoms, a precise anticipation of future possibilities, and finally the selection with a sure grasp of the one most advantageous combination out of a hundred possible ones. To do this the merchant must be able to see with a thousand eyes, to hear with a thousand ears, to feel with a thousand antennae. Here he discovers needy gentlemen or warlike states and offers them a loan at the right moment; there he unearths a heretofore unexploited group of laborers who will work for a few cents less. In one case it is a question of gauging the sales possibilities of a new article and in the other of accurately estimating the influence of a political event upon the temper of the stock market. The merchant's ability immediately to translate all his observations into monetary terms, confidently to combine the thousand separate figures into an integral estimate of the chances of profit and loss, reflects his qualities as a "calculator." And if he be master of the art of instantly reducing every phenomenon to a figure in his ledger he is a "wonderfully shrewd calculator."

In order to succeed the merchant must have not only the sure instinct for a lucrative transaction; he must also be able to carry the transaction through by negotiation. The capacities required resemble those of a skillful mediator between two conflicting parties. For negotiation implies the power to persuade one's opponent, by advancing arguments and refuting objections, to accept a certain proposal. Negotiation is a bout with intellectual weapons. The negotiations carried on by a merchant have to do with the sale or purchase of goods, whether these be shares of stock, a business unit, or a loan. Bargaining in this sense covers the case of a petty peddler who higgles with the cook over a rabbit skin and that of the old clothes man who spends an hour talking the country huckster into buying a pair of pants. Yet it also applies to Nathan Rothschild, when under particularly complicated circumstances he closed a million dollar loan with the Prussian negotiators in a conference that lasted several days, to the representatives of the Standard Oil Company when they conferred on a general rate agreement with the railroad companies of an entire country, and to Carnegie and his men when they discussed with J.P. Morgan and his associates the taking over of the Carnegie plants valued at hundreds of millions. The striking differences between these cases are purely quantitative; the core of the matter remains the same whether the interests involved are measured in millions or pennies. The essence of all modern trading is negotiation, which need not always be verbal or carried on in person. It may be silent as in the case of a seller who by resorting to all sorts of advertising devices succeeds in impressing upon the public the merits of his wares. This is truly a modern example of "silent trade."

Ever present is the problem of convincing the buyer or the seller that the bargain will be to his advantage. The ideal of the seller is realized when an entire population comes to consider as vitally important the purchase of the article which he is advertising, when a panic seizes the mass of the people who fear that they have missed their opportunity to buy (as in times of feverish excitement in the stock market). To arouse interest, to gain confidence, to stimulate the impulse to buy—this is the climactic accomplishment of an effective trader. The way in which he achieves such results is immaterial; it is sufficient for our purposes to know that not physical but merely psychic compulsion is used, that the other party enters the agreement of its own resolve and not against its will.

The Entrepreneur in the Period of Full Capitalism

During the period of full capitalism, which covers approximately the period from 1750 to 1914, the position of the entrepreneur was materially changed in several respects. In the first place, several important tendencies affected the character of entrepreneurial activity. One of these was the tendency to dissociate capital ownership from executive management. The movement away from single ownership or partnership to corporate ownership was paralleled in the substitution of the hired executive for the owner entrepreneur.

Another tendency was that toward increasing functional specialization in entrepreneurial activity. This tendency manifested itself above all in the progressive emergence of the entrepreneur per se, stripped of all subsidiary functions. This process, the beginnings of which may be discerned even in the early capitalist era, was now approaching completion. General supervision, improvement of technique, office organization, and other duties with which the entrepreneur originally had to concern himself came to be cared for by specialists in his employ. Even the question as to whether a certain business proposition would pay, the calculation of probable costs and profits, was delegated by entrepreneurs to special functionaries, the "efficiency experts." Within this more and more narrowly circumscribed sphere of entrepreneurial activity, individuals began to concentrate more intensively in certain fields: the banks developed specialists for contacts with industry, for the flotation of stock issues, for the improvement of deposit banking;

industry demanded specialists in plant organization, in purchasing and marketing, in financial management.

At the same time, however, there was also a tendency toward the integration of functions. There appeared a limited number of universal super-entrepreneurs who combined banking and industrial power. The most popular road to such comprehensive activity was simultaneous membership in boards of directors of several corporations.

The spiritual adjustment of the entrepreneur to this change in the character of his activities took the form of a differentiation among entrepreneurs on the basis of mental type, range of interests, and effectiveness in varying environments. We may distinguish among them three different types: the expert, the merchant or the business man, and the financier.

The expert centers his interest in his particular product. He is definitely tied down to a single branch of production, as is seen most clearly in the case of the entrepreneur who is also a technical inventor. The inventor-entrepreneur aims to bring about widespread adoption of his invention by producing on as large a scale as possible. Plant organization is his major concern, and his chief objective is to procure and make the best use of the proper working forces. Of the three markets—for capital, for labor, and for finished product—the labor market is the one in which he is primarily interested; and of the three possible kinds of competition he prefers the competition in service.

The merchant's starting point is the market demand; he is determined to supply the products which he considers most saleable. Anticipating future demand, which he stimulates with clever propaganda, the ideal merchant creates wants and proceeds to supply the means for their satisfaction. The commodity market rather than the labor market is the main field of his activity, and his important contribution is not organization of the plant but improvement of the sales mechanism. He uses the power of suggestion as his weapon in the competitive struggle.

The financier's important activity is the creation and accumulation of capital by technical manipulations in the stock market. His appropriate milieu is the capital market and his creative powers are expressed in the promotion of new companies or mergers, holding companies and other financial aggregations. His tendency is towards competition of power.

Logically these three types—expert, merchant and financier—represent successive stages of increasing intangibility, of a progressive loss of concreteness in entrepreneurial activity. In a certain sense they follow also a historical sequence. The expert is more a product of early capitalism than of fully developed capitalism, when the other two types appear more and more frequently. The financier becomes really important only after the process of concentration has overtaken that of economic expansion. It must be understood, however, that these ideal entrepreneurial types are seldom encountered in real life. The actual entrepreneur is often a combination of two of these types, generally of expert and merchant or of merchant and financier. It is equally obvious that the demands made upon the entrepreneur and consequently the opportunities offered to each of these types differ in different branches of business. Industries requiring great mechanical precision in the manufacturing process are fertile soil for the expert; the merchant thrives in industries dominated by mass production; and the financier exploits such opportunities as the promotion of new railways.

Something must be said also of the social and national origins of the entrepreneurial class in the period of full capitalism. This period is characterized by an increasing democratization of its economic leadership: entrepreneurs are drawn from a continually growing number of social groups, and in the course of time lower and lower strata of society are tapped for this purpose.

Statistics for a sample of the English cotton industry before the war (Chapman, S.J., and Marquis, F.J., "The Recruiting of the Employing Classes from the Ranks of the Wage-Earners in the Cotton Industry" in *Royal Statistical Society Journal*, vol. lxxv, 1911–12, p. 293–306) offer an apt illustration of the process of democratization. Of 63 manufacturers engaged in the cotton weaving industry, 48 belonged to the "first generation," that is, they were "employers, managers and others…, who have themselves risen from the operative classes or from classes earning no more than operatives." In an industrial city of 100,000 inhabitants, 139 employers who owned 93,400 looms replied to questionnaires. Of these, 88 were of the first generation; they owned 49 per cent of the looms, while the other private employers owned 44 percent of the looms, and corporations accounted for the remaining 7 percent. In the cotton spinning industry dominated by corporations entire boards of directors were questioned; of 45 directors who replied, 33 belonged to the first generation. In addition, among 45 of the mill managers who responded, 38 were of the first generation. In a special investigation dealing with 20 cotton mills in a cotton center it was found that the first generation included 13 percent of the managing directors, 42 percent of the managers (salary range £200–£800), and 67 percent of the assistant managers (salary range £100–£150).

Even many of the great industrial leaders of our day have risen to their high positions from very humble beginnings, as is evidenced in their biographies which are at present in vogue. A number of German business giants came from the middle class of lower social strata and began their careers in subordinate positions. Ballin was an emigration agent; Bosch, the son of a peasant, had an initial capital of 10,000 marks; Dernburg and Helfferich came of families of scholars; Deutsch was the son of a cantor; Fürstenberg's first position was that of a clerk. After his father's fortune was lost Kirdorf began as commercial manager of a small colliery; Isidor and Ludwig Löwe were the children of a grammar school teacher; Emil Rathenau was an engineer in modest circumstances; and Werner Siemens, an artillery lieutenant, founded his plant for the manufacture of telegraphic equipment with a borrowed capital of 6,000 talers. Jandorf, Tietz, and Wertheim, the founders of the large department stores, began as petty shopkeepers in the provincial cities in eastern Germany. In the United States the number of magnates who have risen from the ranks is perhaps even larger: Carnegie was the son of a poor Scottish weaver, Ford the son of a small farmer, and Harriman the son of a minister in a poor Long Island parish.

The reasons for the democratization of the entrepreneurial group are fairly obvious. During the entire period of early capitalism it was necessary either to be wealthy or to affiliate with the possessors of wealth in order to acquire the capital necessary for a start in business. Consequently there must have been many cases in which one man had entrepreneurial ability and no money, and another money but no ability or inclination to engage in business. In the period of full capitalism the man of wealth can easily employ his money as capital without himself being an entrepreneur, and the impecunious man can more easily procure capital by floating stock or borrowing from a credit institution. "Credit institutions are the props of genius," observed the

Bremer Handelszeitung in 1856; it is primarily the credit system that makes it possible for a man without capital to be active as an entrepreneur.

No less important is the change in the national composition of the entrepreneurial class. While in the period of early capitalism the center of gravity of economic life was found in the Romanic countries, industrial leadership in the period of full capitalism shifted to the nations of Germanic origin. Thus in the year 1910–11 the joint share (in percent) of Germany, Great Britain, and the United States in the world's output of the most important raw and semi-manufactured materials was as follows: zinc, 65; lead, 71; crude oil, 71; copper, 76; steel, 78; pig iron, 79; cotton, 80; cotton yarn (number of spindles), 75; coal, 82; and coke, 84.

It is worth noting also that in all countries the Jews have been capturing a growing share in economic leadership. Although the Jews constituted only about 1 percent of the general population in pre-war Germany, 13.3 percent of the directors of industrial enterprises were of Jewish origin. This percentage was as high as 23.1 in the electrical industry, 25 in the metal industries, and 31.5 in the leather and rubber industries. 24.4 percent of the members of supervising councils (*Aufsichtsräte*) in industrial corporations were Jews. They played an even more important part in the management of the banks, which were largely controlled by Jews. There was a similar preponderance of Jews in the large scale retail business: most of the department stores, which in Germany are practically all organized on the Tietz system, were established by Jewish merchants. While these data relate to Germany only, what is true of Germany applies to some extent to all capitalistic countries.

The Importance of the Personal Element in the Capitalistic Economy

It would be erroneous to assume, as is done so frequently, that because of the dominance of the impersonal entity, the capitalistic enterprise, the personality of the capitalistic entrepreneur is submerged and reduced to insignificance. It is true that the prime mover in the economic process has now become the automatic, highly efficient contrivance unrestricted spatially or temporally and unhindered by any personal or organic limitations. The individual, even the individual entrepreneur, inevitably becomes a part of it. The earth is studded with countless factories organized on an identical plan and equipped with machines of delicate precision—all this for the purposes of profit making. Chance, individual and national differences are eliminated. Necessity, uniformity, and homogeneity dominate in this quantitative universe. Yet it must not be supposed that the importance of the human personality is debased in this mechanized world. On the contrary, the individual, if he happens to be outstanding, wields in the economic life of this period an influence far surpassing that of any other age.

Although the categories of striving and action are a necessary part of any abstract conception of the universe, the concrete fact remains that something positive must be striven for and something tangible must be done. If modern economic rationalism is like the mechanism of a clock, someone must be there to wind it up. If the capitalistic enterprise tends to become an ever larger and more complicated machine, still it does not dispense with the need for a human being to tend it; and the more complicated the machine, the more intelligent he must be. The government and the army have developed along similar lines; there too we find a gigantic mechanized apparatus, and yet a leader is more than ever indispensable. It is true, however, that the distribution of forces has changed; a central power station—the leading executive—has superseded, at least in the large business units, the great number of smaller ones.

The Russians grasped less than any other nation the peculiar character of the capitalistic economy when they banished the capitalistic entrepreneur and thereby brought the entire mechanism to a standstill. The Americans, on the other hand, display the keenest understanding of capitalism. They place a particularly high value upon personality in economic life, considering that in the last analysis it is the individual rather than the business enterprise, family, or capital that is the driving economic force. In the large concerns a few eminent personalities hold undisputed sway. Rumor has it that H.H. Rogers, once the leading brain of the Standard Oil group and president of the Amalgamated Copper Company, remarked that on boards of which he was a member the vote was taken first, and discussion followed only after he had left.

The Periods of Capitalism

An economic epoch is the stretch of time during which an economic system is actually realized in history. While every economic system appears first within the framework of another, there are some periods during which economic processes reveal in a comparatively pure form the features of a single economic system. These are periods of the full development of the system; until they are reached the system is going through its early period, which is also the late period of the disappearing or retreating economic system. Applying to capitalism this division into epochs, we may distinguish the periods of early capitalism (*Hochkapitalismus*) and late capitalism.

In the period of early capitalism, which lasted from the thirteenth to the middle of the eighteenth century, economic agents, the capitalistic entrepreneurs, and their subordinates, the workmen, still bear the earmarks of their feudal or handicraft origin; their economic outlook still exhibits the superficial characteristics of pre-capitalist mentality. The economic principles of capitalism are still struggling for recognition; traditionalism and the mediæval idea of working merely for a livelihood still predominate. Likewise the external aspects of economic life frequently resemble those of the earlier period: home industry still prevails; the output of factories and manufactories is still slight; the technology employed is not very far from the traditional rule of thumb. Economic life in general has a decidedly personal cast; the individual and his personal concerns frequently form the center of interest, and the relations between individuals are still for the most part on the old personal basis. In commercial transactions buyer and seller confront each other in person and let their personal likes and dislikes affect their business deals; within the enterprise the employer and workmen are often held together by a personal bond ("patriarchal industrial relations").

In the period of full capitalism, which closed with the outbreak of the World War, the principles of profit and economic rationalism attain complete control and fashion all economic relationships. The scope of economic activity is enlarged (expansion of markets, increase in the size of business units and plants) and scientific, mechanistic technology is widely applied. It is particularly characteristic of this period that relations which originally involved unmediated actions by living persons are now institutionalized; a system of man-made organization eliminates spontaneous contact and forces individual action into a framework imposed from the outside. Thus the relation between seller and consumer loses its personal character in a large retail concern where purchases are made almost mechanically with virtually no human contact (system of fixed prices). The standardization of merchandise and the increasing uniformity of the terms of sale on the basis of established usage (as in the dealings in futures) make the wholesale business quite impersonal. The loss of adaptability to individual differences in factory management takes the form of the standard labor contract. Credit relations are no longer based on personal acquaintance between creditor and debtor; credit transactions are regulated by fixed norms, and the credit instrument is completely standardized. The use of negotiable securities—endorsed promissory notes and bills, banknotes, evidences of debt guaranteed by mortgage, bonds and stocks—by means of which it is possible at a moment's notice to introduce into the situation new creditors unknown to the original debtor, impersonalises and objectifies the credit relation.

Most intimately connected with this tendency toward mediatization and mechanization is the intensified commercialization of economic life, the debasement of all economic processes into the purely commercial transactions or at any rate the subordination of their other constituent elements to the commercial one. This is vaguely expressed by such a phrase as "the domination of business by Wall Street," in which we can substitute for Wall Street the name of the central speculative-financial market of any country. This is made possible primarily by the depersonalization of credit relations and their crystallization in transferable, marketable, liquid credit instruments.

The period of late capitalism, upon which we are at present entering, can be best characterized by describing the changes which capitalism has been undergoing in the past decade. We observe first of all that industrialism is spreading to every corner of the world; the hard and fast division and the resulting peculiar relations between industrial and agrarian countries, both of which were characteristic of the period of full capitalism, are being gradually worn away. In industrial countries the strength of the specifically capitalistic elements of economic life is declining; "mixed" public-private undertakings, state and communal public works, cooperative enterprises, and other forms of non-capitalistic economic endeavor increase in number, size, and importance. The most important changes, however, concern the internal structure of capitalism.

The economic outlook has recently undergone material changes and will continue to change in the future. The capitalistic spirit at its prime was characterized by psychological strains of peculiar intensity born of the contradictions between irrationality and rationality, between the spirit of speculation and that of calculation, between the mentality of the daring entrepreneur and that of the hard-working, sedate bourgeois. At present this strain is relaxing. Rationalism is thoroughly permeating the capitalist spirit, and a completely rationalized mentality is no longer a capitalist mentality in its characteristic sense. Certain special aspects of this change are worthy of mention.

All the differentia of a genuinely entrepreneurial spirit—daring decision, intuitive judgment, instinctive grasp of a situation—become less and less important in the conduct of business. The number of determinable factors is constantly increasing, and the entrepreneur is more and more disposed to build his business upon the foundation of systematized knowledge. This may already be observed in the United States, although only beginnings are discernible in Europe. The budgeting of production, of financial needs, the systematic mapping out of sales campaigns—practises which become increasingly common—represent nothing less than the management of a business in accordance with a system of knowable facts. When such practices are perfected and carried to their logical conclusion, the concern in which they are relied upon ceases to be capitalist in spirit and resembles a public undertaking with a thoroughly systematized and externally regulated management. The manager of such an enterprise resembles a minister of finance, who has to act within a framework imposed upon him from the outside.

It is psychologically plausible that with the increase in the size of the business unit the striving for profit grows less intense; witness such symptoms as the fixed dividend rate, the reinvestment of surplus—in the United States, for example, some concerns provide from 30 to 35 percent of their new capital in this way—the creation of reserves and similar arrangements. Connected with this is the disappearance of the recklessness, daring and aggressiveness of the typical entrepreneur of old. These qualities are paralyzed and fall into disuse with the spread of cartels and trusts and other manifestations of the tendency toward concentration. It is possible that there is a general tendency to gradual decay of the entrepreneurial mentality.

The form of economic life and its objective order are also changing: freedom from external restraint characteristic of the period of full capitalism is superseded in the period of late capitalism by an increase in the number of restrictions until the entire system becomes regulated rather than free. Some of these regulations are self-imposed—the bureaucratization of internal management, the submission to collective decisions of trade associations, exchange boards, cartels and similar organizations. Others are prescribed by the state—factory legislation, social insurance, price regulation. Still others are enforced by the workers—works councils, trade agreements. The relation between employer and employee becomes public and official. The status of the wage worker becomes more like that of a government employee: his activity is regulated by norms of a quasi-public character, the manner of his work approaches that of a civil servant (no overtime), his wage is determined by extra-economic, non-commercial factors. The sliding wage scale of earlier times is replaced by its antithesis, the living wage, expressing the same principle as that underlying the salary scale of civil servants; in case of unemployment the worker's pay continues, and in illness or old age he is pensioned like a government employee. At present this situation is more characteristic of a country of older culture like Germany, but it is bound to become established also in the United States.

The economic process as a whole has changed also. What used to be a matter of spontaneous, natural development is fast becoming a system of external regulations. By and large, flexibility is being replaced by rigidity. Thus regulation of economic life through the market mechanism, a system under which the links of the causal sequence were demand and supply, market conditions, prices of goods, wages, profits, is gradually disappearing. It is being superseded by the price regulation of combinations or even of the government; by wage regulation of the trade unions, who pay little attention to the market conditions; by indirect regulation of the geographic distribution of industry through the intervention of the central and local governments, who disregard the natural rationality implicit in the existing situation.

The cyclical oscillations of the economic system, the rhythm of prosperity and depression characteristic of full capitalism, also become attenuated. A large number of considerations bear upon this change. There is an increasing insight into market conditions and the factors determining them. The currency and credit system has been rationalized, better adapted to serve the needs of the existing order. Conditions of production were affected by important changes in the supply of factors of production; thus, while the economic cycles of the past eighty years were conditioned by railroad building and the introduction of electricity, at present the supply of important equipment has reached the saturation point; business has assumed the corporate form of organization, and there has taken place a concentration of economic power; the reserve army of the unemployed has been reduced by a general decrease in excess population. There is more external regulation of business by government (regulation of the promotion of new enterprises, labor legislation) and by labor organizations. The entrepreneurial group has been consciously striving for stability as in the cartels and trade associations. Public authorities have intervened to offset the business fluctuations by withholding orders in periods of prosperity and granting them more generously in periods of depression; this policy will play an increasingly important role. "Stabilization of business" seems to be both the slogan and the accomplishment of this period.

II

The Diversity of Economic Actors and Motives

2

The Origins of the Capitalist Spirit

The Problem

What is the origin of the capitalist spirit? Whence did it spring? Two ways of answering these questions are possible. The first is by a reference to external facts. You may point to the appearance of a capitalist entrepreneur in a land in which he had come to trade or where he had set up business. Thus you may say the capitalist entrepreneur in a land in which he had come to trade or where he had set up business. Thus you may say the capitalist spirit in China owes its origin to the English; or, the Jews introduced the capitalist spirit into Magdeburg. In this sense the question is answered by the facts of the history of migration. But we shall not deal with this aspect of the question here. What we want to know in this book is, How did a capitalist economic outlook grow up in the minds of men? Why in any particular period did the capitalist spirit dominate economic activities, giving men a certain aim, calling forth in them certain capacities, making them obey certain principles? And what was responsible for the appearance from time to time, now in one generation, now in another, of certain people with strongly marked views and a particular outlook, with a certain will-power and a certain skill?

I am bound to say that many people do not admit that there is any problem at all to be solved. They take it as self-evident that the capitalist spirit was engendered by capitalism. They do not admit that the capitalist spirit has an independent existence. But this is by no means an axiom; it certainly requires proof. It is possible, of course, that an economic outlook may be the result of economic conditions, but the exact relationship between the two has to be most carefully taken into account. We want to know how and why the one springs from the other.

There are other people who admit the problem, but deny that a scientific solution is possible. One of the younger scholars of the day expressed himself on the subject in some such terms as these.[1] The capitalist spirit and all that it conveys are merely very useful descriptive labels. We may talk of the development or the history of morals, but we cannot lay bare the stages in its growth by the aid of documentary evidence. So, in the same way, thrift, self-interest, and all the other qualities contained in the conception "capitalist spirit" have undoubtedly developed, but we cannot trace that development historically.

There is clearly a good deal of truth in this suggestion. No one can definitely show when certain outlooks or opinions first came into existence. It would obviously be an impossibility to demonstrate by reference to sources what the influence (say) of Puritanism was on the capitalist spirit.[2] But what can be done is to differentiate between natural capacities and tendencies and the influence of the environment in general or of specific occurrences in particular. We can even lay down one or two rules to guide us in considering this contrast. These rules will exclude, for example, certain common denominators found among all peoples as sources of a given intellectual outlook; they will make it impossible to account for certain aspects of the capitalist spirit by quoting authorities that come later in point of time. For instance, views of life in the fifteenth century cannot possibly be traced to religious doctrines which were first enunciated in the seventeenth; or, the capitalist spirit of Germany in the nineteenth century cannot be regarded as the fruit of Puritan or Quaker religious teaching.

In order to arrive at a right view of the cause and effects, one or two facts must be born in mind.

1. The component parts of the capitalist spirit vary so much that their origins will vary also. Some of the factors in that spirit may be what are termed "instinctive passions"—acquisitiveness, activity, the desire to plunder your neighbour. All successful entrepreneurs have always had a goodly dose of these instincts. This is common knowledge, and there is ample proof in support of the statement.[3]

Take as an illustration what Gentz, in a letter to Adam Müller, says of the Rothschilds:

> They are just ordinary, ignorant Jews with tolerably good manners, and in their business unspoiled children of nature, understanding the larger aspects of things but little. But they possess a marvelous instinct of always being able to decide upon what is right, and, of two good courses, to choose the better. Their enormous wealth is due entirely to this instinct, which the populace calls luck.

Heine's description of James Rothschild is in almost identical terms: "He has the peculiar capacity of insight, or, if you will, the natural instinct of being able to take the measure of others in all spheres of action."

Again, the capitalist spirit may express itself in certain personal characteristics to which particular business principles or middle-class virtues may be sympathetic. Or we may see acquired skill—say, in rapid calculation or the arrangements of a business or something similar.

Accordingly, when we come to consider the variations in the root elements of the capitalist spirit the question as to the origins of that spirit assumes a twofold importance. In the first place, the manner in which the individual characteristics manifest themselves in one and the same person is different according as the component factors of the capitalist spirit are present in a larger or lesser degree. Instinctive movement, instinctive capabilities are always to be found—they are bred in the bone; they may be either repressed, neglected, or not made use of, or they may be quickened, strengthened, and broadened.

The nature of the two other factors is such that the possibility of their acquirement is patent, and is as a rule the result of tuition. The first factor—molding the character—is due to educative influences; the second—forming the mind—is due to instruction.

In the second place, the question of inheritance divides the various factors into two sharply defined groups. The first consists of those qualities which may be transmitted from one person or from one age to another. The second group is composed of all such characteristics as are so intimately interwoven with the personality of the individual that they can only affect others by the force of example, and their existence ceases with that of their possessor. Instincts and talents can never be accumulated independently of the individual; they are inherited, but though they may have grown and developed, each human has perforce to return to the old starting-point and to pass through all transitory states. On the other hand, virtues and capabilities, though the sum total of man's single and united efforts, are quite distinct from personality, and the stages of their progress may be followed and catalogued in codes and systems. Men die, but these codes continue. In them later generations find the accumulated experience of their ancestors, and profit thereby. It matters not that for a long time any particular precept remains disregarded. So long as it is written down, some one or other may one day be inspired by it. Wise rules for conduct and for craftsmanship are transferable both as to time and space. The latter differ from the former only in that they are added to by each successive generation, seeing that experience is enlarged and technical inventions increased. But rules of conduct can hardly be said to gain by reason of any that were current before.

From all this it now becomes obvious that the process of growth of each of the elements of the capitalist spirit differed enormously among themselves.

2. Secondly, in tracing the origins of the capitalist spirit we must always bear in mind that the conditions vary fundamentally with each epoch of capitalist development. Above all, the era of early capitalism must be sharply distinguished from that of perfected capitalism. If you are to sum up the economic activities of each in a phrase, you might say that in the early capitalist age the entrepreneur produced capitalism, in the perfected capitalist age capitalism produces the entrepreneur. In the young days of capitalism, capitalist organization was by no means general; it was mostly the creation of the non-capitalist genius. Its stock of knowledge and experience was not large; both experience and knowledge had to be gained, garnered, and tested. It had little in the way of capitalist machinery, and that little had to be painfully acquired. As for the primary foundations of all contracts and agreements, they had not yet been laid; long and strenuous was the upward striving of credit and confidence and trust. Does it not stand to sense that under such circumstances the capitalist entrepreneur was bound to act on his own initiative, and possibly with a good deal of caprice? Today all this has been altered. Modern capitalist organization is, in the words of Max Weber, a huge cosmos into which the human unit is born, and which represents for him as such an eternally unmodifiable structure in which he is compelled to live. And this cosmos imposes upon him, in so far as he comes into the marketplace, economic laws of its own. The individual to-day stands face-to-face with a mountain of experience which threatens to crush him—book-keeping methods, calculating systems, wages customs, organization of management, business technics, and what not. All these are so specialized that their application becomes a work of no small difficulty. So much so that specialists have to be called in to carry them through for the capitalist entrepreneur.

What conspicuous changes therefore in the "environment" in which the capitalist spirit grew up then and now! All these distinctions must naturally be taken into account if we are to solve our problem with anything like exactitude.

The material at our command is enormous in extent; it is indeed almost overwhelming. By two methods we may obtain the mastery over it. We may take each element of the capitalist spirit by itself, and try to discover the reasons for its genesis. For instance, what produced the greed of gold; what gave an impetus to the spirit of undertaking; why did the middle-class virtues arise?—and so forth. Or we may trace back the manifold resultants of the capitalist spirit, and thus arrive at the complexity of causes that gave them birth. A good deal of repetition is necessarily involved in the first method, and so I prefer the second, which anyhow promises variety in outlook.

This is the course I propose to follow. One section shall be devoted to the biological foundations on which the history of the whole capitalist spirit is built up. Another section will consider the moral forces which have influenced mankind in determining how much, or how little, of the capitalist spirit it should imbibe. And in the third section the social conditions that have been effective find their place. In the last two sections our aim will thus be to make plain how outward circumstances helped to mold human beings with a capitalist turn of mind. These circumstances will be reviewed in all their details, from the earliest stages down to this very day; and at the end we shall realize how manifold have been the influences at work on the capitalist spirit.

The Biological Foundations

The Bourgeois Temperament

Is one born a bourgeois? Are there people who are naturally "middle class," and thus different from others who are not? If this is so, shall we not have to describe the capitalist spirit as something temperamental? In any event, what is the true relationship between natural gifts and the capitalist spirit?

To answer these questions aright we must pay attention to the following general observations.

There is no doubt that all expressions of the capitalist spirit, as indeed soul expressions in general, may be traced to particular inherent personal characteristics; that is to say, to original, inherited qualities of the organism, which account for the ability and tendency to exercise certain functions, or the inclination to acquire certain qualities.[4] We need not discuss for the moment whether the biological tendencies to capitalism are of a general nature, and so capable of development in various directions and not necessarily only into the bourgeois ideal; or whether from the first they lead to this one goal, and to this only.

I repeat: there can be no doubt that all the expressions of the capitalist spirit, that is to say, the mental constitution of the bourgeois, are rooted in inherited tendencies. This holds good equally of qualities that depend on the will, as of those that are instinctive; of middle-class virtues therefore, as of inherent talents. All spring from certain qualities in the soul. It matters not whether or not these psychic qualities have physical parallels; nor is it of consequence to discover how the tendencies themselves arose in any individual—whether he acquired them, and if so, when and how. It is sufficient for us that they are there at a time when we know capitalism to have been born. That is really the important point—to be alive to the fact that at that given moment man had already made these qualities so much his own that transmission was possible. In short, these qualities, the broader developments of primitive instincts, had become hereditary.

The question now faces us: are these tendencies toward the expression of the capitalist spirit general; are they common in like degree to all mankind? Alike, of course, they cannot be, since no two people possess the same psychological outfit. Even as regards such aptitudes as are almost universal—that of learning languages, for instance—there are differences in degree. Some people are able to acquire languages more easily and quickly than others. You can see it in children learning to speak their mother-tongue; you can see it best of all in grown-ups learning foreign languages.

But I go further and believe that the qualities referred to are not common to humanity. They exist in this and not in that individual. Or, at least, some people possess them in such small doses that for all practical purposes the quantity is negligible; whereas others are so imbued with them as to be at once distinguishable from their neighbors. Is it not obvious that many men have no great capacity or inclination to become freebooters, to organize and supervise the work of a thousand hands, to find a path through the mazes of stock-exchange business, to calculate with lightning rapidity, even to lay by for a rainy day, to economize their time or to lead a regular life? And should we not be agreed that not many people are gifted with a large number, less with all, of the qualities of mind that go to make up the capitalist spirit?

Nevertheless, there are beings who impress you as born capitalist entrepreneurs, who have the bourgeois temperament (even though they may never actually lead a middle-class existence). We have in mind, of course, a more or less perfect bourgeois nature, and we ask, What is its specific mental constitution? How does the blood of such natures vary from that of other folk?

Two souls dwell in the breast of every complete bourgeois: the soul of the entrepreneur and the soul of the respectable middle-class man. The union of the two produces the capitalist spirit. Hence in the bourgeois temperament we may distinguish two contributory factors—the undertaking nature and the nature of the respectable middle-class citizen. We will take each of these in turn.

1. Undertaking natures. What mental or psychological qualities are essential to the capitalist entrepreneur if he is to be successful? I should say he must be intelligent, clever, and imaginative.

Intelligent means quick in comprehension, true in judgment, clear in thought, with a sure eye for the needful, enabling him to recognize the psychological moment (the Greeks called it *Kairos*). He must be endowed with quickwittedness in a large measure, with that nimbleness of spirit which may be compared to the light cavalry of an army; the quality which the French ascribe to all great entrepreneurs—*vivacité d'esprit et de corps*; he must be able to find his way through the complicated conditions of the market, much as the advance posts of an army are expected to render intelligence service. Above all, he must have a good memory—a gift all capitalist entrepreneurs know how to value. Carnegie was glad to possess it; Werner Siemens deplored the lack of it.[5]

Clever means the capacity for forming judgments about the world and men; it postulates shrewdness in weighing up things, and instinctive tact in handling men aright; it denotes ability in arriving at a correct valuation of situations of all kinds, and a knowledge of the weaknesses and disadvantages of one's surroundings. The last especially is a predominant feature which is continually praised in great captains of industry. Pliancy on the one hand and suggestive influence on the other are indispensable to the negotiator.

Imaginative means fertile in ideas, resourceful, gifted with what has been termed the "faculty of combination," as opposed to the "intuitive faculty" of the artist.

All these great gifts of intellect must be accompanied by an abundance of the will to live, by "life energy," by that something (call it what you will) requisite for all undertaking, which produces satisfaction, nay, joy. This joy of work gives the entrepreneur the necessary resolution for the consummation of his enterprise. It makes him want to achieve, so that enforced idleness worries him. Then he must also be robust, with plenty of nerve, unshrinking. You know the type. He has determination, he persists in pegging away, he can hold on indefinitely, he is never at rest, he knows what he wants, he can risk much, and his boldness makes your hair stand on end. In a word, he lives greatly; his vitality is above the average.

It is rather disadvantageous to be blessed with a strong sensitiveness. A capitalist entrepreneur should have no feelings. His intellect alone should rule his conduct if he is to scale great heights.

Contrast the undertaking nature with others, and you will discern its outlines clearly enough. Take the artistic temperament. The entrepreneur, especially where he has carried through some marvelous organizing work, has been compared to the artist. The comparison, to my mind, is a wrong one. The two are opposites, not parallels. All they have in common is a vivid imagination which helps them to create.

But the imagination in each case is of a different quality. Apart from this superficial likeness, the two types differ from each other. Their respective souls draw their strength from very different sources. The entrepreneur works towards a goal; to the artist an end in view is an abomination. The former is dominated by his intellect, the latter by his emotions. The former is hard where the latter is delicate and tender. The entrepreneur is practical and businesslike, the artist is the most unpractical and unbusinesslike fellow in the world. The entrepreneur's eyes look without to the macrocosm beyond, the artist's gaze is fixed on the microcosm within. That is why the entrepreneur is acquainted with men, while the artist knows only man.

Similarly, undertaking natures have little in common with those of craftsmen, private gentlemen living on their means, aesthetic folk, scholars, sybarites, strict moralists, and others of that ilk. On the other hand, they have a good many of the qualities of the general and the statesman, both of whom (more particularly the latter) are in the long run conquerors, organizers, and dealers. Single traits of the capitalist entrepreneur may be found also in the chess-player and the clever doctor. Skill in diagnosis enables you not only to heal the sick but also to do well on the stock exchange.

2. "Middle-Class" natures. Either you are born a bourgeois or you are not. It must be in the blood; it is a natural inclination. We all feel that. Everybody knows the middle-class nature; it has a sort of aroma of its own. And yet it is difficult, we may even say impossible, to analyze its psychological qualities. We shall have to content ourselves with a detailed sketch of the middle-class nature, and a comparison between that and other natures.

It would appear that the contrast between the natures we have described as middle-class and those not so represents a fundamental deviation between the two human types in modern society, anyhow so far as Europe is concerned. People are either of the giving or of the taking sort; either extravagant or economical. Deep down in our natures, as they recognized in classical antiquity and as the mediæval schoolmen philosophized, we are all of us inclined either to *luxuria* or to *avaritia*. Some are naturally spendthrifts, careless alike of material and spiritual riches; others tend them carefully, store them, make the most of them, watch closely over the acquisition and expenditure of mental and bodily strength, of goods and chattels and money. Pergson has also called attention to this contrast; he speaks of *l'homme ouvert* and *l'homme clos*.

These two types—those who spend and those who hoard, the aristocratic and the middle-class natures—stand facing each other in all human life. They appraise the world, they appraise even life itself, from opposite vantage-grounds. The ideals of the one are subjective and personal; those of the other objective and material. The former are born for pleasure, the latter for duty; the former are individualists, loving solitude; the latter are gregarious; for the one aesthetics is the supreme thing in life, for the other ethics. The former are like beautiful flowers wasting their perfume on the desert air; the latter are like healing herbs and edible roots. It is only to be expected that they should hold conflicting views as to any man's occupation in particular, and the sweat of the world in general. The first class regard only those activities as worthy and noble which permit a man to become noble and worthy, which cultivate his personality; the second values all activities alike, provided they contribute to the general good, provided, that is, they are useful. Is it not manifest that it makes an exceeding great difference in the prevailing outlook on life according as the one view or the other is in the ascendant? The ancients had personal values; we middle-class folk have material ones. Recall Cicero's polished statement: "Not what one has achieved is of consequence, but what one is."[6]

The two types are in everlasting contrast throughout life. In his threescore years and ten the one lives, sees, thinks; the other organizes, trains, educates. The one dreams dreams and sees visions; the other calculates. Even as a boy Rockefeller had a reputation for calculations. He made regular bargains with his father, a physician in Cleveland. "From my earliest childhood," so he himself relates in his *Memoirs*, "I had a little book in which I entered what I got and what I spent. I called it my account-book and have preserved it to this day." You notice it was in his blood. No power on earth could have made Byron jot down his income and expenditure in a book, and not only that, but preserve the book!

The first type goes carolling through life; the second is dumb. The first are many-coloured in all they say and do, the second are drab. The first are artists (not necessarily by profession); the second are officials. The first are silk, the second wool. Wilhelm Meister and his friend Werner—there you have the types. The one talks as though he had kingdoms to dispose of, the other like a person who carefully picks up a pin.

It is in the erotic life of each that you find the greatest contrast. After all, the love passion is the mightiest force in human affairs, and the erotic temperament is as far remote from the middle-class nature as pole is from pole. But what is the erotic temperament? It cannot be defined; it can only be felt. Perhaps Goethe pictured it in his "Pater ecstaticus":

Endless ecstatic fire,
Glow of the pure desire,
Pain of the pining breast,
Rapture of God possessed!
Arrows, transpierce ye me;
Lances, coerce ye me;
Bludgeons, so batter me,
Lightnings, so shatter me,
That all of mortality's
Vain unrealities
Die, and the star above
Beam but Eternal Love.*

"I suffered and loved; my heart knew nought else." Everything in the world is nothing worth, save only love. There is only one abiding value: love. Is not this the feeling of the erotic temperament? Sexual love, all-comprehensive, all-embracing love—love of God and love of man: anything beyond is vanity. Nor should love ever be but means to an end. It should not be for pleasure; it should not be for the propagation of the species. "Be fruitful and multiply" expresses the most grievous sin against love.

Love is not lasciviousness. The lascivious and the cold natures are both equally far removed from the erotic temperament. On the other hand, they are closely bound up with middle-class natures. Indeed, sensuality and love are mutually exclusive terms, whereas cold and lascivious natures can easily accommodate themselves to the love of order inherent in the "middle-class temperament." Strong sexual

* [The passage will be found towards the end of the Second Part of *Faust*. The version here given is by Bayard Taylor.]

passion, if restrained and controlled, may even be of great service to capitalism.

It need hardly be pointed out that erotic temperaments vary in strength and intensity, ranging from St. Augustine and St. Francis to the ordinary man of today, who spends his life in amorous adventures. But no matter what their degree, they have little in common with the middle-class nature. For there is only one of two alternatives. Either economic activities are the central interest in life or love is. You live for love or for business. Economic activity implies thrift; while love is usually accompanied by extravagance. It is an old contrast, and the ancient economists did not overlook it. Listen to Xenophon.[7] "I also notice that you seem to think you are rich, that you care nothing for business, that your mind is full of love. I am sorry for you on that account. I am afraid that before long you will be in difficulties." Or again: "Who is the best housekeeper? She who is most capable of exercising moderation in food, drink, sleep, and love." In another passage he says that "those who are in love are useless in business." You will find the same opinion in Columella, the well-known Roman writer on agriculture. "Keep far from amorous adventures," he advises, "for who so enters on them can think of nothing else. Such a one values one prize only—the fulfillment of his desire; he fears only one punishment—to be crossed in love."[8] A good housewife should give no single thought to men; she must be a *viris remotissima*.

These indications must suffice. A more thorough investigation into the relationship between love and capitalism would lead us too far afield. Enough that we have realized that those mental gifts necessary for capitalism lie rooted in the sexual constitution.

We have thus observed how the capitalist spirit thrives in bourgeois natures (these being a hybrid between undertaking and middle-class natures). In other words, we have realized that there are people in the world who are so constituted mentally that they are able to develop the capitalist spirit more rapidly than others; who incline in a more marked degree than those others themselves to become capitalist entrepreneurs; who cultivate the middle-class virtues much more easily; who possess the qualities needful for success in economic life in a larger measure.

The consideration of the problem, however, is not thus exhausted. When all is said, it is of small moment whether one individual or another tends to capitalism. Overshadowing this question is a second of far greater magnitude. What is the aspect of these bourgeois natures in the mass? To what extent are they represented among the different nations? Is one nation more prone than another to develop such natures? And can we say therefore that one nation is more gifted for capitalism than another? Do racial or national characteristics in this respect remain constant, or vary from age to age? If so, why? The answer to these questions will show definitely what the biological foundation of capitalism is; and the following chapter will be devoted to their consideration.

National Traits

We saw in the last chapter that all expressions of the capitalist spirit are due to personal qualities inherent in the individual. And in our survey of the progress of capitalism in Europe we noted that the capitalist spirit manifested itself among all nations, though not in the same degree. In some it was more intense than in others; or again its component parts were commingled in varying proportions in different nations.

Two conclusions follow:

1. All European peoples have the qualities necessary for capitalism; and
2. Each nation has these qualities in a varying degree.

When we speak of a nation having certain qualities, the explanation is that the national group in question possesses a large proportion of individuals with those qualities. Hence the conclusions noted above may be thus further amplified.

1. All peoples have the qualities necessary for capitalism. That is to say that in the course of the history of the European nations there grew up in them a large number of capitalist variants (by which we mean variants specially gifted for the development of the capitalist spirit), and these made it possible for capitalism to thrive and extend.
2. Each nation has the qualities in a varying degree.

That is to say, in the first place, the requisite gifts vary quantitatively in the individuals in each national group; and in the second place, they vary qualitatively.

From a biological point of view, how do these variations spring up?[9] In all probability the nations must from their earliest origins have had a kind of germ-capacity for capitalism, and either all had it in the same degree or the degree varied in each nation. Suppose we take the first assumption. Then the variations that appeared later will have to be accounted for by saying that this germ-capacity was exercised unevenly, and so some nations ended with a strong tendency to capitalism, others with one less strong. As for the second assumption, it suffices itself as an explanation of variations. In theory both views are possible. But history rather shows that the second assumption was probably the correct one, at any rate for all but the prehistoric ages. Certainly the second assumption clears up many a difficulty, and as I see no reason against its adoption, it is on that basis that I shall proceed.

The tribes or races from which the modern European nations have sprung were partly over-inclined to capitalism and partly under-inclined. That the latter must have possessed some individuals with capitalist possibilities goes without saying; it would be absurd to imagine that there is any race wholly without capitalist tendencies of some sort. But these individuals must have been so few in number, and what capitalist tendencies they had so weak, that the capitalist spirit among the under-inclined peoples did not develop beyond its primary stage. The over-inclined peoples on the other hand had many richly-gifted individuals who were capitalistically inclined; in them, therefore, the capitalist spirit developed more rapidly and completely.

We see at once that the assumption of a varied degree of germ-capitalism cannot well be avoided. How else should we account for such different results in the process of development? After all, was there much variation in the growth of Spain and Italy, of France and Germany, of Scotland and Ireland? Yet capitalism, as we have seen, fared differently in each. Varying original national traits seem to be the only explanation for this, as for most other phenomena in the life of a nation. Surely every people has the political system, the religion, even the wars which are in accord with its national qualities.

What peoples may be described as under-inclined to capitalism? I should say the Celts and a few of the Germanic tribes, the Goths in particular.* Wherever the Celtic element predominated capitalism made little headway. The nobility continued to live seigniorially with never a thought for thrift or the virtues of middle-class respectability; and the middle grades of the community went on in the old ruts of traditionalism, preferring a safe billet rather than adventurous careers in the field of commerce and industry. The Highlanders in Scotland are Celts,[10] and more especially the nobility—a knightly race, a little quixotic, a little quarrelsome, holding fast to their ancient class traditions, untouched by capitalism down to this very day. The Scottish chieftain looks upon himself as an old feudal lord, and when the money-lenders begin to remove his possessions one by one, his family heirlooms he guards most jealously.

The Irish are Celts too. Do we not all know the plaint of the capitalist observers that the Irish are no good for business? Even in America, where the economic whirlwind storms, the Irish have managed to maintain their peaceful attitude, preferring above all else the secure harbour of an office in the service of the State.

There is a goodly admixture of Celts among the French. It is the Celtic blood that explains the strongly marked tendency to live on investments and the "plague of office-hunting" (a characteristic of the French people we have already noted). It is the Celtic blood also that probably accounts for that vivacity found more among French entrepreneurs than others. John Law first met with a sympathetic understanding of his ideas in France. Perhaps that was because of his partially Celtic origin. On his father's side Law traced his descent from Lowlanders, on his mother's his family belonged to the Highland nobility.[11]

Lastly, the Spaniards are to some extent Celts. When the Visigoths came to the Pyrenean Peninsula the people there were a mongrel race of Celts, Iberians (a most un-capitalistic folk, for whom gold, desired of almost all peoples, had no attraction), and the descendants of early Roman colonists.[12] The Celts and the Goths were responsible for the slow development of capitalism in the Peninsula after its best strength

* [There is no need to regard all the Germanic peoples as having common traits. No doubt they had many qualities in common which made them different from other races (say, from Jews). But so far as their qualities that bear on economic life are concerned, they differed radically among themselves. Compare in this respect the Goths, the Lombards, and the Frisians.]

had been spent in heroic and adventurous expeditions. What capitalism did thrive in Spain and Portugal was due to Jewish and Moorish influences.

But it is the over-inclined peoples that interest us most. Who were they?

Two groups meet our gaze. The one was more talented for forcible, all-conquering undertakings on a large scale, smacking somewhat of freebooting; the other for successful peaceful trading, with a tendency to middle-class respectability. The first we will call Heroic peoples, the second, Trading peoples.

The first introduced a touch of the heroic even in their economic activities. The warlike or semi-warlike entrepreneurs with whom we have already made ourselves acquainted sprang from them. First in order we must mention the Romans, who formed an ethnical element in Italy, in parts of Spain, in Gaul, and in Western Germany. Their method of trading rested on force, and was governed by the idea that economic success can be won by the aid of the sword.[13] It was in accord with this idea that the different sorts of undertakings were variously appraised in classical antiquity. The attitude then was the same as that in England and France at a later period. There the shipping-merchant, with more in him of the soldier than the trader, was socially superior to the mere tradesman. Cicero's excellent contrast between the two is well known. "Oversea commerce to distant lands, bringing commodities from all quarters, taking no mean advantage over customers or talking their heads off, is by no means to be despised."[14] Put this into the terminology used in our pages, and what does it amount to? A conqueror-entrepreneur—that is something, certainly; a tradesman-entrepreneur—no one with any self-respect can sink so low.

Side by side with the Romans must be placed several of the Germanic races. The Normans, the Lombards, the Saxons, and the Franks all appear to have had the same all-conquering spirit within them, and their influence will account, together with the Romans, for undertakings, whether of the freebooting or the feudal sort, that were found among the Venetians and the Genoese, the English and the Germans.

You may see the true nature of these peoples by comparing them with others equally gifted for the development of capitalism, but in another way. I mean the essentially trading peoples, who have the capacity strongly marked of doing successful business by peaceful contract-making, by diplomacy and by clever calculation. We have already noted what peoples helped to develop this aspect of the capitalist spirit in Europe: the Florentines, the Scotch, and the Jews. It remains only to adduce some testimony to prove that in all probability—and the evidence at our disposal suffices for a probability only—these peoples became what they were because of certain primary qualities which were theirs from the earliest times.

The Florentines became traders, became the foremost and greatest trading community in the Middle Ages, because of their Etruscan and Greek (i.e., Oriental) blood.

It is somewhat difficult to estimate exactly the influence of the Etruscans on the inhabitants of Tuscany throughout the ancient period of their history. But authorities seem to agree that the city on the Arno was more Etruscan in Character than its neighbours.[15] Certainly Etruscan blood flowed in the veins of very many Florentines. Now the Etruscans,[16] possibly even more than the Phoenicians and Carthaginians, were the trading people of antiquity, and their commercial policy, so far as can be judged, was much like that of the Florentines in a later day. From the earliest times their trade was mainly peaceful land-trade, particularly with their northern neighbours. When Rome conquered their country, the Etruscans continued to ply their trade, seeing that the Romans scorned trafficking and allowed the inhabitants in the conquered territories to live their life as heretofore.

What manner of ideal was the Etruscan's? The most trustworthy authorities describe it as rational and practical.[17] They were also a religious folk with a national church.[18] Is it not curious that the same can be said of the Florentines, no less than of the Jews and the Scotch?

During the Roman sway the Etruscan ethnical layer had superimposed upon it another of Asiatic origin, which was probably of the same quality, seeing that the newcomers wandered into Italy as traffickers. The influence of the two elements continued right into the Middle Ages. "The number of Greeks or Hither-Asiatics in Florence," says one writer,[19] "was considerable. Of 115 tombstones of the pre-Christian period, the inscriptions on 21 are in Greek, and of 48 epitaphs of Christians 9 are in Greek....In one of these it is recorded that the grave contains a man born in Asia Minor." The same authority holds that the Greek inscriptions would seem to point to the conclusion that traders from Hither-Asia must have settled in Florence. As late as the eleventh century there is evidence pointing to the same fact. At baptisms the priest asked whether the formulas were to be pronounced in Latin or in Greek.

As for the Scotch, if there is any truth in the hypothesis[20] that the Frisians settled on the eastern shores of Scotland, are we not justified in asserting that the Scotch too have possessed their peculiar national traits from the very earliest period in their history? The Frisians, so much is certain, were a clever and skillful race of traders.[21] On this basis it is perfectly easy to trace the peculiar characteristics of the English to the influence of the Romans, Saxons, and Normans; that of the Lowland Scotch to the Frisians. It is a racial or blood difference.

One other nation is indebted to the Frisians for its national bent—the Dutch. From their earliest history the folk in the Low Countries were devoted to trade, traffic, and calculations. The Frisians, indeed, may be regarded as the paramount commercial race in the Germanic family, by whose side later the Alemanni took up a similar position. The Alemanni were the ancestors of the Swiss.

As for the Jews, I believe that in my treatise on *The Jews and Modern Capitalism* I have established the fact that the racial characteristics of this gifted people, as we perceive them when they first began to exercise an influence on capitalism (say about the seventeenth century), were inherent in their blood from the earliest times. Jews were traders from the first.

Summing up our considerations, we arrive at this important conclusion: that the capitalist spirit in Europe was cultivated by a number of races, each with different characteristics of its own, and that of these races the Trading peoples (Etruscans, Frisians, and Jews) may be divided off from those we have termed Heroic.

Now, the original traits of a people are only a starting-point in the consideration of its biological development. In every generation the original traits are influenced anew, and two processes are responsible for the change. The one is selection, the other admixture with other races.

So far as our knowledge goes, it would seem that among the trading people the process of selection left the fittest to survive; that is to say, those who possessed the trading characteristic in a high degree. Of the Jews it may even be said that among them selection was hardly active at all, for they were from the first a pure trading people. The

Florentines, on the other hand, had a trace of Germanic blood, which flowed in the veins of the nobility. So long as the influence of this social group predominated, Florence had the appearance of a military town. But slowly the foreign element was shed, nowhere so soon and so thoroughly as in this city. A large part of the nobility vanished. Did not Dante mourn the decline of numerous noble families? What was left was removed by force. As early as 1292 the people with the true commercial spirit in them succeeded in establishing a law that no grandee should be a member of the Senate. What was the result? Those of the nobility that possessed the quality of adaptation had themselves put down among the commons; the others, those in whom we must suppose the seigniorial temperament to have been strong, whose natures were averse to traffic, emigrated. The later history of Florence showed that its public life became more and more democratic, that from the fourteenth century on its citizens were all bourgeois.

Some such similar process must have taken place in the Scotch Lowlands, from which the Celtic nobility were eliminated before long. Their decline commenced in the fifteenth century; it was due to their "eternal want of pence," and their inability to dispense with them.

> The day had gone by when a following of rudely armed retainers made a great man of Bell-the-Cat or Tiger Earl. As things now went, what had been a source of strength was fast becoming a source of weakness. Retainers had to be maintained, and their maintenance was a drain on the lord's resources which his extended wants made ever more undesirable....A noble lord with broad domains and a scanty purse was a stranded leviathan, impotent to put forth his strength in the new conditions in which he found himself.[22]

Those of the nobility that could, saved themselves by removing to the Highlands. The result was that the Frisian trading element became predominant in the Lowlands.

The process of selection was the same, if slower, among the other peoples. Probably there were two stages among them. First the non-capitalist elements were eliminated, and then from the residue those that had a strong tendency to trade. The process went on in so far as the more gifted in the lowest social grades worked their way up and became capitalist entrepreneurs. They could only do so by skill in negotiating, by economy, and by careful calculation.

So much for selection. Blood-admixture had the same results, and they may already be perceived in the Middle Ages. From the sixteenth century onward the admixture of blood in countries like France and England had important consequences. To explain these it is necessary to assume that as a general rule, when nobles and commoners intermarried, the blood of the latter was the stronger and prevailed. How else are we to account for a man like Leon Battista Alberti? The Albertis were among the highest and purest of the Germanic nobility in Tuscany, spending their lives in martial undertakings. Many of its branches we know something about;[23] The Contalbertis may be mentioned as an instance. Leon Battista's own clan was proud and mighty. It sprang from Castello di Catenaia in Val d'Arno; beside their own family estate they were the lords of many others; and they had intermarried with distinguished Germanic noble families. Defeated in a local quarrel, they moved into the town (in the thirteenth century), where the first of the Albertis joined the Gild of the Giudici, and gradually they became the most famous drapers in Florence. It was the descendant of such a line that wrote a book second to none in its bourgeois sentiments, a book which already breathed the spirit of Benjamin Franklin. How many shopkeeper families must have crossed the noble breed to produce a result like this? In Leon Battista's own case the crossing was certain: he was an illegitimate child and born in Venice. His mother must have been a woman of the middle class sprung from a trading stock.

One other point before we conclude these considerations. Every increase of capitalist variants denoted an extension of the capitalist spirit. But it also denoted its greater intensity, for every additional variant increasingly facilitated the expression of that spirit. In a word, the reaction on each other of the variants with similar traits increased the possibilities of their expression.

It only remains for us now to consider the historical aspect of our problem. We must discover what it was that enabled the original inherent national tendencies to capitalism to grow and expand. I see two groups of such forces, internal and external, if you like to call them so—though the terms are hardly exact, seeing that the internal group is influenced from without and the external can scarcely be conceived without internal, psychological processes. Still, the moral forces press more from within outwardly, and the social circumstances exercise their influence more from without inwards.

The influence of nature I have not considered separately. I refer to the influence of the land, climate, geographical position, mineral wealth. In so far as these must be noted, we shall take cognizance of them under the group of forces we have termed "social circumstances." For example, the effect of particular callings, the exploitation of mineral deposits, the development of technical science, and so forth.

One word more before we leave the debatable problem of biology—a word of comfort to the skeptical. The historical considerations that we are about to enter upon are of value even if the biological arguments have failed to carry conviction. The most devoted advocate of the environment theory will find nothing to object to in them. For those who, like us, believe in latent tendencies, these historical investigations will demonstrate what forces developed them, and how unsuitable variants were shed; whereas for those who pin their faith to the environment theory they will explain how capitalism came into being (out of nothing apparently). But both sides will agree that the trend of history has resulted in the development of the capitalist spirit; both, therefore, will attach the utmost importance to the historical factors in the problem.

Notes

1. Ludwig Feuchtwanger, "Die ethischen Grundlagen der Nationalökonomie," in Schmoller's *Jahrbuch*, vol. 37 (1913), p. 961.
2. See F. Rachfahl, "Kalvinismus und Kapitalismus" in *Internationale Wochenschrift* (1909), p. 1,293.
3. Cf. for instance Rathenau, *Reflexionen* (1908), p. 92.
4. Consult the *Handwörterbuch der Philosophie*, by Dr. Rudolf Eisler (1913), for "natural gifts." Also H. Kurella, *Die Intellektuellen und die Gesellschaft* (1913).
5. Werner Siemens, *Lebenserinnerungen*, p. 296.
6. Cicero, *Brutus*, p. 257.
7. Xenophon, *Œeconomicus*, chaps. 2, 9, and 12.
8. Columella, *De re rustica*, lib. xi. ch. I.
9. Cf. H.E. Ziegler, *Die Naturwissenschaft und die sozialdemokratische Theorie* (1893), p. 251.
10. For the ethnography of Scotland, see W.F. Skene, *Celtic Scotland*, 3 vols (1876–80); John Mackintosh, *History of Civilization in Scotland*, 4 vols (1892).
11. A.W. Wiston-Glynn, *John Law of Lauriston* (1907), p. 3.
12. For a good account of the ethnology of the Iberian Peninsula see H. Schurtz, "Die Pyrrhenäen-Halbinsel," in Helmholts' *Weltgeschichte*, vol. 4.

13. Cf. J. Jung in Helmholts, vol. 4, p. 366.
14. Cicero, *De officiis*, I, c. 42. Cf. Otto Neurath, "Zur Anschauung der Antike über Handel, etc.," in *Jahrbücher für Nationalökonomie,* Series 34, p. 577.
15. G. Toniolo, *Dei remoti fattori della potenza economica di Firenze* (1882), pp. 12, 46.
16. For the Etruscans, see Müller-Deecke, *Die Etrusker*, 2 vols (1877). Cf. also Pauli, "Die Urvölker der Apenninhalbinsel" in Helmholts *Weltgeschichte*, vol. 4; also H. Genthe, *Über den etruskischen Tauschhandel nach dem Norden* (1874).
17. Müller-Deecke, ibid., vol. 2, p. 325.
18. Livy, v. I.
19. Davidsohn, *Geschichte von Florenz*, vol. 1 (1896), p. 39.
20. Skene, *Celtic Scotland*, vol. 1, pp. 145, 191, 231.
21. J. Klumker, *Der friesische Tuchhandel zur Zeit Karls des Grossen* (Doctorate dissertation, University of Leipzig).
22. T. Hume Brown, *Scotland in the Time of Queen Mary* (1904), p. 182.
23. Cf. Luigi Passerini, *Gli Alberti di Firenze. Genealogia, storia e documenti,* 2 vols, 1969.

3

The Proletariat

My task is to sketch the historically peculiar circumstances of life amid which the industrial proletariat lives. By the industrial proletariat I mean the body of wage-earners in the service of modern industrial capitalism. And I intend to point out the relation of these conditions to modern progress in general. This problem might be attacked in either of two ways,—first by making prominent those phenomena, such as state interference, that have a peculiar significance in the establishment of a definite social ideal and that furnish encouragement, as well, for undertaking definite reforms. This is the political point of view.

A second method would be to correlate such of these phenomena as we are able to recognize as the points of departure, the occasions, or the conditions from which arise the movements of the laboring class itself. This is the evolutionary point of view, from which can be answered the question, What makes the social movement possible? In the language of Hegel and Marx this sort of inquiry would be called the dialectic method. And this is the method of inquiry which will be adopted here.

In order rightly to judge the conditions of existence of the modern proletariat we must first of all understand what it has lost as compared with other groups of people, what it no longer possesses of the conditions of living of its own former generations. hence I must pay special attention to European conditions, which indeed are necessary to an understanding of all social phenomena. My discourse cannot be more than an introduction to a big subject.

Estrangement from nature is the most important feature of the proletarian existence. The contact of the country lad with nature ceases,—the friendly relation with the animal world, the growing up with the elements, rain, storm, and inclement weather, the dependence upon the events of nature, the rotation of summer and winter, of day and night. The modern industrial wage-earner becomes a characteristic representative of that artificial race of men now growing up in cities. Away from his natural environment, that is, away from home, the thousand-fold spiritual ties and tender sentiments are lost. His home is the world, he is a child of the world.

Another feature of the laborer's existence is his liberation from old institutions which confined him but restrained him as well. Among these was the village community with its customs and its usages, its festivals and fashions, which in part survive in the smaller towns. *Propinquitas!* But the proletariat has cosmopolitan customs and usages. Thanks to the development of commerce, provincial manners are abandoned.

There was also the family group. Not only is the old family connection, with its far-reaching interdependence, giving way, but the immediate family is also losing its binding power because the economic basis upon which it rests is disappearing owing to labor away from home, night work, and the labor of children and women who no longer find satisfactory employment at home. The early employment of children and youth makes them independent at an early age, and thus is weakened the discipline over children by parents. To this must be added the sordidness of the dwelling-houses in cities, for this narrows even more the basis of family life.

We must note, also, the decay of trade-associations built up by the medieval handicrafts, by which membership in a definite craft provided the individual ample internal and external status. Membership in a trade, however, is losing its hold as a result of the frequent change of occupation. For an individual passes with greater ease than formerly from one occupation to another, while the array of labor arrangements mobilized for a united productive activity has to be constantly remarshaled owing to the influence of the modern revolutionizing technique. The mechanical arrangement of individual operations which constitute an industry leads to a constant change, just as surely as a personal classification leads to the stereotyping of the industry.

Another cause of the decay of the trade fellowship is the dissolution of the intimate relation of the worker and his work. Activity is no longer the expression of a lively human interest, it is only the mechanical turning-off of some one simple process. The empirical technique of the olden time rested upon personal skill; the modern technique rests upon objective science. The organization of industry upon the principle of the division of labor separates the laborer from his work and makes him a mere soulless piece-worker in the social process of production. The capitalistic organization also separates the worker economically from his work. He is no longer economically interested in the results of his work.

The old servile rights and obligations have been destroyed. Every earlier time has recognized mutual responsibilities with respect to the dependent man, which indeed bound him, made him unfree, but gave him physical and moral support, protected him from hunger, and helped him over crises in his life, such as sickness. Even the slave or serf had this claim upon his lord. The journeyman of the Middle Ages was united to his master by a close fellowship supported by the feeling of moral obligation. This relation is disappearing. The modern workman is a "free" laborer, legally free, who now stands only in a business relation with his employer; services are rated on both sides at a money value. Therewith he is free to go hungry because without protection from commercial crises. He must win his bread from day to day and be prepared at any time to lose his position. In other respects his freedom is a mere formality; he cannot exercise it by not working; he can at best change masters. But this is becoming closed to him because capital is being monopolized in trusts. As soon as he succeeds in finding work, he is for the greater part of his life driven to the hardest drudgery in the service of the capitalistic employer. He is then less free than any Turkish peasant who plows with his oxen in a free field.

How will, how can this "free," that is to say, uprooted cosmopolitan live? This is the question which presents itself for him as well as for all who have experienced the same process of emancipation. This is the question of the time, which receives only one definite response from the proletariat. The recovery of the content of life is to be sought in two ways: by means of pleasure and by means of labor. Pleasure as one of the features of life is necessarily denied to the great mass, clearly from external causes, perhaps also from internal causes, because people are still too "sensible" to find a motive of life in pure pleasure, material or spiritual, i.e., in estheticism! They still require self-sacrifice, an object, morals. There remains clearly open only the second way—labor. "To labor and not to despair," has been proclaimed as the watchword for our hollow age. And the poet sings so sweetly

> Tis labor alone that helps us along
> Over this wilderness of gloomy doubt:
> It gives to each passing moment a go
> Which our life itself is without.

But how is it with the labor of the wage-earner? Often enough he has no work at all. The condition known as "being out of work" has established itself as a matter-of-course accompaniment of capitalism,—another novelty of our age. But also, by the time he finds work its power of yielding satisfaction has for the most part been lost. This is, perhaps, the most significant consequence of modern civilization. Labor as the sanction of life, as the director of energy, has ceased to round out the worker into the complete man and hence to make him peaceful and contented. The reason for this lies in the peculiarity of modern technique as well as the organization of modern business, for the modern factory labor is in large measure destructive of health, above all because it calls for too intense an exertion, and because of that disregard for the limits of human endurance which characterizes the modern technical development.

Moreover, labor has frequently become a disagreeable, repulsive act, in the depths of the earth and amid the noise, dust, and heat of many modern factories. Labor has become more and more monotonous and arrhythmic, mere piece-work of unvarying nature in the modern great industries built up by division of labor and consolidation. The laborer is now separated from his work, he creates no longer, he fashions no longer, he brings nothing to completion, nothing appears as his work, nothing in which his labor is embodied. He is no more than a secondary wheel in a gigantic mechanism.

The labor of the modern industrial wage-worker has thus lost all concreteness, all qualitative significance, and so has for him only an abstract and hence purely quantitative significance. And so it becomes a burden of which he seeks to be relieved as much as possible. (If we realize this we come to comprehend the endeavors for shortening the hours of labor, which give the characteristic impress to the modern labor movement.) And so also it comes to be measured in the terms of the money for which it is exchanged. Thus it was that the wage-earner was involved in the circle of ideas of the capitalistic world. The mechanism which accomplished his inclusion was the piece-wage system, after the pure money-wage had already accustomed him to value all labor power in terms of money. This valuation in money is imbued in him from early youth, for he enters "service" early, at a period of life when hitherto a youth lived without responsibility as a dependent member of a family.

Here lie the roots of all class strife between proletariat and entrepreneurs, who are now at odds regarding their respective shares in the joint product. "The right to the whole produce of labor!" The foregoing sketch of the peculiarities of proletarian life explains what we mean by the modern "social movement," wherein the proletariat struggles against the position into which capitalism has brought it.

When we observe the proletariat setting forth to emancipate itself from its position, and see how the movement is carried on with the passions of hatred and envy, the conviction forces itself upon us that the origin of the movement is not hopeless misery, for this is no characteristic of the proletariat. The cause is rather the contrast which the laborer observes between his own frequently pinched position and that superabundance of wealth in which many of the employing class live, wealth which the laborer has, in his own opinion, produced. For in their service he wears himself out. And this contrast is constantly brought to his attention, not so much because he sees that insolent wealth used in display, oftentimes vain enough,—the poor serfs of the Middle Ages endured that sight,—but rather because he daily witnesses the accumulation of new fortunes, whose possessors grow rich before his very eyes. Frederick Albert Lange accurately and forcibly express this attitude when he once said, "The spirit of jealousy never completely disappears while a poor man lives in the neighborhood of a rich man; it may, however, be rendered very dull by constant relative wealth." But by fluctuating relations and by every occasion which makes the present contrasts more striking, the feeling of envy is quickened. To this, what we might call objective insecurity of wealth relations, which is characteristic of our times, and which the proletariat observes, is added another insecurity which for the laborer is a subjective one. This is the uncertainty as to the means of his livelihood, the fact that he does not know from day to day whether he is going to earn his bread. For an industrial depression may result in the wholesale discharge of laborers, and thus in widespread famine.

It is this continual change which brings to a member of the proletariat a consciousness of his position. The increasing intellectual training, to which his life in great cities powerfully contributes, enables, and inspires him to reflect upon the causes of this insecurity and upon the contrast between his own position and that of the rich. And then a secret is revealed to him, the discovery of which becomes the ground of justification for the modern agitations of the laboring class, the secret, namely, that all the circumstances of his existence are not founded in unchangeable, natural relationships. On the contrary, they are based upon the peculiarities of the prevailing social and economic organization. "No man can assert any right against nature, but in society distress at once assumes the form of an injustice inflicted upon this or that class" (Hegel). Thus the ground is prepared upon which a social movement may be developed, for now a point of attack is found,—the existing social order.

And to the extent that social criticism of this sort becomes refined and sharpened, as discontent and the desire for improvement become intensified, another circumstance which defines the position of the wage-earner becomes more and more intolerable. This is his dependence upon his employer. This dependence is no longer a legal one, as in the time of slavery, but is no less complete on that account.

It appears in the fact that the laborer is assigned to his position by the entrepreneur through stress of hunger; it appears in the humiliating subordination under the command of an entrepreneur. It often assumes a mediæval form when the factory-owner regards himself as the "patriarch" of his people and seeks to guide and determine their lives. It reaches out into the sphere of political right when the capitalist classes use their power in order to limit the participation of the wage-earners in the activity of the state.

Apparently these are the causes of the proletarian criticism of the existing organization of society, yet we must attend to some other special conditions of life among the modern laboring classes in order to understand the peculiar current of ideas which we continually meet with in all clamors for the "emancipation" of the proletariat. These might be distinguished on the one hand as a tendency toward communistic dreams, and on the other as a love for the masses.

The love of the masses and regard for the masses follows immediately from the association of each individual wage-earner with his thousands of fellow workers, all of whom are united by no other tie than their common labor in the service of the entrepreneur. They are grouped together without distinction, like grains in a heap of sand, and outside the factory undertake no higher social activity than some sort of union. What capitalism has tossed together, in crowds, in great cities and centers of industry, is, as we say, an inarticulate mass of individuals who have completely broken with the past, who have cut themselves loose from all communal ties, from home, village, and kindred, beginning life anew with a complete destruction of their old ideals. The laborer's only support is the comrade of his fate, who signifies as little as he, and who like himself does not belong to any historic community. With this individual he allies himself, and becomes his confederate. Hence arises a host of confederates who are distinguished by one thing above all others, not by individuality, not by common tradition, but by their mass, their massiveness. Never in the history of the world have so many individuals stood together for united action. Never in history has the impetus of mass-action so characterized any movement as has this of the proletariat. Everywhere we hear "the heavy tramp of the labor battalion" with which Lassalle sought to frighten his opponents. And if we would picture to ourselves the social movement of our day, it invariably appears to us as an inexhaustible stream of men hardly one of whom stands out clearly, flowing over the whole land as far as the eye can see, to the farthest horizon where the last of them roll away into the darkness. Translated into psychological terms, it signifies that there has grown up in the individual a tremendous strengthening of the consciousness of combined power, and a strong mass-ethical feeling to conflict with class-ethical doctrine. Membership in his class, therefore, signifies for the wage-earner exactly what for others membership in a noble rank, in a community, a city, or a state has implied. With pride, he proclaims, *Proletarius sum.*

This dissolution of all quantitative or individual distinction in the mass, now viewed and, therefore, now valued only qualitatively, is parallel with and affects in the same manner, the development of modern technique in other directions. Only he who has familiarized himself with their peculiarities will be in a position to understand the important features of the proletarian movement, and above all to comprehend the above-mentioned communistic tendency.

The increasing differentiation and integration of separate economies, their absorption into an indissoluble whole, on the one hand, and on the other, the progressive specialization and organization of labor in the modern "great industries" constitute what has been called the socialization of the process of production. This socialization has brought it about that a particular commodity appears no longer as the product of individual labor but as the joint product of common labor. Formerly the cobbler who made a pair of boots regarded himself as the fashioner of this particular article. The laborer in a modern shoe factory, who pursues only a single task in the general process, has lost this personal relation to the particular product. Today the actual process is collective for individual articles, and, therefore, to the task laborer engaged in it, the conception of a collective organization of general production is no more strange. In the same way, however, and at the same time, the idea occurs to the laborer in the great city of a common, of a communistic consumption. This idea is made more and more familiar to him by the character of his own home surroundings.

The separate dwelling, which satisfies man's original instinct for privacy, loses for the poor man in his congested tenement more and more of its charm. Instead, he feels a growing liking for public places where he can satisfy more completely his material and immaterial needs. Workingmen's clubs, public reading-rooms, concert-halls, and beer-gardens become a new home for the masses in great cities. The aggregated advantages of the public institutions, the public gardens and parks, and museums, with their uninterrupted series of pleasures and delights, rise in the estimation of the laborers as the charm of their private or family life diminishes. The family itself dissolves under the influence of the excessively long day or night work away from home, through woman's labor, and the early employment of children. The result is that the proletariat is involuntarily led to transfer the weight of its interest from the individual to the social life.

Now, however, to gain a full understanding of the modern social movements, we must become acquainted with the general conditions of the time under which they operate. Here also a few remarks are necessary. That which distinguishes the modern time is, above all, an alertness such as I can think of in no other time. A current of life flows through present-day society, of which no other time has known, and thus a stimulus between individual members of society is made possible, which was before inconceivable. This has been brought about by the machinery of commerce which capitalism has provided. The possibility of communicating across a great country within a few hours by means of the telegraph, the telephone, and the newspaper; the possibility of transferring from one place to another great masses of people by the modern facilities of transportation, has brought about an appreciation of the solidarity of the great masses, and a sense of omnipresence that to earlier times was unknown. This is especially true of the great towns of the present. The possibility of great mass-movements is thus extraordinarily increased. And in like manner is attained that development within the mass which we are accustomed to call education. Knowledge, and with knowledge pretensions.

Closely connected with this activity, however, is that phenomenon which we call the nervousness of our time, the lack of composure, the hurrying, the restlessness pervading all the walks of life. Through the peculiarity of business relations in all branches not only of economic, but also of social life, this restless spirit prevails. The era of free competition is manifest in all fields. Every one vies with his neighbor. No one longer finds joy in life. Beautiful contemplative peace is gone.

And finally, one more suggestion. This might be called revolutionism. For there never has been a time which has experienced such a complete subversion of every form of existence. Everything is in a fluid state, business, science, art, morals, religion; all ideas are in such a ferment that we are finally driven to the conclusion that there is nothing certain left. And this is one of the most important criteria for the interpretation of the modern social upheaval. For it explains two different things. In the first place it accounts for that destructive criticism of existing conditions which seeks to throw a bad light upon everything; which casts to the scrap-heap all former ideas in order to bring new ones to market. This critical spirit first took its rise among the bourgeoisie, who applied it to political, moral, religious, and esthetic relations. The proletariat is now adopting the same critical spirit, and applying it to the whole intricate field of economic and social institutions.

That revolutionary spirit produces, furthermore, fanatical ideas concerning the possibility of a blissful future state. Since miracles have been realized before our own eyes, such as none could have hoped for; why not still more? Why not anything we wish? Thus the revolutionary present becomes the breeding-ground for the social Utopias of the future. Edison and Siemens are the spiritual fathers of Bellamy and Bebel. Here we have at hand the elements of which are constructed the "Socialism and Social Movements" of our time.

4

The Bourgeois—Past and Present

The Bourgeois—Old Style

By now we have come to know the component parts of the employer's soul as it aspires to perfection. Acquisitiveness and enterprise, middle-class respectability and calculation all go to compose the complex entity, though various combinations are possible owing to the variety of shade in each element, or owing to the way the elements are combined. That is why we have reviewed the different resultant types of capitalist employer. Moreover, we have also observed that in different countries the development of the capitalist spirit varied considerably. There remains one further question. Is the capitalist spirit constant? Does the bourgeois remain immutably the same? In other words, is there anything common to all the types that have come under our notice, and to all the national expressions of capitalism, so that it may be possible to sketch the picture of the bourgeois from them?

With one qualification the answer is in the affirmative. And the qualification is that we should be allowed to divide one age of capitalist growth from another according to its characteristic spirit, for it was this that marked of one type of bourgeois or employer from another. This means that there was not one persistent type of employer at all times, but different sorts at different times.

Now, so far as I can judge, capitalist employers from the first dawn of capitalism to about the middle of the eighteenth century—the period which I have christened that of early capitalism—had, with all their variation in details, a good many characteristics in common. These were so definite that they form a clear dividing line between the employer of the early capitalist period and his prototype in modern times. What manner of man, then, was he, this bourgeois of old?

To begin with, he also was a capitalist employer. Profit was his end, undertakings his means; he speculated and calculated; and ultimately he cultivated the middle-class virtues, though not all in the same degree. What, then, was his distinguishing mark, you ask? How did he differ from his modern brother? You may sum it up in a sentence: in all his thoughts and actions, in all that he did or left undone, he was actuated by the weal or woe of the living, breathing human being. The central doctrine of the pre-capitalist period had not lost its efficacy. *Omnium rerum mensura homo*; man still continued to be the measure of all things. Life was still natural. Even the bourgeois as yet walked bolt-upright on his two feet; he did not yet run about on all fours.

Of course, only fragments remained of the pre-capitalist man who was still met with in the first faint beginnings of capitalism, when the Genoese noble merchants built them towers, or when Sir Walter Raleigh sallied forth in search of El Dorado. These fragments you may come across in Defoe or Benjamin Franklin. But the remainder of that early natural man with his healthy appetites has disappeared; he has been forced to accustom himself to the strait-waistcoat of middle-class respectability and the tyranny of the calculating habit. His claws have been trimmed, his carnivorous teeth blunted, and his horns encased in leather.

But all those who bowed the knee to capitalism—the rich land-owner and the great oversea trader, the banker and the speculator, the manufacturer and the draper—all these never ceased to accommodate their economic activities to the healthy demands of life; for all of them business was but a means of livelihood. Their own interests and those of their fellow-men, for whom and with whom they labored, determined the extent and direction of what they did. In support of this, you need only examine the views of these old-fashioned bourgeois.

1. First and foremost, consider their conception of riches and their attitude towards profit. Wealth was undoubtedly prized, and to obtain it was the

> passionate desire of every heart. But wealth was not an end in itself. Its only virtue lay in the creation or preservation of life-values. This is the tune on which all our informants harp, from Alberti to Defoe and Franklin.

The true value of money, says Alberti, can be appreciated only by him who has at any time been obliged to say to another "that bitter word, which all free spirits hate—'I pray thee'."[1] Riches should bring you independence and liberty, should get you friends, should make you honored and renowned.[2] On the other hand, "What you cannot make use of is but a heavy burden."[3]

It will suffice to add to these expressions of opinion, dating from the childhood of capitalism, others that were current in the latest period of this early capitalist era. The similarity in sentiment will be apparent.

Our first witness shall be Benjamin Franklin. A man, he says, who has been granted wealth and a soul to use it aright has received a special and splendid gift of grace. Once in possession of riches it is a paramount duty to use them well. "A wise man will desire no more than what he may get justly, use soberly, distribute cheerfully, and live upon contentedly."[4] Riches must be constantly increasing through industry and skillful application. They should never be allowed to lie fallow, but always be adding to their owner's wealth and spreading happiness all around. It is sensible to accumulate goods and money; but to use them well is wise. It is not riches that give happiness, but rather their proper utilization.[5] Riches bring fame, guarantee security, and provide means for many an honorable and useful undertaking. Moreover, wealth must be acquired in just and right ways,[6] for only those riches bring joy that are gotten honestly, or *onestamente*, as Alberti says.[7] If you are selling anything for profit, hearken to the still, small voice of conscience, and be content with fair gain; and take no advantage of the buyer's ignorance.[8]

Now, it may quite rightly be objected that this wise counsel is easily given. In all probability it is the leisure-thought of the writers; possibly the voice of conscience heard in the quiet of the study but neglected in the stress and heat of the day. Consequently, it is evidence that must be ruled out of court.

2. To see that such an objection would be invalid, observe (and this is the second point) the attitude of all our authorities to business itself, their conduct as business men, the way they carried on their affairs; in a word their "style" (as it may be called), and you shall find the same spirit in it as that in their attitude towards wealth.

Their business pace was as yet slow; their whole activity was calm and unruffled. There was no stormy whirlwind in their work. Recall Franklin's decision to spend his time as profitably as possible and his view that industry was the prime virtue. His working-day was mapped out thus: six full hours were devoted to his business; seven to sleep; the rest he gave up to prayer, reading, and social diversions. And this was the type of the diligent employer, though Franklin was then only in a small way of business. His own words are worth recording.[9]

THE MORNING. *Question.* What good shall I do this day?	5, 6, 7	Rise, wash, and address Powerful goodness. Contrive day's business, and take the resolution of the day; prosecute the present study and breakfast
	8, 9, 10, 11	Work.
NOON.	12, 1	Read, or overlook my accounts, and dine.
	2, 3, 4, 5	Work.
EVENING. *Question.* What good have I done to-day?	6, 7, 8, 9	Put things in their places. Supper. Music or diversion, or conversation. Examination of the day.
NIGHT.	10, 11, 12, 1, 2, 3, 4	Sleep.

The precept of order requiring that every part of my business should have its allotted time, one page in my little book [cf. p. 119 above] contained the following scheme of employment for the twenty-four hours of a natural day.

Or take the case of the wholesale traders of Bozen. They closed their businesses for the whole summer and spent the time in the health resort of the highlands near.

Leisure was thus appreciated. And just the same as you left yourself an abundance of it during the day and during the year, so, too, you sought to obtain the maximum amount of leisure for life as a whole. It was a common practice for people who had amassed a fortune in business or in industry (even though it were not of great proportions) to retire in middle age, and if possible purchase a country seat where they might end their days in contemplative ease. Jacob Fugger with his "Let me earn so long as I am able"—a dictum typically characteristic for a full-blown capitalist economic outlook—was undoubtedly far in advance of his age. It was for holding such a view that Anthony Fugger described him as a queer fish. He was regarded as abnormal. And so he was, judged from the standpoint of those who in their demands on life placed the ideal of the retired private gentleman first and foremost.

This yearning for a peaceful existence in a country house may be found in all the Italian books on trade; in the German Renaissance there was the same tendency to feudalize the traders; and in the eighteenth century the English commercial world still continued to look longingly at this end-all of business. The ideal of the retired private gentleman may thus be regarded as an article of faith in the early capitalist economic creed everywhere. That it had yet another significance we shall see presently.

The domination of this ideal in England in the first half of the eighteenth century is attested by Defoe's remarks[10] on the common English practice to retire from business comparatively early. When a man has amassed £20,000, "why should he trade any farther? and what need he desire any more, that has such a bank? 'Tis time to leave off and have done; 'tis time to leave labouring for the world, when he has the world, as they call it, on a string." Such a one "changes his situation in the world, that is to say, he lays down the tradesman and takes up the gentleman with a £1,000 a year estate." Defoe gives him two "seasonable hints." Let him live within the compass of his income. Of his £1,000 a year he should spend half and lay up the remainder, thus ensuring "a rising family under him." Secondly, he should keep far from speculation, for has he not retired from business to enjoy what he has got? Why then adventure it? All he has to do is to be "quiet when he is arrived at this station of life." After all, "if a tradesman is leaving off, it is with the usual saying of the rich men that withdraw from the world—That he may enjoy himself; that he may live in quiet and peace at the latter end of his days, without noise and without hurry."

That was all very well when they had made their fortune. But while making it, what of their work? Let it be said at once that it was slow. Business methods were such that in any given time you accomplished the least possible transactions. The extensive development of commerce was small; its intensive development was only in accord with it. The spirit in which business was carried on appears to me to be exemplified in the ancient saw to demand as high prices as possible so as to obtain a great rate of profit on a small capital. Small turnover, large profits, seems to have been the ruling principle of the employers of those days. And not merely of the lesser men, some of whom had not yet thrown off entirely the shackles of the gild system; the very big trading companies had it too. Thus it was the policy of the Dutch East India Company to carry on "small transactions that brought in a great deal." That was why it always destroyed spice plants, burned rich harvests and the like; though another motive was to deprive the poor of the opportunity of enjoying colonial products.

Quite generally it was the aim of all business to satisfy the demands of the wealthy, which is always easier than to deal with demand on a large scale.[11] This was quite justifiable according to the economic theory of the seventeenth and eighteenth centuries, which made out a good case for high prices.[12]

The dignified aspect of the old-fashioned bourgeois, his stiff and pedantic bearing, were only the outward garb of his inward calm. Can you imagine a man in the long fur cloak of the Renaissance, or in the knee-breeches and powdered wig of the subsequent centuries, as ever being in a hurry? Reliable authorities, indeed, describe the old-fashioned tradesman as one who walks with careful step and slow, who is never in haste just because he is occupied. Messer Alberti, himself a very busy man, tells us that he had never observed a busy person walking otherwise than at a slow pace,[13] and this applied to fifteenth-century Florence. Of eighteenth-century Lyons a contemporary tells the same tale. "Here," he says, "our walk is slow because every one is busy; in Paris people are in one continuous haste—because there is nothing to do there."[14] So in Glasgow about the same time. We read of its merchants "how in scarlet coats, cocked hats, and powdered wigs, they strutted up and down the Planistanes, the only bit of pavement then in Glasgow, covering three or four hundred yards of road in front of the Town Hall and the adjoining offices, talking grandly to one another and nodding haughtily to the humbler folk who came to do them homage."[15]

3. The attitude of the old-fashioned traders towards competition and to their customers sprang naturally from their business style. Above all else they wanted quiet. This "static principle," which had dominated the whole of pre-capitalist economic activities, had not yet lost all its influence in the early capitalist period. And the circle of your customers was like a fenced-off preserve; it was wholly yours—to be compared to the territory assigned to the trading company in lands beyond the sea for its exclusive exploitation.

With this point I have dealt fully in another book;[16] it must here suffice, therefore, to indicate its importance briefly. Let me refer to one or two business principles, all of them naturally resulting from a static economic order, all of them included in the economic outlook of the old-fashioned bourgeois.

All "custom hunting" was looked at askance; to take away your neighbor's customers was contemptible, unchristian, and immoral. A rule for "Merchants who traded in commodities" was: "Turn no man's customers away from him, either by word of mouth or by letter, and do not to another what you would not have another do to you." It was, however, more than a rule; it became an ordinance, and is met with over and over again. In Mayence its wording was as follows: "No one shall prevent another from buying, or by offering a higher price make a commodity dearer, on pain of losing his purchase; no one shall interfere in another's business undertaking or carry on his own on so large a scale as to ruin other traders." In Saxony it was much the same. In the Ordinances of 1672, 1682, and 1692, paragraph 18 reads: "No shopkeeper shall call away the customers from another's shop, nor shall he by signs or motions keep them from buying."[17]

It followed from this that all tricks to increase your custom, of whatever sort they were, were rather despised. Right into the nineteenth century there was still a certain prejudice in many a high-class firm against even the simplest form of advertisement. Some houses in New York had not got rid of the prejudice by the middle of the century. "No respectable house would overdo the thing. There was a sort of self-respect about the articles advertised."[18]

But even in an advertising age it was for long considered nefarious to praise your goods or to point out wherein your business was superior to others. The last word in commercial impropriety was to announce that your prices were lower than those of the man opposite. "To undersell" was most ungentlemanly: "No blessing will come from harming your neighbour by underselling and cutting prices."

Bad as underselling itself was, it was beneath contempt to advertise it. "Since the days of our author," remark the editors of the 5th edition (1745) of Defoe's *Complete English Tradesman* (Defoe died in 1731), "this underselling practice is grown to such a shameful height that particular persons publicly advertise that they undersell the rest of the trade."

For France there is extant a particularly valuable document, dating from the second half of the eighteenth century, which proves even more strikingly how heinous this offence was thought to be, even in Paris. It is an ordinance of the year 1761, and it proclaims to all and sundry in the French capital that to advertise that you are selling your goods at a price below the customary one must be regarded as the last resource of a merchant in difficulties, and that such action deserved severe condemnation. The ordinance proceeded to forbid the wholesale and retail traders of Paris and its suburbs "to run after one another" trying to find customers, and above all to distribute handbills calling attention to their wares.

Other methods of drawing advantages for yourself at the expense of your neighbors or of poaching on others' preserves were equally disreputable. The author of the *Complete English Tradesman* has some reflections on this manner of competition which help us exceedingly in gaining a true estimate of the business ethics of those days. They prove that economic activities were still in a static state and that tradition and custom ruled them. Remember that Defoe was not unskilled as a trader, and that generally he is filled with the capitalist spirit.

This is his story.[19] Before Wiltshire broadcloth reaches Northampton, where it is retailed, four people find employment. "The clothier, when it is finished, sends it up by the carrier to London to Mr. A, the Blackwell hall factor, to be sold. Mr. A, the factor, sells it to Mr. B, the woolen-draper; Mr. B, the woolen-draper, sells it to Mr. C, the shopkeeper at Northampton, and he cuts it out in his shop and sells it to the country gentlemen about him...also 'tis sent down by the carrier from London to Northampton."

Now in Northampton is another shopkeeper, "perhaps an Alderman, a rich overgrown Tradesman," who has more money than his neighbors and therefore wants no credit. "Prying about into all the secrets of the trade," he discovers where the cloth comes from, communicates with the clothier in Wiltshire, and buys his goods direct, then has them brought by horse-packs to Northampton. Possibly by tempting the clothier with ready money he obtains the cloth a penny per yard cheaper than the factor in London sold it to the woolen-draper. What is the result? The overgrown tradesman will save in cost of transport, so much so that his cloth will cost him half-a-crown per yard less than his neighbor. Hence he will be able to undersell, and thus obtain his neighbor's custom. Not only that, but he will have taken away the occupation of several people: the carrier who brought the goods to London from Wiltshire, the carrier who took them from London to Northampton, and finally Mr. A, the Blackwell Hall factor, who "also loses his employment and may sit and blow his fingers for want of trade." Mr. B likewise is ruined by the loss of his wholesale trade. "And what is all the benefit which is made by this spoil upon trade? Only this, that Squire D.E. of Northamptonshire buys his suits half-a-crown a yard cheaper," and a covetous man has been made richer. And the moral? "This is cutting off the circulation of trade; this is managing trade with a few hands; and if this practice, which is indeed evidently begun, was to come to be universal, a million of people in England that now live handsomely by trade would be destitute of employment and their families in time might want bread."

This passage speaks volumes. How utterly inconceivable must the line of thought appear to a modern business man!

Like the producers, the consumers also received attention. In a certain sense the consumer received even more, for the conception that all production was in the interests of consumption had not yet disappeared. It was the old "natural" view; production for use was still the rule of all economic activities. Hence the stress laid throughout the whole of the early capitalist period on *good* wares, and on the principle that commodities should really be what they pretended. Innumerable were the ordinances that were everywhere promulgated to this intent, more especially in the seventeenth and eighteenth centuries; and the state deemed to part of its work itself to regulate the quality of wares. It is idle to assert that this very state control is evidence of the decline of the "natural" view; in other words, that the custom of producing for use was on the decline. Such was not the case. The interference of the state was intended to check the conduct of some few unscrupulous manufacturers. For the rest, the old tradition prevailed that you should make good and genuine commodities; it was the tradition of the gild system, and industry in the early capitalist period continued to be tinged with it.

It was long before the purely capitalist notion gained acceptance that the exchange value of any commodity was what influenced the employer most. We may observe how slow its progress was from the conflicting opinions on the subject in the eighteenth century. Sir Josiah Child appears to have been in the minority on this, as on most other questions, when he formulated the demand that every manufacturer should be allowed to judge for himself as to the kind of commodity, and the quality, that he brought into the market. It is curious enough nowadays to read Child's plea for the right of the manufacturer to make shoddy goods. "If we intend to have the trade of the world," he cries,[20] we must imitate the Dutch, who make the worst as well as the best of all manufacturers, that we may be in a capacity of serving all markets and all humours."

4. Finally, the attitude of the old-fashioned bourgeois to technical inventions is significant for the spirit within him. The old view of life appears once more: technical improvements are to be welcomed if only they do not overthrow man's happiness. True, they may cheapen commodities; but the odd pence thus gained are too high a price for the tears and the sufferings of the families of the workmen who are thrown out of employment. Once more, then, human welfare is the pivot of the whole economic organism, even though this time it be but the welfare of the wage-earning class. The interests of this class were by no means absent from men's thoughts in those days, although the reason for this may have been a selfish one.

There is abundant testimony to the dislike of labor-saving machinery in the early capitalist period. Let us glance at one or two instances.

In the second year of Elizabeth's reign a Venetian inventor (a type whose acquaintance we have already made) offered a labor-saving machine to the Court of the London Clothworkers' Company (whose industry by that time was already capitalistic in its organization). The Court carefully considered the offer and decided to refuse it, for the new invention would probably have deprived many a workman of his living. "It wolde be a grete decay unto the companye, whereupon the Master and Wardens gave the said stranger grete thanks and also *xxs.* in money towards his charge, and so parted."[21]

In 1684 the knitting-frame for stockings was forbidden to be used (again in a capitalistically organized industry), and once more the reason was that it might reduce the wages of the craftsmen.[22] Even a professional "projector" and inventor like John Joachim Becher shared this view. "I should certainly advise no one to invent instruments that might do away with human labor or reduce wages; but there can be no objection to such as are of advantage and utility, especially in those places where there is more work than workers can accomplish."[23] Colbert's language is stronger still; the inventor of time-saving devices is a "foe of work." And these are the sentiments of Frederick the Great: "It is not by any means my intention that the spinning machine should be generally used....If it were, a large number of people who depended for their livelihood on spinning would be thrown out of employment into starvation—which cannot possibly be tolerated."[24] After all this we shall not be surprised to find that a man of such noble sentiments and good taste as Montesquieu should be conservative in this respect. He believed that machines, even including water-mills, were not an unmixed blessing.[25] Finally, so thorough a business man as Postlethwayt is very reserved in his judgment on new inventions. A people without commerce may safely refuse to admit machines, but commercial states should only allow them after careful scrutiny and should anyhow exclude such as manufacture goods for home consumption. "What we gain in expedition, we lose in strength."[26]

What comes to the fore throughout? The old conception of producing in order to satisfy wants, no more and no less, the traditional way of life, or moral scruples. But be the reason what it may, it is always a stumbling-block to the unfettered development of acquisitiveness, of the undertaking spirit, and of economic rationalism.

With the dawn of the nineteenth century all this changed, at first slowly, then with a rush. The results of the change will form the subject of the succeeding chapter.

The Modern Business Man

How has the economic outlook changed in the last century? What characterizes the capitalist spirit of our own day—the zenith of capitalism; and how does that spirit differ from the one which filled the old-fashioned bourgeois?

Before attempting to answer these questions, let us realize that there is no one single type of employer today, any more than in earlier epochs; that, as in the early capitalist period, a different spirit moves different capitalist employers. Let us, then, place the various types in groups. Surprising as it may seem, they are the types we already know as having existed in the past. Today, too, we find the freebooter, the ground landlord, the bureaucrat, the speculator, the trader, and the manufacturer.

Recall the career of a Cecil Rhodes. Does it not remind you of the Genoese merchants on their towers, or possibly even more of Sir Walter Raleigh and Sir Francis Drake? Cecil Rhodes was of the stuff that robber-knights were made of. He was a discoverer and a conqueror whom no stumbling-blocks could retard; beside the word and the rifle he wielded another mighty weapon—modern stock-exchange gambling. He was partly politician, partly capitalist employer; rather more of a diplomat than a trader; he recognized no other power than brute force. It is strange to find in him even one iota of the Puritan spirit. And if we are to compare him with earlier generations, he must be placed alongside the men of the Renaissance.

How different from Cecil Rhode's world is that of (say) Stumm, or some Silesian mine-owner! Here we are in the atmosphere of the old feudal landed nobility; the ancient relationship between master and man is still met with; the staff of the establishments are arranged in a kind of hierarchy, and business is deliberate and cumbersome. Such are a few of the characteristics of these concerns, the directors of which have much in common with the capitalist landed proprietor of days gone by.

Then there is a third kind of employer nowadays who reminds us of the bureaucrat of old—exact in his work, methodical to a degree, nicely balanced in his judgments, highly gifted as an organizer, very careful before committing himself, an excellent executive official, who today may be town clerk of a large town and tomorrow manager of a bank, who frequently enough gives up the control of a Government department for that of a trust.* You will find him at the head of state and municipal enterprises.

Different from all these is the speculator of our time, who appears to be twin-brother to the eighteenth-century projector. Recently the daily papers reported the exploits of a French speculator, and the story is worth recalling. Rochette was the man's name; his age scarcely thirty. Yet he had allowed millions to slip between his fingers. He started life as an under-waiter in a railway station restaurant; before long he was a full-fledged waiter in a café in Melun. Coming to Paris, he made himself acquainted with bookkeeping, and entered the service of Berger, the financial swindler. On his master's bankruptcy Rochette took over the business with the 5,000 francs dowry brought him by a typist whom he married. He then began to float companies, and in the space of four years no less than 13 came into existence. There was the Crédit Minier, with a capital of 500,000 francs; the Laviana Coal Mines, with 2 millions; the Liat Coal Mines, with the same amount; the Banque Franco-Espagnole, with 20 millions; the Minier Trust, with 10 millions; the Union Franco-Belge, with 2 ½ millions; the financial paper *Le Financier*, with 2 millions; a number of copper and tin companies; a Moroccan Fishery Company; an incandescent lamp company, with 4½ millions; and many more. He issued altogether some 60 million francs' worth of shares, which by skilful manipulation rose to 200 millions, though a tenth of that figure was more nearly their true value. He had opened no less than 57 branch establishments in France; and the total number of people who participated in his scheme was close upon 40,000. Most of them were ruined, their total losses amounting to more than 150 millions. Why, it may be asked,

* [This is a type common in Germany. Perhaps Bernard Dernburg is the best known. He was Director of the Darmstädter Bank from 1901 to 1906, and German Minister for the Colonies from 1907 to 1910. On his resigning his portfolio he again became a banking magnate.]

was Rochette able to take in so many people? The explanation will be found in his marvelous power of surrounding himself with "solid," respectable folk. Just to show how cunning he was in blinding his victims, it may be mentioned that he founded a large factory for utilizing a filament lamp patent. Everybody rushed to get shares in the company; the huge factory was the talk of the town; its tall chimneys belched forth smoke day and night, to the great satisfaction of the shareholders. In reality, however, there was only one solitary individual working in the building, and he was the stoker!

Does not this story read like a report of doings in England in the 1720s?

How different is the preserving tradesman who makes a fortune because of his sure eye for the right conjuncture, or by clever calculations and advantageous agreement with his wholesale house, his customers, and his employees. What has such a man, say a Berlin draper, in common with Cecil Rhodes? What the director of a multiple shop with gold-mine speculator? And what all these with the manufacturer who runs his factory as was done 100 or 200 years ago, in Bradford or Sedan?

These old friends are still among us, and seemingly their form is unchanged. Nor are they the only types of the modern employer. Others have joined the group, which thus becomes quite picturesque. A very common one, usually found in America, may be termed the master-employer (since super-employer is an ugly word). His great characteristic is that he unites within himself several independent types. He may be freebooter, unscrupulous calculator, landlord, and speculator all in one. Any trust-magnate will serve as an illustration.

Finally, a phenomenon of our age is the collective employer, who is not an individual at all, but a group of capitalist employers at the head of a giant enterprise. They form a kind of syndicated employer, each of them exercising special functions, and in their corporate capacity they represent undertaking in all its comprehensiveness. We need only think of such industrial organizations as our electrical concerns, our iron foundries, our cannon factories.

In short, modern undertaking in all its types presents a variegated picture. But in our own days, as in those of long ago, all the types have certain features in common, all are filled with the same spirit. It is only a difference of degree that distinguishes the one from the other.

In the old times, as we saw, the employers were children of the early capitalist spirit; in modern times, they are the children of the perfected capitalist spirit.

What manner of thing is this perfected capitalist spirit? And what have all the types of the modern capitalist employer in common?

1. The ideal of both must be our first consideration. What is it? What are the life-values that govern the latter-day business man? What strikes us here is that there has been a peculiar change of perspective in the evaluation of man, a change of perspective which seems to have affected the whole of the rest of life. Man, the flesh-and-blood man, with his joys and sorrows, with his needs and demands, has been forced from his place as the center round which all economic activities rotate; his throne is now occupied by a few abstractions, such as Acquisitiveness and Business. Man has ceased to be what he was until the end of the early capitalist period—the measure of all things. The economic subjective agent now aims at as high a profit as he can, and strives to make his business flourish exceedingly. The two aims are closely intertwined, as we shall presently observe. Their relationship may be expressed thus: The employers wish to see business thriving; as for acquisitiveness, it is forced upon them, even though they may never have set out with that as their goal.

The real interest of undertaking does not always lie in mere gain, certainly not for the dominating personalities who determine the type. Walter Rathenau was, as I think, perfectly right when he once said: "I have never yet met with a business man whose chief aim was to acquire wealth. I will even go so far as to assert that he who is out to make money cannot possibly be a great business man."[27] Something very different occupies the thoughts of the employer. His heart is set on seeing his business thrive. Once more Walter Rathenau has expressed it well.

> The object of the business man's work, of his worries, his pride and his aspirations is just his undertaking, be it a commercial company, factory, bank, shipping concern, theatre or railway. The undertaking seems to take on form and substance, and to be ever with him, having, as it were, by virtue of his book-keeping, his organization, and his branches, an independent economic existence. The business man is wholly devoted to making his business a flourishing, healthy, living organism.[28]

This view is shared by all the capitalist employers of the day in so far as they have expressed themselves on the inner meaning of their activity.

Now, what is really meant by making a business, that is, a capitalist undertaking, flourish? Observe that a business begins with a sum of money and ends with the same, and that therefore its existence is bound up with the realization of a surplus. Success in business can only mean success in realizing this surplus. No profits, no business success. A factory may make very dear or very cheap goods, and their quality may establish their maker's name as a household word throughout the globe, but if the business continues to show a deficit from year to year, it is a failure from the capitalist point of view. To flourish, a concern must be profitable; to prosper, it must pay.[29]

You see now what I meant when I made the statement that the employers wish to see business thriving, and as for acquisitiveness, it is forced upon them.

Such being the goal of the capitalist employer, the end of his activities is necessarily projected into infinity. In earlier times, when the needs of the community determined economic activities, these had natural boundaries or limits. There can be no such limits when economic activities are determined by acquisitiveness and by flourishing businesses. There is never a point in the future when the total profits are sufficiently great for the employer to say: It is enough. Should the development of a business be such that its prosperity ceases to increase, the many-sidedness of modern enterprise will see to it that before long a second, and possibly a third, business is added to the original one. Thus it is that in modern days two equally strong tendencies show themselves—expansion of one and the same business, and the branching out into subsidiary or additional businesses. This very often leads to a kind of inner pressure in the mind of the employer. It frequently happens that he really does not want to expand further, but he must. Many a captain of industry has confessed as much. We were always hoping, says Andrew Carnegie in his Autobiography, that there would come a time when extension of business would no longer be necessary; but we invariably found that to put off expanding would mean retrogression.[30] Rockefeller tells the same tale. The first reason for starting his trusts was the desire to unite his capital and his capacities

> to carry on a business of some magnitude and importance in place of the small business that each separately had heretofore carried on. After some time, when the possibilities of the new conditions became apparent, we found that more capital was necessary. This we provided, as also the people, and founded the Standard Oil Company with a capital of a million dollars. Later we discovered that even more money could be profitably invested, and we raised our capital to 3 ½ millions. The more the business grew the more capital we put into it, the object being always the same: to extend our business by furnishing the best and cheapest products.[31]

A kind of monomania this; capital is piled on capital *because* the business grows. Extension of business is the end; furnishing cheap and good products the means. A famous German employer—Strousberg—says exactly the same thing. "The first wedge calls as a rule for a second, and so the great railway I was building made further demands upon me. To satisfy these I extended my activities, departed more and more from my original intention, and, finding so much promise in the new prospect, I devoted myself wholly to my business."[32]

Most capitalist employers think of nothing else but this constant desire for extension and expansion, which to the outside observer appears so meaningless. If you ask them what purpose the expansion is intended to serve, they will regard you with a kind of mild surprise and reply a little testily that the purpose is self-evident; it is to make economic life more vigorous, and, moreover, is demanded by economic progress.

But what is meant by "economic progress" in this quite general and fairly stereotyped answer? What is the association of ideas in the minds of the people who give it? Examine carefully and you shall find that it means an expansion in what may be called the "economic apparatus"—the production of largely increased quantities at the cheapest possible price; enormous output; enormous extent of communications; the quickest transportation of goods, people, and news.

But the answer, like the phenomena that prompted the question, sounds meaningless too. It is therefore unsatisfactory. There must be method in all this madness; it must surely be explicable. The people concerned in the activities do not seem to be alive to any life-values at their base. But life-values in them there must be, or you would not find whole generations of men intellectually sound and strong engaged in the activities mentioned. An analysis of the soul of the modern capitalist employer therefore repays the trouble, and at the very outset you stumble across—the child. In very truth, the psychology of the modern employer appears to me to resemble greatly that of the child. Understand the one and you will understand the other. For all the processes in the mind of the employer (and indeed of modern man generally), if reduced of their simplest elements, show a kind of relapse into the days of childhood.

Let us consider the matter more in detail.

The child possess four elementary "values"; four ideals dominate its existence. They are—

a. Physical bigness, as seen in grown-ups and imagined in giants;
b. Quick movement—in running, bowling a hoop, riding on a roundabout.
c. Novelty—it changes its toys very quickly; it begins something and never completes it because another occupation attracts it; and
d. Sense of power—that is why it pulls out the legs of a fly, makes Towzer stand on his hind legs and beg nicely, and flies its kite as high as it can.

Curious as it may sound, these ideals, and these only, will be found in all modern "values." Let us take them in turn.

A. WE ATTACH IMPORTANCE TO QUANTITIES, TO MERE SIZE. It is what interests us, what we admire most. That, I fancy, will be generally admitted. There is a universal tendency (to use the words of Lord Bryce) "to mistake bigness for greatness." It matters not wherein the bigness consist: it may be the population of a town or a country, the height of a monument, the breadth of a river, the frequency of suicide, the passengers carried by a railway, the size of a ship, the number of players in an orchestra, or what not. Of course our greatest admiration is reserved for a huge sum of money. Besides, money makes it possible to measure the size of otherwise immeasurable things and to compare them. It is a natural and easy step from this to the belief that that is valuable which costs much. We say this picture or this jewelry is twice as valuable as that. In America, where this modern tendency may be studied better than anywhere else because there it has reached its greatest perfection, people come to the point at once, and prefix to every commodity its monetary value. "Have you seen the 50,000-dollar Rembrandt at Mr. A's house?" is a not unusual question. "Today Mr. Carnegie's 500,000-dollar yacht entered the harbor of" (say) Boston—so you may read in the daily paper.

Get into the habit of looking at the mere quantity of things and you will naturally tend to compare any two phenomena that may come under your notice; you will weigh the one against the other and pronounce the larger to be the more valuable. Again, if of two things the one becomes larger than the other in a given space of time, it is said to have been successful. So that the inclination towards what is measurably big brings with it necessarily another tendency—worship of success. The modern businessman is appraised only in accordance with his success. Now success means to overtake others; to do more, to achieve more, to possess more than others; in a word, to be great. The pursuit of success holds out the same unlimited possibilities as the chase of profits; the one complements the other.

To illustrate the influence on the inner workings of the mind of this quantitative valuation of things, so characteristic of our day, let us refer to the attitude of people to sport. What is invariably the main question of interest? Is it not, who will win? Who will score most? A match is but a quantitative balance between two results. Imagine such a standpoint in an ancient Greek wrestling school! Imagine it at a Spanish bull-fight! The thing is impossible. In both these cases qualitative values were looked for, e.g. the highest personal artistic skill.

B. SPEED IS OF ALMOST THE SAME CONSEQUENCE TO THE MODERN MAN AS MASSIVENESS. To rush on in a 100-h.p. motor-car is one of the most supreme ideals of our age; and he who cannot speed madly along contents himself with reading of record-breaking velocity. Perhaps the express between Hamburg and Berlin was ten minutes in advance of its scheduled time; perhaps the latest ocean-liner reached New York three hours earlier than it was expected; perhaps the postman now comes at 7:30 instead of at the customary 8 o'clock; perhaps one newspaper published a declaration of war (probably a fictitious one) an hour before its competitor—all these things are of tremendous interest to the queerly constituted folk of our day; they seem to be of vital importance to them.

Moreover, a curious concept has sprung into existence, that of "beating the record." In terms of record-breaking you impress on your memory the speediest achievements as the most valuable ones. In its fullest meaning the new concept refers to great size and great speed combined. All the megalomania, all the mad hurry of our time, is expressed in record-beating. I think it most likely that the future historian of our time will speak of it as "The Age of Record-breaking."

C. WHATEVER IS NEW NOWADAYS ATTRACTS MERELY BECAUSE IT IS A NOVELTY. It attracts most when the assurance is possible, "There never has been anything like it." Sensational we call its effect on the mind. That the love of sensation is a marked feature of the age requires no expatiation. Modern journalism is perhaps the best proof. But recall also how fashions in dances, no less than in clothes, change from season to season. Is it not because nothing is so attractive as what is new?

D. THE SENSE OF POWER IS THE FOURTH CHARACTERISTIC OF THE MODERN SPIRIT; it is felt in the consciousness of superiority over others. But in reality it is only an expression of weakness; hence its importance in the child's world. For, after all, any one gifted with true greatness, which is usually inward, will be hardly likely to estimate the outward semblance of power at all highly. Power has no temptation for Siegfried; only a Mime thirsts for it. Bismarck in all probability did not bother much about the power he exercised; but in Lassalle the desire for power must have been tremendous. A king possesses power; it is therefore of small moment in his sight. But the financier of humble origin, who keeps a kingly borrower waiting in his ante-chamber for some little time, suns himself in this power because his soul has none of it. An employer who employs 10,000 men and experiences a sense of power in consequence is like a little boy who makes his doggie bring back the stick he keeps on throwing from him. Moreover, when neither by money nor any other outward force power over mankind is given us, we talk of the conquest of nature. That is why our age is so childishly delighted with epoch-making discoveries—say, the mastery of the air, and such-like achievements. The truly great man, however, will be comparatively unmoved at the sight of a big plane in the air. A truly great generation concerned with the deepest problems of life will not be enraptured because it made some discoveries in technical science. Power of this sort it will assuredly regard as "superficial." Our own age lacks true greatness; accordingly, like a child it admires the power which new inventions bestow, and it overrates those who possess it. Hence the high esteem in which the populace holds inventors and millionaires.

It is just possible that these visions float before the gaze of the employer more or less clearly. But certain it is that they take form and substance in his goal—the expansion and growth of his business. Acquisitiveness and interest in his enterprise thus direct his activities as a capitalist employer.

2. *His ideal we have reviewed. It remains now to review these activities as influenced by the ideal.* In essence the activities of the modern capitalist employer remain the same as before. He must conquer, organize, deal speculate, and calculate. But the extent of each of these factors varies, and consequently the resultant whole is not quite like that of an earlier age.

In modern times the trading function has become of more and more significance. I use the word "trading" in the sense indicated earlier in the book of dealing or negotiating. It is on this that commercial success now increasingly depends; on the skill and strength of suggestion in making contracts of all kinds. In olden days knots were cut; today they must be unraveled.

Next in importance to dealing comes skilful speculation—by which I mean stock-exchange manipulations. Modern undertakings are drawn more and more into the vortex of stock-exchange activities. Trust development such as we find in the United States is in reality only the transformation of manufacturing and commercial enterprises into purely stock-exchange speculative concerns. Consequently the directors and managers of such businesses have new problems to solve, and this opens up new activities for them.

As for calculation, it becomes more and more delicate as well as increasingly difficult, both because of the need for absolute exactitude and also because it has become so extensive.

Finally, the activities of the capitalist employer have become much more many-sided; that is to say, in so far as specialization has not set in. Economic activities have branched out in all directions; what wonder then that those who direct them should be called upon to be many-sided?

So much for the nature of the activity itself. What is new is its boundlessness. So long as the needs of the living human being governed economic activities, so long did these have a limit. But with the disappearance of the governing factor, the natural limit fell away. Accordingly the activities of the capitalist employer have no bounds. *Non sunt certi denique fines.* Which means that the expenditure of human energy in modern economic activities, extensively and intensively, is strained to the uttermost. Every minute of the day, of the year, nay, of life itself, is devoted to work; and during this working period every power is occupied at highest pressure. Everybody is acquainted with the hard-worked man of today. Whether employer or employed, he is constantly on the verge of a breakdown owing to overwork. That he tends to be excited, that he is always on the move, is generally known too. Speed and yet more speed—such is the cry of the age. It rushes onward in one mad race.

The influence of such a life on body and soul is not difficult to gauge. It corrodes the former and dries up the latter. Everything is sacrificed to the Moloch of work; all the higher instincts of heart and mind are crushed out by devotion to business. How much the inner life of modern man has been shattered is best seen if we cast a glance at the kernel of all natural life—the relationship to women. These men have no time for the enjoyment of delicate passions, nor even for gallant flirtations. They seem to be quite incapable of deep erotic emotions. Either they are wholly apathetic so far as love is concerned, or they are content with a brief sensual intoxication. They either do not bother about women at all, or they buy what they require in this respect.

3. Business principles likewise have undergone a change. That was only to be expected when the goal of enterprise has become different. Today, it may be said, five main rules regulate economic activities.

A. Absolute rationalism is the first. Economic activities are ruled by cold reason, by thought. As we have already seen, that has always been the case; it showed itself in the making of plans, in considering whether any policy was likely to be successful or no, and in calculation generally. The modern capitalist spirit differs from its predecessors only in the degree in which this rule is obeyed. Today the rule is strictly, one might almost say sternly, enforced. The last trace of traditionalism has vanished. The man of today (and the American employer may stand as the most perfect type) is filled with the will to apply cold reason to economic activities; moreover, he possesses the determination to make the will effective. Accordingly, he is ever ready to adopt a newer method if it is more rational, whether in the sphere of organization, of production, or of calculation. This naturally implies that, no matter what the cost may be, he is able to leave the old methods the moment the newer ones are available.

B. Production for exchange (as opposed to production for use) is the motto of economic activities. As much profit as possible is their ideal; consequently what matters is not the goodness or the kind of commodities produced but their salability. How they are sold is secondary, so long as they are sold. Consequently the employer is wholly indifferent to the quality of his wares; he will make shoddy goods or cheap substitutes, if only it pays. If cheap and nasty boots yield more profit than good ones, it would be a deadly sin against the holy spirit of capitalism to manufacture good ones. It is no argument against the truth of this to point to a movement in certain industries (the chemical industry is one), the object of which is to improve quality. As well say that the bonuses which the general store offers to its employees on the sale of more expensive articles proves the same thing. What both instances do prove is that they are cases where there is more profit from high-class goods than from inferior articles. The greatest gain is the only criterion in these matters, and an employer will make now cheap goods, now dearer, according as the one or the other yields more profit. From the capitalist's standpoint that is only natural.

What follows from this is plain. Since it is inherent in acquisitiveness to enlarge revenues to the uttermost; and since, again, the greater the sale the larger the profits, it is only to be expected that the employer will try all he can to increase his sales. Apart from the greater gain, more extended sales will give him certain advantages over competitors. Hence it is by no means remarkable that the desire for greater sales, for new markets, for more customers, is one of the mightiest motive powers in modern capitalism. It is directly responsible for a number of business principles, all of which have one end in view—to make the public buy. The more important of these principles deserve to be mentioned.

C. The first (and the third in the general scheme) may be enunciated as follows: Search out the customer and attack him. That is today as self-evident a maxim in all branches of business as it was strange and wrong in the age of early capitalism. In practice it means that you set out to attract the customer's attention and to stir up within him the desire to purchase. You attract his attention by shouting in his ears, or catching his eye by loud, colored indicators; you strive to make him purchase by suggestion; you seek to convince him that the articles for sale are extraordinarily good or valuable. Advertisement serves both ends—as every one knows; and advertisements, as every one knows also, shatter all sense of propriety, of taste, of good manners, and of dignity. Is it not true to say that modern advertising in its extreme forms in both unæsthetic and immoral?

D. Secondly, sell as cheaply as you can; reduce price to the lowest possible figure so as to attract the public. In the early capitalist age low prices were an abomination. The motto then was (as we have already noted) little business but great profits. Today we are at the opposite extreme: as much business as possible but small profits. Small profits, quick returns—is not this nowadays the universal motto?

E. Elbow-room is demanded in order to arrive at the wished-for goal. Which means, first, that you require freedom of action, liberty to enter upon or to abstain from any course, as seems best to you. It means emancipation from the trammels of law or morality; it means that you should be allowed to poach on your neighbor's preserves just as he may be allowed to poach on yours; it means that you should be allowed to oust him if you can; it means that you object to interference either from the state or from working men's organizations in making your contracts. You want none of the restraints of an earlier age. The free exercise of your powers shall alone determine economic success or failure. And in the second place it means—what follows quite naturally—unrestricted competition. If acquisition is the first consideration, unrestricted competition is a matter of course. You need no longer be bound by considerations of any kind, whether moral æsthetic, or social. Unscrupulous is the adjective for your actions.

Look at the extensive American trusts and you will see what unrestricted competition means. The recent doings of the American Tobacco Company are a case in point; they outdistanced the accepted practices of Europe and illustrate to what lengths an unscrupulous employer will go. No considerations give him pause; he leaves no road untried that promises success. The trust threw its goods away at ridiculous prices in order to conquer new markets; middlemen received enormous commissions; well-known brands were imitated and poor quality wares were sold in wrappers that misled the public. If it became involved in litigation, the trust by its superior financial strength was able to draw out the cases until its opponents were utterly exhausted. Even retail trading received careful attention, for the trust opened shops at effective points, and by underselling forced the old-established tobacconists to close their doors. Finally, the trust monopolized the raw material, and so came into conflict with the tobacco-growers of Kentucky. In 1911 the trust was proceeded against under the Sherman Law, and the presiding judge in delivering sentence characterized the activities of the undertaking against their competitors as having been carried on with extraordinary cunning, precaution, and devilry. Every human creature that by energy or skill threatened to stand in the way of the trust was mercilessly crushed.

Perhaps the most perfect type of the unscrupulous, smart business man was Edward H. Harriman, who died a few years ago. An obituary notice[33] was declared that the secret of his victorious career was his utter lack of moral scruples. Had he not cast these overboard he would have stumbled almost at the very first step he took. He began by breaking the man who had opened for him the gates of the railway paradise; following this up by his brutal campaign against Moran, who, however, knew how to utilize for his own ends the capacities of his opponent. Harriman's fight with Hill was as unscrupulous as the policy that brought him into the Standard Oil Trust. But Harriman's delinquencies were not merely personal; they form part and parcel of American speculation.

Of the great victors on the racecourse of modern capitalism it may be asserted, what was recently said of Rockefeller, that they know how to glide over every moral restraint with almost childlike disregard. The mirror of this naïve view of life will be found in the memoirs of John Rockefeller, who once summed up the faith within him by saying that he was willing to pay a substitute a salary of a million dollars, if beside other positive qualities he had no scruples whatsoever, and was ready to kill off thousands of victims without a murmur.

Another employer, this time a German, who considered himself rather backward in this respect because he was "too good-natured and considerate"—I refer to Werner Siemens—urged his brother Charles to become a smart business man in these terms: "Always be determined and unscrupulous. That in so large a concern is called for. Once begin to be considerate of private interests and you will fall into a morass of demands and intrigues" (letter of March 31, 1856).

4. The middle-class virtues—industry, frugality, and honesty—are they of any consequence for the modern capitalist employer? It is as difficult to reply to the question in the affirmative as in the negative. The place of these virtues in modern economic life is so very different from what they occupied in the early capitalist system. As a matter of fact, they have ceased to be necessary to the employer. Nevertheless, they still play their part in undertaking. Before, these virtues were still in the sphere wherein personal will-power was exercised; now they have become part of the mechanism of business. Before, they were characteristic of living beings; now, they have turned into objective principles of business methods.

This may sound difficult. I will explain my meaning by considering each of the virtues in turn.

In the olden days when industry was preached as a prime virtue in the tradesman, it was necessary to implant a solid foundation of duties in the inner consciousness of men. Everybody had to be urged to exercise his will-power in a certain direction, and when the habit was once formed the industrious tradesman went through his day's work in conscious self-mastery. Today all this is changed. The business man works at high pressure because the stress of economic activities carries him along in spite of himself.

He is no longer exercising a virtue; necessity drives him to this particular course. The general business pace determines what his own business pace shall be. He can no more be idle than a man at a machine; whereas a craftsman with his tools can be idle or industrious as he chooses.

The objectiveness of frugality is even more marked, for the private and the business "housekeeping" of the employer are now separate. In the latter frugality is needful more than ever. "Extravagance even in the smallest things should be avoided. It is not petty to have a care of this, for extravagance is a consuming disease difficult to localize. There are great undertakings whose existence depends on whether all the sand is removed from the carts or whether one shovelful is left behind."[34] Recall the careful, almost miserly, economy of Rockefeller in his management of the Standard Oil Company; recall how not a drop of oil was wasted; the wooden boxes in which tin was brought from Europe were sold to florists or were used as firewood.[35] But in the private housekeeping of the employer you will find none of this fanatical thrift. Neither Rathenau's nor Rockefeller's castle is a center of that frugality so much beloved of Benjamin Franklin; and the festive boards of our rich employers know nothing of sufficiency and moderation. And if the head of the family is content to go on in the old-fashioned bourgeois style of his youth, his wife, his sons, and his daughters will all see to it that luxury and superfluity and pomp become part and parcel of the new bourgeois spirit. Bourgeois the style of life still is even in the case of the wealthiest. The old doctrines of Alberti still hold sway. Never let your expenditure exceed your income, he urged his disciples. And calculate. Today this advice is faithfully obeyed by the modern bourgeois. Herein his mode of living differs from the seigniorial. The seignior scorns money.

Commercial honesty comes last. Can any one doubt that honesty is today—today perhaps more than ever—a factor in business life? In business life only, however. For the conduct of the employer as a man may differ widely from his conduct as a tradesman. Commercial honesty is a complexity of principles that are intended to apply to business but not to the personal conduct of the business subject. An honest tradesman today may certainly be unmoral in his private life. When you say he is "good," you mean that he is reliable in his business; that he will pay; that his firm has a good name. You pass no judgment on his personal conduct, which is governed by other principles. Indeed, the firm may not have an individual head at all. It may be an impersonal limited company, the directors of which change from time to time. Their personal morality stands in no relationship to the business, the "name" of the business is all that matters. Thus, here, too, what before was a personal quality has now become a matter of business routine. You can see it best by considering modern credit. A bank in olden days was relied upon because it could point to an ancient and honored name; it was "good" for personal reasons. Today a bank inspires confidence by the size of its invested capital and its reserves. Today you assume that business is carried on honestly—anyhow until some swindle comes to light to prove the contrary. In this virtue then, as in the others, what before was organic has now become mechanical.

All this applies to the large undertakings. In the small and middle-sized enterprises, however, you may still find the principles prevalent in the early days of capitalism. The middle-class virtues are still cultivated, and the employer's personal characteristics determine his economic progress. It is in the large undertakings and their directors and managers that we find the spirit of capitalism fully developed in all its shining purity.

Now, why has the capitalist spirit developed in this fashion? Why did it not take on another guise? What forces molded it? What nourished it during its growth? These are questions that require consideration by themselves, and so the sources whence the capitalist spirit sprang will be reviewed in the following section of this book.[#]

Notes

1. Leon Battista Alberti, *I libri della Famiglia*, (Florence 1908), p. 49.
2. Ibid., p. 139.
3. Ibid., p. 49.
4. *The Economy of Human Life* (1785), p. 338.
5. *The Way to Wealth* (edition by Dr. Bergk, 1838).
6. Ibid.
7. Alberti, *op. cit.*, p. 242.
8. *The Economy of Human Life*, p. 121.
9. Albert Henry Smyth (ed.), *The Writings of Benjamin Franklin* (1907), vol. 1, p. 332
10. *The Complete English Tradesman,* part 2 (1727 ed.), pp. 97, 161, and 213.
11. G. Smith, Diss. de privilegiis societatis India orientalis (1786), quoted by Laspeyres, *Geschichte der volkswirtschaftlichen Anschauungen der Niederländer* (1863), p. 91.
12. Laspeyres, *op. cit.*, p. 87.
13. Alberti, *op. cit.*, p. 165.
14. Cf. J. Godard, *L'ouvrier en soie*, vol. 1 (1899), pp. 38–9.
15. Cf. Fox Bourne, *English Merchants* (1886), p. 394.
16. *The Jews and Modern Capitalism*, p. 122.
17. See *Allgemeine Schatzkammer der Kaufmannschaft* (1741), vol. 3, p. 148; vol. 4, p. 677; vol. 3, p. 1325; vol. 1, p. 1392.
18. W. Barrett, *The Old Merchants of New York City* (1863), pp. 22, 25.
19. *The Complete English Tradesman* (ed. 1727), part 2, p. 111.
20. Josiah Child, *A New Discourse of Trade* (4th ed.), p. 59.
21. See George Unwin, *Industrial Organisation in the 16th and 17th centuries* (1904), p. 117.
22. See Levasseur, *Histoire de l'industrie, etc.* vol. 2, p. 257.
23. J.J. Becher, *Närrische Weisheit* (1686), p. 15.
24. Cf. Carl Ergang, "Untersuchungen zum Maschinenproblem in der Volkswirtschaftlichen Lehre," in *Freiburger Volkswirtschartliche Abhandlungen,* vol. 1, section 2 (1911), pp. 4 and 10.
25. Montesquieu, *Esprit des Lois*, bk. 23, ch. 15.
26. Postlethwayt, *Dictionary of Commerce*, vol. 2, p. 121.
27. Walter Rathenau, *Reflexionen* (1908), p. 81.
28. Ibid., p. 82.

[#] Not included in this collection.

29. See my essay in *Archiv für Soziale Wissenschaft*, vol. 29, p. 700, where I have elaborated this subject.
30. Andrew Carnegie's *Autobiography*.
31. Report of the Indiana Commission (1900), p. 795.
32. *Dr. Strousberg und sein Wirken*. By himself (1876), p. 397.
33. L. Jolles, "Eine wirtschaftliche Personlichkeit" in *Der Tag*, no. 215 of 1909.
34. W. Rathenau, *Reflexionen*, p. 99.
35. John R. Rockefeller's *Memoirs*.

5

The Significance of the Jewish Religion in Economic Life

Introductory Note

Three reasons have actuated me in devoting a special chapter to the consideration of the religion of the Jewish people and the demonstration of its enormous influence on Jewish economic activities. First, the Jewish religion can be fully appreciated in all its bearings from the economic standpoint only when it is studied in detail and by itself; secondly, it calls for a special method of treatment; and thirdly, it occupies a position midway between the objective and the subjective factors of Jewish development. For, in so far as any religion is the expression of some particular spiritual outlook, it has a "subjective" aspect; in so far as the individual is born into it, it has an objective aspect.

The Importance of Religion for the Jewish People

That the religion of a people, or of a group within a people, can have far-reaching influences on its economic life will not be disputed. Only recently Max Weber demonstrated the connexion between Puritanism and Capitalism. In fact, Max Weber's researches are responsible for this book. For any one who followed them could not but ask himself whether all that Weber ascribes to Puritanism might not with equal justice be referred to Judaism, and probably in a greater degree; nay, it might well be suggested that that which is called Puritanism is in reality Judaism. This relationship will be discussed in due course.

Now, if Puritanism has had an economic influence, how much more so has Judaism, seeing that among no other civilized people has religion so impregnated all national life. For the Jews religion was not an affair of Sundays and Holy Days; it touched everyday life even in its minutest action, it regulated *all* human activities. At every step the Jew asked himself, Will this tend to the glory of God or will it profane His name? Jewish law defines not merely the relation between man and God, formulates not merely a metaphysical conception; it lays down rules of conduct for all possible relationships, whether between man and man or between man and nature. Jewish law, in fact, is as much part of the religious system as are Jewish ethics. The Law is from God, and moral law and divine ordinances are inseparable in Judaism.[1] Hence in reality there are no special ethics of Judaism. Jewish ethics are the underlying principles of the Jewish religion.[2]

No other people has been so careful as the Jews in providing for the teaching of religion to even the humblest. As Josephus so well put it: Ask the first Jew you meet concerning his "laws" and he will be able to tell you them better than his own name. The reason for this may be found in the systematic religious instruction given to every Jewish child, as well as in the fact that divine service partly consists of the reading and explanation of passages from Holy Writ. In the course of the year the Torah is read through from beginning to end. Moreover, it is one of the primary duties of the Jew to study the Torah. "Thou shalt speak of them when thou sittest in thine house and when thou walkest by the way and when thou liest down and when thou risest up" (Deut. vi.5).[3]

No other people, too, has walked in God's ways so conscientiously as the Jews; none has striven to carry out its religious behests so thoroughly. It has indeed been asserted that the Jews are the least religious of peoples. I shall not stay to weigh the justice of this remark. But certain it is that they are the most "God-fearing" people that ever were on the face of the earth. They lived always in trembling awe, in awe of God's wrath. "My flesh trembleth for fear of Thee, and I am afraid of Thy judgments," said the Psalmist (Ps. cxix.120), and the words may be taken as applicable to the Jews in every age. "Happy is the man that feareth alway" (Prov. xxviii.14). "The pious never put away their fear" (*Tanchuma Chukkath*, 24).[4] One can understand it when one thinks of the Jewish God—fearful, awful, curse-uttering Jehovah. Never in all the world's literature, either before or since, has humanity been threatened with so much evil as Jehovah promises (in the famous 28th chapter of Deuteronomy) to those who will not keep His commandments.

But this mighty influence (the fear of God) did not stand alone. Others combined with it, and together they had the tendency of almost forcing the Jews to obey the behests of their religion most scrupulously. The first of these influences was their national fate. When the Jewish State was destroyed the Pharisees and Scribes—i.e., those who cherished the traditions of Ezra and strove to make obedience to the Law the end and aim of life—the Pharisees and Scribes came to the head of affairs and naturally directed the course of events into channels which they favoured. Without a State, without their sanctuary, the Jews, under the leadership of the Pharisees, flocked around the Law (that "portable Fatherland," as Heine calls it), and became a religious brotherhood, guided by a band of pious Scribes, pretty much as the disciples of Loyola might gather around them the scattered remnants of a modern State. The Pharisees now led the way. Their most distinguished Rabbis looked upon themselves as the successors of the ancient Synhedrium, and were indeed so regarded, becoming the supreme authority in spiritual and temporal affairs for all the Jews in the world.[5] The power of the Rabbis originated in this fashion and the vicissitudes of the Jews in the Middle Ages only helped to strengthen it. So oppressive did it eventually become that the Jews themselves at times complained of the burden. For the more the Jews were shut off, or shut themselves off, from the people among whom they dwelt, the more the authority of the Rabbis increased, and the more easily could the Jews be forced to be faithful to the Law. But the fulfilment of the Law, which was urged upon them by the Rabbis, must have been a necessity for the Jews for inner reasons: it satisfied their heart's desire, it appeared the most precious gift that life had to offer. And why? Because amid all the persecution and suffering which was meted out to the Jews on all sides, that alone enabled them to retain their dignity, without which life would have been valueless. For a very long period religious teaching was enshrined in the Talmud, and hence Jews through many centuries lived in it, for it, and through it. The Talmud was the most precious possession of the Jew; it was the breath of his nostrils, it was his very soul. The Talmud became a family history for generation after generation, with which each was familiar.

> The thinker lived in its thought, the poet in its pure idealism. The outer world, the world of nature and of man, the powerful ones of the earth and the events of the times, were for the Jew during a thousand years accidents, phantoms; his only reality was the Talmud.[6]

The Talmud has been well compared (and the comparison to my mind applies equally to all religious literature) to an outer shell with which the Jews of the Diaspora covered themselves; it protected them against all influences from without and kept alive their strength within.[7]

We see then, what forces were at work to make the Jews right down to modern times a more God-fearing people than any other, to make them religious to their inmost core, or, if the word "religious" be objected to, to keep alive among high and low a general and strict observation of the precepts of their religion. And for our purpose, we must regard this characteristic as applicable to all sorts and conditions of Jews, the Amarannos of the sixteenth, seventeenth, and eighteenth centuries included. We must look upon these too as orthodox Jews. Says the foremost authority on that period of Jewish history,[8]

> The great majority of the Marannos were Jews to a much larger extent than is commonly supposed. They submitted to force of circumstance and were Christians only outwardly. As a matter of fact they lived the Jewish life and observed the tenets of the Jewish religion... This admirable constancy will be appreciated to the full only when the wealth of material in the Archives of Alcalia de Henares, Simancas and other places has been sorted and utilized.

But among professing Jews, the wealthiest were often enough excellent Talmudic scholars. Was not a knowledge of the Talmud a highway to honour, riches, and favour among Jews? The most learned Talmudists were also the cleverest financiers, medical men, jewelers, merchants. We are told, for example, of some of the Spanish Ministers of Finance, bankers, and court physicians that they devoted to the study of the Holy Writ not only the Sabbath day but also two nights of each week. In modern times, old Amschel Rothschild, who died in

1855, did the same. He lived strictly according to Jewish law and ate no morsel at a stranger's table, even though it were the Emperor's. One who knew the Baron well says of him that

> he was looked upon as the most pious Jew in all Frankfort. Never have I seen a man so afflict himself—beating his breast, and crying to Heaven—as Baron Rothschild did in the synagogue on the Day of Atonement. The continual praying weakens him so that he falls into a faint. Odorous plants from his garden are held to his nose to revive him.[9*]

His nephew William Charles, who died in 1901 and who was the last of the Frankfort Rothschilds, observed all the religious prescriptions in their minutest detail. The pious Jew is forbidden to touch any object which under certain circumstances has become unclean by having been already touched by some one else. And so a servant always walked in front of this Rothschild and wiped the door-handles. Moreover, he never touched paper money that had been in use before; the notes had to be fresh from the press.

If this was how a Rothschild lived, it is not surprising to come across Jewish commercial travellers who do not touch meat six months in the year because they are not absolutely certain that the method of slaughtering has been in accordance with Jewish law.

However, if you want to study orthodox Judaism you must go to Eastern Europe, where it is still without disintegrating elements—you must go there personally or read the books about it. In Western Europe the orthodox Jews are a small minority. But when we speak of the influence of the Jewish religion it is the religion that held sway until a generation ago that we mean, the religion that led the Jews to so many victories.

The Sources of the Jewish Religion

Mohammed called the Jews "the people of the Book." He was right. There is no other people that lived so thoroughly according to a book. Their religion in all its stages was generally incorporated in a book, and these books may be looked upon as the sources of the Jewish

---

* Sombart in the German text quotes this as an occurrence on the Sabbath. It is obvious that the description refers to the Day of Atonement.—Trans.

religion. The following is a list of such books, each originating at a particular time and supplementing some other.

1. The Bible, i.e., the Old Testament, until the destruction of the Second Temple. It was read in Hebrew in Palestine and in Greek (Septuagint) in the Diaspora.
2. The Talmud (more especially the Babylonian Talmud), from the second to the sixth century of the Common Era, the principal depository of Jewish religious teaching.
3. The Code of Maimonides, compiled in the twelfth century.
4. The Code (called the *Turim*) of Jacob ben Asher (1248–1340).
5. The Code of Joseph Caro—the *Shulchan Aruch* (sixteenth century).

These "sources" from which the Jewish religion drew its life appear in a different light accordingly as they are regarded by scientific research or with the eyes of the believing Jew. In the first case they are seen as they really are; in the second, they are idealized.

What are they in reality? The Bible, i.e., the Old Testament, is the foundation upon which the entire structure of Judaism was built up. It was written by many hands at different periods, thus forming, as it were, a piece of literary mosaic.[10] The most important portion of the whole is the Torah, i.e., the Pentateuch. It received its present shape by the commingling of two complete works some time in the period after Ezra. The one was the old and the new (the Deuteronomic) Law Book (650 B.C.) and the other, Ezra's Law Book (440 B.C.).* And its special character the Torah owes to Ezra and Nehemiah, who introduced a strict legal system. With Ezra and the school of *Soferim* (scribes) that he founded, Judaism is the form which it has today originated; from that period to the present it has remained unchanged.

Beside the Torah we must mention the so-called Wisdom Literature—the Psalms, Job, Ecclesiastes, Ecclesiasticus, and the Proverbs. This section of Jewish literature is wholly post-exilic; only in that period could it have arisen, assuming as it did the existence of the Law, and the prevailing belief that for obeying the Law God gave Life, for transgressing it Death. The Wisdom Literature, unlike the Prophetic Books, was

* I.e., Deut. v.45–xxvi..69 (about 650 B.C.) and Exod. xii.25–31, xxxv. to Lev. xv.; Numb. i.–x.; xv.–xix; xxvii.–xxxvi. (about 445 B.C.).

concerned with practical life. Some of the books contain the crystallized wisdom of many generations and are of a comparatively early date. The Book of Proverbs, for example, the most useful for our purpose, dates from the year 180 B.C.[11]

Two streams flow from the Bible. The one, chiefly by way of the Septuagint, ran partly into Hellenistic philosophy and partly into Pauline Christianity. That does not concern us further.

The other, chiefly by way of the Hebrew Bible current in Palestine, ran into Jewish "Law," and the course of this we shall have to follow.

The specifically Jewish development of the Holy Writ already began as early as Ezra's day; it was due to the first schools of *Soferim* (scribes), and the later schools of Hillel and Shammai only extended and continued the work. The actual "development" consisted of explanations and amplifications of the Holy Writ, arrived at as the result of disputation, the method in vogue in the Hellenistic World. The development was really a tightening of the legal formalism, with the view of protecting Judaism against the inroads of Hellenistic Philosophy. Here, as always, the Jewish religion was the expression of a reaction against disintegrating forces. The Deuteronomic Law was the reaction against Baal worship; the Priestly Code against Babylonian influences; the later Codes of Maimonides and Rabbenu Asher and Caro against Spanish culture; and the teaching of the *Tannaim* [Tannai-teacher] in the century preceding and that commencing the Common Era against the enervating doctrines of Hellenism.[12]

The old oral tradition of the "Wise" was codified about the year 200 A.D. by R. Judah Hanassi (the Prince), usually called Rabbi. His work is the *Mishna*. Following on the Mishna are further explanations and additions which were collected and given a fixed form in the sixth century (500–550 A.D.) by the *Saboraim* [Saborai—those who give opinions]. Those portions which had reference to the Mishna alone were termed the *Gemara*, the authors of which were the *Amoraim* [Amorai-speaker]. Mishna and Gemara together form the Talmud, of which there are two versions, the Palestinian and the Babylonian. The latter is the more important.[13]

The Talmud, as edited by the Saboraim, has become the chief depository of Jewish religious teaching, and its universal authority resulted from the Mohammedan conquests. To begin with, it became the legal and constitutional foundation for Jewish communal life in Babylon, at the head of which stood the "Prince of the Captivity" and the Presidents of the two Talmudic colleges, the *Gaonim* [Gaon—Excellency]. As Islam spread further and further afield the Jewish communities in the lands that it conquered came into closer relation with the Gaonate in Babylon; they asked advice on religious, ethical, and common law questions and loyally accepted the decisions, all of which were based on the Talmud. Indeed, Babylonian Jewry came to be regarded as the new centre of Jewish life.

As soon as the Gemara was written down, and so received permanent form, the development of Judaism ceased. Nevertheless we must mention the three codes which in the post-Talmudic period embodied all the substance of the religion, first, because they presented it in a somewhat different garb, and secondly, because in their regulation of the religious life they could not but pay some heed to changed conditions. All the three codes are recognized by Jews as authoritative side by side with the Talmud, and the last, the *Shulchan Aruch*, is looked upon today by the orthodox Jew as containing the official version of religious duties. What is of interest to us in the case of all the codes is that they petrified Jewish religious life still more. Of Maimonides even Graetz asserts as much.

> A great deal of what in the Talmud is still mutable, he changed into unmodifiable law....By his codification he robbed Judaism of the power of developing...without considering the age in which the Talmudic regulations arose, he makes them binding for all ages and circumstances.

R. Jacob ben Asher went beyond Maimonides, and Joseph Caro beyond Jacob ben Asher, reaching the utmost limit. His work tends to ultra-particularism and is full of hair-splitting casuistry. The religious life of the Jews "was rounded off and unified by the *Shulchan Aruch*, but at the cost of inwardness and unfettered thought. Caro gave Judaism the fixed form which it has retained down to the present day."[14]

This, then, is the main stream of Jewish religious life; these the sources from which Judaism drew its ideas and ideals. There were, of course, tributary streams, as, for instance, that of the Apocalyptic literature of the pre-Christian era, which stood for a heavenly, a universal, an individualistic Judaism,[15] or that of the Kabbala, which busied itself with symbols and arithmetical figures. But these had small share in the general development of Jewish life, and may be neglected so far as their effect on historic Judaism is concerned. Nor were they ever recognized by "official" Judaism as sources of the Jewish religion.

So much for the realistic conception of these sources. But what of that current in orthodox Jewish circles? In many respects the belief of the pious Jew touching the origin of the Jewish system is of much more consequence than its real origin. We must therefore try and acquaint ourselves with that belief.

The traditional view, which every orthodox Jew still holds, is that the Jewish system has a twofold birth; partly through Revelation and partly in the inspiration of the "Wise." Revelation refers to the written and the oral tradition. The former is contained in the holy books of the Bible—the Canon as it was fixed by the members of the Great synagogue. It has three parts:[16]—the Torah or Pentateuch, the Prophetical Books, and the "Writings" (the remaining books). The Torah was given to Moses on Sinai and he

> gradually instructed the people in it during their forty years' wandering in the wilderness....It was not until the end of his life that he finished the written Torah, the five books of Moses, and delivered them unto Israel, and we are in duty bound to consider every letter, every word of the written Torah as the Revelation of God.[17]

The remaining books were also the outcome of divine revelation, or, at any rate, were inspired by God. The attitude towards the Prophetical literature and the Hagiographa, however, is somewhat freer than that towards the Torah.

The Oral Tradition, or the Oral Torah, is the explanation of the written one. This, too, was revealed to Moses on Sinai, but for urgent reasons was not allowed to be written down at once. That took place at a much later date—only after the destruction of the second Temple—and was embodied in *Mishna* and *Gemara*, which thus contain the only correct explanation of the Torah, seeing that they were divinely revealed. In the Talmud are included also rabbinic ordinances and the *Haggada*, i.e., the interpretation of those portions of Holy Writ other than the legal enactments. The interpretation of the latter was called the *Halacha*, and *Halacha* and *Haggada* supplemented each other. Beside these were placed the collection of decisions, i.e., the three codes already referred to.

What was the significance of all this literature for the religious life of the Jews? What was it that the Jew believed, what were the commands he obeyed?

In the first place it must be premised that so far as I am aware there is no system of dogmas in Judaism.[18] Wherever compilation of such a system has been attempted it was invariably the work of non-Jews.[19] The nature of the Jewish religion and more especially the construction of the Talmud, which is characterized by its lack of order, is inconsistent with the formulation of any dogmatic system. Nevertheless certain principles may be discovered in Judaism, and its spirit will be found expressed in Jewish practices. Indeed, it will not be difficult to enumerate these principles, since they have remained the same from the very beginning. What has been termed the "spirit of Ezekiel" has been paramount in Judaism from Ezra's day to ours. It was only developed more and more, only taken to its logical conclusions. And so to discover what this "spirit" is we need only refer to the sources of the religion—the Bible, the Talmud and the later Rabbinic literature.

It is a harder task to determine to what extent this or that doctrine still finds acceptance. Does, for example, the Talmudic adage, "Kill even the best of the Gentiles," still hold good? Do the other terrible aphorism ferreted out in Jewish religious literature by Pfefferkorn, Eisenmenger, Röhling, Dr. Justus, and the rest of that fraternity, still find credence, or are they, as the Rabbis of today indignantly protest, entirely obsolete? It is obvious, of course, that the single doctrines were differently expressed in different ages, and if the whole literature, but more especially the Talmud, is referred to on particular points, opposite views, the "pros" and the "cons," will be found. In other words, it is possible to "prove" absolutely anything from the Talmud, and hence the thrust and counter-thrust between the anti-Semites and their Jewish and non-Jewish opponents from time immemorial; hence the fact that what the one proved to be black by reference to the Talmud the others proved to be white on the same authority. There is nothing surprising in this when it is remembered that to a great extent the Talmud is nothing else than a collection of controversies of the different Rabbinical scholars.

To discover the religious ordinances which regulated actual life we must make a distinction which, to my mind, is very real—the distinction between the man who by personal study strives to find out the law for himself, and the one who accepts it on the authority of another. In the case of the first, the thing that matters is that some opinion or other is found expressed. It is of no consequence that its very opposite may also be there. For the pious Jew who obtains edification by the study of his literature the one view was enough. It may have been the spur to a particular course of action; or it may have provided him with an additional reason for persisting in a course upon which he had already entered. The sanction of the book was sufficient in either event, most of all if it was the Bible or, better still, the Torah. Since all was of divine origin, one passage was as binding as another. This held good whether applied to the Bible, to the Talmud, or to the later Rabbinic writings.

The matter assumes a different aspect if the individual does not, or cannot, study the sources himself but relies on the direction of his spiritual adviser or on books recommended by him. Such a one is confronted with only one opinion, arrived at by the proper interpretation of contradictory texts. Obviously these views must have varied from time to time, in accordance with the Rabbinic traditions in each epoch. Hence, to find the laws that in any period were binding we must search for its Rabbinic traditions—no great task since the publication of the Rabbinic law-books. From the eleventh to the fourteenth century we have the *Yad Hachazaka* ["Strong Hand"] of Maimonides, from the fourteenth to the sixteenth the *Tur* of R. Jacob ben Asher, and after the sixteenth the *Shullchan Aruch* of Caro. Each of these gives the accepted teachings of the age, each is the decisive authority. For the last three hundred years the *Shulchan Aruch* has thus laid down the law wherever there were differences of opinion. As the text-book I have already quoted says, "First and foremost the *Shulchan Aruch* of R. Joseph Caro, together with the notes of R. Moses Isserlein and the other glosses, is recognized by all Israel as the Code on which we model our ritual observances." The Law is also summed up in the 613 precepts which Maimonides derived from the Torah and which even today are still in force.

> According to the tradition of our Teachers (of blessed memory) God gave Israel by the hand of Moses 613 precepts, 248 positive and 365 negative. All these are binding to all eternity; only those which have reference to the Jewish State and agricultural life in Palestine and to the Temple service in Jerusalem are excepted, as they cannot be carried out by the Jews of the Diaspora. We can obey 369 precepts, 126 positive and 243 negative; and in addition the seven Rabbinic commands.[20]

The lives of Orthodox Jews were governed by these manuals during the last century and still are so today, in so far as the guidance of the Rabbinic law was followed and opinions based on a personal study of the sources were not formed. From the manuals we have mentioned, therefore, we must gather the ordinances which were decisive for each individual instance in religious life. Hence Reformed Judaism is of no concern to us, and books trimmed to suit modern ideas, such as the great majority of the latest expositions of the "Ethics of Judaism," are absolutely useless for our purpose—which is to show the connexion between capitalism and genuine Jewish teaching, and its significance in modern economic life.

The Fundamental Ideas of the Jewish Religion

Let me avow it right away: I think that the Jewish religion has the same leading ideas as Capitalism. I see the same spirit in the one as in the other.

In trying to understand the Jewish religion—which, by the way, must not be confused with the religion of Israel (the two are in a sense opposites)—we must never forget that a *Sofer* was its author, a rigidly minded scribe, whose work was completed by a band of scribes after him. Not a prophet, mark you: not a seer, nor a visionary nor a mighty king; a *Sofer* it was. Nor must we forget *how* it came into being: not as an irresistible force, not as the expression of the deepest needs of contrite souls, not as the embodiment of the feelings of divinely inspired votaries. No; it came into being on a deliberate plan, by clever deductions, and diplomatic policy which was based on the cry "Its religion must be preserved for the people." The same calm consideration, the same attention to the ultimate goal were responsible in the centuries that followed for the addition of line to line and precept to precept. That which did not fit in with the scheme of the *Soferim* from before the days of Ezra and that which grew up afterwards, fell away.

The traces of the peculiar circumstances which gave it birth are still visible in the Jewish religion. In all its reasoning it appeals to us as a creation of the intellect, a thing of thought and purpose projected into the world of organisms, mechanically and artfully wrought, destined to destroy and to conquer Nature's realm and to reign itself in her stead. Just so does Capitalism appear on the scene; like the Jewish religion, an alien element in the midst of the natural, created world; like it, too, something schemed and planned in the midst of teeming life. This sheaf of salient features is bound together in one word: Rationalism. Rationalism is the characteristic trait of Judaism as of Capitalism; Rationalism or

Intellectualism—both deadly foes alike to irresponsible mysticism and to that creative power which draws its artistic inspiration from the passion world of the senses.

The Jewish religion knows no mysteries, and is perhaps the only religion on the face of the globe that does not know them. It knows not the ecstatic condition wherein the worshipper feels himself at one with the Godhead, the condition which all other religions extol as the highest and holiest. Think of the Soma libation among the Hindoos, think of entranced Indra himself, of the Homa sacrifice of the Persians, of Dionysus, the Oracle of Greece and of the Sibylline books, to which even the staid Romans went for advice, only because they were written by women who in a state of frenzy prophesied the future.

Down to the latest days of the Roman Empire, the characteristic of religious life which remained the same in all aspects of heathenism continued to manifest itself—the characteristic which spread far and wide and infected large masses of people, of working yourself up by sheer force to a pitch of bodily or mental excitement, often becoming bacchanalian madness, and then regarding this as the deity's doing and as part of his service. It was a generally accepted belief that certain sudden impulses or bursts of passion or resolutions were roused in the soul of a man by some god or other; and conduct of which a man was ashamed or which he regretted, was usually ascribed to the influence of a god.[21] "It was the god who drove me to it"—so, in Plautus's comedy, the young man who had seduced a maiden excused himself to his father.

The same thing must have been experienced by Mohammed in his morbid condition when his fits of ecstasy were upon him, and there is a good deal of mysticism in Islam. At least Mohammedanism has its howling dervishes.

And in Christianity, too, so far as it was not Judaism, room was found for emotional feeling—witness the doctrine of the Trinity, the sweet cult of Mariolatry, the use of incense, the communion. But Judaism looks with proud disdain on these fantastic, mystical elements, condemning them all. When the faithful of other religions hold converse with God in blissful convulsions, in the Jewish synagogue, called a *School* [i.e., School] not without significance, the Torah is publicly read. So Ezra ordained, and so it is done most punctiliously.

> Ever since the destruction of the State, study became the soul of Judaism, and religious observances without knowledge of the ordinances which enjoined them was considered as being of little worth. The central feature of public service on Sabbaths and Holy Days was the lesson read from the Law and the Prophets, the translation of the passages by the *Targumists* [Interpreters] and the homiletic explanation of them by the *Haggadists* [Preachers].

> Radix stultitiae, cui frigida sabbata cordi
> Sed cor frigidus relligione sua
> Septima quaeque dies turpi damnato veterno
> Tanquam lassati mollis imago dei.
>
> [The Sabbath—monstrous folly!—fills the need
> Of hearts still icier than their icy creed,
> Each seventh day in shameful sloth they nod,
> And ape the languor of their weary God.]

Such was the Roman view.[22]

Judaism then looked askance at mysteries. With no different eye did it regard the holy enthusiasm for the divine in the world of feeling. Astarte, Daphne, Isis and Osiris, Aphrodite, Fricka, and the Holy Virgin—it would have none of them. It banished all pictorial art from its cult. "And the Lord spake unto you out of the midest of the fire: ye hear the sound of words but ye saw no form" (Deut. iv.12). "Cursed be the man that maketh a graven or molten image, an abomination unto the Lord, the work of the hands of the craftsman..." (Deut. xxvii.15). The command, "Thou shalt not make unto thee any graven image" finds acceptance today, and the pious Jew has no statues made, nor does he set them up in his house.[23]

The kinship between Judaism and Capitalism is further illustrated by the legally regulated relationship—I had almost said the businesslike connexion, except that the term has a disagreeable connotation—between God and Israel. The whole religious system is in reality nothing but a contract between Jehovah and His chosen people, a contract with all its consequences and all its duties. God promises something and gives something, and the righteous must give Him something in return. Indeed, there was no community of interest between God and man which could not be expressed in these terms—that man performs some duty enjoined by the Torah and receives from God a *quid pro quo*. Accordingly, no man should approach God in prayer without bringing with him something of his own or of his ancestors' by way of return for what he is about to ask.[24]

The contract usually sets forth that man is rewarded for duties performed and punished for duties neglected; the rewards and punishments being received partly in this and partly in the next world. Two consequences must of necessity follow: first, a constant weighing up of the loss and gain which any action needs must bring, and secondly, a complicated system of bookkeeping, as it were, for each individual person.

The whole of this conception is excellently well illustrated by the words of Rabbi [164–200 A.D.]:

> Which is the right course for a man to choose? That which he feels to be honourable to himself and which also brings him honour from mankind. Be heedful of a light precept as of a grave one, for you do not know what reward a precept brings. Reckon the loss incurred by the fulfilment of a precept against the reward secured by its observance, and the gain gotten by a transgression against the loss it involves. Reflect on three things and you will not come within the power of sin. Know what is above thee—a seeing eye, and a hearing ear, and all your deeds written in a book.[25]

So that whether one is accounted "righteous" or "wicked" depends on the balance of commands performed against commands neglected. Obviously this necessitates the keeping of accounts, and each man therefore has his own, in which his words and his deeds, even the words spoken in jest, are all carefully registered. According to one authority (*Ruth Rabba*, 33*a*) the prophet Elijah keep these accounts; according to another (*Esther Rabba*, 86*a*) the duty is assigned to angels.

Every man has thus an account in heaven: Israel a particularly large one (*Sifra*, 44*b*). And one of the ways of preparing for death is to have your "account" ready (*Kohelet Rabba*, 77*c*). Sometimes "extracts" from the accounts are forthcoming (by request). When the angels brought an accusation against Ishmael, God asked, "What is his position at present? Is he a righteous man or a wicked?" (i.e., do the commands performed outweigh those neglected?). And the angels replied, "He is a righteous man." When Mar Ukba died, he asked for a statement of his account (of the money he had given to charity). It totalled 7000 zuzim. As he was afraid that this would not suffice for his salvation he gave away half of his fortune in order to be on the safe side (*Kethuboth*, 25; *Baba Bathra*, 7). The final decision as to the righteousness or wickedness of any man is made after his death. The account is then closed, and the grand total drawn up. The result is inserted in a document (*Shetar*) which is handed to each individual after it has been read out.[26]

It is not difficult to perceive that the keeping of these accounts was no easy matter. In biblical times, so long as rewards and punishments were meted out in the life on earth, the task was no great one. But in the period that followed, when rewards and punishments were granted partly in this life and partly in life everlasting, the question grew to be troublesome, and in the Rabbinic theology an intricate and artistic system of bookkeeping was evolved. This distinguished between the capital sum or the principal, and the fruits or the interest, the former being reserved for the future world, the latter for this. And in order that the reward which is laid up in heaven for the righteous may not be diminished, God does not lessen the stock when He grants him ordinary earthly benefits. Only when he receives extraordinary, i.e., miraculous, benefits on earth does the righteous man suffer a diminution of his heavenly reward. Moreover, the righteous is punished for his sins at once on earth, as the wicked is rewarded for his good deeds, so that the one may have only rewards in heaven and the other only chastisements.[27]

Another conception is bound up with this of divine bookkeeping and is closely akin to a second fundamental trait of capitalism—the conception of profit. Sin or goodness is regarded as something apart from the sinner. Every sin, according to Rabbinic theology, is considered singly and by itself. "Punishment is according to the object and not the subject of the sin."[28] The quantity of the broken commandments alone counts. No consideration whatever is had for the personality of the sinner or his ethical state, just as a sum of money is separated from persons, just as it is capable of being added to another abstract sum of money. The ceaseless striving of the righteous after well-being in this and the next world must therefore take the form of a constant endeavour to increase his rewards. Now, as he is never able to tell whether at a particular state of his conscience he is worthy of God's goodness or whether in his "account" the rewards or the punishments are more numerous, it must be his aim to add reward after reward to his account by constantly doing good deeds to the end of his days. The limited conception of all personal values thus finds no admission into the world of his religious ideas and its place is taken by the endlessness of a pure quantitative ideal.

Parallel with this tendency there runs through Jewish moral theology another which regards the getting of money as a means to an end. The conception is frequently found in books of religious edification, the authors of which realizing but seldom that in their warnings against the acquisition of too much wealth they are glorifying this very practice. Usually the treatment of the subject is under the heading "covetousness," forbidden by the tenth commandment. "A true Israelite," remarks one of the most popular of modern "helps to faith,"[29]

> avoids covetousness. He looks upon all his possessions only as a means of doing what is pleasing in the sight of God. For is not the entire purpose of his life to use all his possessions, all enjoyment as the means to this end? Indeed it is a duty...to obtain possessions and to increase one's enjoyments, not as an end in themselves but as a means to do God's will on earth.

But if it is urged that this is no conclusive proof of the connexion between the religious idea and the principle of getting gain, a glance at the peculiar ordering of divine service will soon be convincing. At one stage in the service there is a veritable public auction. The honorary offices connected with the reading of the law are given to the highest bidder. Before the scrolls are taken from the Ark, the beadle walks round the central platform (the *Almemor*) and cries out: "Who will buy *Hazoa vehachnosa*? (i.e., the act of taking the scrolls from the Ark and of replacing them). who will buy *Hagboha*? (the act of raising the scroll in the sight of the people). Who will buy *Gelilah*?" (the act of rolling up the scroll when the reading is finished). These honours are knocked down to the highest bidder, and the money given to the synagogue poor-box. It need hardly be said that today this practice has long been eliminated from synagogue worship. In days of long ago it was quite general.[30]

Again, the words of some of the Talmudic doctors, who at times dispute over the most difficult economic questions with all the skill of experienced merchants, cannot but have a curious connotation, and must lead to the conclusion that they preached the getting of gain. It would be fascinating to collect those passages of the Talmud wherein the modern practice of making profit is recommended by this or that Rabbi, in many cases themselves great traders. I will quote an instance or two. "R. Isaac also taught that a man should always have his money in circulation." It was R. Isaac, too, who gave this piece of good advice. A man should divide his fortune into three parts, investing one in landed property, one in moveable goods, and holding the third as ready cash (*Aba Mezia*, 42*a*). "Rav once said to his son, Come let me instruct thee in worldly matters.

Sell your goods even while the dust is yet upon your feet." (What is this but a recommendation to have a quick turnover?) "First open your purse and then unloose the sack of wheat....Have you got dates in the box? Hasten at once to the brewer" (*Pesachim*, 113*a*).

What is the meaning of this parallelism between the Jewish religion and capitalism? Is it a mere chance? A stupid joke perpetrated by Fate? Is the one the effect of the other, or are both traceable to the same causes? Questions such as these naturally suggest themselves to us, and I hope to answer them as we proceed. Here it will suffice to have called attention to them. Our next step will be the comparatively simpler one of showing how individual customs, conceptions, opinions, and regulations of the Jewish religion influenced the economic conduct of Jews, of showing whether they facilitated the extension of capitalism by the Jews, and, if so, to what degree. We shall limit ourselves in this to primary psychological motives, avoiding all speculative difficulties. Our first problem will be to discover the goal set up by the Jewish religion and its influence on economic life, and the next section is devoted to it.

The Idea of Rewards and Punishments

The idea of contract, which is part and parcel of the underlying principles of Judaism, must perforce have the corollary that whoever carries out the contract receives reward, whoever breaks it receives punishment. In other words, the legal and ethical assumption that the good prosper and the evil suffer punishment was in all ages a concept of the Jewish religion. All that changed was the interpretation of prosperity and punishment.

The oldest form of Judaism knows nothing of another world. So, weal and woe can come only in this world. If God desires to punish or to reward, He must do so during man's lifetime. The righteous therefore is prosperous here, and the wicked here suffer punishment. Obey my precepts, says the Lord, "so that thou mayest live long and prosper in the land which the Lord thy God hath given unto thee." Hence the bitter cry of Job, "Wherefore do the wicked live, become old, yea, wax mighty in power?....But my way He hath fenced up, that I cannot pass....He hath broken me down on every side....He hath also kindled His wrath against me" [Job xxi.7;8,10,11]. "Why hath all this evil come upon me, seeing that I walked in His path continually?"

A little after Ezra's time the idea of another world (*Olam Habo*) finds currency in Judaism, the idea, too, of the immortality of the soul and of the resurrection of the body. These beliefs were of foreign origin, coming probably Persia. But like all other alien elements in Judaism they, too, were given an ethical meaning, in accordance with the genius of the religion. The doctrine grew up that only the righteous and the pious would rise up after death. The belief in eternity was thus made by the *Soferim* to fit in with the old teaching of rewards and punishments, in order to heighten the feeling of moral responsibility, i.e., of the fear of the judgement of God.[31]

The idea of prosperity on earth is now extended. It is no longer the only reward of a good life, for a reward in the world to come is added to it. Still, God's blessing in this world is no small part of the total reward. Moreover, the very fact that a man is prosperous here was proof positive that his life was pleasing to God, and that therefore he might expect reward in the next world also. Then, too, the idea of a blind fate is no longer troublesome. What appeared as such is now regarded as God's punishment on earth to the righteous for his transgressions, so that his heavenly recompense may suffer no diminution.

The "doctrine of possession" (if the term may be allowed in connexion with the Jewish religion) received some such shape as this, more especially through the Wisdom Literature. The great aim of life is to obey God's commandments. Earthly happiness apart from God has no existence. Hence it is folly to seek to obtain earthly possessions for their own sake. But to obtain them in order to use them for divine ends, so that they become at one and the same time the outward symbols and guarantees of God's pleasure, as signs of His blessing—such a course is wise. Now earthly possessions in this view of them include a well-appointed house and material well-being—in a word, wealth.

Look through Jewish literature, more especially through the Holy Writ and the Talmud, and you will find, it is true, a few passages wherein poverty is lauded as something higher and nobler than riches. But on the other hand you will come across hundreds of passages in which riches are called the blessing of the Lord, and only their misuse or their dangers warned against. Here and there, too, we may read that riches alone do not necessarily bring happiness, other things are essential in addition (such as health, for example), that there are "goods" (in the broadest use of the word) more valuable or as valuable as riches. But in all this nothing is said *against* riches; and never is it stated that they are an abomination to the Lord.

I once gave expression to this view in a public lecture, and it was severely criticized on all sides. Just this point more than any other was controverted—the statement that riches are in the Jewish religion accounted as a valuable good. Many of my critics, among them several distinguished Jewish rabbis, went to the trouble of compiling lists of passages from the Bible and Talmud which confuted my opinion. I admit that there are many places in the Bible and the Talmud which regard wealth as a danger to the righteous, and in which poverty is extolled. There are some half-dozen of them in the Bible; the Talmud has rather more. But the important thing is that each of these passages may be capped by ten others, which breathe a totally different spirit. In such cases numbers surely count.

I put the question to myself in this way. Let us imagine old Amschel Rothschild on a Friday evening, after having "earned" a million on the Stock Exchange, turning to his Bible for edification. What will he find there touching his earnings and their effect on the refinement of his soul, an effect which the pious old Jew most certainly desired on the eve of the Sabbath? Will the million burn his conscience? Or will he not be able to say, and rightly say, "God's blessing rested upon me this week. I thank Thee, Lord, for having graciously granted the light of Thy countenance to Thy servant. In order to find favour in Thy sight I shall give much to charity, and keep Thy commandments even more strictly than hitherto"? Such would be his words if he knew his Bible, and he did know it.

For his eye would rest complacently on many a passage in the Holy Writ. In his beloved Torah he would be able to read again and again of the blessing of God.

> And He will love thee and bless thee and multiply thee, He will also bless the fruit of thy body and the fruit of thy ground, thy corn and thy wine and thine oil...thou shalt be blessed above all peoples (Deut. vii.13–15).

And how moved he would be when he reached the words,

> For the Lord, thy God, will bless thee, as He promised thee: and thou shalt lend unto many nations, but thou shalt not borrow (Deut. xv.6).

Then suppose he turns to the Psalms, what would he find there?

> O fear the Lord, ye His saints: for there is no want to them that fear Him. (Psa. xxxiv.10).
>
> Blessed is the man that feareth the Lord.... Wealth and riches are in his house (Psa. xc.1–3).
>
> Our garners are full, affording all manner of store, our sheep bring forth thousands and ten thousands in our fields (Psa. cxliv.13).

He would rejoice with Job when on concluding the story of his trials he found that his latter end was more blessed than his beginning, and that "he had 14,000 sheep, 6,000 camels, 1,000 yoke of oxen, and 1,000 she-asses" and the rest. (Happily our friend Amschel knew nothing of modern Biblical criticism, and was not aware therefore that this particular portion of Job is a later interpolation in the story.)

The prophets also promised Israel earthly rewards if it kept to God's way and walked therein. If Amschel turned to the 60th chapter of Isaiah he would find the prophecy that one day the Gentiles should bring their gold and silver to Israel.

But perhaps Amschel's favourite book would be Proverbs,[32] "which expresses in a most pregnant form the ideas of life current in Israel" (as a rabbi wrote to me who quoted this book in proof of my error, Prov. xxii.1,2: xxiii.4; xxviii.20,21; xxx.8). Here he would be warned that riches alone do not bring happiness (xxii.1,2), that God must not be denied amid great wealth (xxx.8), that "he that maketh haste to be rich shall not be unpunished" (xxviii.20). (Perhaps he will say to himself that he does not "hasten" to be rich.) The only verse that may disquieten him is when he reads "Weary not thyself to be rich; cease from thine own wisdom" (xxiii.4). But only for a moment, for his mind will be eased when he observes the connexion with the preceding passage. Possibly these six little words may not after all trouble him much when he remembers the numerous passages in this very book which commend riches. So numerous indeed that it may be said they give the tone to the whole of Proverbs.[33] A few only shall be quoted:

> Length of days are in her right hand; in her left are riches and honour (iii.16).
>
> Riches and honour are with me; yea, durable riches and righteousness (viii.18).
>
> The rich man's wealth is his strong city (x.15).
>
> Their riches are a crown unto the wise (xiv.24).
>
> The reward of humility and the fear of the Lord is riches and honour and life (xxii.4).

The Wisdom Literature included Ecclesiastes and the Wisdom of Solomon. The first[34] certainly does not breathe a uniform spirit; the many accretions of later times make it full of contradictions. Yet even here the pious Jew found never a passage which taught him to despise wealth. On the contrary, wealth is highly valued.

> Every man also to whom God hath given riches and wealth, and hath given him power to eat thereof ... this is the gift of God (v.19).
>
> A feast is made for laughter and wine maketh glad the life: and money answereth all things (x.19).

The Wisdom of Solomon likewise praises riches. No less does the Book of Jesus, the son of Sirach, that fund of wise saws, which old Amschel must have conned with delight. If any Rabbi had told him that Ben Sirach's books regard the wealthy man almost as a sinner and wealth as the source of evil, instancing chapters x.–xiii. in proof, Amschel would have replied, "My dear Rabbi, you are mistaken. Those passages are a warning against the dangers of wealth. But a rich man who avoids the dangers is thereby the more righteous.

> Blessed is the rich that is found without blemish...his goods shall be established and the congregation shall declare his alms (xxxi.8,11).

"And why, my dear Rabbi" (so Amschel might continue), "do you not mention the passages which speak of the man who has amassed millions, passages like the following?

> Better is he that laboureth and aboundeth in all things, than he that boasteth himself and wanteth bread (x.27).
>
> The poor man is honoured for his skill, and the rich man is honoured for his riches (x.30).
>
> Prosperity and adversity, life and death, poverty and riches come of the Lord' (xi.14).
>
> Gold and silver make the foot stand sure (xl.25).
>
> Riches and strength lift up the heart (xl.26).
>
> Better it is to die than to beg (xl.28).

"Should I be ashamed of my millions, my dear Rabbi" (Amschel would conclude the imaginary conversation), "should I not rather look upon them as God's blessing? Recall what the wise Jesus ben Sirach said of great King Solomon (xlvii.18): 'By the name of the Lord God, which is called the Lord God of Israel, thou didst gather gold as tin, and didst multiply silver as lead.' I also will go, Rabbi, and in the name of the Lord God will gather gold as tin and silver as lead."

In the Talmud the passages that express the same point of view are frequent enough. Riches are a blessing if only their owner walk in God's ways, and poverty is a curse. Hardly ever are riches despised. Let us quote a few Talmudic sayings on the subject.

> Seven characteristics are there which are "comely to the righteous and comely to the world." One of them is riches (*Aboth*, vi.8).
>
> In prayer a man should turn to Him who owns wealth and possessions.... In reality both come not from business, but according to merit (*Kidushin*, lxxxiia).
>
> R. Eleazer said, "The righteous love their money more than their bodies" (*Sota*, xiia).
>
> Rabba honoured the wealthy, so did R. Akiba (*Erubin*, lxxxvia).
>
> In time of scarcity a man learns to value wealth best (*Aboth de Rabbi Nathan*).

Doctrines concerning wealth such as these could not but encourage a worldly view of life. This the Jewish view was, despite the belief in another world. There were indeed attempts at ascetic movements in Judaism (e.g., in the ninth century the Karaites combined to live the life of monks;* in the eleventh century Bachja ibn Pakuda preached asceticism in Spain), but none of them ever took root. Judaism even in times of great affliction was always optimistic. In this the Jews differ from the Christians, whose religion has tried to rob them all it could of earthly joys. As often as riches are lauded in the Old Testament they are damned in the New, wherein poverty is praised. The whole outlook of the Essenes, turning its back upon the world and the flesh, was incorporated in the Gospels. One can easily recall passage after passage to this effect. (Cf. Matt. vi.24; x.9,10; xix.23,24.) "It is easier for a camel to go through a needle's eye than for a rich man to enter into the Kingdom of God." This is the keynote of Christianity on the point, and the difference between it and Judaism is clear enough. There is no single parallel to the saying of Jesus in the whole of the Old Testament, and probably also none in the entire body of Rabbinic literature.

---

* Sombart is mistaken in this. The characteristic of the Karaites was that they accepted and lived by the *letter* of the Torah.—Trans.

There is no need to expatiate on the different attitude of the good Jew and the good Christian towards economic activities. The Christian is forced by all manner of mental gymnastics to interpret away the Essene conception of riches from his Scriptures. And what anxious moments must the rich Christian live through as he thinks of heaven locked against him! Compare with him the position of the rich Jew, who, as we have seen, "in the name of the Lord God" gathers gold as tin and silver as lead.

It is well known that the religion of the Christians stood in the way of their economic activities. It is equally well known that the Jews were never faced with this hindrance. The more pious a Jew was and the more acquainted with his religious literature, the more he was spurred by the teachings of that literature to extend his economic activities. A beautiful illustration of the way religion and business were fused in the mind of pious Jews may be found in the delightful Memoirs of Glückel von Hameln, to which we have already referred. "Praise be to God, who gives and takes, the faithful God, who always made good our losses," she says. And again, "My husband sent me a long, comforting letter, urging me to calm my soul, for God, whose name be blessed, would restore to us what we had lost. And so it was."

The Rationalization of Life

Since Judaism rests upon a contract between God and His people, i.e., upon a two-sided legal agreement, each party must have definite responsibilities. What were those of the Jews?

Again and again was the answer to this question given by God through His servant Moses. Again and again the Israelite was informed that two great duties were his. He was to be holy and to obey God's law. (Cf. Exod. xix.6; Deut. iv.56.) God did not require sacrifices of him; He demanded obedience (Jer. vii.22,23).

Now it is generally known that in the course of events the Jews came to regard righteousness as a minute fulfilment of the Law. The inward holiness that may have existed in early days soon vanished before formalism and legalism. Holiness and observation of the Law became interchangeable terms. It is generally known, too, that this legalism was a device of the Rabbis to protect the Jews against the influences first, of Hellenism, then of Christianity, and finally, when the Second Temple was destroyed, to maintain by its means the national consciousness. The struggle with Hellenism resulted in Pharisaism; the struggle with Pauline Christianity which aimed at replacing the Law by faith, transformed the religion of the Pharisees into that of the Talmud, and the old policy of the Scribes "to encompass the whole of life with regulation" made greater progress than ever. In their political isolation, the Jewish communities submitted entirely to the new hierarchy. They desired to see the end attained and so accepted the means. The school and the Law outlasted the Temple and the State, and Pharisaic Rabbinsim had unlimited sway. Righteousness henceforth meant living in strict accordance with the Law. Piety, under the influence of the legally minded Scribes, was given a legal connotation. Religion became the common law. In the Mishna all this finds admirable expression. The commands of the Pentateuch and the commands deduced from these are all divine ordinances which must be obeyed without questioning. More and more stress is laid on externals, and between important and insignificant commands there is less and less differentiation.[35]

So it remained for two thousand years; so it is today. Strict orthodoxy still holds to this formalism and the principles of Judaism know no change. The Torah is as binding today in its every word as when it was given to Moses on Sinai.[36] Its laws and ordinances must be observed by the faithful, whether they be light or grave, whether they appear to have rhyme or reason or not. And they must be strictly observed, and only because God gave them. This implicit obedience makes the righteous, makes the saint.

> Saintly or holy in the Torah sense is he who is able to fulfil the revealed will of God without any struggle and with the same joy as carrying out his own will. This holiness, this complete fusion of the will of man with the divine will, is a lofty goal attainable in its entirety by a few only. Hence the law of holiness refers in the first instance to the striving towards this goal. The striving all can do; it demands a constant self-watchfulness and self-education, and endless struggle against what is low and vulgar, what is sensual and bestial. And obedience to the behests of the Torah is the surest ladder on which to climb to higher and higher degrees of holiness.[37]

These words show clearly enough how holiness and legalism are connected; they show that the highest aim of Israel still is to be a kingdom of priests and a holy nation; and that the path to that end is a strict obedience to God's commandments. Once this becomes apparent, we can imagine the importance the Jewish religion has for the whole of life. In the long run, external legalism does not remain external; it exercises a constant influence on the inner life, which obtains its peculiar character from the observance of the law.

The psychological process which led to the shaping of Judaism appears to me to be this. At first God's behests were those that mattered, regardless of their contents. But slowly the contents must needs make themselves manifest to the observer, and a clearly defined ideal of Life evolved itself from the word of God. To follow this ideal, to be righteous, to be holy was the heart's desire of each believer.

Before continuing, let us strive to obtain some notion of what the pious Jew meant, and means, by holiness in the material sense.

Let us recall what was said in the last section about the "worldliness" of the Jewish religion. In accordance with this it can scarcely be holy to deny the natural instincts or to crush them, as other religions teach—e.g., Buddhism or Primitive Christianity. Other-worldly asceticism was always antagonistic to Judaism. "The soul which has been given thee—preserve it, never kill it"—that is the Talmudic maxim on which to build up the conduct of life and which found currency at all times.[38]

The negation of life cannot therefore be holiness. Nor can the exercise of man's passions and appetites be holiness. For if it were, it could not be put as an ideal before the righteous; it would then be accessible to everybody. There remains therefore only one other possibility—to live your life of set purpose in accordance with some ideal plan based on supernatural rules, and either utilizing the desires within you or crushing them. In fine, holiness is the rationalization of life. You decide to replace the natural existence with its desires and inclinations by the moral life. To be holy is to become refined, and to realize this is to overcome all your natural tendencies by means of moral obedience.[39]

A rugged Dualism—the terrible Dualism which is part and parcel of our constitution—characterizes the Jewish conception of ethical worth. Nature is not unholy, neither is she holy. She is not yet holy. She may become holy through us. All the seeds of sin are in her; the serpent still lurks in the grass as he did long ago in the Garden of Eden. "God certainly created the evil inclination, but he also created the Torah, the moral law, an an antidote to it."[40] The whole of human life is one great warfare against the inimical forces of Nature: that is the guiding principle of Jewish moral theology, and it is in accordance with it that the system of rules and regulations was instituted by which life might be rationalized, de-naturalized, refined, and hallowed without the necessity of renouncing or stifling it. In this we see the marked difference between the Christian (Essene) and the Jewish (Pharisaic) ideas of morality. The former leads quite logically away from the world into the silent hermitage and the monastery (if not to death); the latter binds its faithful adherent with a thousand chains to the individual and social life. Christianity makes its devotee into a monk, Judaism into a rationalist; the first ends in asceticism outside the world; the second in asceticism within it (taking asceticism to mean the subjugation of what is natural in man).

We shall gain a clearer insight of what Jewish Ethics (and therefore also the Jewish religion) stands for if we examine its regulations one by one.

The effect of Law is twofold. Its very existence has an influence; so have its contents.

That there is a law at all, that it is a duty to obey it, impels one to think about one's actions and to accomplish them in harmony with the dictates of reason. In front of every desire a warning finger-post is set; every natural impulse is nullified by the thousand and one milestones and danger-signals in the shape of directions to the pious. Now, since obedience to a multifariousness of rules (the well-known commands compiled by Maimonides number 365—of which 243 are still current—and his prohibitions 248) is well-nigh impossible without a pretty good knowledge of what they are, the system includes the command to study the Holy Writ, and especially the Torah. This very study itself is made a means of rendering life holy. "If the evil inclination seizes hold of you, march him off to the House of Study," counsels the Talmud.

The view that all the enactments were for the purpose of ennobling the life of the faithful was accepted at all times, and is still held today by many orthodox Jews.

> God wished to refine Israel, therefore He increased the number of the commandments (*Makkoth*, 23*b*).
>
> The commandments were given by God to ennoble mankind (*Vajikra Rabaa*, 13).[41]
>
> It would have been better for a man never to have been born, but once he is in the world let him continually examine his actions (*Erubin*, 13*b*).
>
> Every night a man should critically examine his deeds of the day (*Magen Abraham on Orach Chajim*, 239, §7).[42]

"Observe" and "remember" were ordained in a single utterance.[43]

Deum respice et cura[44] is still the motto of the Jew. If he meets a king or sees a dwarf or a Negro, passes a ruined building or takes his medicine or his bath, notes the coming storm or hears its roaring thunder, rises in the morning and puts on his clothes or eats his food, enters his house or leaves it, greets a friend or meets a foe—for every emergency there is an ordinance which must be obeyed.

Now what of the contents of the ordinances? All of them aim at the subjugation of the merely animal instincts in man, at the bridling of his desires and inclinations and at the replacing of impulses by thoughtful action; in short, at the "ethical tempering of man."

You must think nothing, speak nothing, do nothing without first considering what the law about it is, and then apply it to the great purpose of sanctification. You must therefore do nothing merely for its own sake, spontaneously, or from natural instinct.

You must not enjoy Nature for the sheer pleasure of it. You may do so only if you think thereby of the wisdom and the goodness of God. In the spring when the trees put on their blossom the pious Jew says, "Blessed art Thou, O Lord our God,...who hast made Thy world lacking in nought, but hast provided therein goodly creatures and trees wherewith to give delight to the children of men." At the sight of the rainbow he brings to mind the Covenant with God. On high mountains, in vast deserts, beside mighty rivers—in a word, wherever his heart is deeply moved by Nature's wonders—he expresses his feelings in the benediction, "Blessed art Thou, O Lord our God,...who hast made the Creation."

You must not enjoy art for its own sake. Works of plastic art should be avoided, for they may easily lead to a breach of the second commandment. But even the poet's art is not looked upon with favour, except it refer to God. All reading is good, provided it has some practical end in view.

> It is best to read books of the Torah or such as refer to them. If we desire to read for recreation, let us choose books that are able to teach us something useful. Among the books written for amusement and to while away the time there are some that may awake sinful wishes within us. The reading of these books is forbidden.[45]

You must not indulge in harmless pleasures. "The seat of the scornful [Psa. i.1],—the theatres and circuses of the heathen are meant." Song, dance, and wine, save when they are connected with religious ceremonial, are taboo. "Rabbi Dosa ben Hyrkanus used to say, Morning sleep and midday wine and childish talk and attending the houses where the ignorant foregather put a man out of the world."[46] "He that loveth pleasure shall be a poor man; he that loveth wine and oil shall not be rich" (Prov. xxi.17).

If this be so, those qualities which may lead a man to "unseemly" conduct are useless or even harmful. Such are enthusiasm (for while a man is in this state he may do something useless),[47] kindness of heart (you must exercise kindness only because the idea of benevolence actuates you; you must never let pity carry you away, so that the nobility and dignity of the ideal law may always be before you);[48] a sensual temperament ("the source of passion—and of sin—is in sensuality"),[49] ingenuousness, in short anything that marks the natural (and therefore unholy) man.

The cardinal virtues of the pious are, on the other hand, self-control and circumspection, a love of order and of work, moderation and abstemiousness, chastity, and sobriety.

Self-control and circumspection especially and in regard to your words is a constant theme of the moralists. "In the multitude of words there wanteth not transgression: but he that refraineth his lips doth wisely" (Prov. x.19).[50]

No less insistent was the later tradition. "Raba held that whoso carries on an unnecessary conversation transgresses a command" (*Joma*, 19*b*). "Our sanctification," says a modern book for popular edification, "depends to a large extent on the control of our tongues, on the power of holding our peace. The gift of speech...was given to man for holy purposes. Hence all unnecessary talk is forbidden by our wise men."[51]

But self-control and circumspection generally are urged on the pious Jew.

> Who is the strongest of the strong? He who controls his passions (*Aboth de R. Nathan*, xxiii.1).
>
> The thoughts of the diligent tend only to plenteousness: but every one that is hasty hasteth only to want (Prov. xxi.5).
>
> He that hasteth with his feet sinneth (Prov. xix.2).

And as for industry and thrift, innumerable are the exhortations to that end.

The Jew must wake the day, not the day the Jew—so taught the Rabbis, as a homily on Psalm lvii.9.[52]

It is just the strongest instincts of man that must be curbed, directed into right channels, deprived of their natural force and made to serve useful ends. In short, they must be rationalized.

Take the instinct which desires to satisfy hunger. It is forbidden to appease the appetite merely because it happens to be there; it should be appeased only for the body's sake. And when the good man sits down to eat, let him do so according to the precepts of his Maker. Hence the large number of rules concerning food; hence the command to be serious at meals—to begin and to close with prayer; hence the advice to be moderate and the appeal to banish the pleasure of feeding.

> It is only through God's goodness that you are enabled to use His creatures as food, and therefore if your entire eating and drinking is not to be beastly, it must be hallowed; it must be looked upon as the getting of strength for His service.[53] The Jew should make the satisfaction of his appetite for food a sacrament; should regard his table as an altar and the food thereon as sacrifice, which he enjoys only in order to obtain more strength for the fulfilment of his duties.[54]

(Jewish cooking, by the way, is excellent.)

Finally—and this of curse matters most—just like hunger, Love also must be rationalized, that is to say, its natural expression must be held in check. Nowhere more than in the erotic sphere does the hard dualism show itself so well. The world, and certainly the civilized nations, owes this conception of the sexual to the Jews (through the agency of Christianity, which was infected with the idea). All earlier religions saw something divine in the expression of sex, and regarded sexual intercourse as of the nature of a heavenly revelation. All of them were acquainted with Phallus-worship in a grosser or finer form. None of them condemned what is sensuous, or looked upon women as a source of sin. But the Jews from Ezra's day to this held, and hold, the opposite view.

To sanctify himself, to make himself worthy of his converse with God, Moses "drew not nigh unto his wife." And Job mentions as being in his favor that he made a covenant with his eyes not to look upon a maid. The whole Wisdom Literature abounds in warnings against women,[†] and the same spirit dominates the Talmud. "Better to die than to be guilty of

---

[†] Sombart instances Prov. v.3-4. But does not the passage clearly refer to *bad* women?—Trans.

unchastity" (*Sanhedrin*, 75*a*). Indeed, the three capital crimes for which even death does not atone are murder, idol-worship, and adultery. "Hast thou business with women? See to it that thou art not with them alone" (*Kiddushin*, 82*a*). This dread runs through all the codes. The *Eben Ha-ezer* condemns to death by stoning any one who has had guilty intercourse with a woman related to him within the prohibited degrees. The very clothes or the little finger of a woman of such close consanguinity must not be looked at "to get pleasure from it." It is forbidden a man to allow himself to be waited on by a woman, or to embrace his aunt or his grown-up sister.

Teachers of today are no less explicit. "Guard yourself against any contact with impurity," says one of the most popular of them.

> Look at nothing, hear nothing, read nothing, think of nothing which may in any wise occupy your thoughts unchastely or make you familiar with what is not clean. Do not walk in the street behind a woman; if you cannot help yourself, look not at her with desire.[‡] Do not let your eye rest longingly on a woman's hair, nor your ears on her voice; do not take pleasure in her form; yea, a woman's very clothes should not be looked at if you know who has worn them. In all things go out of the way of Opportunity...The two sexes should not jest together. Even in make-believe little pressures of the hand, winking of the eyes, embracing and kissing are sinful.[55]

Warnings such as these were not neglected, as may be seen from the autobiographies of pious Jews, some of which may now be read in modern languages.[56]

But the point of it all must not be overlooked. Other religions also show signs of being terrified at women. Ever since the notion became prevalent that woman brought sin into the world there have always been morbid souls who spent their lives exciting themselves with all manner of lascivious imaginings but avoiding woman as though she were the devil incarnate. In other religions the man fled to the hermit's cave in the wilderness or to a monastery. In either case, his religion forced "chastity" upon him, with all the horrid resultants well known to students of monastic life. Not so Judaism. Judaism does not forbid sexual intercourse, it rationalizes it. Not that it does not regard sexual intercourse as sinful. Sinful it must always be, but its sinfulness may to some extent be

---

‡ Cf. Robert Louis Stevenson: "To remember the faces of women without desire,...is not this to know both wisdom and virtue?"—Trans.

removed by sanctification. Hence Judaism advocates early marriages and regulates the relationship between husband and wife as something "ever in the great Taskmaster's eye."

"A man should not be without a wife, nor a woman without a husband; but both shall see to it that God's spirit is in their union." That is the motto, and in accordance with it the Talmud and the later codes have multiplied rules and regulations for the guidance of married couples. In the eleventh century (to mention but a few) R. Eleazar ben Nathan compiled a special code on the subject, the *Eben Ha-ezer*, and in the thirteenth century R. Nachman wrote a famous work on the sanctification of marriage.[57] The laws of the *Eben Ha-ezer* were incorporated in the *Shulchan Aruch* and together with the glosses upon them receive recognition today. The main ideas throughout are those we have already considered: hallow thy body's strength in accordance with God's will; be careful of thy manhood; be God's servant at all times.[58]

Such was the Jewish view of marriage, which has continued for more than two thousand years. It is well illustrated by that touching story in the Book of Tobit, which may form a fitting conclusion to our considerations under this head.

> And after they were both shut in together, Tobias rose out of the bed, and said, Sister, arise, and let us pray that God would have pity on us.
>
> Then began Tobias to say, Blessed art Thou, O God of our fathers, and blessed is Thy holy and glorious name for ever; let the heavens bless Thee, and all Thy creatures.
>
> Thou madest Adam, and gavest him Eve his wife for an helper and stay: of them came mankind: Thou hast said, It is not good that man should be alone; let us make unto him an aid like unto himself.
>
> And now, O Lord, I take not this my sister for lust, but uprightly therefore mercifully ordain that we may become aged together.
>
> And she said with him, Amen.
>
> So they slept both that night.—Tobit vii.4–9.

It may be asked, Why have I treated this aspect of Jewish life at such great length? My answer is simple. I really believe that the rationalization of life, and especially of the sexual life, which the Jewish religion effects cannot be too highly estimated for its influence on economic activities. If religion is at all to be accounted a factor in Jewish economic life, then certainly the rationalization of conduct is its best expression.

To begin with, a number of good qualities or virtues which are indispensable to any economic order owe their existence to rationalization—e.g., industry, neatness, thrift. But the whole of life, if lived in accordance with the ordinances of the "Wise," ministers to the needs of wealth-getting. Sobriety, moderation, and piety are surely qualities which stand the business man in good stead. In short, the whole ideal of conduct preached in Holy Writ and in Rabbinic literature has something of the morality of the small shopkeeper about it—to be content with one wife, to pay your debts punctually, to go to church or synagogue on Sunday or Saturday (as the case may be), and to look down with immeasurable scorn on the sinful world around.

But Jewish moral teaching did not spend itself in the mere production of this type of the small respectable shopkeeper. It may even by questioned whether the type is altogether its work. At any rate, it is not of much consequence for economic development. Middle-class respectability as a matter of fact owes its origin to the narrow outlook of the petty trading class. Hence it can have but little to do with capitalism, except in so far as the qualities which that class possessed were the foundation on which capitalism could be built up. But capitalism did not grow out of the qualities, and therefore we must search in other directions for the causes which made the Jews pioneers of capitalism.

The first that suggests itself is the cultivation of family life among Jews, calling forth as it did energies so necessary to economic growth. The cultivation and refinement of family life was undoubtedly the work of the Jewish Rabbis, assisted, it must be added, by the vicissitudes of the Jewish people. In Judaism woman was first held in that high esteem which is the prime postulate for the existence of a sound family life and all that it means for man's conduct. The Rabbis by their laws and regulations affecting marriages, the marital relationship and the education of children and the rest, did all that was humanly possible in the way of outward limitation and influence to establish family life in all its purity. That marriage is considered more sacred among pious Jews than among people of other denominations is demonstrated by the statistics of illegitimate births. These are considerably fewer among Jews than among Christians.[59]

Illegitimate Births Per Thousand

Year	Country	General Population	Jews
1904	Prussia	2.51	0.66
1905	Würtemberg	2.83	0.16
1907	Hesse	2.18	0.13
1908	Bavaria	4.25	0.56
1901	Russia	1.29	0.14

If the figures for Russia be looked into a little more carefully it will be seen that illegitimate births among Jews vary very much from those among non-Jews. At the same time it must not be forgotten that there is a slight lowering of the standard in sexual morality among Jews. Thus, the following table shows the percentage of illegitimate births in Russia.

Illegitimate Births Per Hundred In Russia

Year	Greek Orthodox	Catholics	Protestants	Jews
1868	2.96	3.45	3.49	0.19
1878	3.13	3.29	3.85	0.25
1898	2.66	3.53	3.86	0.37
1901	2.49	3.57	3.76	0.46

Such then was one result of the family life current among Jews and introduced by them. The man contributed to it the best that was in him, and in return he drew from it invigorating strength, courage, and an inducement to maintain and to expand his position in life. Family life of this kind generated centers for masculine energy large enough to set in motion such a mighty economic system as capitalism. For this system calls for great energy, and we can scarcely imagine it being produced except through the agency of psychological influences which appeal not only to the social instincts but also to the family ideal.

It may perhaps be necessary to look below the psychological influences to the physical ones. How curiously moulded must the constitution of the Jew have become through the rationalization of his married life! We see this phenomenon—that a people with strong sexual inclinations (Tacitus speaks of it as *proiectissima ad libidinem gens*) is forced by its religion to hold them in complete restraint.

Extra-marital connexions are absolutely forbidden; every one must content himself with one wife, but even with her intercourse is restricted.

The result of all this is obvious. Enormous funds of energy were prevented from finding an outlet in one direction and they turned to others. Knowing as we do the condition of the Jews throughout the Common Era, we shall not be wrong in assuming that economic activities were their chief channel. But we may go further. It is possible to prove that, quite generally, restrained sexual desires and the chase of profits go hand in hand. For the present we have had but little scientific investigation of this fact, so important for all modern sociological problems.[60] That a lordly way of life is usually accompanied by lavishness of money and of love, whereas such qualities as niggardliness, avarice and a setting of much store by money are the ubiquitous partners of a stunted sexual life—these are everyday experiences, and though it would be presumptuous to attempt to solve this most interesting problem with the aid of observations which must perforce be limited, yet for the purpose of my argument they ought not to be omitted, at least as an hypothesis.

We see then that a good deal of capitalistic capacity which the Jews possessed was due in large measure to the sexual restraint put upon them by their religious teachers. The effect of the rationalization of the whole of life on the physical and intellectual powers of the Jew must still be gone into by scientists,[61] at present we have only beginnings of such studies. I refer to the influence of the very wise regulations of sexual intercourse, of eating and drinking and so on. (Incidentally it is worthy of note that Jewish law has long restricted the marriage of the unfit.)

One other point in conclusion. The rationalization of life accustomed the Jew to a mode of living contrary to (or side by side with) Nature and therefore also to an economic system like the capitalistic, which is likewise contrary to (or side by side with) Nature. What in reality is the idea of making profit, what is economic rationalism, but the application to economic activities of the rules by which the Jewish religion shaped Jewish life? Before capitalism could develop the natural man had to be changed out of all recognition, and a rationalistically minded mechanism introduced in his stead. There had to be a transvaluation of all economic values. And what was the result? The *homo capitalisticus*, who is closely related to the *homo Judoeus*, both belonging to the same species, *homines rationalistici artificiales*.

And so the rationalization of Jewish life by the Jewish religion, if it did not actually produce the Jewish capacity for capitalism, certainly increased and heightened it.

Israel and the Nations

One of the causes to which the Jew owed his economic progress was, as the reader will remember, the fact that Israel was for generations a stranger and an alien. If we seek to account for this aloofness we shall find its roots in the ordinances of the Jewish religion, shall find that this religion always maintained and broadened the line of separation. As Leroy-Beaulieu, who has studied this aspect of Jewish history with great success, has so well said, "La loi leur donnait l'esprit de clan." The very fact that they had their Law forced the Jews to live apart from the Gentiles. For if they desired to observe the Law they must keep to themselves. The Jews created the Ghetto, which from the non-Jewish point of view was a concession and a privilege and not the result of enmity.

But the Jews wished to live separated from the rest because they felt themselves superior to the common people round them. They were the Chosen Race, a People of Priests. The Rabbis did all that was required to fan the flame of pride—from Ezra, who forbade intermarriage as a profanation of Jewish purity, down to this very day, when the pious Jew says every morning, "Blessed art Thou, O Lord, King of the Universe, who has not made me a Gentile (stranger)."

And so they lived separate and apart all through the centuries of the Diaspora, despite the Diaspora and (thanks to the bands which the Law laid upon them) because of the Diaspora—separate and apart, and therefore a group by themselves, or, if you will, a group by themselves and therefore separate and apart.

A group by themselves—they were that already at the time of the Babylonian Exile, which in reality established the internationalism of the Jew. Many of them, especially the wealthier ones, remained behind in Babylon of their own free will, but they retained their Judaism and professed it zealously. They kept up a lively intercourse with their brethren who had returned home, took a sympathetic interest in their fortunes, rendered them assistance and sent them new settlers from time to time.[62]

The bonds of union were in no way relaxed in the Hellenistic Diaspora.

> They kept closely together in the cities and throughout the world. No matter where they pitched their tents, their connexion with Zion was upheld. In the heart of the wilderness they had a native land where they were at home....By means of the Diaspora they entered into the world. In the Hellenistic cities they adopted the Greek tongue and Greek manners even if only as the outer garb of their Jewishness (Wellhausen).

So it continued throughout the centuries of their exile. If anything the bond became strengthened. "*Scis quanta concordia*"—"You know how they hang together!" cries Cicero.[63] So it was; so it still is. "All the Jewries in the Empire and beyond," we read of the rebellion of the year 130 A.D., "were stirred and more or less openly supported the insurgents on the banks of the Jordan."[64] Is it any different today when a Jew is expelled from some Russian town or other?

A group by themselves and therefore separate and apart—this is true from earliest antiquity. All nations were struck by their hatred of others, of which they were for the first time accused by Hekateus of Abdera (300 B.C.). Many other ancient writers repeat the indictment,[65] almost always in the same words. Perhaps the best known passage is in Tacitus:

> *Apud eos fides obstinata, misericordia in promptu. Sed adversus omnes alios hostile odium. Separati epulis discreti cubilibus, proiectissima ad libidinem gens, alienarum concubita abstinent* (Historia, V, i.5). [Amongst themselves they are doggedly faithful and quick to pity, but all strangers they hate as enemies. They neither eat nor intermarry with strangers; they are a people of strong passions, yet they withhold themselves from other men's wives.]

Jewish apologetics never attempted to combat these views:[66] there must therefore have been some foundation for them.

It is true that the Jews kept together so closely and shut themselves off very often on account of the unfriendly treatment they received at the hands of their hosts. But it was not so originally. The Jews wanted to live secluded from their neighbors because of their religion. That this was so appears from their attitude in those lands where they were well treated. Witness one or two instances in the ancient world, of which I have just given illustrations [Tacitus, etc.]. Witness the same tendency in the Middle Ages. Take Arabia in the first century. The Jews there at the period named lived according to the religion which the *Tanaim* and *Amoraim* had formulated—keeping the dietary laws and festivals, the great White Fast and the Sabbath.

> Although they could not complain of anything in this hospitable country they yet longed for the return to the Holy Land and awaited the advent of the Messiah every day.... They were in direct communication with the Jews of Palestine.[67]

Or take Moorish Spain. While the Christians who lived among the Mohammedans forgot their mother tongue (Gothic Latin), no longer understood their sacred books, and were rather ashamed of their Christianity, the Spanish Jews were more and more devoted to their national language, their Holy Writ, and their ancient religion.[68] This attitude was clearly reflected in the Jewish poetry and philosophy of the period, the greatest perhaps that mediæval Jewry can boast. In the midst of an Arabic-Spanish world in which they lived and enjoyed the respect of their fellow-citizens, they were strictly "national," that is religious; they drew poetic inspiration from the Messianic hopes and were filled with an unconquerable longing for Zion.[69] One need only mention the great Jehuda Halevy, whose Odes to Zion are the highest expression of the genius of neo-Hebrew poetry.

Like a cloud sailing in the blue of the sky above, Judaism winds its way through history, refreshed by the memories of its hoary and holy past as by a soft breeze. To this very day the pious Jew blesses his children with the words, "The Lord make thee as Ephraim and Manasseh."

What was the effect on economic life of this seclusion and separation of the Jewish social organism? Directly the Jews stepped outside the Ghetto gates their intercourse was with strangers. We have already dealt with the point elsewhere; my reason for calling attention to it again is to show that this attitude was a direct consequence of the teaching of Judaism, that in treating the people among whom they lived as "others," the Jews were but obeying a divine behest. Here, too, their conduct was hallowed, and it received a sanction from the peculiar system of laws relating to "strangers."

The most important and most frequently discussed legal ordinance in this system was that affecting the taking of interest. In the old Jewish theocracy, [70] as in every society in early civilization, loans without interest were the regular means of rendering assistance by a man to his neighbor. But it may be observed that even in the earliest collection of laws interest was allowed to be taken from "strangers."

The Jewish code was no exception. The best example of this may be found in Deuteronomy xxiii.20. Other passages in the Torah that have reference to interest are Exodus xxii.25 and Leviticus xxv.37. They all form the theme of a lively discussion which has been carried on from the days of the *Tanaim* down to the present. The chief instance and at the same time the crux of the matter is in the Talmud, in *Baha Mezia*, 70*b*, and my own feeling is that for the most part it is an attempt to discount the very clear statement of the Torah by all manner of sophistries. For what does the verse in Deuteronomy say? "Unto a foreigner thou mayest lend upon usury; but unto thy brother thou shalt not lend upon usury." The only doubt is the wording of the original, which may mean with equal grammatical exactitude, "thou *mayest* lend upon usury" or "thou *shalt* lend upon usury." (It need hardly be added that "usury" with the translators was nothing more or less than our "interest.")

Inn either case, the pious Jew was allowed to take interest from non-Jews—that is the significant thing as far as we are concerned. Right through the Middle Ages he was not oppressed by the burden of the anti-usury prohibition which weighed upon the Christian. The Jewish law on the subject was never to my knowledge questioned by the Rabbis.[71] On the other hand, there were periods when the "mayest" in the Deuteronomic passage was read as "shalt," periods when the Jew was urged to become a money-lender.

The authors who have dealt with this subject in modern times appear to have overlooked the fact that the Deuteronomic command has been received as one of the laws that regulate the life of the Jew, and that Tradition sanctions money-lending to a stranger on payment of interest. Of the 613 commandments, this is the 198th and may be found likewise in the *Shulchan Aruch*. Modern Rabbis,[72] to whom the perfectly clear ordinance in Deuteronomy is somewhat inconvenient (one cannot quite understand why), attempt to explain it away by asserting that "strangers" in the passage is intended not for all non-

Jews but only for heathens or idol-worshippers. If this be so, let it not be forgotten that there never was any very distinct conception as to who was, and who was not, an idol-worshipper. Besides, the pious Jew who has committed the 198th command to memory is not likely to draw the fine distinction urged by the learned Rabbis. Sufficient for him that the man to whom he lent money was no Jew, no "brother," no neighbor, but a Gentile.

Now think of the position in which the pious Jew and the pious Christian respectively found themselves in the period in which money-lending first became a need in Europe, and which eventually gave birth to capitalism. The good Christian who had been addicted to usury was full of remorse as he lay a-dying, ready at the eleventh hour to cast from him the ill-gotten gains which scorched his soul. And the good Jew? In the evening of his days he gazed upon his well-filled caskets and coffers, overflowing with sequins of which he had relieved the miserable Christians or Mohammedans. It was a sight which warmed his heart, for every penny was almost like a sacrifice which he had brought to his Heavenly Father.

Apart from this particular question, the stranger was accorded special consideration in the Jewish legal code. Duties towards him were never as binding as towards your "neighbor," your fellow-Jew. Only ignorance or a desire to distort facts will assert the contrary. True, the conception of law and morality as it affected the "stranger" varied from age to age. But there was no change in the fundamental idea that you owed less consideration to the stranger than to one of your own people. That has remained the same from the day when the Torah first became current to our own. That is the impression that is conveyed by an unprejudiced study of the law concerning strangers in the Holy Writ, the Talmud, the Codes, and the Responsa literature. There certainly are passages in the Torah which breathe equality between the homeborn and the stranger (Exod. xii.49, xxiii.9; Lev. xix.33,34, xxv.44–6; Deut. x.18,19). But in a question of *halacha* (legal enactment) such as this is, the oral tradition cannot be neglected. Secondly, the passages instanced above all refer to the *Ger*, the non-Jew who had settled in Palestine, seeing that the Jews knew the heart of a *Ger*, "for ye were *Gerim* in the land of Egypt." [In the sentence about interest the word used is *Nachari*, some one from another nation.] As time went on it was but natural that there should be an increase of the cases in Jewish law in which the non-Jew was at a disadvantage as compared with the Jew. So much so that in the latest code they occupy a good deal of space.[73]

What was the importance in economic life of the laws concerning strangers? It was twofold. First, intercourse with strangers was bereft of all considerations, and commercial morality (if I may put it so) became elastic. I admit that there was no absolute necessity for this to come about, but all the conditions were given for it to do so, and it must have been an everyday occurrence in certain circles. "If a non-Jew makes an error in a statement of account, the Jew may use it to his own advantage; it is not incumbent upon him to point it out." So we may read in the *Tur*, and though Joseph Caro did not include this in his law-book, it crept in later as a gloss from the pen of Isserlein. Is it not obvious that the good Jew must draw the conclusion that he was not bound to be so particular in his intercourse with non-Jews? With Jews he will scrupulously see to it that he has just weights and a just measure,[74] but as for his dealings with non-Jews, his conscience will be at ease even though he may obtain an unfair advantage. It is not to be denied that in some cases honesty towards non-Jews was inculcated.[75] But to think that this should have been necessary! Besides, this is the actual wording of the law: "It is permissible to take advantage of a non-Jew, for it is written, Thou shalt not take advantage of thy brother." (The context refers not to overreaching, but only to the asking of higher prices from a non-Jew.)

This conception must have been firmly rooted in those districts (e.g., in Eastern Europe) where the study of the Talmud and the casuistry it engendered were universal. The effect it had on the commerce of the Jew has been described by Graetz, surely no prejudiced witness.

> To twist a phrase out of its meaning, to use all the tricks of the clever advocate, to play upon words, and to condemn what they did not know...such were the characteristics of the Polish Jew....Honesty and right-thinking he lost as completely as simplicity and truthfulness. He made himself master of all the gymnastics of the Schools and applied them to obtain advantage over any one less cunning than himself. He took a delight in cheating and overreaching, which gave him a sort of joy of victory. But his own people he could not treat in this way: they were as knowing as he. It was the non-Jew who, to his loss, felt the consequences of the Talmudically trained mind of the Polish Jew.[76]

In the second place, the differential treatment of non-Jews in Jewish commercial law resulted in the complete transformation of the idea of commerce and industry generally in the direction of more freedom. If we have called the Jews the Fathers of Free Trade, and therefore the pioneers of capitalism, let us note here that they were prepared for this rôle by the free-trading spirit of the commercial and industrial law, which received an enormous impetus towards a policy of *laissez-faire* by its attitude towards strangers. Clearly, intercourse with strangers could not but loosen the bonds of personal duties and replace them by economic freedom. Let us glance at this in greater detail.

The theory of price in the Talmud and the Codes, in so far as it affected trade between Jew and non-Jew, is exactly parallel to the scholastic doctrine of *justum pretium* which was prevalent in Europe throughout the Middle Ages. But as between Jew and non-Jew, there was no just price. Price was formed as it is today, by "the higgling of the market."[77]

Be that as it may, the important thing to observe is that already in the Talmud, and still more distinctly in the *Shulchan Aruch*, conceptions of the freedom of industry and enterprise, so entirely alien to the Christian law of Mediæval Europe, are met with. It is a subject deserving of close study and should be taken up by a specialist. For my part, I can do no more here than refer to a few instances. But few though they be, they seem to me to be conclusive evidence on the point in question. My first reference is to a passage in the Talmud which fully recognizes free competition among sellers.

Mishna.—R. Judah was of opinion that a shopkeeper should not distribute nuts among children, because by so doing he gets them into the habit of coming to him. But the Rabbis allow it. Moreover, it is not lawful to spoil prices. But the Rabbis say, "Blessed be his memory."

Gemara.—The question at once arises, what was the reason for the attitude of the Rabbis in the first case? The answer is that the shopkeeper may say to his competitor, "I give the children nuts, you can give them plums." And what is the reason of the Rabbis in the second case? The Mishna forbids price alteration, and yet they say, "Blessed be his memory." The answer is, they bless his memory because he reduces prices (*Baba Mezia*, 60*a* and *b*).

In the Codes the reasons have been omitted, and the dry statement of law only is found.

> A shopkeeper is allowed to make presents of nuts and other things to the children who come to purchase in his shop, in order to win their custom. Moreover, he may sell at a price below the current one, and the competing tradesmen can do nothing (*Choshen Mishpat*, 225, §18).

Similarly, in the laws regulating the conduct of traders who bring their goods to the market town, the following may be read:

> Should the strangers sell more cheaply than the native dealers, or should their goods be of a better quality, the natives may not prevent them, for the Jewish public derives benefit therefrom (*Choshen Mishpat*, 156, §7).

Once more.

> If a Jew is prepared to lend money to a non-Jew at a lower rate of interest than some one else, the latter can do nothing against it (*Choshen Mishpat*, 156, §5).

Finally, Jewish law favours industrial *laissez-faire*. So we find in the *Shulchan Aruch*:

> If any one commenced a handicraft in his street and none of his neighbours protested, and then one of the other residents in the street wishes to carry on the same calling, the first may not complain that the new-comer is taking the bread out of his mouth, and try to prevent him (*Choshen Mishpat*, 156 §5).

Clearly, then, free trade and industrial freedom were in accordance with Jewish law, and therefore in accordance with God's will. What a mighty motive power in economic life!

Judaism and Puritanism

I have already mentioned that Max Weber's study of the importance of Puritanism for the capitalistic system was the impetus that sent me to consider the importance of the Jew, especially as I felt that the dominating ideas of Puritanism which were so powerful in capitalism were more perfectly developed in Judaism, and were also of course of much earlier date.

A complete comparison of the two "isms" is not within my province here. But I believe that if it were made, it would be seen that there is an almost unique identity of view between Judaism and Puritanism, at least, on those points which we have investigated. In both will be found the preponderance of religious interest, the idea of divine rewards and punishments, asceticism *within* the world, the close relationship between religion and business, the arithmetical conception of sin, and, above all, the rationalization of life.

Let me refer to an instance or two. Take the attitude of Judaism and Puritanism to the problem of sex. In one of the best hotels of Philadelphia I found a notice in my room to this effect: "Visitors who may have to transact business with ladies are respectfully requested to leave the door of their room open while the lady is with them." What is this but the old dictum of the Talmud (*Kiddushin*, 82*a*), "Hast thou business with women? See to it that thou art not with them alone"?

Again, is not the English Sunday the Jewish Sabbath?

I would also recall the words of Heine,[78] who had a clear insight into most things. "Are not," he asks in his *Confessions*, "Are not the Protestant Scots Hebrews, with their Biblical names, their Jerusalem, pharisaistic cant? And is not their religion a Judaism which allows you to eat pork?"

Puritanism *is* Judaism.

Whether the first was influenced by the second, and if so, how, are most difficult questions to answer. It is well known, of course, that in the Reformation period there was close intercourse between Jews and certain Christian sects, that the study of Hebrew and the Hebrew Scriptures became fashionable, and that the Jews in England in the seventeenth century were held in very high esteem by the Puritans. Leading men in England like Oliver Cromwell built up their religious views on the Old Testament, and Cromwell himself dreamed of a reconciliation between the Old and the New Testaments, and of a confederation between the Chosen People of God and the Puritan English. A Puritan preacher of the day, Nathaniel Holmes by name, wished for nothing better than, in accordance with the letter of the prophetic message, to become a servant of God's people and to serve them on bended knee. Public life became Hebraic in tone no less than the sermons in churches. And if only speeches in parliament had been in Hebrew, you might have believed yourself in Palestine. The "Levellers," who called themselves "Jews" (in opposition to their opponents whom they termed "Amalekites"), advocated the adoption of the Torah as the norm of English legislation. Cromwell's officers suggested to him to appoint seventy members of his Privy Council according to the number of the members of the Synhedrin. To the

Parliament of 1653 General Thomas Harrison, the Anabaptist, was returned, and he and his party clamoured for the introduction of the Mosaic legislation into England. In 1649 it was moved in the House of Commons that the Lord's Day should be observed on Saturday instead of on Sunday. On the banners of the victorious Puritans was inscribed "The Lion of Judah."[79] It is significant that not only the Bible, but the Rabbinical literature as well, was extensively read in large circles of the clergy and laity.

Altogether, then, there appears to be sufficient evidence for the deduction of Puritan doctrines from Jewish sources. The specialists must decide. Here I have been able to do no more than give a hint or two. And in conclusion I would draw attention to a little humorous publication, which appeared in the year 1608 and the contents of which would seem to demonstrate the close connexion between Judaism and Calvinism (which is only Puritanism). It is called, *Der Calvinische Judenspiegel* (the Calvinistic Jewish Mirror), and on page 33 a comparison is drawn between the two religions in the following droll fashion. [The old German is delightful.]

> If I am to say on my honour why I am become a Calvinist, I shall have to confess that the one and only reason which persuaded me was that among all the religions I could find none which agreed so much with Judaism, and its view of life and faith. (Here follow a number of parallel statements, partly serious and partly satirical.) 8. The Jews hate the name of Mary and tolerate her only when she is made of gold and silver, or when her image is impressed on coins. So do we. We too like Mary farthings and crowns, to which we pay all due respect, for they are useful in business. 9. The Jews everywhere are at pains to cheat the people. So are we. For that very reason we left our country to wander in other lands where we are not known in our true colours, so that by our deceit and cunning...we might lead astray the ignorant yokels, cheat them and bring them to us...

Notes

1. M. Lazarus, *Ethik des Judentums* (1904), pp. 67, 85, etc. [There is an English edition of this book issued by the Jewish Publication Society of America.]
2. Hermann Cohen, "Das Problem der jüdischen Sittenlehre. Eine Kritik (adverse) von Lazarus' Ethik des Judentums," in *Monatsschrift*, vol. 43, p. 385.
3. *Orach Chajim*, §8.
4. Quoted by F. Weber, *Altsynagogale Theologie* (1880), p. 273.
5. J. Wellhausen, *Israelitische und jüdische Geschichte*, p. 340.
6. Graetz, *Geschichte der Juden, von den ältesten Zeiten bis auf die Gegenwart*, vol. 4, p. 411. Graetz also has an excellent appreciation of the Talmud (one-sided of course, and optimistic), and its influence in Judaism.
7. J. Fromer, *Vom Ghetto zur modernen Kultur* (1906), p. 247.
8. M. Kayserling, *Columbus* (1894), ch. vi.
9. *Das Haus Rothschild*, vol. 1 (1857), p. 186.
10. This is not the place to enter into an account of the results of Biblical criticism. All I can do here is to mention a few books that may serve as an introduction to the subject: Zittel, *Die Entstehung der Bibel* (5th ed., 1891); for the history of the Pentateuch, Adalbert Merx, *Die Bücher Moses and Josua* (1907), and Ed. Meyer, *Die Entstehung des Judentums* (1896).
11. W. Frankenberg, "Die Sprüche, übersetzt und erläutert," in *Handkommentar zum Alten Testament*, herausgegeben von D.W. Nowack. On p. 16 there is a list of books for the Wisdom Literature. See also Henri Traband, *La loi mosaïque, ses origines et son développement* (1903), p. 77.
12. Cf. M. Friedländer, *Geschichte der jüdischen Apologetik* (1903).
13. Books about the Talmud form a small library in themselves. I can only mention one or two to serve as an introduction to the subject. The best is H.L. Strack's *Einleitung in den Talmud* (4th ed., 1908), which also contains a pretty full bibliography. For Talmudic Ethics, see Salo Stein's *Materialien zur Ethik des Talmud* (1904). Talmudic scholars, however, do not apprize this book very highly. A more recent book is by J. Fromer, who has occupied himself with Talmudic and later Jewish literature. See his *Die Organization des Judentums* (1908), which is intended to serve as an Introduction to a big Encyclopedic Dictionary of the Talmud, which Fromer has planned. Another book which deals with the sources is E. Schürer, *Geschichte des jüdischen Volkes im Zeitalter Jesu Christi*, in 3 vols. The first (2nd ed. 1890) in §3 contains an extensive bibliography. In addition, the standard Jewish histories, especially Graetz, deal with this aspect of Jewish Literature.

    To comprehend the spirit of the Talmud it is necessary to read the text itself. There is a German translation (almost complete) by Lazarus Goldschmidt. The Talmud has this characteristic: that although the sections follow each other in some fixed order, yet not one of them is strictly limited as regards its subject matter. They all deal with practically the whole field of Talmudic subjects. Hence by studying one or more of the (63) Tractates, it is comparatively easy to obtain a fair notion of the contents of the whole, and certainly, to find one's way about in the great sea. Specially to be recommended is the Tractate *Baba Mezia* and its two sister tractates [*Baba Kama* and *Baba Bathra*]. There is a good edition of *Baba Mezia*, with an introduction and a translation by Dr. Sammter (1876).

A special branch of Talmudic literature is composed of the so-called "Minor Tractates," usually found in an appendix to the Talmud, though often published separately. These are *Derech Erez Rabba* (third century), *Aboth, Aboth de R. Nathan, Derech Erez Zutta* (ninth century, according to Zunz). Zunz calls them Ethical *Hagadoth* because of their obvious intention of teaching practical wisdom. They have had no small influence on the development of the Jewish people and are therefore of great interest to us here. Next to the Bible, these tractates enjoyed a widespread popularity. They formed the principal reading of the layman, unacquainted with the Talmud. They were (are) found in Prayer Books and devotional literature. Some of them have been issued in German translations. *R. Nathan's System der Ethik und Moral*, translated by Kaim Pollock (1905); *Derech Erez Zutta*, translated by A. Tawrogi (1885); *Derech Erez Rabba*, translated by M. Goldberg (1888). We must also mention the *Tosephta*, which contains the teaching not included in the *Mishna*. This also dates from the period of the *Tanaim* and is arranged like the *Mishna*.

Finally, a word as to the Rabbinical commentaries or *Midrashim*, which are partly *halachic* [i.e., legal] and partly *hagadic* [i.e., moral and edifying]. The oldest of them, mostly *halachic*, are *Mechilta* (on Exodus), *Siphra* (on Leviticus), and *Siphre* (on Numbers and Deuteronomy).

The *Targumim* are the Aramaic translations of the O.T.

14. There is no good translation of the *Shulchan Aruch*. The only available one is by Löwe (1837), which is incomplete and one-sided. On the other hand, the *Orach Chajim* and the *Jore Deah* have been published in a German dress by Rabbi P. Lederer (1906 and 1900), but not in a complete form.

    As for works on the *Shulchan Aruch*, they are mostly of the nature of apologetic pamphlets. Anti-Semites have turned to the S.A. for material to attack Jews and Judaism; and Jewish scholars have naturally replied. We may mention, for instance, A. Lewin, *Der Judenspiegel des Dr. Justus* (1884), and D. Hoffmann, *Der Schulchan Aruch und die Rabbiner über das Verhältniss der Juden zu Andersgläubigen* (1885). Thus there is no subjective treatment of the *Shulchan Aruch*, though it deserves as thorough a consideration as the Talmud. The only strictly scientific book with which I am acquainted and which should be mentioned in this connexion is S. Bäck's *Die religionsgeschichtliche Literatur der Juden in dem Zeitraume vom 15–18 Jahrhundert* (1893), reprinted from Winter and Wünsche, *Die jüdische Literatur seit Abschluss des Kanons*, vol. 2. But Bäck's book is not big and his treatment therefore can only be of the nature of a sketch.
15. Paul Volz, *Jüdische Eschatologie von Daniel bis Akiba* (1903).
16. Fürst, *Untersuchungen über den Kanon des Alten Testaments nach den Überlieferungen in Talmud und Midrasch* (1868).
17. L. Stern, *Die Vorschriften der Thora, welche Israel in der Zerstreuung zu beobachten hat. Ein Lehrbuch der Religion für Schule und Familie* (4th ed., 1904), p. 28. This book, which may be looked upon as a type, gives the view current in strictly orthodox circles.
18. Cf. Rabbi S. Mandl, *Das Wesen des Judentums* (1904), p. 14. Mandl relies on J. Gutmann, *Über Dogmenbildung und Judentum* (1894). Cf. also S. Schechter, "The Dogmas of Judaism," in J.Q.R., vol. 1 (1889), pp. 48, 115. As is well

known, Moses Mendelsohn was the first to express (in his *Jerusalem*) the idea that Judaism has no dogmas, with some degree of insistence.
19. The best that I am acquainted with is Ferdinand Weber's *System der altsynagogalen palästinensischen Theologie aus Targum, Midrash und Talmud* (1880).
20. Stern, *op. cit.*, p. 5.
21. Döllinger, *Heidentum und Judentum* (1857), p. 634.
22. Rutilius Namatianus, "De reditu suo," in Reinach's *Textes d'auteurs grecs et romains relatifs au judaisme*, vol. 1 (1895), p. 358.
23. Stern, *op. cit.*, p. 49; S.R. Hirsch, *Versuche über Jissroëls Pflichten in der Zerstreuung* (4th ed., 1909), §711.
24. Cf. Weber, *op. cit.*, p. 49. Weber has worked out this idea of contract in Judaism better than any other writer. The treatment in the text owes much to him as will be apparent. I have also utilized his references. In this particular instance, cf. *Sifre*, 12*b*. *Wajjikra Rabba*, ch. 31.
25. *Aboth*. II, near the beginning.
26. Cf. Weber, *op. cit.*, pp. 270, 272.
27. *Ibid*., p. 292.
28. R. Joseph Albo, *Ikkarim*, a book on the principles of Judaism, dating from the fifteenth century. W. and L. Schlesinger have issued a German translation [of the Hebrew] (1844). This particular problem is dealt with in ch. 46.
29. S.R. Hirsch, *op. cit.*, ch. 13, especially §§100 and 105.
30. J.F. Schröder, *Talmuldisch-rabbinisches Judentum* (1851), p. 47.
31. Graetz, vol. 2, p. 203 and note 14; J. Bergmann, *Jüdische Apologetik im neutestamentlichen Zeitalter* (1908), p. 120. For the spirit of ancient Judaism, see Wellhausen, *op. cit.*, ch. 15.
32. H. Deutsch, *Die Sprüche Salomons nach der Auffassung in Talmud und Midrasch* (1885).
33. J.F. Bruch, *Weisheitslehre der Hebräer* (1851), p. 135.
34. Rabbi S. Schiffer, *Das Buch Kohelet. Nach der Auffassung er Weisen des Talmud und Midrasch* (1884).
35. Cf. Graetz, vol. 4, p. 233; Wellhausen, *op. cit.*, pp. 250, 339: and also the well-known works of Müller, Schürer, and Marti.
36. Mandl, *op. cit.*, p. 14.
37. S.R. Hirsch, *op. cit.*, §448.
38. A number of similar extracts from Talmudic literature will be found in S. Schaffer, *Das Recht und seine Stellung zur Moral nach talmudischer Sitten- und Rechtslehre* (1889), p. 28.
39. M. Lazarus, *op. cit.*, p. 22. Lazarus has worked out the idea that to be holy means to overcome your passions, exceedingly well, though he approaches very closely to Kant's system of Ethics.
40. *Kiddushin, 30b, aba Bathra, 16a.*
41. Cf. Schaffer, *op. cit.*, p. 54.
42. Cf. Fassel, *Tugend- und Rechtslehre des Talmud* (1848), p. 38.
43. Albo's *Ikkarim* [note 28], ch. 24, deals fully with this.
44. Cf. S. Bäck, *op. cit.*, Preface; also M. Lazarus, *op. cit.,* p. 20.
45. Stern, *op. cit.*, p. 126.
46. *Aboth de R. Nathan*, xxi.5 [also *Aboth*, III, 14].
47. G.F. Oehler, *Tehologie des A.T.* (3rd ed., 1891), p. 878.

48. Lazarus, *op. cit.*, p. 40.
49. *Aboth de R. Nathan*, xvi.6.
50. Cf. Eccles. 1.8; Prov. x.8; x.10; x.31; xiv.23; xvii.27,28; sviii.7,21; xxi.23, Ecclus. iv.34(29); v.15(13); ix.25(18); six.20,22.
51. Stern, *op.cit.*, No. 127*a*
52. Cf. also Prov. xii.27; xiii.11; xviii.19; xxi.20. For further passages in praise of labor, cf. L.K. Amitai, *La sociologie selon la lègislation juive* (1905), p. 90.
53. Hirsch, *op. cit.*, §448.
54. *Ibid.*, §463; and Stern, *op. cit.*, p. 239.
55. Hirsch, *op. cit.*, §443, almost identically expressed by Stern, *op. cit.*, Nos 125, 126.
56. J. Fromer, *op. cit.*, p. 25.
57. *Iggeret ha-Kodesh*, first published in 1556; translated into Latin by Gaffareli; cf. Graetz, vol. 7, p. 46.
58. Hirsh, *op. cit.*, §263. Cf. also §264, §267.
59. The figures are taken from Hugo Nathansohn, "Die unehelichen Geburten bei den Juden," in Z.D.S.J., vol. 6 (1910), p. 102.
60. We may mention as one of the foremost authorities S. Freud. See his *Sammlung kleiner Schriften zur Neurosenlehre* (2nd series, 1909).
61. See Dr. Hoppe, "Die Kriminalität der Juden und der Alkohol," in Z.D.S.J., vol. 3 (1907) p. 38; H.L. Eisenstädt, "Die Renaissance der jüdischen Sozialhygiene," in *Archiv für Rassen- und Gesellschaftsbiologie*, vol. 5 (1908), p. 714; L. Cheinisee, "Die Rassenpathologie und der Alkoholismus bei den Juden," in Z.D.S.J., vol. 6 (1910), p. 1. It can be proved with great certainty that the Jew's freedom from the evil effects of alcohol (as also from syphilis) is due to his religion.
62. Wellhausen, *op. cit.*, p. 119.
63. Cicero, *Pro Flacco*, ch. 28.
64. Mommsen, *Römische Geschichte*, vol. 5, p. 545.
65. The passages may be found in Felix Stähelin, *Der Antisemitismus des Altertums* (1905). Cf. Reinach, *op. cit.*
66. J. Bergmann, *op. cit.*, p. 157.
67. Graetz, vol. 5, p. 73.
68. Graetz, vol. 5, p. 321.
69. Graetz, vol. 6, pp. 140, 161.
70. A comprehensive account of laws on interest in the old Jewish legal system will be found in J. Heicl, Das *alttestamentliche Zinsverbot* (*Biblische Studien*, herausgegeben von O. Bardenhewer, vol. 12, No. 4, 1907).
71. Cf. a collection of "Responsa" by Hoffmann, in *Schmollers Forschungen*, vol. 152.
72. Cf. Fassel, *op. cit.*, p. 139; E. Grünebaum, *Die Sittenlehre der Juden andern Bekenntnissen gegenüber* (2nd ed., 1878), p. 414; the same writer's "Der Fremde nach rabbinischen Begriffen" in *Eigers jüdische Zeitschrift*, vols 9 and 10; D. Hoffmann, *op. cit.*, p. 129; Lazarus, *op. cit.*, §144. Lazarus is curiously incomplete. What he says in his third chapter about the duty of Israel towards non-Jews does his heart all credit, but it is hardly in accord with historic truth.
73. Cf. *Choshen Mishpat*, §§188, 194, 227, 231, 259, 266, 272, 283, 348, 389, etc.
74. "When he appears before the divine Judge, the first question that man is asked is, Have you been straightforward and honest in business?" *Sabbath*, 31*a*. This

Talmudic quotation is the motto of a little book (privately printed) dealing with passages concerning honesty. Das *Biblisch-rabbinische Handelsgesetz*, by Rabbi Stark.

75. *Choshen Mishpat*, §231. The passage given in the text is from §227.
76. Graetz, vol. 10, pp. 62, 81.
77. *Choshen Mishpat*, §227; *Baba Mezia,* 49*b*.
78. In addition, see John G. Dow, "Hebrew and Puritan," in J.Q.R., vol. 3 (1891), p. 52.
79. Graetz, vol. 9, pp. 86, 213; vol. 10, p. 87; Hyamson, p. 164; J.Q.R., vol. 3, p. 61.

III

The Culture of Economic Phenomena and the Economy of Cultural Processes

6

The City

Sources And Literature

I am unacquainted with any literature on the history of the city which could be used in connection with our study. A great many writings dealing with the history of individual cities are at best mere histories of municipal law or of monuments. The economic and cultural points of view are almost never taken into consideration. It would hardly be of use, then, to cite these books here.

The material presented in the following pages on the origin and the organization of the early capitalistic city has been compiled almost entirely from original sources. Travel books and descriptions of other kinds take first place among the sources used. Needless to say that Mercier's *Tableau de Paris* (1781), 12 vols, has no counterpart for any city. Still, we find reasonably accurate information about London in the seventeenth and eighteenth centuries in the descriptions by Defoe-Richardson, Miege-Bolton, Archenholtz, etc.

The sources for Naples in the sixteenth century are to be found in E. Gothein, *Culturentwicklung Süd-Italiens* (Breslau, 1886); Naples in the eighteenth century is described in *Essai sur la société et les moeurs des Italiens* (1782), Letter LV, *et seq*.

With regard to Madrid in the seventeenth century, some travel journals and the memoirs of Mme d'Aulnoy[1] are adequate for our purposes. (Cf. also, Karl Justi, *Diego Velasquez und sein Jahrhundert* [Bonn, 1888]; English tr., *David Velasquez and His Time* [London, 1889].)

The Cities in the Sixteenth, Seventeenth, and Eighteenth Centuries

One of the most significant events in the whole history of our civilization (which is essentially a result of the processes described in the preceding chapter) is the rapid increase in population of a number of towns at the beginning of the sixteenth century. The product of this development is the city with a population running to six figures. Toward the end of the eighteenth century this type of city, exemplified by London and Paris, comes close to the modern metropolis.

During the sixteenth century the number of cities with 100,000 inhabitants and over increased to thirteen or fourteen.[2]

The first group to be considered are the Italian cities: Venice (1563: 168,627; 1575–77: 195,863), Naples (240,000), Milan (about 200,000), Palermo (1600: about 100,000), and Rome (1600: about 100,000). On the other hand, Florence, in 1530, had a population of only 60,000.

The next are the Spanish-Portuguese cities: Lisbon (1629: 110,800) and Seville (at the end of the sixteenth century it had 18,000 households representing a population of about 100,000), and the cities of the Netherlands: Antwerp (1560: 104,972) and Amsterdam (1622: 104,961).

Let us finally consider Paris and London. Paris, against whose expansion royal edicts had already been issued by the middle of the sixteenth century (I shall revert to them presently) obviously decreased in population because of the religious wars; in 1594 the population of Paris was about 180,000. London grew rapidly and by the end of the sixteenth century exhibited all the signs of an overpopulated city, as we may gather from a decree by Queen Elizabeth in 1602.[3] We must place its population for that period at about 250,000.

During the seventeenth century a few of the formerly large cities decreased in population. Lisbon and Antwerp fell below the 100,000 mark, and the population of Milan and Venice likewise shrank considerably. On the other hand, Vienna (1720: 130,000) and Madrid grew into big cities.

Rome, Amsterdam, Paris, and London continued to expand. Rome had a population of 140,000 at the end of the seventeenth century; Amsterdam, one of 200,000. At the same time, Paris reached half a million, while London, in 1700, exceeded this mark with 674,350.

While London grew only gradually during that century, Paris developed more rapidly, particularly in the reign of the first two Bourbons. Now we frequently meet with those odd edicts, to which I have referred above, forbidding the erection of new houses with a view to checking the growth of the city. They usually begin with phrases like "Whereas the increase in size of our good city of Paris is highly prejudicial," or "Whereas it has been the intention of His Majesty that the city of Paris be of a fixed and limited size..." (These prohibitive edicts express a spirit kindred to that of the guilds of the Middle Ages: opposition to an unrestrained growth of an organic structure, opposition to the tendency to unrestrained expansion and quantification inherent in the capitalistic system, opposition of the old frugality, and conservatism to the boundless urge to expand inherent in the commercial spirit.)

As might have been expected, these prohibitions proved useless. In spite of their reiteration (1627, 1637), Paris kept on growing mightily during these very decades. Baudrillart, a judicious historian, holds that there is a greater difference between the Paris of Louis XIII and that of the League than between the Paris of the League and that of the Third Republic. The awareness of contemporaries of this change is expressed by Corneille in his comedy, *Le Menteur*, written in 1642 (II:5):

> Tout un ville entière, avec pompe bâtie
> Semble d'un vieux fossé par miracle sortie
> Et nous fait présumer, à ses superbes toits,
> Que tous ses habitants sort des dieux ou des rois.

The eighteenth century brought the following changes: The 200,000 mark in population was passed by Moscow, St. Petersburg, *Vienna,*

* An asterisk before the name of a city in the text indicates that the relevant figures are taken from the article by Inama-Sternegg in *Handwörterbuch der Staatswissenschaften*.

*Palermo (1795: 200,162), with Dublin not far behind (1798: 182,370, as against 8,159 in 1644 and 128,870 in 1753).

The 100,000 mark was reached by Hamburg, Copenhagen, Warsaw; Berlin, and *Lyon grew to 141,283 (1783) and 135,207 (1787), respectively.

*Naples approached the half-million mark (1796: 435,930), London the million mark (864,845 according to the census of 1801), while *Paris had a population of between 640,000 and 670,000 at the outbreak of the Revolution.

Origin and Inner Structure of the Cities

When we inquire into the reasons for the gigantic growth of these cities we discover the same kind of city-building factors at work which we have found in the growth of the towns in the Middle Ages. Moreover, this is worth noting—the large cities of the early capitalistic epoch are basically consumer cities. The most important consumers are familiar to us; the princes, prelates, and nobles, who are now joined by a new group, "haute finance" (which may be regarded as a class of consumers without disparaging its "productive" function in the politico-economic organization). The largest cities have attained that degree of expansion because they were the residence of the largest number of great consumers. Hence, the expansion of the cities is essentially due to a concentration of consumption in the urban centers of a given country.

The correctness of this view can be proved negatively by pointing out that the "producers," commerce and industry, were unable to develop the cities in which they were situated beyond mere middle size.

Purely commercial cities as, for example, Bristol, which a traveler, about the middle of the eighteenth century, called the "largest, most populous and flourishing place in the island, and one of the principal cities in Europa,"[4] or the other flourishing commercial cities of England at that period, Exeter, Lynn, Norwich, Yarmouth, etc. numbered no more than 30,000 to 40,000 inhabitants when London had long passed the half-million mark. In general, industry had no inherent ability to develop large cities. The industrial centers of the eighteenth century, the mining cities or the centers of the household industries, like Newcastle, Glasgow, Leeds, Manchester, and Birmingham in

England; Iserlohn, Paderborn, Jauer, and Hirschberg in Germany, are middle-sized or smaller cities. Neither Great Britain nor Germany, with the exception of their capitals, could boast of a city with a larger population than 100,000 before the end of the eighteenth century.

When we closely examine the so-called commercial cities, for instance, Amsterdam or Hamburg, it is not long before we discover that they owe their rise to city status to forces other than trade. Hence, we can name but one commercial town which, prior to the nineteenth century, had risen to the rank of a city: Lyon, the site of the greatest luxury industry of the early capitalistic epoch. And even in the case of Lyon, banking activities probably have played an important part in the growth of the city.

It will now be easy to show conclusively that it was the concentration of consumption which brought about the early development of the cities. Such a development occurred everywhere under the pressure of a germinating capitalistic system, irrespective of the peculiar character of the country.

Using the most important cities of the seventeenth and eighteenth centuries as illustrations, I shall proceed now to test my assertion.

1. Berlin is the model of the purely residential city, in which only the court, the government official, and the military appear as urbanizing factors. The first signs of an accelerated rate of growth appeared in the latter half of the eighteenth century; it was not until the beginning of the 1760s that its population passed the 100,000 mark. But even at the end of the eighteenth century, Berlin was almost exclusively a city of soldiers and officials and, consequently, of necessity a poor city. In 1783 the garrison, including the families of officers and soldiers, numbered no less than 33,088 people, or 23 percent of the total population of 141,283. (In 1895 this same group comprised 29,448 persons, or 1.8 percent of the entire population.) The state and municipal officials totaled 3,433 or, with their dependents, about 13,000. In addition to these two groups there was an extraordinarily large number of servants (10,074). These three sections of the population, and the section depending directly on the court, formed a group totaling 56,000 persons, or two-fifths of the entire population of the capital.[5] How poor these salaried employees of the king of Prussia were is evidenced by the fact that they, in turn, could give employment and homes to a group no more numerous than their own. During that period, 50,000 salaried employees in London or Paris would have fed a population from 200,000 to 300,000 at least.

2. Amsterdam, too, began as the residence of a prince. We gather this from the fact that the departure of the court toward the end of the seventeenth century resulted in great losses in every direction.[6] The gap was soon bridged, however. Amsterdam became the home of the creditors of all European states, a city which consumed the surplus of the wealthiest colonial empire of the world.

3. Venice is similar in character to Amsterdam. The extensive possessions acquired in the early colonial days of the Republic produced in due course a smug, over-wealthy class with incomes from abroad, which swelled the substantial group of land owners. A writer of the fifteenth century informs us with respect to the colonial families of Crete: "A number had accumulated large fortunes and lived in Venice on their income."[7] Nor should it be overlooked that Venice, prior to the loss of her colonies, was the capital of the third largest state in Europe. The great wealth spent in Venice was conducive to a rich, lavish life of pleasure which attracted many foreign visitors. Next to Rome, Venice was the most celebrated city in the sixteenth century: *sede principalis-sima del piacere* (principal pleasure resort), as it is described in a letter of the year 1565; *paradisus delitarum* (paradise of delights), as it is called in Hentzner's Itiinerarium (1617).[8] The greatest attractions of Venice were amusements and women.

4. Rome, in the opinion of Gregorovius, "the only metropolis" because of its physical extent, combined a multitude of important consumers of various kinds:

I. The pope, with the numerous court attendants, who relied on Peter's pence and, in most cases, on a very considerable private income.

II. The pilgrims. Two hundred thousand are said to have been in Rome in 1500.

III. The cardinals and the prelates. Cartesius de Cardinalatu estimates[9] that as early as the fifteenth century a cardinal had to have an income of 12,000 gold florins and a staff of about 140 persons. Some of the cardinals had income of 30,000 ducats, and more.[10]

IV. The relatives of the popes on whom riches were lavished. Pietro Riario, the son of Sixtus IV, drew an annuity of 60,000 gold florins.

V. The great noble families, the Orsini, Colonna, etc., who had huge estates and a correspondingly great income from ground rents.

In the period when the popes resided in Avignon, Rome threatened to decay. Cardinal Napoleone Orsini assured the French king after the death of Clement V that, through the departure of the popes, Rome was brought to the verge of ruin. In 1347, Cola di Rienzi held that Rome resembled a robbers' den rather than a habitation fit for respectable people.[11]

5. Madrid. What Rome and Venice meant to the fifteenth and sixteenth centuries, Madrid became in the seventeenth century—the Metropolis. The mightiest king on earth held court in Madrid; it was the center of the greatest empire in the world, and to it flowed all the silver treasures of America. No wonder, then, that Madrid attracted all who represented power and riches in Spain. Nothing was more keenly coveted than the honor of being received in the king's household. The court offices bestowed by the king were the especial goal of the younger sons of the nobility. It is fairly easy to trace the growing importance of Madrid to the congregation of the great of the country in that city, particularly since the accession of Phillip III. "The rural districts," we learn from a contemporary, "are being abandoned by the rich notables."[12] It also seems that Madrid, next to Rome, was the first modern city to have an appreciable influx of pleasure-bent foreign visitors. For this reason Madrid was called "the noble inn of foreigners."[13]

6. Naples. If Madrid, in the seventeenth century, was the third, or perhaps the second, largest city in Europe (it is estimated to have had 400,000 inhabitants at the height of its glory), Naples now grew so rapidly that during the following century it ranked immediately behind London and Paris.

Naples is a textbook example of the vindication of the thesis advanced here, namely, that the early development of the cities is based on the concentration of consumption in them. Naples was never anything but the residence of a prince. It owes its status as a city to this circumstance and to the fact that it was the capital of Italy's first unified state, possessing a centralized administration and judiciary.

The greatness and wealth of Naples flowed from two sources: the royal court and the church. These facts were well recognized in their time. "*Regis servitum nostra mercatura est*" (Serving the king is our business), says Caracciolo, in whose writings we see mirrored the social structure of Naples. Indeed, the number of offices in Naples was infinitely large, for centralization led to hypertrophy of offices. The payment of fees was worked out as a system, which was likewise recognized by contemporaries as an essential source of income. An observer moving in the higher strata of Naples' society must have gained the impression that there was hardly anything besides the "unlimited number of jurists, lawyers and clerks" (Folieta). With the definite establishment of Spanish rule, Caracciolo at once notes the wane of that influence which had been exerted by the court. The king is now far away, he says, and the city is declining. The barons have given up their large retinues, and, in consequence, public life has lost rhythm and brilliance. No longer does anyone here display princely splendor. The city loses its population, rents are falling, and all merely because Naples has ceased to be the residence of the king.

Later, everything changes again. Naples had another period of prosperity under Spanish rule. When the nobility resumed its lavish mode of life, Naples witnessed a greater pomp than ever before and the population again increased rapidly.[14]

7. Paris. When Lavoisier, the founder of modern chemistry, dedicated his not inconsiderable faculties to the "public good" and fought in the National Assembly for the fiscal reform of France, he made an extremely interesting calculation in order to ascertain the quantity and value of the goods brought into Paris for local consumption. His very accurate computations disclose that every year the people of Paris bought necessities worth 260,000,000 livres for themselves, and feed worth 10,000,000 livres for their horses. Of course, all this had to be paid for. The answer which Lavoisier gives to the question as to the sources from which the 250,000,000 livres were paid interests us because it contains a remarkable estimate of the composition of the population of Paris at the outbreak of the Revolution. The answer, after eliminating certain obviously erroneous statements which crept into Lavoisier's computations, presents the following picture.[15]

Export industries and trade brought in about 20,000,000 livres; 140,000,000 livres constituted the share of Paris in the interest paid on the public debt (*revenu des intérêts et dépenses payé par le trésor public*); 100,000,000 livres represented ground rents and profits from industries outside of Paris spent in the city (*revenu des propriétaires de terre, de biens ruraux et de manufactures*). Brilliant indeed! What depth of insight and comprehension! Paris, with a negligible exception, is revealed as purely a consumers' city which drew its livelihood from the court, the officials, the public creditors, and the receivers of ground rents.

The same idea is advanced by all well-informed contemporaries. And in the absence of statistical material we must, to our regret, depend on their statement for the correctness of our opinion.

Mirabeau the Elder, the author of *L'Ami des hommes*, estimated that the population of Paris would be reduced by about 200,000 if, in conformity with his proposal, the following persons were to be ordered back to the provinces: (1) the court officers who are drawing large salaries; (2) all the large landowners who have come to Paris to carry on their litigation before the courts. They should be made to understand that the cases could best be handled in their own rural districts, where they would enjoy greater consideration and more ease; (3) mischievous litigants.[16]

In his opinion, and that of all physiocrats, there is "a false distribution of population and wealth," for,

> all the gentlemen, all the rich people, all those who have independent incomes or pensions which enable them to live comfortably, install themselves in Paris or some other large city where they spend almost the entire interest from the bonds of the state. This spending of money attracts a host of merchants, artisans, servants and laborers.[17]

These wealthy people of independent means, with whom the "financiers who maintain a direct connection with the royal treasury..."[18] and others were associated, stimulate the growth of a highly developed and, in the opinion of the physiocrats, an overrefined luxury industry. "The landowner, a rustic when on his estate, becomes in Paris an *arbiter elegantiarum* and gives new ideas to the artisan who, thus lifted above routine work, becomes eminent in his line..."[19]

To what extent all industries and businesses thrived only on the expenditures of the wealthy, who thus become the founders of the city in the sense which we have given to this term, is again told by Mercier, in his usual incisive manner:

> How are we to help this mass of needy who have no other guarantee of livelihood than the depraved luxury of the great...

> We see in this capital men spending their whole life making toys for children; varnishing, gilding, and tufting occupies a whole army of workers; a hundred thousand are busy day and night mixing sweetmeats or making ornamental pastries. Fifty thousand other men, comb in hand, wait for the moment of awakening of those idlers who vegetate under the impression that they are alive and who make their toilet twice a day to overcome the boredom which weighs them down.[20]

In most cases the physiocrats forget to stress in their discourses the fact that a not inconsiderable portion of the population of Paris lived on the income of the Church and her servants. It is Mercier again who serves as the most valuable source on this point also:

> Paris is filled with abbés, tonsured clerics, serving neither Church nor State, who lie in continuous idleness, whiling away their time with futility and inanities ... In many a house we find an abbé who is called 'friend of the family' but is only simple valet in charge of servants ... Then come the tutors who are also abbés...[21]

> The bishops violate without much concern the residence laws and leave the posts assigned to them by the holy canons. Boredom drives them from their dioceses which they look upon as places of exile. Most of them come to Paris to enjoy their wealth.[22]

We are indebted to the same authority for the only reliable account of the various strata which made up the population of Paris at the end of the early capitalistic period. In conclusion, I shall present the survey furnished by Mercier. In order to bring out the picture in sharper relief, and also for the sake of greater clarity, I shall reproduce the survey in schematic form.

Paris has eight distinct classes of inhabitants:

1. Prince and nobles
2. Gentlemen of the robe
    a. bar
    b. church
    c. medical profession
3. Financiers, from the farmer-general to those who lent money on estates; the stockbrokers, those new vultures, occupying the center of this predatory brotherhood, despicable and despised
4. Business men or merchants, living exclusively on the great, who, being gentlemen, never buy anything for cash, and are obliged to humiliate themselves daily before them or their servants

5. Artists
   - Painters, Architects, Sculptors } inferior rank
   - Music composers, ranking high
   - Men of letters, ranking highest, the *nobilitas literata*
6. *Artisans, wealthy artisans deriving their comfort* exclusively from the work performed for the wealthy (as I have shown elsewhere)
7. Laborers
8. Servants
9. Populace

(There are nine classes for all?!)

Above all there are also a great number of unproductive people, such as the monks performing religious services in private chapels; and so many nobles, court clerks, bailiffs, constables, attorneys' clerks, armed guards, beadles, people of independent means, coachmen, postilions, grooms, and, moreover, the foreigners who come to Paris in droves.[23]

8. London. A great royal court, surrounded since the end of the sixteenth century by a circle of feudal lords spending their income there, is still the core of London when we enter the seventeenth century. We sense the power of attraction of the capital for the nobility and gentry in the seventeenth century from the numerous decrees issued—strangely enough, by the first two Stuarts—against the tendency of country gentlemen to reside in London. One of these decrees, from the year 1632, runs as follows:

> The King's Most Excellent Majesty hath observed, That of late yeares a great number of the Nobility and Gentry, and abler sort of his People with their Families have resorted to the Citties of London and Westminster, and places adjoyning, and there made their Residence more then in former tymes...by their Residence in the said Citties and Parts adjoyning, they have not imployment but live without doing any Service to his Majesty or his People, a great part of their Money and Substance is drawn from the severall Countries whence it ariseth, and is spent in the Citty in excess of Apparell provided from forraigne parts ... and of the great Numbers of loose and idle People, that follow them and live in and about the said Citties, the disorder there groweth so great...[24]

However, these residence prohibitions suffered the fate of all decrees that purport to drive the river upstream; they were simply disregarded. During that century the migration of landowners to

London must have taken place with increasing frequency. This movement was the chief factor in the growth of London in the seventeenth century, for at the turn of the following century, London was described as "the might Rendez-vous of Nobility, Gentry, Courtiers, Divines, Lawyers, Physicians, Merchants, Seamen and all kind of excellent Artificers of the most refined Wits and the most excellent Beauties."[25]

Since the end of the seventeenth century and the beginning of the eighteenth century, a new element appeared as a city builder, the creditors of the state and the big financiers. As early as the seventeenth century, London had a well-established banking business. What great amounts of cash could be mobilized on short notice is demonstrated, for instance, by the fact that the subscription of the capital stock of the Bank of England (£1,200,900) was completed between June 21 and July 2, 1694. D. Hume recognizes, with profound acumen, the power of the state debts to promote the growth of the city: "...[Our] national debts cause a mighty confluence of the people and riches to the capital, by the great sums levied in the provinces to pay the interest [on these debts]."[26]

In the middle of the seventeenth century we find society still living in the city, as evidenced by the complaints of city ladies with sensitive olfactory nerves about the nuisance of coal smoke (coal was then beginning to be widely used): "O Husband wee shall never bee well, wee nor our children while wee live in the smell of this Cities Sea-coale smoke."[27]

This period inaugurates the transfer of the mansions of the nobility to the suburbs. Bolton, who continued the work of Guy Miege, has left us a vivid picture of this process of transformation which the city of London underwent in the middle of the eighteenth century. "The Nobility and chief among the Gentry are at this time much better accommodated in fine Squares and Streets where they breath a good Air and have Houses built after the modern way." He lists a great number of these new houses. We also conclude from his descriptions that the character of elegant London was, in his time, still determined by the establishments of the gentry.[28] The nobility was living at that time in the immediate vicinity of London. Defoe counts seventeen localities in the outskirts of London, "all crowded and surrounded with fine houses or rather palaces of the nobility and gentry of England."[29]

In attempting statistically to ascertain the part played by the several urbanizing elements of the population in the development of London in the eighteenth century, I have sought to do for that city what Lavoisier has similarly done for Paris, although by quite a different method. The conclusions arrived at by me naturally make no claim to absolute accuracy. Undoubtedly, however, they gain considerably in credibility by the fact that the components calculated closely approximate those given for Paris by Lavoisier. The apparent disparity exists only insofar as the turnover of trade in London exceeded that of Paris.

We can readily understand why descriptions of London, as the one by Chamberlayne, for instance, place such great emphasis on the importance of trade as a city-forming element. Trade impressed all observers as the most prominent feature of English life. Statistics, however, plainly show that trade could have supported only a small part of the population of London. In 1700, the imports and exports of England amounted to about RM 214,000,000, (about £10,500,000), a figure reached by the trade of the city of Bremen around the middle of the nineteenth century. The tonnage of incoming and outgoing vessels in all harbors of England in 1688 totaled 285,000 tons, equaling Hamburg's traffic about the year 1800, or one-fiftieth of its present volume.[30] With all due respect to the commercial greatness of London in that day, we should not uncritically accept the extravagant statements of contemporary writers who speak of the "infinite number of ships, which by their masts resemble a Forest, as they lie along this Stream" (Themas), or of the "infinite number of great wellfurnished Shops" (Chamberlayne). In order to appreciate the true part that trade shared in the development of London, we should present the following calculation.

In 1700, the imports and exports of all England amounted to not quite £11,000,000. Assuming a net profit of ten percent, which is high enough even for that period, this will give us a profit of £1,100,000. Assuming London's share to be two-thirds of the total English trade, which is certainly ample, we arrive at the round sum of £750,000 as the yearly profit of the London merchants. Considering, as King does, that in 1688 the average income of an artisan's family was £40, and that of a laborer's family £15 a year, the foregoing sum could have furnished an income for only about 7000 artisans' families and 24,000 workers' families, or 12,000 families in each category. King holds that the average number of persons in these families was three and a half or four. Hence, it is unlikely that trade could have supported much more than a population of 100,000 souls, i.e., from one-seventh to one-sixth of the total population of London at that period.

Moreover, we must not lose sight of the fact that trade transacted in London could be a factor in the promotion of the growth of the city only insofar as it was not engaged in merely supplying the needs of the population of London itself. When we deduct that portion from the total trade, the part which was operative in the growth of the city is considerably reduced.

The civil lists of the English kings of that period may serve as a basis of comparison. In 1696 Parliament granted William III a civil list of £700,000. Queen Anne received the same sum. Under George I the civil list was increased to £800,000 and under George II to £900,000 (£100,000 for the separate household of the queen). In addition to this, the prince of Wales had a private income of £100,000. Thus, the king, the queen-mother, and the heir apparent disposed of a combined income of approximately the same amount as that of all the merchants of the realm together and consequently, constituted a source of income for as large a population as that supported by the merchant class. The figures here are taken from the above-mentioned work by Miege-Bolton.[31] This work offers in an appendix ("A regular collection of series of lists containing all the offices and the whole establishment civil, military and ecclesiastical in Great Britain and Ireland"), a nearly complete roll of the salaries of the military and civil officers of the kingdom, which reveals salaries of almost incredible size, especially in the upper brackets. Not infrequently these salaries rise to £1000, £1500, and even £2000. Continuing our calculation, we find that if £2000 had to be earned as profit, such a profit, even assuming a rate of 20 percent and two complete capital turnovers a year, would have necessitated an investment of £200,000 or one-fortieth of the yearly turnover of all goods in London. If we assign the various portions, by their source of income, to the several city-forming strata, we may effect the following distribution: two-sixths of the population derive their livelihood from the king and his court, one-sixth from the officials, two-sixths from people of landed and indirect income from the state (high finance), and one-sixth from trade and industrial activities.

Theories of the City in the Eighteenth Century

The sketch of the social structure of the city in the early capitalistic epoch, which I have attempted to draw in the preceding pages, finds unequivocal corroboration in the numerous "city theories" of the eighteenth century, from which we may infer the character of the city at that time. For, although most authors believed they were describing the origin and the conditions promoting the development of the city or the metropolis, their theories are in reality only generalizations regarding the actual municipal structures accessible to their observation. For this reason I shall now, in conclusion, quote some of the most widely read and respected contemporary authorities on the theory of city growth.

Cantillon, as far as I can see, is the pioneer in this field as in so many other fields of political economy in the eighteenth century. He assigns the origin of the city to the following causes:

> If a Prince or Nobleman...fixes his residence in some pleasant spot, and several other Noblemen come to live there to be within reach of seeing each other frequently and enjoying agreeable society, this place will become a City. Great houses will be built there for the Noblemen in question, and an infinity of others for the Merchants, Artisans, and people of all sorts of professions whom the residence of these Noblemen will attract thither. For the service of these Noblemen, Bakers, Butchers, Brewers, Wine Merchants, Manufacturers of all kinds, will be needed. These will build houses in the locality or will rent houses built by others...all the little houses in a City such as we have described depend upon and subsist at the expense of the great houses....The City in question will increase still further if the King or the Government establish in it Law Courts....A Capital City is formed in the same way as a Provincial City....Thus, all the Lands in the State contribute more or less to maintain those who dwell in the Capital.[32]

A similar train of reasoning is found with minor modifications in almost all contemporary treatises on the formation of the city. This concept was developed with particular emphasis by the physiocrats, who made it the foundation of their theory, but it was also taken up by many non-orthodox physiocratic writers.

The politico-economic literature of the eighteenth century is devoted to the discussion of the most desirable way of spending incomes from ground rent. This subject is the theme of a host of pamphlets and treatises dealing with luxury, which are as characteristic of the politico-economic literature of the eighteenth century as the treatises on the subject of population.

Since this economically important portion of the national income is expended in towns and, especially, in the large cities, the problems posited by luxury and the cities soon coalesced. In almost every instance the discussions of luxury are extended to an examination of what caused the cities to become populous, to the very composition of this population, to the specific items and the distribution of the expenditures of the rich, with the resulting economic effects.

In order to ascertain the connection between theories of luxury and the city, one need only refer to Quesnay's "Questions intéressantes sur la population, l'agriculture et le commerce,"[33] which deals, in the twenty questions set forth in the section "Ville," with the nexus between city formation and economic circulation. Question XV,[34] for instance, propounds: "Are the great fortunes forming in the city not prejudicial to agriculture...does their existence not prove that they accumulate in the cities and do not return to the country?" Then in Question XVIII: "Does the restoration of the income from landed property permit the proprietors and all other people, who are able to spend lavishly, to live in the country?",[35] etc. Or, in the section "Richesse," Article VI: "Ever since the great and rich have gone to the capital, have their expenses not augmented enormously, and would one not judge therefrom that luxury has increased? Has luxury not always been a measure of the wealth of a nation?",[36] etc. Quesnay, too, bases his argumentation on Cantillon, whose brilliant treatise, in its first part, is concerned with many of the same problems. See, for example, Chapter XIV,[37] the title of which constitutes a whole program.

For comparison with the theory of Cantillon, I quote the following passage from Helvétius: "The wealth of the city has attracted pleasure seekers: the rich landowners who want to enjoy themselves leave their estates and spend several months in the city where they have mansions built for themselves. The city will grow with every day....Eventually it will become a capital."[38] We have already seen a similar view expressed by Quesnay. Wholly kindred in spirit are the arguments of Count Mirabeau.[39]

Of Italian writers, Beccaria and Filangieri should be mentioned.

> The big landowners, with their greater needs and a life more refined than the lowly and simple customs of the common people, became victims of ennui—the plague of the rich. In order to distinguish themselves from others and to assert their superiority over the working class, which are just as good as they are, they eventually had to congregate and live near one another at the sources of the law, near the highest courts of the land where, while extending the sphere of their pleasures, they extended their powers as well. This is the origin of the large cities and, in consequence of the capitals.[40]

Filangieri, likewise, attributes the formation of the city to the rich landowner:

> In that place (the city), in order to display his luxury he (the landowner) prostitutes the canvas of the painter, the chisel of the sculptor, the talent of the architect, the imagination of the poet, and all sorts of artisans. In the city he also maintains a band of idlers, more for the sake of display than for his own convenience. In the city, he eats up finally his own income as well as that of future generations.[41]

The English theory of Stuart is but a restatement of Cantillon's ideas with only this modification. Stuart recognizes as free, city-forming elements not only the landlords ("to whom this surplus [of food] directly belongs") but also the new class of financiers, i.e., people with a vested claim to the nation's income ("with a revenue in money already acquired") around whom are grouped tradesmen and artisans ("those who purchase it [their food] with their daily labor or personal service").[42]

Notes

1. Marie d'Aulnoy, *La Cour et la ville de Madrid* (Paris, 1874).
2. The figures are taken from the painstaking inquiry by F. Beloch, "Die Entwicklung der Grosstädte in Europa," published in *Comptes rendus du VIIIe Congrès International d'Hygiène et de Démographie*, pp. 55 *et seq.* The census figures of Dublin have been taken from A. Moreau de Jonnèes, *Statistique de la Grande-Bretagne…* (Paris, 1837), 1, p. 88. The last figure for London is that of the census of 1801; the figures given for Berlin are those in the compilation of Normann, cited by H.G.R. Mirabeau, *De la Monarchie prussienne* (London, 1788), 1, pp. 395 *et seq.*
3. The edict is cited in T. Rymer's *Foedera*...(London, 1726–35), 16, p. 448.
4. Daniel Defoe, *A Tour Through the Islands of Great Britain* (London, 1778), 2, p. 253.
5. Mirabeau, *op. cit.*
6. Berg, *De Refugiés in de Nederlande…* (Amsterdam, 1845), 1, pp. 269, *et seq.*

7. Gerland, "Kreta als venetianische Kolonie" (1204–1669), in *Historisches Jahrbuch* (München, 1899), 20, p. 22.
8. Cf. the descriptions of Venice in H. Simonsfeld, *Der Fondaco dei Tedeschi in Venedig...* (Stuttgart, 1887), 2, pp. 265 *et seq.*
9. Gregorovius, *Geschichte der Stadt Rom im Mittelalter* (Stuttgart 1859–72), 7, p. 236; English tr. by Annie Hamilton, *City of Rome in the Middle Ages* (London, 1900), 7, p. 247, note.
10. *Ibid.*, 8, p. 287; English tr., 8, p. 302.
11. Ludwig Pastor, *Geschichte der Päpste...* (Freiburg, i.B., 1901), 1, pp. 78 *et seq.*
12. "Conservación de monarquías y discursos." Discurso XIV, cited in L. Ranke, *Fürsten und Völker von Südeuropa* (Berlin 1837–45), 1, p. 458. Cf. K. Haebler, *Wirtschaftliche Blüte Spaniens...* (Leipzig, 1888), pp. 53, 153, 155, and *passim.*
13. Cf. the interesting description of Madrid in her Golden Age, based on good sources, which W.F. von Gleichen-Russwurm gives in *Das galante Europa...* (Stuttgart, 1910), p. 19.
14. The descriptions in E. Gothein, *op. cit.*, pp. 317 *et seq.*, pp. 342 *et seq.*, make pleasant reading. Cf. J. Burckhardt, *Die Cultur der Renaissance* (Leipzig, 1878), 2, pp. 106, 166; English tr. by S.G.C. Middlemore, *The Civilization of the Renaissance* (London, 1909), p. 371. Hippolyte a Collibus, *Incrementa urbium...* (Helmestadii, 1665), 11, p. 207.
15. L. Lavoisier, "Essai sur la population de la ville de Paris, sur sa richesse et ses consommations,'' in *Mélanges d'école politique*, ed. Daire (Paris, 1847), 1, pp. 601 *et seq.*
16. R. Mirabeau, *op. cit.* (Avignon, 1756), 2, p. 408.
17. Quesnay, "Fermiers," in *Encyclopédie*, ed. Oncken (Frankfurt and Paris, 1888), p. 1, Sq. Authors speak of the unnaturally large size of Paris as early as the sixteenth century. Cf. V.R. Mirabeau, *op. cit.*, 2, p. 408. The same applies to London in the seventeenth century. John Graunt, *Natural and Political Observations...* (London, 1662), *passim.*
18. R. Mirabeau, *op. cit.*, 2, p. 442.
19. *Ibid.*, p. 412. Cf. H. Taine, *Les Origines de la France contemporaine* (Paris, 1885), 1, p. 52, for figures on the enormous incomes of the high church and secular dignitaries. Strangely enough, the authority from whom Taine derives his information on the absenteeism of the French nobility and its gathering in Paris is none other than Arthur Young who speaks of French conditions as if conditions in England were different.
20. S. Mercier, *op. cit.*, 1, pp. 67–68.
21. *Ibid.*, Chapter XC.
22. *Ibid.*, Chapter XCI.
23. *Ibid.*, 2, pp. 39 *et seq.*, 44 *et seq.*
24. Rymer, *op. cit.*, 19, p. 374.
25. Chamberlayne, *Angliae Notitia: The Present State of England* (London, 1687), p. 200.
26. David Hume, *Essays* (London, 1882), 3, p. 364.
27. "Artificial Fire" (1644). Ms. in the British Museum, cited in W. Cunningham, *The Growth of English Industry and Commerce* (Cambridge, 1907), 2, p. 319.
28. Guy Miege, *The Present State of Great Britain and Ireland*, ed. by Bolton (London 1745), p. 101.
29. Daniel Defoe, *A Tour...*, 2, pp. 136–36.

30. See the figures in J. Goldstein, *Berufsgliederung und Reichtum* (Stuttgart, 1897), p. 143, quoting Chalmers and Price Williams.
31. *Op. cit.*, p. 236.
32. Richard Cantillon, *Essai sur la nature du commerce en général* (London, 1755), pp. 17 et seq; English tr. by Henry Higgs (London, 1931), pp. 16–17.
33. In: *Oeuvres économiques et philosophiques*, ed. Oncken (Frankfort and Paris, 1888), pp. 250 *et seq.*
34. *Ibid.*, p. 297.
35. *Ibid.*, p. 298.
36. *Ibid.*, p. 302.
37. Cantillon, *op. cit.*
38. "De l'Homme," *Oeuvres*, 2, p. 360.
39. Mirabeau, *op. cit.*, pp. 403 *et seq.*
40. Beccaria, *Economia pubblica* (1771) Paragraph 30. Custodi, P.M. 11, pp. 58–59. See also p. 86, where the author deals with the origin of luxury industries in the great cities.
41. Gaetano Filangieri, *Leggi politiche e leggi economiche* (1780). Custodi, p.M. 32, pp. 185–86.
42. Sir James Stuart, *Inquiry*... (London, 1767), 1, p. 48.

7

The Secularization of Love

Sources and Literature

A.

I. The Renaissance. The works of Capellanus, Petrarca, Boccaccio, L. Valla, Bembo, Castiglione, Beccadelli, Firenzuola, Arentino, Montaigne, and Rabelais.

II. The seventeenth century. The collection: *Cabinet satyrique ou recueil parfait des vers piquants et gaillards de ce temps*, printed in many editions, one of them in Paris in 1632; the books by Auvray and by P. de Brantôme (*Vie des dames illustres, Vie des dames galantes*, were recently published in German by Insel Verlag, 1905 and 1907), etc.

III. The eighteenth century. The works of Restif de la Bretonne, especially *Le Palais royal* (1790), 3 vols. New edition in the collection: *Les Moeurs légères au XVIII*[e] *siècle*, introduction and notes by Henri d'Alméras; above all, the extensive literature of memoirs.

B.

I. The Middle Ages. A. Schultz, *Das höfische Leben zur Zeit der Minnesänger* (2d ed.; 1889).

II. The Renaissance. Of prime importance are the well-known historical works of general character by Burckhardt, Gregorovius, Grimm, and others, also Chledowski's fine work, *Die Menschen der Renaissance* (Rome, 1912), tr. from Polish; the recent literature on the life of the great courtesans of the Renaissance is particularly extensive: C. Biagi, *Un Etera romana, Tullia d'Aragona* (1897); P. L. Bruzzone, *Imperia e I suoi ammiratori, Nuova antologia* (1906), fasc. 828; even the letters of these ladies have found editors: L. A. Ferrari, *Lettere di cortegiane del secolo XVI* (1884); Lothar Schmidt, *Renaissancebriefe* (n.d.), vol. IX of "Kultur."

III. The seventeenth and eighteenth centuries. Besides the universal works on cultural history: Imbert de Saint-Amand, *Femmes de Versailles: Les femmes de la cour de Louis XV* (1876), 2 vols., and *Les femmes de la cour de Louis XVI* (1876), 2 vols.; Arsène Houssaye, *Galerie du XVIIIe siècle*, 6th ed., second series: *Princesses de comédies et déesses d'opéra*, fourth series: *Hommes et femmes de cour*, (1858), very witty and clever.

IV. Le régime des dames. Theodor Griesinger: *Das Damenregiment an den verschiedenen Höfen Europas in den zwei letztvergangenen Jahrhunderten*, first series: Die grossen französischen Vorbilder (1866–7), 2 vols.; second series: *Versailles in Deutschland* (Dresden and Hanover, 1869–70), 2 vols., extensive material, but compiled in the form of anecdotes, and containing no sources. Albert Savine, *La Cour galante de Charles II* (1908), good, authoritative.

A good introduction into the world of the theatre star is *Souvenirs de Mlle Duthé de l'opéra* (1748–1830), apocryphal; new edition by Paul Ginisty with an instructive preface.

V. The Goncourts. The superb and instructive works of the brothers Goncourt place them in a class by themselves. *Portraits intimes du XVIIIe siècle*, new ed. (1873), 2 vols. *Les Maîtresses de Louis XV* (1860). *La Femme au XVIIIe siècle*, 1862. *L'amour au XVIIIe siècle* (1875), and particularly the two works, *La Pompadour* and *La Du Barry.*

VI. Famous Mistresses. Each of the famous mistresses, particularly those of the kings, has become the subject of an extensive literature. The most important works are on *La Pompadour* by Capefigue, Compardon, Goncourt, and others. The *Montespan* by Arsène Houssays, Clément, Bonnassieux (*La Château de Clagny et Mme de Montespan*, 1881), and others.

VII. Various Courts. The literature on the history of the various rulers is also to be mentioned, but cannot be cited here, just as we cannot cite the literature on the various courts. Vehse's work of ill-fame, *Geschichte der deutschen Höfe seit der Reformation* (1851–8), 48 vols., on account of its size, takes first place among the latter.

VIII. French Kings. For France should be noted: Saval, *Les Galanteries des rois français sous plusieurs races*.

IX. French Financiers. H. Thirion's *La Vie privée des financiers au XVIII*[e] *siècle* portrays the régime of the mistresses of the high financiers in detail.

X. Influence of Women. The (not very informative) works on the history of women should also be mentioned. Comte de Ségur: *Les Femmes* (1803), 3 vols. G. Klemm: *Die Frauen. Kulturgeschichtliche Schilderungen des Zustandes und Einflusses der Frauen in den verschiedenen Zonen und Zeitaltern* (1859), 6 vols. The title is the best part of the book. Only the second volume is of interest. In it the author has compiled some articles on the "cocu" (p. 355). H. Scheube, *Die Frauen des achtzehnten Jahrhunderts* (1876), 2 vols., and the well-known works by Scherr, Henne am Ryhn, and others.

XI. Manners and Customs. The books on the history of manners and customs are generally instructive: R. Günther, *Kulturgeschichte der Liebe* (1899); Eduard Fuchs, *Illustrierte Sittengeschichte vom Mittelalter bis zur Gegenwart; Renaissance* (1909); *Die galante Zeit* (1910), with supplementary volumes containing the obscenities, valuable on account of their illustrations; E. Dühren, *Sittengeschichte, Englands* (2d ed.; 1912), 2 vols.

XII. Art. Naturally the literature on the history of art belongs here but I cannot enumerate the various books. I will only mention one book because it does not belong to any special class and for that reason is most enlightening: Virgile Josz, *Fragonard: Moeurs du XVIII*[e] *siècle* (1901).

XIII. Love and Marriage. The recent books on love, on sex problems, and on marriage offer us very little information because they do not deal with historical data. A good introduction into this literature is: Max Rosenthal, *Die Liebe, ihr Wesen und ihr Wert* (1912).

XIV. Prostitution. Of the books on the history of prostitution, the best known is by the Frenchman Dufour, translated into German by Adolf Stille and Bruno Schweiger and brought up to date by Franz

Helbing (5th ed.; 1910), 6 vols. Because of the author's moral conceptions, according to which all love relations without benefit of clergy or the marriage register are termed "prostitution," Lucrezia Borgia and Madame d'Etoiles, for instance, are classified as prostitutes. The book treats the subject expansively; unfortunately, it is carelessly written and lacks references.

XV. Bibliography on Erotic and Obscene Literature. Hugo Hayn, *Bibliotheca Germanorum erotica. Verzeichnis der gesamten deutschen erotischen Literatur,...* (2d ed., 1885); and (more important) *Bibliotheca erotica et curiosa Monacensis, Verzeichnis französischer, italienischer, spanischer, englischer, holländischer, und neulateinischer Erotica und Curiosa* (1887*). Bibliographie des ouvrages relatifs à l'amour, aux femmes, au mariage et des livres facétieux, pantsgruéliques, scatalogiques, satyriques...*, par M. le Cte D'I***; par J. Lemonnyer, fourth ed. (Paris 1894–1900) the chief work, 4,595 columns of encyclopedia size!

The Triumph of Illicit Love

I know of no event of greater importance for the formation of medieval and modern society than the transformation in the relations between the sexes which occurred during the Middle Ages and through the eighteenth century. In particular, comprehension of the genesis of modern capitalism is closely bound up with a correct appreciation of the basic changes in this most important domain of human activity.

The change in the conceptions of love and love relations was in the beginning, of course, an internal process. We have two sources of information which help us to appreciate that process fully: observations of representative men (in this instance, of women as well) and characteristic acts of contemporaries. These observations appear in a great variety of forms; they may be made *ex professo* in treatises on love, "*ne'quali si ragiona d'amore*," as they say in the dialogues of Asolani; we may find them also in the poetry and other works of art that reflect the "spirit of the times." Moreover, it goes without saying that the "spirit of the times" is but the "spirit" of a certain social class, in this case, the society of the courts and the nobility and their sycophants. The love life of the burgher develops in a fundamentally opposite direction to that of the courtiers; and these social contrasts give birth eventually to the capitalistic entrepreneur.

The changing modes of life follow one another like waves of the sea. The wave carrying us at the moment has nothing in common with the one whose rise and fall we wish to study. Social and moral attitudes emanate from the guildhalls and from the sermons of Calvin and John Knox to whom we owe all concepts of middle-class respectability. Development never takes an absolutely linear course, not even within one and the same cultural circle, for now and then the direction is diverted by counter-tendencies. Only in a general way is it possible to speak of a fundamentally uniform and linear development which has influenced the conception of love and its manifestations in our era.

Europe, during the Middle Ages, subordinated the cosmic phenomenon of sexual love, like every other human activity, to the service of a higher order: God—either worldly love received its religious consecration and was diverted to heavenly goals (as in Mariolatry) or love became institutionalized and this institution (marriage) was recognized as willed and blessed by God—a sacrament. All love which was not sanctioned and institutionalized became branded with the stigma of "sin."

A fundamentally different conception of the nature of love first becomes palpably evident in the period of the *Minnesänger*. This would set the date in the eleventh century, which marked, in every respect, the beginning of the secularization of love. The year of terror, 1000, had passed, new silver mines had been opened, and the trade connections with the Orient had been extended and consolidated. Provence, which during the eleventh and twelfth centuries, was likened to a "peaceful, gaily blossoming island in a stormy sea" was the first to hear the airs of a free, worldly love in the songs of the troubadours who appeared about the year 1090, flourished, and reached their highest peak between the middle of the twelfth and the middle of the thirteenth century. They are followed by the German minnesinger but, above all, in Italy by a large number of lyrical poets, singing of nothing but love. In a collection from the century preceding that of Dante, which I have at hand, I count no less than 126 names of these love minstrels.[1]

Today the whole lyric of the troubadours (the feelings expressed in these lyrics) impresses us as false, affected, and stilted. But it is exactly in this that they are the worthy precursors of modern love. They are a distinct example of adolescent eroticism, which exhausts itself in the glorification of the beloved one, in languishing, sighing, yearning, and adoring. It is not until the beginning of the thirteenth century that we reach the firm ground of natural sensuality. We even cannot state definitely whether the era of the minnesingers finds its direct continuation in the societies forming the papal court at Avignon or assembled about Boccaccio's Fiametta. If we are to believe an authority like Ulrich von Lichtenstein, the amorous period of minnesong was an episode which ended during the thirteenth century. In his *wrouwenbuch* (1257), he complains that women were no longer free in the society of men, did not don pretty costumes any more, covered their faces with heavy veils, and piously wore rosaries around their necks. Ulrich von Lichtenstein feels that women have been estranged from the joyous spirit of living which gave so much zest to former years. The men found pleasure only in hunting; they set out with their dogs at the break of dawn, and when they returned weary at nightfall, they spent their time throwing dice and drinking with their boon companions instead of devoting themselves to the ladies.[2]

Perhaps this condition concerned Germany only. Germany, with few exceptions, is lost to the history of love until the birth of another era, Goethe's Weimar. It is much more in keeping with the spirit of the countries of Southern Europe to have perpetuated a mode of life which had been ushered in by the troubadours. In any event, a spirit like that which pervades the *Decameron* appears to us as the direct continuation of the rapturous lyrics of the preceding centuries. It is the reaction of a healthy sensuality against an overstrained idealism, still expressing itself at the outset in childish forms: the allure of sexual pleasures is rediscovered, as it were, and the lifting of veils and garments causes undreamed-of delights. The keynote to which everything is attuned can be found in the words of the pious and lascivious nun of Boccaccio: "I have heard from several women, who came to see us, that all delights in the world are quite worthless in comparison with those given by woman to man." Woman, in the imagination of man, appears still fully clothed; let us remember that the *Decameron* is a product of Giotto's times.

Realistic representations of nude figures in the guise of religious myths, predominantly Adam and Eve, appear as harbingers of a new conception in art.[3] The paintings and illustrations of the first half of the fifteenth century already give clear evidence of the fact that the eye has begun to perceive flesh and blood again. The Adam and Eve by Jan and Hubert van Eyck on the panels of the altar in St. Bavon's in Ghent (now in the Museum of Brussels), in Jacopo della Quercia's reliefs on the doorjambs of S. Petronio in Bologna (c. 1425), Massaccio's frescoes in the Brancacci Chapel of Santa Maria del Carmine in Florence, but above all Ghiberti's (1378–1458) reliefs on the bronze gates of the baptistery in Florence are like the dawn of a new era.

But only the late quattrocento sees women in complete nakedness and discovers the intimate beauties of the female body and drinks in to the full the charms of sensual love. One fights for love and for woman: the painters have a partiality for the subject of "The combat of love against chastity" (Pietro Perugino, Sandro Botticelli), but the issue never is doubtful; in the frescoes which Francesco Cossa paints in the Palazzo Schifanoia, in Botticelli's "Primavera" and "Birth of Venus" the love of woman and her beauty triumphs.

What Lorenzo Valla came near to expressing theoretically, in his treatise *De Voluptate* (1431), now emerges palpably from the works of painters and poets as the spirit of concrete life: "What is sweeter, what is more delightful, what is more worthy of love than a beautiful face. The gates of Heaven cannot be a greater pleasure to man's eyes."[4] Valla is indignant that women do not bare to the world the most beautiful portions of their bodies. The manner in which he describes the female body reminds us of the beautiful stanzas in the *Hohe Lied* by Heinrich Heine. (A hundred years later Valla would have found many of his demands fulfilled.) Firenzuola, in the cinquecento, almost canonized the ideal of beauty of the new era.[5] To love means to enjoy these pleasures. "Love is nothing but pleasure. I love women as I love wine, games, and the sciences. The ultimate meaning of life is pleasure. We do not enjoy pleasure for the sake of an ulterior end. Pleasure itself is its own end... ."[6] Love becomes the essence of life. The poets Boiardo, Poliziano, Ariosto devote their works to love and women. The words of the poet: "I sing of women, lovers, our clean swords, love, gracious manners, and adventure" might be inscribed on the gates to this era, which, as Ariosto sings, "... was submerged up to the eyes in a sea of delights and beautiful things." Love impels men through life as depicted symbolically by a woodcut in the Poliphilo.[7]

One of the most glamorous illustrations of the amorous character of those days is transmitted to us by Thomas Garzoni in the ninety-seventh discourse of his *Piazza Universale* (1587), dedicated to Alfonso II of Este:

> These fools do not know what calamities disguise themselves under the name of women friends and ladies. I would not say that they revere them, nay, they worship them as their goddesses who are responsible for so many whims, illusions, and vanities, and with this weak foundation the mansion of love crumbles into an ocean of misery and sorrow. These women are also the idols and godheads, deities of the third heaven and the Graces of the tenth heaven, the beautiful lithe nymphs and the virginal followers of Diana to whom men offer their arduous tears as an incense, their afflicted hearts as censers, their cringing souls as host and sacrifice, their protestations of love as incantations, as their hymns, amorous sonnets and madrigals and the sight of weak, confused countenances as rituals. As oblation they bring the submission of a dog who fears neither cold nor heat, neither night nor daylight, undismayed by pain or by sorrow, who returns when repulsed, does not remain to be protected, never counts the wrongs and insults, never thinks of harm done him, does not think of revenge because like the dead he is blind and mute as to his own interest. They run after these savage beasts, willing to become the prey of these she-bears, ready to submit to these she-panthers and to love these tigresses.

In this manner he continues for pages and pages which glitter and sparkle like a rapid stream so that one feels tempted to copy the entire chapter. In general, one can see how the good Garzoni must have singed his wings if he has gathered so much wisdom in the fires of love.

The century of Titian dawns—a century in which soul and senses unite in a hitherto unknown harmony, in which to love woman means to love beauty and to love beauty means to love life. To what height of refinement love is developed is not so much revealed by the works of poets, painters, and sculptors as by the "theoretical treatise" on love which that period has produced. I mean the writings of the Asolanian Pietro Bembo: "Love is the first cause of everything" we hear; "love is the sweetest of all sweet things."[8] And what is love but a longing for beauty? All wise men agree on this. Beauty, then, is nothing else but gracefulness, born of propriety, symmetry, and harmony in all things. The same idea holds true for body and soul. "As the body with well-proportioned limbs is a thing of beauty, so is the soul with harmonizing virtues." "Love spreads its wings toward beauty—and two windows are opened to love in its flight; the ear, through which it reaches the soul; the eye, through which it is carried to the body."[9]

At that time Italy was probably the only country where the cults of love and beauty found a home; France was still in a chrysalid stage. Montaigne bitterly bewails the awkwardness of the French in the conventions of their love life; the younger France was still too impetuous to enjoy fully the pleasures of love as Montaigne would have liked to see them enjoyed. Next to the Italians, he considers the Spaniards to be masters of the pleasures of love: "They are more given to preamble and, thus, make love linger; a twinkling of the eye, a nod, a word, or a slight gesture becomes a favor or a reward."

But this situation was to be radically changed. With the Valois dynasty, Italian art came to France and with it the woman cult. Brantôme extols the amatory art of the French. Needless to say, in the seventeenth and eighteenth centuries France became the recognized school of love which she has remained up to the present day; it was in France that love life attained the ultimate refinement which approaches perversion. The true essence of the eighteenth century was life for love's sake, which found its highest consummation in Paris.

In the works of Fragonard, Boucher, and Greuze, we see the culmination of an era which began with Boccaccio and Pietro Perugino; or better yet, the glamorous finale, because Tintoretto, Rabelais, Ariosto, and Rubens really mark the zenith of that period. The theorists of love, first the minnesingers, Cappellanus, then Lorenzo Valla, and finally Bembo, now become Brantôme and Restif de la Bretonne and also perhaps the marquis de Sade.

These stages seem to mark the normal development which has been repeated in numerous civilizations. "The emancipation of the flesh" begins with timid attempts; this is followed by an epoch of strong natural sensuality in which a free, naive love life reaches its full climax. Then follows a certain refinement, then debauchery, finally perversion. This necessary cycle seems to encompass the deepest tragedy of human destiny; that all culture, being an estrangement from nature, carries in itself the terms of dissolution, destruction, and death.

Ein wenig besser würd' er leben,
Hätt'st du ihm nicht den Schein des Himmelslichts gegeben;
Er nennt's Vernunft und braucht's allein,
Um tierischer als jedes Tier zu sein.*

Evidently, this purely hedonistic aesthetic conception of woman and of love of her, as it gradually emerged after the fifteenth century, stood in an irreconcilable opposition to the religious or institutional restraints to which love had been subjected in former times. Possibly religious ecstasy may yet be reconciled with a detached view of love, e.g., the marvelous poem ascribed to Saint Francis of Assisi, beginning with the words:

In foco l'Amor mi mise:
in foco l'Amor mi mise:
in foco d'amor mi mise
Il mio Sposo novello...†

Such lines could have been written by every worldly lover. The ecstasies of the Mary cult certainly were not far removed from the "free love" of that time. What free love, however, could never become reconciled to was the institutionalization of love by marriage. The cosmic love instinct as well as the refined pleasures of love recognize no legal barriers. By its very nature "free love" is illicit or, better, nonlicit. And the ability of a woman to be womanly, beautiful, and lovable can neither gain nor lose an iota of its penetrating power by any man-made social institution such as marriage.

Men, pondering at that time on love problems, could not help but realize that, in marriage, two quite heterogeneous elements were combined—love and order: thus we find this problem thoroughly treated

---

* Life somewhat better might content him
But for the gleam of heavenly light, which Thou hast lent him:
He calls it Reason—thence his power's increased,
To be far beastlier than any beast.
(From the Prologue to Goethe's *Faust*.)—Trans.

† Love has thrust me in the furnace
Love has thrust me in the furnace
He has plunged me in the furnace of love.
(From Frederick Ozanam, The Franciscan Poets in Italy in the Thirteenth Century (London, 1914), p. 85.)

by all "theorists" of love. Probably one of the first to accept the inevitable conclusions arising from his natural conception of love and to declare the relations of the sexes to be non-licit, was Lorenzo Valla. He says, without circumlocution, that it does not concern anyone if two people choose to love each other: "*Si mulier mihi et ego mulieri placeo, quod tu tanquam medius non dirimere conaberis*?"[10] Therefore, says Valla, it is of no consequence whether a woman has intercourse with her husband or her lover. This conception then finds its free expression in the belles-lettres of the period, particularly those of lighter genre. Boccaccio still had a semblance of respect for marriage, but now derision of marriage and mockery of the duped husband is not only admissible but almost good form; even in the less lascivious novels, which were introduced with Piccolomini's *Euryalus* as well as in the less obscene comedies, adultery is always the "predominant theme."[11]

Montaigne carries this thought one step further. If love is pleasure and marriage a social or ecclesiastical institution with many very noble aims (Montaigne always speaks of marriage with the greatest respect, and precisely because of his opinion of marriage, he arrives at his radical views regarding the interrelation of love and marriage), then the achievement of the goal of love is not only independent of previous matrimonial alliance, but the two, love and marriage, are mutually exclusive. He bases his conception on the following reasoning: Love loathes anything which deals with other matters and shuns every relation contracted for other reasons, such as marriage, where connections and wealth are at least as important as charm and beauty. We do not marry for marriage's sake alone but principally for reasons of offspring and family connections. So it would be short of incest to give free rein to the extravagance of amorous passions in this honorable and holy institution of marriage. A good marriage rejects the association with love and seeks the pleasures of friendship. To love and to bind oneself are two fundamentally different matters which contradict each other.[12]

What Titian and Georgione expressed in their paintings, what Ariosto and Rabelais declaimed in their writings was formulated in these views. Love finds in itself its highest and only justification and must necessarily dwell outside and beyond all institutions created by man for social and moral purposes, even though sanctified by the Church.

It is, however, more important and decisive for the development of culture that society had lived for centuries in accordance with these ideas; that for centuries, in certain classes, marriage and love had been regarded, almost as a matter of course, as distinct entities which existed side by side, possessing equal rights. In the latter instance we see actually only the resumption of the mode of life of Greek (and late Roman) antiquity. This continuity will be traced more exactly in the following section, especially insofar as it introduced the *hetaera* into European society.

The Courtesan

When free love becomes established in society beside institutionalized love, the women serving this new cult are either seduced daughters of respectable families, adulteresses, or prostitutes. What significance purely erotic love has attained among the upper strata of European nations since the period of the minnesingers may be gathered from the fact that seduction, adultery, and prostitution have shown a great increase.

Figures for the first two forms of free love are not available. But we may infer from the opinions of contemporaries and from many other indications that, for centuries, free love played indeed an important role. Petrarch believes that the festering sore of adultery came to a head in his time. It became good form for a young man to seduce a married woman; he must do it lest he be laughed at by his friends, hence, the feverish craving of young men for gallant adventures, which springs less from sensual needs than from an erotic ambition. Too often the success does not repay the efforts.[13]

It is the same period in which princes ceased to be embarrassed about their natural offspring and, on the contrary, began to boast about them, as Jacob Burckhardt and Luigi Cibrario prove by numerous examples.

From that time until the end of the epoch, premarital or extramarital sexual relations steadily supplemented marital relations in all circles desirous of being in "style." It is unnecessary to adduce evidence from contemporary biographies; every general "history of morals" is replete with the subject. I will, however, point out one significant symptom which makes adultery appear almost as a social institution; the public recognition of the cuckold, as it appeared in Italy during the fourteenth century and in France in the reign of Francis I.

It is also known that prostitution greatly increased in extent and importance after the close of the Middle Ages. Naturally, prostitution finds its best markets in the large cities. Starting in Avignon, this institution reaches its height in London and Paris. Petrarch, in his magnificent Latin, complains that Avignon is invaded by a veritable flood of harlots. Rome was long famous for the abundance of public women within its walls; a reasonably reliable census of the year 1490 lists 6800 *meretrice*. Considering that the population of Rome at that period had not yet reached the 100,000 mark, this proportion is considerably higher than that for London and Paris, at the end of the eighteenth century, with a count of 50,000 and 30,000, respectively.

Still more important, especially for the development of our external culture, is the circumstance that with the spread of illegitimate love, love for its own sake, a new class of women appeared and took a position between the "respectable woman" and the *putain*. In the Romance languages these women are designated by a multitude of names: *cortegiana, courtisane*, *concubine*, *maîtresse, grande amoureuse, grande cocotte*, and *femme entretenue*, etc. (The German language and perhaps the English have no single expression for them, although the rather indefinite German word *buhlerin* might be acceptable. This is, perhaps, proof that the entire question was confined to countries of the Romance tongue or was introduced by them.)

Through these women, love—having become a free art—emerges again from the dilettantism of the preceding centuries, and its cult is now placed in the hands of its "vestals." While talent and long practice are necessary to the execution of every art, they are particularly needed in the art of love. Thus, the art of loving could reach its climax only after eminently gifted women, through a natural process of selection, had been elevated from the great mass and given the opportunity to become masters of that art by devoting their whole life to its practice.

Courtisane, cortegiana, meant in the beginning merely "court lady." There were also ladies at the court with purely legitimate love relations. In the third epistle of his book on the courtier, which Castiglione devoted to the court lady, Magnifico goes so far as to say that the love relations between gentlemen and ladies of the court should only be of a licit character. Certainly, most members of the inner circle smilingly contradicted him. They must have known why, for Magnifico's demands were far removed from reality. There seems little doubt that the illicit relations of illustrious ladies were identified at an early date with the social life at the courts. I presume that life at the papal courts had a considerable influence in the formation of this idea. In Avignon (where probably the modern courtesan originated), we find a set of clever, witty, and beautiful women at the courts of the pope and the princes of the church. Such a situation led many to designate the courts *académies de femmes aimables*. We have but to recall such names as Mabille de Villeneuve, Briande d'Agoult, Huguette de Forcalquier, Beatrix de Sault, Laure de Noves, Blanche de Flassans, Isnarde de Roquefeuille, Doucette de Moustiers, Antoinette de Cadenet, Magdeleine de Salon, Blanchefleur de Pertais, Stephanette de Gantelme, the Beautiful Adelise of Avignon, the cousin of Laura, to realize the justification of this phrase.

It is natural that a woman in the entourage of the princes of the church could only be a mistress if her relations to the high dignitaries went beyond the merely intellectual, and this, indeed, was probably not unusual. The *cortegiana*, for purely extrinsic reasons, had to become a courtesan.

What Avignon began, Rome continued. For here, too, the lady at the court was "illegitimate" by her very nature. This outward compulsion towards illegitimacy did not exist at the secular courts; the inner urge, however, amply replaced it. The selection of concubines by princes was not an innovation of the Renaissance; the princes had done it at all times. But the daughters of commoners, whom Louis XI of France invited to his royal chambers were not "courtesans" by any means; they became so only when they were received at court and given official recognition as favorites of the ruler. The first tyrants who elevated their mistresses to princely rank are believed to have been Bernabò and Gian Galeazzo Visconti. But the reign of the *cortegiana* does not actually begin until the time when we see Cossa painting the frescoes in the Palazzo Schifanoia; when the court, as we understand that term today, was formed by women and with women. After this period, gallantry became the soul and the ornament of court life. "No court, however great, can sparkle or be gay without women, nor can a courtier be, or achieve, anything of importance without being filled with or urged on by love of women." Thus, Castiglione in his book *Il Cortegiano*.

Taking into account the temper of that period, it is self-evident that our author did not have in mind connubial love; thus, one *cortegiana* after another became the mistress of a *cortegiano* until the term *cortegiana* became identical with courtesan (in its modern connotation).

At this stage we enter the era of the unrestricted sway of the *maîtresse* which, in view of what we have found to be the prevailing relations between the sexes, was the inevitable concomitant of monarchic rule. In the measure that small courts grow, the system takes on larger proportions. We know that from the beginning of the Reformation, France took the lead in this most important matter also; the lady-loves of Francis I are the first royal mistresses who appear as such in history, for it was this king who, as we have seen, conceived the essence of court life to be gallantry and "the most significant act of gallantry was that he made his mistresses the most important personages at the court."[14]

The entire guild of the professional priestesses of Venus was ennobled, as it were, in the persons of the king's *maîtresses attitrés* who now began to govern the world. Thus, also, was the outward stigma removed from these illicit relations, at least from those at court.

In that epoch the influence of the court on any one wishing to belong to society was so great that the legalized illicit behavior gradually resulted in freer love relations outside of the court circles also. Women, in the growing cities, began to live like ladies of the court. This condition produced the courtesans who had nothing to do with the court. They were *femmes entretenues*, if they bestowed their favors on one man, or cocottes, if they were more promiscuous. In the upper crust of the demimonde the term "venal love" becomes slightly blurred.

The courtesan, who was not a courtesan at all, emerged at about the same time as her sister at court (from whom she received her name) and in the same localities, above all in the large Italian cities, especially Rome and Venice. Conditions here were particularly propitious to the creation of a new type of woman; wealth, delight in the revival of antiquity, and the idea that its *hetaera* could be brought back to life. The spirit of the large city, together with the general liberality of that period, was conducive to surrounding a few selected prostitutes, a small upper stratum, with a halo of distinction. (This liberality always refers to the upper social strata, for there were in those times also respectable tradespeople and merchants who, no doubt, shunned the glittering courtesan just as a Sunday school teacher or purity crusader would avoid her modern sister today.) These were the "honest harlots," the *honeste cortigiane* or *cortesane famose* as they are called in a fragmentary register of Roman prostitutes of the year 1500. The two hundred listed in that register were contrasted with the prostitutes of the lower class, *cortesane puttane* or *cortesane de la minor sorte.*[15]

This document indicates conclusively that the process of differentiation to which I have referred had been completed already.

Much has been written lately regarding the *cortesane famose* of the Renaissance. Many new sources have been made available. We now know by name all the famous cocottes who lived in Rome, Florence, or Venice during the period of the reign of Sixtus IV, Alexander VI, and Leo X. There are even learned discussions regarding the degree of their "education," which they displayed ostentatiously, and the quality of their poetry, which they wrote more or less with the assistance of "ghosts." As if this were so important! Certainly it was only a very superficial education, and their verses were poor. Be that as it may, the significance of this new species of humanity does not lie in these items, but in facts such as, for instance, that a Tullia d'Aragona could, for years, make a fool of Filippo Strozzi and that an Imperia could make the richest man in Italy, Agostino Chigi, keep her during many years of her life. Such achievements are certainly not due to their proficiency in poetry; rather, they require, as Maupassant says, other *qualités rares*, which they amply possessed. And through these qualities they became a power which has had considerable influence on the development of culture. The significance of this class of women is not embodied in the fact that an Imperia could inspire one of her distant admirers to compose the following glorifying epitaph: "Imperia, Roman Courtesan, how worthy are you of this name. Seldom has nature created a being of such beauty"; nor does this significance lie in other manifestations of gallantry bestowed on the *grandes amoureuses* in the Italy of that period. The evidence of their sway is found in facts such as the privilege of interment in the chapel of Santa Gregoria granted to the same Imperia and the solemnization by the pope and fourteen cardinals of the baptism of Agostino Chigi's first son by his new Venetian mistress, Francesca Andreosia.

Like the courtesan and favorite, the woman of the town first attained her full development in France. It is there that she became that definite type with which all European countries are now familiar.

It is of particular significance for the formation of the type of the modern courtesan that, at the turn of the sixteenth century, women appeared on the stage of Paris theaters. In England this custom was introduced in the reign of Charles II. Now, at last, this era had a substitute for the glamour which had surrounded the Renaissance cocotte, herself emulating the hetaera of antiquity; the theater provided the nimbus, which seems to be so essential for free love relations on a higher level. The actress, the prima donna, and the dancer at the Grand Opera took the place of the versifying and painting courtesans of the fifteenth century.

The number of "women of the town" steadily increased during the seventeenth and eighteenth centuries, particularly in cultured centers such as London and Paris, where it became "the thing" to keep an elegant mistress instead of, or besides, a lawful spouse. If we are told that at least fifteen out of every twenty court dignitaries did not live with their wives, but with their mistresses,[16] we may rest assured that this estimate approximated pretty nearly the actual situation. But it is not only the courtier who keeps a mistress; the Turcarets also believe they owe it to themselves to be in the good graces of ladies of easy virtue, the *demoiselles de moyenne vertu*, as they were called. The expenses incurred through these liaisons (I shall discuss this later) constituted the largest items in the budgets of the financiers, as we are reliably informed by Thirion who has made a thorough study of these "affairs." The annals of gallantry in the eighteenth century reveal the close relations between illicit love and the tax farming system.[17] London is not different from Paris. We are told that a bachelor with an income of £2000 spends scarcely £200 for his immediate needs; the rest go for pleasure, which means girls, first and last (Archenholz.)

In view of such judgments we cannot but accept the figures given us by reliable observers regarding the number of the "women of the town" in Paris and London. Mercier, for instance, estimates that in his time 10,000 women were "kept" in Paris. In one single parish of

London (Marylebone), 1,700 courtesans lived in their own town houses at that period.

The prominent place held by venal love in eighteenth century society is best revealed by the custom of publishing, every year, directories of the better class of cocottes, giving names, addresses, and various other information regarding facial pulchritude, deportment, and talents. In London, one printing (8,000 copies) of Harry's List of Covent-Garden Ladies was sold as fast as it came off the press. In Paris, a "similar guide" was published with the following title: *Almanac des adresses des demoiselles de Paris de tout genre et de toutes les classes. Calendrier du Plaisir. A Paphos.*

One outgrowth of the new prominence of the elegant courtesan in social life was that bourgeois wives followed her example in style and taste. Not directly though. First, it is the court society which shapes the habits and manners of all good society: "Paris apes the court," says La Bruyère. Court society in turn is molded by the acknowledged favorite of the prince, who thus puts her stamp on all strata of society. The court favorite is above all the model which is copied by the ambitious woman of the town, the *grande cocotte*. At the outset, the latter almost becomes a competitor of her sister at court.

Ninon de l'Enclos follows in the footsteps of Madame de Maintenon: she carries on the old traditions of gay life when her predecessor grows old and pious; the rue de Tournelles challenges St. Cyr.

On the other hand, the respectable lady had to adjust herself to competition with the mistress; the alternative was complete elimination from social life. From this more or less open struggle resulted certain minimum standards of culture to which every lady, whatever her superior social position, had of necessity to conform.

It does not seem improbable that it was the cocotte who indirectly compelled the respectable lady to wash. Marieu de Romieu, who lived in the sixteenth century, advises, in her *Instruction to Young Girls*, "all women to keep their bodies clean, be it only for their own good or that of the husband." The "salon," an institution through which, in the seventeenth and eighteenth centuries, the woman of the world exercises her greatest influence, is probably only the successor of the meetings of great minds at the houses of the great Italian courtesans in the fifteenth century.

But the most important result of this development is that the style of life of the demimonde determined that of the women of the world, i.e., society. Hardly anything has changed in this respect since then. Even in the respectable middle-class world of today, the woman of secure position (I am not referring to the eccentric people in "rational" dresses, vegetating in three-room apartments) studies the costumes worn by the *grandes cocottes* at the Spring races in Paris. All the follies of fashion, luxury, splendor, and extravagance are first tried out by the mistresses before they are finally accepted, somewhat toned down, by the reputable matrons. In those bygone days which we discuss here, when the burgher lived in a sphere of his own, far removed from what was then "society," the courtesan in her respected circle naturally exercised an influence which was more thoroughly and directly felt than is possible today.

Notes

1. Ludovico Valeriani and Urbano Lampredi, *Poeti del primo secolo...* (Firenze, 1816), 2 vols.
2. Alwin Schultz, *Das Höfische Leben zur Zeit der Minnesinger* (Leipzig, 1889), 2, p. 423.
3. For an interesting description see Joseph Kirchner, *Die Darstellung des ersten Menschenpaars in der bildenden Kunst,...*(Stuttgart, 1903).
4. Lorenzo Valla, *Opera...* (Basel, 1590). (*De Voluptate*, lib. I, c XXII.)
5. Aug. Firenzuola, "Discorso delle bellezze delle donne," cited in: J. Burckhardt, *Die Cultur der Renaissance* (Leipzig, 1878), 2, p. 64; English translation by S.G.C. Middlemore, *The Civilization of the Renaissance* (London, 1909), p. 345; and in R. Günther, *Kulturgeschichte der Liebe* (Berlin, 1899), pp. 298 *et seq*. In view of such evidence it is strange that Burckhardt, (*op. cit*., p. 63; English tr., *op. cit*., p. 344), should have said: "Whether the fifteenth century has left any written account of its ideal of beauty, I am not able to say." Evidently, when writing this book the quoted passages must have slipped his mind.
6. Lorenzo Valla, *op. cit*., p. 668.
7. Francesco Colonna, *Poliphili Hypnerotomachia,...*(Venice, 1499).
8. Pietro Bembo, *Gli Asolani* (Venice, 1575), p. 134.
9. *Ibid*., pp. 189–90.
10. Lorenzo Valla, *op. cit*., libl. I, c. xxxviii.
11. F. Gregorovius, *Lucrezia Borgia* (Stuttgart, 1875), I, p. 96.
12. These passages are in the famous fifth chapter of the third book of the Essays. Were such views entirely new then? Or better, was it the first time that such views were integrated into a system? (After all, since the decline of the minnesingers people did live in accordance with them). This seems rather unlikely when we think of many a decision of the *Minnehöfe*. Cf. K. Weinhold, *Die Deutschen Frauen in dem Mittelalter* (Wien, 1897).

13. I shall give here the original passage because it so admirably reflects the spirit of the time, and because to my knowledge, it has never before been cited:

> Quae tunc pestis incipiens nunc adeo certa est, ut adolescens cui non feliciter adulterium successerit, quamvis dives, quamvis formosus ac nobilis, coaevorum iudicio inter miseros habeatur, quasi abiectus ac repulsus non pudicitia sed contemptu; et quasi dilectio casitatis convicium sit amantis. Hinc ille iuvenum fervor et sollicitudo improba, tanquam non de libidine sed de gloria sit certamen: hinc labores, hinc suspiria, hinc repentinae repulsae amarissimae: saepe tamen successus amarior.

Epistolae de rebus familiaribus et variae, ed. by Joseph Fracassetti (Florence, 1862), 2, liber nonus, epistola IV, p. 10.

14. Heinrich Laube, *Französische Lustschlösser* (Mannheim, 1840).
15. Extract from the periodical "Gli studi in Italia" (1882), in F. Gregorovius, *op. cit.*, 7, p. 722.
16. E.J.F. Barbier, "Journal historique...," 4, p. 496, in R. Günther, *op. cit.*, p. 397.
17. See the long list of mistresses of the farmer-general in: Paul Ginisty, *Mlle Duthé et son temps* (Paris 1909), p. 11.

8

Travel in Germany in 1800

How One Traveled

Traveling at that time was not such a simple affair as it is today. He who did not wish to travel through the countryside on foot, which the seasoned walker who did not care too much about time often preferred, would either, equipped with boots and spurs, have to mount a horse or harness his own nag to his travel carriage and take the reigns himself, or finally, if all these options of trans-locating were unavailable, he might have to revert to the last resort: the mail or stage-coach. This method of transportation, in turn, put considerable strain on the psychological and physical condition of those taking advantage of such an offer. I.N. Hecht, the Bädeker of that time considers it essential that a "serious passenger" is above all in good bodily shape and has the unlimited patience of Christ. Therefore, these skills required practice. And those who did not possess these virtues were, according to competent observers, actually able to acquire them during the course of a lengthy coach journey. "Those without a wife and thus with less patience," as opined by one of the most traveled men of that time (the author of the "Papiere eines lachenden Philosophen," i.e., "Essays of a Smiling Philosopher") "mark my word and travel to the North," of Germany that is, which was particularly disreputable among travelers. One traveled slightly better in Southern Germany and clearly conditions in Austria's countryside were considered less adverse. Mail service in particular was more reliable over there, along the Danube. How times are changing!

And the many complaints about the hardships of traveling which echo from each and every travel report of that time (and there are almost as many in the form of books as there are nowadays in the feuilletonistic form of the so-called "Reisebriefe," i.e., "Travel Letters"), seem to be entirely understandable if we consider the circumstances under which journeys were undertaken.

The roads! For heaven's sake! What misery! Only a few limited stretches of main roads or paved streets. By 1816 in all of the kingdom of Prussia only 523 and 3/8 miles of main roads existed (today more than 10,000 miles are available in the same area); Westphalia and the Rhine Palatine claimed 3/5 thereof, whereas the provinces of Pomerania and Poland had no main roads whatsoever, and Prussia had already 1 mile. Thus, as a rule: sand, clay, turf mean dust during summer, morass in the winter; deep potholes, stumps, and stones everywhere. Hence, report after report about carriages getting stuck, occasionally even about stage coachmen suffocating in swamps. Quite often no attempts were made to improve the roads. Mail and freight coaches were to proceed slowly through a region so that the inn-keepers and tradesmen could profit from them substantially.

And the carriages measured up to the reputation of the roads. The postal coaches were among the most popular and most often cited objects of jokes for the witty newspaper editors in those days. It would be worthwhile to write a doctoral thesis in modern German philology collecting from contemporary literature the many citations, which a) in witty humor and b) in bad temper deal with the inadequacies of the postal coaches at that time. May I just point out Lichtenberg:

> They are painting the postal coaches red (obviously referring to those of Taxis) as the color signifies pain and torture, and are covering them with wax linen, not as one might assume to protect the travelers against sun and rain (for, the travelers' enemy is to be found below, meaning the roads and the carriages), but rather for the same reason one places a hood over the head of the condemned to be hanged: so that the onlookers will not see their faces twisted in agony.

However, Ludwig Börne even wrote at the beginning of the third decade of the nineteenth century his standard "Contribution to the

Natural History of the Mollusks and Testaceans" ["Beitrag zur Naturgeschichte der Mollusken und Testaceen"], "Monography of the German Snail Mail" ["Monographie der deutschen Postschnecke"], where he states:

> On previous journeys I have had my best satirical ideas about postal carriages, but lost them all. My capacity of storing ideas is too small and not enough room is left to save thoughts which I do not immediately process and, by writing them down, apply. Thoughts about postal coaches, however, I was unable to put down on paper immediately because impacts to the latter used to coincide with the impetus to the former.

Yet an almost inexhaustible source of all kinds of fun and satire was the speed with which the postal coach traveled. If you wish to inform yourself, study the essay by Ludwig Börne mentioned above, which includes many delightful stories. The journalists at that time still worked at their profession thoroughly and with a lot of passion. Indeed, the monograph of our source is not lacking in "statistical references"; the author himself translates statistics of the postal coach with "science of no motion." Below are the statistics taken down during a journey from Frankfurt to Stuttgart. The travel time was 40 hours; the stopovers were:

	Hours	**Minutes**
In Sprendingen	—	12
In Langen	—	50
In Darmstadt	—	45
In Bickenbach	—	30
In Heppenheim	1	15
In Weinheim	—	30
In Heidelberg	3	15
In Nekargemünd	1	15
In Wiesenbach	—	12
In Sinzheim	—	15
In Fürfeld	—	30
In Heilbronn	3	10
In Besigheim	—	1
In Ludwigsburg	1	—
Total:	14	44

That Börne did not overstate his report is evident from many other reports and time-tables which match. One traveled one and a half days from Berlin to Leipzig, to Breslau four days, to Königsberg over a full week. And all in all one can see from the following rendition by Ludwig Rellstabs given in his Early Memoirs [Jugenderinnerungen] that it made no difference whether one started out from Berlin or Frankfurt a. M.

> One traveled in that time admittedly somewhat differently than now.—We departed from Berlin by the 'standard mail' (at that time the official term). A covered carriage, which in itself was already considered an oriental luxury of the standard mail service, welcomed us. The carriage without shock springs had upholstered seats and arm rests, covered with smooth leather and contained many luggage-pieces in the back which, at the same time, served as back-rests. (On side roads partially covered or completely uncovered carriages were commonly used.) One was not seated too comfortably, however for such a young enthusiastic traveler as myself, it was wonderful, and the strong pushing and shaking was probably healthier than the nerve-wrecking vibrations of today's train compartments. One also had sufficient time to get acquainted with land and people. One rarely traveled in a moderate trot, except on a very leveled road; the slightest elevation triggered a cumbersome stride. The travel time to Zehlendorf—we were taking the route via Potsdam to Wittenberg—was three hours, followed by a one-and-a-half-hour stop-over because at each station all luggage was counted and the carriage completely reloaded. Having started out at 8 or 9 o'clock in the morning we, therefore, arrived safe and sound late in the evening in Belitz, a town three miles from Potsdam.

The idea, therefore, could arise to charge the travelers with waiting fees and to take not the mourners but the corpses themselves to the funeral in stately Thurn-and-Taxis' postal coaches, "so that they might gain time to awaken from their death-like state, because, if not more than a spark remains in the ashes of life, the hurtling of the coach is bound to set it aflame."

What was responsible for the snail-pace was, according to Börne, not only the consideration that a sudden change of pace from slow to fast and vice-versa was harmful to the horses and that since a slower pace was required while traveling through cities and villages this pace was retained on country roads as well. There were more plausible reasons. The difficult road conditions have been mentioned already. Then, on top of it, the continuous hassle with customs and toll clearance took much of the time. By the end of the eighteenth century, for example, there were still 16 toll stations between Dresden and

Magdeburg, and 7 from Wertheim to Mainz; this was the case everywhere. One should remember that until 1803 still more than 300 princes and lords ruled German regions which then were amalgamated to 38. But even these "thirty-eight monarchs" considered the neighboring county or duchy still as foreign territory liable to excise (in modern terminology), and German roads had almost as many turnpikes as nowadays telegraph poles. "However, the Germans confine themselves all the more," complains Frederick List in 1819.

> Thirty-eight toll and excise borders paralyze the traffic within Germany and bring about approximately the same effect, as if each limb of the human body is tied off to make sure that no blood flows between them. In order to trade between Hamburg and Austria, Berlin and Switzerland, one has to cross through ten states, study ten excise and toll regulations, and pay ten transit fees. But the unfortunate, who lives at a border, where three or four states collide, spends his whole life among hostile-minded custom agents and duty collectors; he has no fatherland. This is a desolate situation for men who wish to wheel and deal and enviously look across the Rhine River, where a great nation is trading unhindered on free rivers and open highways from the Channel to the Mediterranean Sea, from the Rhine to the Pyrenees, from the Dutch border to Italy without encountering a single toll collector.

And the plagued traveler, who crossed several of these sovereign empires, did not only constantly have to battle with customs officers: what must have driven him to despair was the annoyance of having to deal with hundreds of coins which had to be exchanged constantly. Those who are interested in the motley world of German numismatics at the beginning of the nineteenth century and do not wish to consult some tedious technical literature, I refer to the respective chapters in the book by the previously mentioned "German traveling in Germany" ["in Deutschland reisenden Deutschen"], which even today is worth reading. They are found in the fourth volume of his collected works. In short: it is of no surprise if the nervous traveler à la Börne, who had been tortured in such a manner, exclaimed: "I want to jump out of my skin, if only there was room for escape as I am completely filled with fury."

And even when he rested from his ordeal and did not stay with good friends, he did not experience much comfort. Guest-houses and inns were most inadequate. I recall a travel description by an upright country-parson who stayed in Halle for a few days and cannot stop complaining about the bad meals: and he found it specially annoying that the rooms of his inn looked out onto the place of executions, where within the distance of a few steps the recently hanged were still dangling in the wind. Thus one often preferred to travel at night: much more than today, mainly because of the longer duration of the trip.

> We traveled the whole night alone
> in the dark mail coach.

But of course: one also saw more on such a trip. It was an adventure in itself. Slowly one would take in the impressions; pondered deep inside on what one observed, and instead of writing postcards in dispatch-style, one wrote detailed letters to loved-ones at home; instead of three columns in the entertainment section of the "Daily" casually jotted down in a speedy train, the experiences of several months were finally put down in a formidable volume. Nowadays, books are, if at all, only written if the subject is a trip through Siberia or Africa. From that earlier time we have entire series of volumes with descriptions of trips to Rügen or from Berlin to Dresden; of walking excursions in Brandenburg or in some other small corner of Germany. This was brought about by the technology in news communication and news-publication.

But how intimate was the traveler's experience of the natural landscape through which he drove, rode, or walked! How close was his relationship with people of all ranks! A lovely description of this atmosphere is given in a chapter of Johann Friedrich Zöllner's "A Journey through Pomerania" ["Reise durch Pommern"] (1797): "Up to here we traveled throughout the night and shortly before arriving at the village were pleasantly awakened from our morning-slumber by our sentimental coachman." (Sentimentality [Empfindsamkeit]: a favored word at that time, one may recall the well-known book by Stern, which had been translated in 1768 and—upon Lessing's suggestion—received the title "Nork's Sentimental Journey" ["Norks empfindsame Reise"]; 1776 Moser's satire "For Sentimentalists" ["Für die Empfindsamen"]; 1776 Goethe's "The Triumph of Sentimentality" ["Triumpf der Empfindsamkeit"]; etc.)

> Next to the administrator's house stands a tower with ruins of antique masonry. The good man stopped opposite this and blew a fine tune on his horn. The echo bounced back repeating each theme in its entirety and clearly. Changing between

shorter and longer passages he observed the time needed for the echo to bounce back so closely, that we enjoyed the rare beauty of it completely. I especially appreciated that during all of this he spoke not a single word to draw our applause but surrendered completely to his own feelings and let us surrender to ours. His playing seemed also to grow in intensity, which convinced me that he must have made many attempts before he was satisfied; and after several minutes he drove on silently and slowly, heading towards the rising sun. Upon parting, as we had increased his tip for this display, he said with a content smile: 'Yes, it is a splendid echo!'

What One Experienced While Traveling

In my imagination, dear lady reader, we have repeatedly walked, ridden, and driven together through the many provinces of the German fatherland as depicted above: with a sensitive mind and an open eye for everything offered to the observer. Unlike Madame de Staël, that is, who actually saw nothing of Germany but rather read and heard more about it and therefore, naturally, missed the main thing.

Furthermore I visualize that we first of all write down our impressions as a preliminary draft just as they came to mind, refined and enhanced, if at all, with some details as they are found in commonly used geographic handbooks; and that only after we are back home sitting near the warm stove we will sort out our travel impressions and try to enrich them through the thorough study of socio-economical works. We shall then see how observant we have been.

It goes without saying that we are undertaking our trip with a distinct interest in matters of economical concern and anything related to these. Otherwise you would have to put yourself in the care and company of a naturalist or poet or antiquarian which, however, you would certainly dislike.

Though traveling may have been strenuous: it was certainly never boring. And even if one could not pass the time by reading newspapers as one can today, one did not miss it. In fact life on country roads leading through regions that were more or less densely populated proved to be quite colorful.

In the first place, traveling itself created peculiar 'branches of certain industries,' pan-handling in particular, which increased considerably after the military campaigns in the 1820s and 1830s. Panhandling in all its variations popped up, quite often accompanied by all kinds of entertainment and displays; not unlike nowadays when traveling from Naples to Pompeii.

But we also encounter a multitude of different people on the country roads, going about their business.

> These include:
> The anxious merchant and the sparsely
> clad pilgrim—the devoted monk,
> the shady robber and the merry musician,
> the packer with his heavily packed horse
> who traveled far from remote countries,
> as each road leads to the end of the world!

And above all the many heavy wagons on these country roads, with canvas tops, often stretching in long trains, one behind the other. In their midst the agile journeyman and the peddler moving from village to village with his pack on his back.

You ask what the purpose of the strange wooden structures may be, towering next to the road, lifting their arms up into the fog like ghosts. What you have observed is the optical telegraph. Here are more details about it according to Geistbeck: After several years of research in which he was supported by his brothers, the French engineer Claude Chappe (1792) was the first to succeed in constructing useful optical telegraphs. Its basic design consisted of three beams mounted on a frame in a spot that could be seen over a great distance; arranged in a multitude of combinations they were able to relay a great number of signals. The observation and reproduction of a signal required 20 seconds under favorable conditions. A signal from Toulon to Paris (approximately 300 km) required 20 minutes. The first telegraph line of this kind was completed between Paris and Lille in 1794. One by one lines of a total length of 5000 km were constructed in France which all ended in Paris. Other countries soon followed with similar constructions, such as England, Sweden, Denmark, Prussia, etc. In Germany the most important of these telegraph lines was the one from Berlin to Cologne.

By the way, the optical telegraph suffered from an all too human failure: at crucial moments it broke down; at night and during fog, when it rained and snowed it was, of course, impossible to convey messages.

The surrounding landscape through which the journey went was as picturesque and colorful as life on the road itself; and totally different from nowadays. Indeed I would describe it as still in its natural state, randomly created, with all the imperfections of a real cultivation.

The road still continues between irregularly planted rows of trees, through picturesque narrow passages with blossoming blackthorn extending its growth into their paths; through creeks and rivers or over half-collapsed bridges, their hewn stones covered with patches of moss and grass. The landscape is often interrupted by swamps and moors with croaking frogs and the characteristic booming cry of the bittern. Quite often a quarry or a sand pit interrupts the monotony of the landscape; and at the roadside you might find a bush providing shade for the resting wanderer, or in the middle of a field you will see a hedge whit songbirds nesting in its bushes. Wild roses are winding round old ruins of unknown origin whose purpose no one knows. Much of the landscape seems to have "no real purpose"!

A peculiarity which the traveler is sure to notice is the wealth of heath and pastures and herds. Not only does the wanderer encounter large flocks of sheep wherever he goes: but he just as often meets flocks of geese, pigs, goats, grazing horses, and cattle.

The farm-land looks like a chess board: one tiny strip of ploughed acre follows the next, except that neighboring stretches bear the same crop or remain untilled. What makes these fields particularly colorful during the summer time are the many blue and yellow patches dotting billowing grain fields; beds of flax and rape.

And more frequently than it is the case today, a forest receives the wanderer into its shady growth. The ancient giant trees have not yet been cut; the undergrowth still grows wild entangled with all kinds of "useless" shrubs, the "weeds of the forest," as the picturesque invasive plants are called today. The forest plays another quite different role in the life of a people who make the forest the center of legends and fairy tales and often look upon it as the sole source of earning a living. The old German culture as it was still basically maintained in the beginning of the nineteenth century had actually derived from this ideal of a forest; the murmuring brook, the rustling oak tree are synonymous of the German soul, which in those very days when our imagination travels through the German countryside created the romantic notion of the magic *Blaue Blume* ("blue flower"). The sensitive, the fragile, the feelings of dread, the deep sentimental disposition, and whatever else differentiates the Germans from all other nations: Its primary cause lies in the forest, in the untended wild grown forest, where the birds sang in the bushes during springtime, where fog moved across clearings in the fall.

But also the material culture of the Nordic countries is rooted in the forest before iron and other inorganic matter created a new culture. An observant traveler crossing the country had to become aware of this. Everywhere he went he encountered common people collecting brushwood, berries, straw, and other forest products. The small farmer's pigs are searching for acorns as feed, his cow and goats graze near the edge of the woodlands. He uses the wood supply as base material for products to trade, offering these for sale at fairs and markets: all sorts of shovels and other tools, tubs, wooden clogs, and various carvings. The forest also supplies most raw materials to the craftsman in the city: tanning bark and wood. Our forebearers' culture, that is, was very much a wooden one. Wood for burning; wood for housing, bridges, and planks; thousands of utensils used in daily life were made of wood, by the cooper in particular, articles which we nowadays only know by name: the wooden bathtub, the wooden milk- and beer-tankards, the wooden wash-tub, the wooden pail, the wooden fire-tub, the wooden brine and beer barrels. Viktor Hehn in his witty way once attributed the different mentalities of inhabitants of the South and the North to the contrast between stone and wood. Certainly this contrast was more significant for the times one hundred years ago than at the present time which is in the process of obliterating all national and local differences.

To what extent the entire material culture depended on the forest at that time must have become even more imprinted on the observer's mind when he became aware of the fact that even numerous commercial products that are not made of wood required wood for their production; primarily iron which was smelted from the ore by means of charcoal and forged in the same manner; also glass, porcelain etc. We have to visualize that industrial installations (on a small scale) were, much more so than today, spread throughout the country, and especially in the middle of the forest next to a gushing forest-brook (whose water power was used before steam became predominant). We have a nice description of such an idyllic ironworks from that time, which you, my dear lady friend, will probably have cited often without noticing that it is a typical description of the old iron industry:

Water and fire power
as allies are seen here;
The mill-wheel, pushed by the stream,
turns round and round;
The wheels rattle day and night,
The hammer pounds and beats in rhythm,
And slowly from those mighty strikes
even the iron gives in and softens.

Also upon arriving at a village we perceive a greater number of commercial activities than today: we observe the farmer's wife at the spinning wheel, hear the weaving shuttle clacking, find farmers behind the joiner's bench and vice or occupied at the tannery-pit and the shoemaker and tailor at the farmer's table. Our learned books will tell us that our observations are not based on deceptions and were also not incidental.

And the villages, what did they look like? That on its own would make an interesting chapter, but it would probably turn out too long. After all, what characterizes those earlier times are precisely the differences in the design of the villages and the style of the houses. Some of it remains even until today: Lower Saxon and Alpine farmers used to settle on single farms, the Swabian, the Thuringians, the Silesian, and other tribes live in villages, today as in the past. However, the characteristic styles of the houses have gradually disappeared: thatch and shingles have been replaced by tiles and slates and the townhouse style also took over in the villages. A hundred years ago we could clearly differentiate between cultural zones, ethnic regions, borders of settlement according to their style of farmhouses, of which the Lower Saxony, Alemannic, and Thuringian houses are the most characteristic ones. Whoever wishes to obtain more information about these stylistic variations will find the desired explanations in Friedrich von Hellwald's book, "House and Farm" ["Haus und Hof"] (1st vol., 1888). The various traditional costumes of the regions are, of course, part of these characteristic types of houses of past times. The reader will already know more about them than I could tell.

There were many small towns; later on I will mention some figures.

The difference between them and the larger towns was often only the way they were administered. In economical terms the smaller ones among those in particular had a semi-rural character; which means: the population lived primarily on farming and gardening. Today we would say: most of them were country towns, similar to the town where Hermann's parents had their inn. You will certainly remember the scene from "Hermann and Dorothea" and more precisely the verse:

> Praise the burger of the small town,
> who combines the farmer's and the townsman's trade.

There you have your typical smaller, and in many cases probably also medium-sized, towns of that time!

It is my goal not to overburden the reader with too many numbers. Nonetheless you will not be able to escape some "statistical data" now and then as we call it in our formal and affected official jargon; but I will attempt to restrict myself to figures which even the unsophisticated mind is able to comprehend on first glance. Listen therefore: At the beginning of the century (1802/3) there still were 63,486 barns (and storage-houses) in the towns of Prussia. You see, that leads to the conclusion that the townspeople used to engage in extensive agricultural activity. In addition there were 14,088 "untended places" in the towns of that time. For example in the Department of Breslau towns still had 4,400 barns and 5,492 stables; in the region of Glogau 1,796 barns and 4,074 stables, etc. Therefore, it should not surprise us to learn that in the year 1801/02 the towns in the State of Prussia still had revenues of 10.5 million thalers from agriculture and almost 7 million thalers from cattle breeding.

In the smaller and medium-sized towns half-timbered houses were still predominant; by the beginning of the century not more than 24,643 houses of a total of 1,454,475 buildings and hearths in all of Prussia were made of brick, i.e., approximately 17 per thousand. But even the thatched and shingled roof had not entirely disappeared from towns, especially east of the Elbe river. For example, in the towns of the Department of Posnia, apart from 1,350 houses with tiled roofs, 20,393 houses with thatched and shingle roofs were counted; in the towns of the Department of Breslau the numbers were 7,425 and 20,342 respectively, and even in the towns of the region of Paderborn,

1,588 roofs were thatched and shingled, 3,443 tiled and 204 slated.

Even the Weimar of Goethe's later years was a town of not more than 8,000 inhabitants who lived in 800 houses. The houses must have been rather small: they sheltered two families at the most. Some houses still had thatched roofs, most of them were shingled. They were mainly inexpensive structures: 150 at a cost of 200 thalers each, another 150 at a cost of 400 thalers each. Only four private homes were valued at between 10 and 20,000 thalers.

But even the larger and largest towns still looked a lot less "urban" than today. At the beginning of the century most German cities had hardly expanded beyond the size they had reached in the late Middle Ages. Beyond the old town walls, which in their majority still existed, only a few scattered houses were to be found in the midst of gardens and fields. Often enough, these gardens and fields even reached into the center of town. Imagine, for instance, Breslau encircled by its town-moat, which was part of the rampart. When General Tauentzien was dying, he asked to be laid to rest far away from all the hustle and bustle of the city outside the city gates. Now, as you know, his monument stands in the middle of the city surrounded by roaring traffic.

And what did it look like in Berlin, the largest German (now Reichs-German) city which in 1800 had almost 200,000 inhabitants (1800: 172,023; 1804: 182,157)! It will interest you to hear the report of a contemporary observer who compares Vienna with Berlin. Even in those days Vienna had already reached a totally different level of cultural development than Berlin, even though according to today's standards it seemed lacking in comfort. The person reporting is the councilor of defense from Cölln; his comparison originates from the year 1800 and reads in its characteristic paragraphs as follows:

> Vienna is located in a fertile garden, surrounded by high mountains, among them the Schneeberg in the Steiermark (6–8 stations away from Vienna), with its permanent snow-cover towering majestically.
>
> In contrast, Berlin lies in the deserts of Arabia; from whatever side one chooses to enter, from east or west, from south or north, one is dragged through an ocean of sand by wheezing coach horses; in the summer the sun burns twice as strong on this sand and some pine trees, half-eaten by caterpillars, offer the only meager shade available. Not a trace of a mountain can be spotted as far as the eye can see, and where water is finally found, it turns out to be a swamp surrounded by a flock of pleasantly screeching lapwings. What you see on the fields are single stalks of grain whose seeds seemed to have been dropped there by birds.

The scene turns even more exciting when a storm arises, for then entire fields of fruits and seeds are whirled up into the air and deposited at a different site. Although we now have paved streets, their paltry surroundings remained.

One is glad to finally catch sight of Berlin's spires. Now, however, nearing the gates the traveler is hit by a pestilential odor because the people of Berlin unload all of their garbage outside the city's gates; and as if this were not enough, the knacker has set up his workshop at the road coming from Frankfurt: Everyone can imagine what a delightful mixture of stench originating from Berlin's excrement and the carcasses of dead pets is greeting the traveler.

Once one has survived the unbearable inspection by the customs officers and answered the hundred questions from the officer-on-duty to satisfy public curiosity (as this is their sole purpose), one is surrounded by shabby huts, meadows and fields (unless you enter through the gates of Friederichsstadt). Frequently you see nothing however, because the slightest zephyr stirs up such an unbearable amount of dust that you have to close your eyes.

Vienna does not have any palaces or official buildings which would match the Berlin castle, or its opera and armory, or the Palais Heinrich palace and other buildings in Berlin. In short: Vienna cannot be compared with Berlin as far as architecture and the regular and broad design of its streets are concerned, and in fact the latter excels by far. Nevertheless, Vienna has one advantage even in this respect which is lacking completely in Berlin. The pavement in Vienna consists of squared stones and one does not find any foul smelling and dirty gutters as in Berlin because in Vienna these gutters are all underground. It is a disgrace how little the police of Berlin interferes in this respect. The chamber pots are emptied into the gutters and so is all kitchen garbage and even dead pets, spreading an insufferable stench. The streets of Vienna are as clean as the hallways of a big mansion. Wagons are constantly driving around, picking up all kinds of waste, other wagons with big water barrels sprinkle the streets freeing them from all dust. In Berlin, in contrast, one is constantly wading in excrement or in dust.

Vienna actually has underground sewers which empty into the Danube, where all waste is discharged. Day-laborers are working in the many different lanes, sweeping up the waste; they are followed by a water-tank on wheels which flushes the garbage into the next sewer opening. In Berlin you constantly need to protect your nose with a handkerchief because towards the morning, you are met by the foul odor of last night's chamber pots having recently been emptied into the gutters; or if a villager is collecting one household's accumulated waste, the air of the entire street is polluted.

One cares little to dispose of dead dogs and cats, and I have often seen dead horses left on very busy streets for as long as half a day. There are also some locations which have been converted into public toilets, and pedestrians beware if by mistake you end up here after dark. After a rainfall, piles of excrement are heaped up in the streets and because these often are not picked up for many days and nights, it can easily happen that one mistakenly steps knee-deep into these in the dark.

A similar description of the conditions in Berlin in the year 1798 is given by a "candid Berlin citizen":

> The pavement of our streets is so bad and irregular that every visitor complains about aching foot soles. The ups and downs of the sidewalks are like hills and valleys and on evenings you run the risk of falling and breaking your leg. The paths leading over gutters are miserable and even in the center of Cölln-Berlin there are entire areas without one burning lantern. Thefts and robberies on the open street are therefore not unusual during the evening. Neither the bridges of Berlin's Spree River nor those of Potsdam's Havel River have safe railings. A recent accident at the Hundebrücke (now called Schloßbrücke) has again proven how vital such a construction is, since a local merchant fell straight into the Spree river on a dark evening as he came directly from the Lustgarten.

Repeatedly one hears complaints about the impassable streets of the cities of that time. No or poor pavement, no sidewalk, therefore dust in the summer and mud in the winter. But one also needs to consider that what we now call inner-city traffic did not exist then. Except for the few civil servants walking back and forth between home and office, by whose movements the residents along their route could set their watches, some errand-boys, travelers, and a few others, the inhabitants of even a larger city still led domestic lives without the constant hustle as nowadays. Laborers did not have to walk for miles to their workplace which most often was at the same location as their home; the thousands of items daily required were not obtained in an endless running about, shopping had not yet become a favorite pastime of ladies of all ranks because they were still predominantly occupied with home and garden and the care of their children, and strolling through the city was completely out of question.

In the evening one sat outside in front of the house, in the gazebo, or on Sundays one headed beyond the city gates, to one's own garden which all families that were better off still had, or walked through the fields and woods. After all, what kind of enjoyment would it be to take a walk in the city? There were no "fancily decorated" shop-windows along the streets, except for a simple showcase here and there displaying a few pairs of satin shoes or some scissors and knives or a number of horse harnesses: the craftsmen's array. In addition most streets were still narrow with many angles and corners and were by no means "leveled" so the line-up of houses was constantly interrupted by stone steps leading to the house entrances or by the protruding "window displays" of the craftsmen or some other structural obstacle.

The same is true for the means of transportation in the city. Either they did not exist at all, or if so, they were extremely primitive. At the beginning of the ninteenth century, Berlin had hardly any carriages; only a few coaches were available for public transport at the end of an opera performance or a play. Otherwise a carriage had to be hired from the home of a coach-driver: as it is still common in smaller towns today. In 1814 Breslau introduced the first city owned coaches stationed at Salzring Street and Neumarkt. And even that cultural phenomenon, the "omnibus," belongs to a far later time period (the "omnibus," this hallmark of our modern time epitomizes its peculiarity more than any other means of transportation): it appears in Hamburg 1843, in Berlin 1846, in Munich 1854, in Breslau 1862. But the people of those days had no need to be carted around in a 'monkey cage' a few times daily. I reminded you earlier that city dwellers, their prettier half in particular, were less mobile. Distances were short and one had not yet completely forgotten how to walk.

In addition to the impassable streets and the non-existent transportation system, street lights were inadequate as well. Only larger cities had something similar to a "public lighting system": the main streets had dim oil lamps a few hundred steps apart on wooden posts or hung from a chain across the street, which often were not even lit "when the calendar promised moonlight." At the end of the eighteenth century Berlin possessed 2,354 lanterns which were serviced from September to May. Those who found this insufficient took their own lantern when leaving the house in the evening or had their servant (if they could afford one) precede them or their 'sedan chair' with a torch.

What mental pictures are now appearing before our eyes! The deserted town, silent as early as nine or ten o'clock in the evening, with its romantic corners and lanes, barely lit by the moonlight, where in the shadow of a fountain or an alcove a late-night pair of lovers shyly hides and here and there a night reveller with his light passes furtively like a jack-o'-lantern. It was a major event when this silence was broken by the large bell pounding its hollow fire signal from the tower high above and calling the sleepy citizens from their beds to the water barrels and the clumsy manual fire-pumps. Usually the peace of the sleeping town was disturbed by nothing more than the moaning of tomcats in love and the hooting of an owl fluttering around the church walls. And then of course: every hour on the hour the stately tune which the slowly wandering night watchman produced with his horn. I am inclined to state that if the omnibus and nowadays the streetcars, transit lines, and subways are symbols of the modern city, the symbol of old-fashioned city life, as it was up to the nineteenth century in Germany, was the night watchman with his pike and horn: an expression of a child-like clumsiness and a backward attitude towards technical matters. But on the other hand full of originality and close to the soil as is no longer known nowadays. Today one blows a shrill whistle for a signal, whereas one sang in those days! Can you comprehend what this means?!

The elder among us may still have the distinct sound of the night watchman's horn in their ears. You, dear lady reader, have probably never heard of such a person. It may therefore be of interest if I give you the text and melody of the well-known song heard in almost all German cities night after night, as a quasi leitmotiv of German city culture at the beginning of the nineteenth century. I found it in a booklet by Otto Bähr, "A German City Sixty Years Ago" ["Eine deutsche Stadt vor sechzig Jahren"] (2nd ed., 1886), whose reading I would like to recommend at this point if you want to know more about the customs and habits of that time, of which I could only give a sketchy description here. He started out at 10 o'clock in the evening by singing:[#]

> Listen folks and let me tell you the bell has tolled ten,
> take care of the fire and also the light
> so that the town may come to no harm,
> and praise God, the Lord.
>
> [Hört ihr Herrn und lasst euch sagen,
> die Glock' hat zehne geschlagen,
> bewahrt das Feu'r und auch das Licht,
> damit der Stadt kein Schaden g'schicht,
> und lobet den Herrn.]

In the hours in between he sang the verse: "The bell has tolled."

At four o'clock in the morning he sang for the last time, ending with the following verse:

> The day banishes the gloomy night.
> You faithful Christians be cheerful and wide awake,
> and praise God, the Lord.

[#] *Note*: In the German version Sombart printed the musical score with the text.

9

The Emergence of Fashion

I.

Not every increase in demand leads to standardization. It could grow in quantity and widen in ever increasing diversities depending on its nature. Not every massive demand is a *mass demand* in the sense understood here, i.e., a demand for uniform or homogeneous goods. Here, we only need to examine if within the course of modern development mass demand is created.

In fact we are only interested in as far as the creation of modern demand is standardized independently from production. However, those cases will not be considered here where the producer in his own interest imposes homogeneous consumer goods on the buyer. For example, if a hardwood floor manufacturer influences good taste in such a way that instead of introducing creative patterns only the so-called capuchin floors, namely floors made of the tile-shaped diagonally placed small square oak boards attached to each other are marketed. These small boards represent an item perfectly suitable for machine automated production. All are of the same size and because they are solid, quality control during the selective process does not require a particularly high standard. But to us only the spontaneous change of demand within consumer circles is of interest.

One would possibly think that such simplification would merely be *a result of increasing population and wealth.* And indeed, this is most often the case. If more people now have a higher demand than they used to, such a conclusion can easily be substantiated, for example, if a hospital expands from formerly 20 beds to now 200 beds, all kinds of institutional requirements, the demand for the same kind of goods, increase tenfold. Also if more people can buy goods at a certain price due to the general increase of prosperity, a certain commodity which previously only sold in small numbers may then easily mushroom into a "mass article." All so called democratic items and "luxury" goods fall in this category. The famous silk stockings are an exemplary illustration. As Schopenhauer already mentioned, it was once the status symbol of a queen to own two pairs of silk stockings. Today, a coquettish girl would not be dressed up to date if she did not possess silk stockings.

On the 31st of August 1899 the *Confectionär* writes about a certain feminine type of clothing comparable to silk stockings—the silk *Jupon*:

> One would certainly not be accused of exaggerating if one places pure silk skirts of *moiré* and *glacé* taffeta among the rows of ready-made clothes goods, thus reflecting the immense demand of such wholesale wear. The public's luxurious inclinations are particularly well identified by this example, a wide preference for silk *Jupons* nowadays exists, comparing present day's consumption with the one of a few years earlier.

But one would certainly not mention the standardized demand as a trend of modern times, would this not be a consequence of increasing population and wealth. This tendency of standardization created by the latter would certainly be derailed by increasingly prominent different tastes in the course of cultural development. Consequently other factors play a role if we can actually state that the result of present developments—without doubt at least in some areas—is a concentration of variable requirements of standardized mass demand. Such a tendency of standardized demand is created through:

1. Formation of large conglomerates in the area of production and supply of consumer goods. Such a type of created demand among large industrial or commercial buyers naturally caters to a more standardized demand as opposed to formerly existing numerous smaller producers, smaller dealers, or individual owner-operated businesses. For example: if "canning"

fruits, vegetables, etc. by housewives and individual gardeners is taken over by large canneries, a demand for uniform or standard tin cans is therefore created. Or, if a shoe factory buys leather in bulk worth many hundred thousands Marks, whereas earlier thousands of individual shoemakers bought leather in quantities of single hides. Or, if large breweries now require many barrels of one size, whereas previously each small brewery maintained their own cooper workshop. Or if large establishments of the textile industry, the shoe industry, or garment makers require large number of cartons of the same size and type for dispatching. Or, if the expansion of modern business practices require standardized accounting, therefore requiring a larger demand of standard bookkeeping journals.

Case studies of a shifting demand belong to this category, which cannot be defined as clearly as steps of standardization from a previously existing individual demand, but which they basically are. If businesses tend to expand, they also require larger production facilities. In most cases the growth tendency of industrial and commercial companies leads to a tendency of expanding the premises. As a result, larger buildings create a demand for many standard components: bricks, doors, windows, hinges, flooring, staircases, lighting and heating fixtures, tables, chairs—all this requires larger standardized quantities for outfitting larger buildings instead of equipping many small ones.

But here I also consider the dimensional expansion of individual articles as a result of tendencies within large industries: the iron construction scaffold for a train station or exhibition pavilion is an example of standardized demand of previously diverse small scaffolds used for the same purpose. And if larger boilers, larger machines are needed, one may conclude the same aspects of development. Or would it be anything else than a uniform effort, if instead of several dozens of scythes—each of which would practically be of different shape—a mower combine is used; instead of hundreds of single ploughs, one steam powered plough is operated, etc.

2. The proletariat follows big capitalistic companies like a shadow. This development means nothing more than a new tendency towards standardized demand. The huge uniform masses of predominantly poor buyers with a past history of uniformed thinking and acting, and who were hardly left any time to form their own individual taste, are the logical buyers of massive consumer goods of poorest quality. One needs to pay special attention to the inevitable succession of individual development stages of production with regards to their capitalistic character. One must be aware that capitalistic shoemakers, tailors, carpenters, etc. could only thrive after the old traditions of craftsmanship in the textile and steel industry were crushed by the mills of capitalism, as will be explained below.

3. With the expansion of large capitalistic ventures, demand for *governmental administration* grows at the same time which again in many cases leads to a tendency of standardization. Is it always concentration of demand in some areas where individual taste gives in or was it only chance which covered individual's requirements? To the extent to which government and community activities expand, the need for many items will have a uniform character in future. One could call this bureaucracy of consumption. One interesting example of thought of such a causality follows: it is well known that in Switzerland school books and learning materials are under public ownership. This has caused standardization of these items to such an extent that only large companies can compete as suppliers in this market.[1]

4. Just as big capitalistic ventures cannot expand without increasingly hiring laborers, the activity of public institutions cannot expand without increasing an army of *civil servants*. This is another aspect leading to a tendency of standardized demand. Bureaucrats and civil servants can be labeled as part of the population who experience and share certain common uniform inner and outer characteristics. This is evident by looking at their official and private requirements: a uniform dress code is their dominant appearance. No doubt hundreds of town clerks or hundreds of post office employees, or hundreds of railway conductors have a more uniformed individual need than hundreds of shoemakers, tailors or even farmers. Their uniformed pattern of thinking is far more advanced thanks to their completely similar working environment and, therefore, a uniformity in their taste and judgment; but also their income is equalized by their budgeted salaries of completely equal amounts which is not the case with non-civic people whatever they may be.

   In the discussed cases standardized demand caused by the appearance of new special consumer groups is what can be defined as:

5. *Collective Consumption*, an appearance evenly noticeable in all consumer groups, certainly in regions of modern civilization, in large cities. This includes all such cases where now a satisfactory demand by larger groups of people is uniformly met which was previously only acquired by individuals or families. This development, as it also could be addressed, progresses toward the socialization of our existence, as commonly known, simultaneously in thousands and thousands of areas: here actually as a result of urban city planning such as the rise of apartment blocks, entertainment pubs, there especially as a consequence of progressive techniques in the community utilities of water, gas, and electricity supply; often as a result of a symptom of large city developments eliminating formerly family owned businesses. It may be that less family businesses are actually created: an increase of singles, relationships, or even marriages without a foundation of a so-called home, so that family run businesses attempt to and are able to free themselves

from the burden of crafting goods, repairing, etc.

The main activity of satisfying natural demands change over from the kitchen and rooms of single households to restaurants and cafés,[2] i.e., whatever is still consumed at home is now delivered almost completely ready-made to the individual household.

Obviously, all this has a similar impact on creating demand by standardizing it. Certainly, as much as the menus of a restaurant or canteen show a larger variety than household menus: they are definitely not as diverse as all household menus together of the families dining out on an evening. Even if this would be the case, the wholesale demand of each individual food item: bread, meat, potatoes, poultry, vegetables, etc. would require far larger quantities of each single staple.

Much more important than all other previously mentioned developments of standardizing demand is the inherent change of taste, the obvious

6. *taste standardizing* as a consequence of urban spreading with increasing commercial activities in modern countries. In the old days each region developed its own taste and each villager was proud of his traditions; the city dweller is different from the farmer or the nobleman. The break-up of estates' and rural lifestyle caused by modern capitalistic development leads to leveling out diverse taste. Now fashion and household furnishings, as well as every other specific demand of consumer goods throughout the region is dominated by the large centers of social life, the cities. Certainly here too, the influence of large industrialists had its impact. But on the whole, such standardization of taste is a logical consequence of economical development.[3]

II.

Of importance is how city life itself changes demand entirely. I call this evolving process here *urban demand* or in other words, *consumption*. The quality demands of our consumer goods change and in the same way as need alters, the general opinion about usefulness and fashion alters as well. Everyone has a certain opinion associated with expressions as country style or city style or intellectual taste. Summarizing the difference in one word, one might phrase that the preference for coarse, solid, durable goods declines in favor of enjoying fashionable, soft, gracious, *chic*. The peasant girl's traditional costume of heavy pleated skirts, coarse leather shoes, colorful thick woollen socks, bodice made of stiff felt, a rough linen shirt and extensive hair decoration, even with metal plates integrated in the braids as can be seen in Holland, contrasting with the city girl wearing a light batiste blouse with a yellow leather belt, light low-heeled shoes with transparent laced stockings, the colorful batiste shirts with sailor hats on their head and open curly hairdo—all this strikingly shows extremes in both directions of demand and taste shifted and developed over time. The history of shoes gives a good example about the change of usefulness influencing taste. People living in the countryside, or in small towns with badly cobble stone pavements all needed durable, sturdy, and waterproof shoes. Old-fashioned boots—as can be observed still worn by professors and privy councilors in cities—originate from a time when road conditions occasionally required trousers to be tucked into the boots to protect them from being soiled and becoming wet. In the past, when one often crossed the country on horseback, the high-shafted riding boots for men were common. Nowadays such heavy clothing with thick fur and ear muffs is only seen in weather-beaten regions east of the Elbe river. The constantly cleaned well-paved city with slab sidewalks, or traveling in heated trains, the invention of rubber boots, etc. have diminished the demand for durable and waterproof footwear and instead increased demand for light-footed more elegant though less sturdy footwear. The old-fashion knee-boot, the "long-shaft" vanishes. In accordance with hygienic needs, *chic* and comfort, the low heeled shoe, boots with buttons and lacing take over as practical footwear. Also the very light dress-shoes made of patent, soft goat skin or taffeta, thanks to the protecting galoshes, exceedingly gain market share. In previous times only the ladies in their carriages or nobility could risk wearing these.

But what really seems to characterize the city-like demand in contrast to the one of rural small-town regions is a much higher fluctuation and faster pace of change. This leads us to a tendency of diversity or change in modern *forms of demand* of a more generalized character and often originates from habits that are not indirectly city related but have a direct impact. Thus, it is necessary to separately address a third large tendency in the *change of modern demand* of commercial goods, i.e., a form of development which I would like to summarize under the definition of "Mobility of Consumption (and Demand)."

III.

A well-known fact observed by everyone is that nowadays most products have a shorter shelf life than before. The ancestors' household plays only a minor role nowadays. The young *nouveau* household starts completely newly furnished whereas our parents still used furniture, beds, linens, cutlery, and all household utensils during their marriage which still lasted at their golden wedding anniversary—and only in rare circumstances were these replaced. Today, as a rule, specially in better households the cycle of renewal already starts after ten to twelve years. We ourselves wore the home-made clothes of our parents and brothers and sisters, and the famous man's "tuxedo" or the wedding gown of the woman played a dominant role especially among the commoners. These robes lasted a lifetime and were passed on over generations like a permanent malady. Dealing with used goods and commodities, refurbishing old items was a flourishing trade in earlier times still around the middle of the nineteenth century. In most cities second-hand dealers even formed their own guild. In the old days trading with used items must have been booming when we hear that around the sixteenth century the nobility of France complained about the fierce competition for the local traders when shiploads of old hats, boots, shoes, etc. came from England![4]

Today the second-hand dealer plays only a minor role. In second-hand stores there are now rows of new suits and coats straight from the factory; next to old rummage one finds more often new mirrors and modern tables of freshly varnished fir.

A rapid turnover of commodity goods, furniture, clothing, jewelry can be noticed everywhere. One is labeled conservative, if shoes are soled a second time, and the bride is ridiculed if she stacks shirts, table cloths, and linens by the dozen in her closets or dressers, as the old custom used to be.

What is the reason for such a change, the joy of replacement and modification?

What is it, that has caused such a "Mobilization of Demand" indeed?

The superfluous observer will have a quick answer. He wants the reason for such change of consumption to be solely seen in the *new techniques* of production of consumer goods. "New goods do not last as long as before," "with such low prices it is not worthwhile to spend much time repairing items; you discard them if they are broken and buy new ones." Regarding this more closely, this attempt of an explanation turns out to be a hollow phrase: that the goods today are less durable in relation to their price paid in earlier times generally is not correct: an additional explanation is needed why one would make a change if enticed to change thanks to lower prices.

This may be because of the multitude of *changed living conditions* under which namely the city dwellers live today. A large impact on the kind of demand required came obviously from the common rental housing expanding. It created modern mobility and with it a declined desire for long-lasting, permanent, solid furniture. The fact that these are almost fully "mobile"—now even the stoves (long-burning stoves!) are mobile—whereas previously window nooks, the oven corner bench, even the bed and other household items were fixed permanently in the house, thus creating a tendency to design the goods to be of lightweight and not to be everlasting. And even the mobility of the people themselves: constantly moving from place to place, from street to street within the same city, does this not bring about the wish for lightweight transportable furniture? It seems to be almost unbelievable when one reads about the extent of restlessness of the population. In the city of Breslau with a population of 400,000 (1899) a total of 194,602 people moved, whereas within Hamburg within the same year even 211,783 parties (!) changed their domicile. In (1899) the following were registered (NB not including travelers)[5]

At	Arrived	Left
Berlin	235,611	178,654
Breslau	60,283	54,231
Hamburg	108,281	86,245

But more important is the fact that with the change of technology and general living conditions, as mentioned several times, a *new generation* has taken over. People tend to transform their inner restlessness and mobility toward their surrounding living conditions. We would like a change of our daily used appliances. We are irritated if we constantly wear and see the same clothing. People are driven by a need for change which often leads to acts of discarding used household items. Without remorse, a couple might completely refurbish their home on their Silver Wedding Anniversary, as if the twenty-five years of joint usefulness with thousands of closely knot ties between the inhabitants and their furniture never existed; this might appear barbaric to a sensitive person. But the new generation lacks sentimental and emotional feelings of the past. Times are tougher and consequently such a relationship between the individual and the daily personal belongings has been stripped of its emotional and romantic charm which once radiated warmth from our parent's home even if one calls it kitsch. Nowadays this—very often!—lacks in the glamorous salons of our grandchildren.

To a great extent the constant change of daily used goods is not necessarily the result of a conscious decision. Many times the individual is bound by customs or influenced by his group or peers. He makes changes because he has to. Change has turned from an individual into a social factor winning the far reaching importance gained today. The reader notices the level this research has attained: we are confronted with the problem of change of fashion and the issue has to be resolved; this phenomenon requires an explanation: a *fashion theory*.

Much has been said and written about fashion by sophisticated historians,[6] intellectual psychologists,[7] and ingenious aesthetics.[8] Usually, when consulting economists who have dealt with this issue we hardly find thorough research, often only repetitions of what laymen have written.

In all compendia and textbooks we trace the mediocre joke of Storch who has labeled fashion as "opinionated consumption." As far as I can see, this has not yet been surpassed. Occasionally one argues if and to which extent "fashion" should be banned from an ethical point of view—and that is it.

As such, the following major aspect must be observed in an *economic theory of fashion*. Foremost the question has to be asked what important role does fashion play in the economy; and soon the answer could be found in the influence it has on creating the type of need. One does not need to argue much about the definition of fashion. Without further concerns one can accept Vischer's definition "Fashion is a general expression for a complex cultural creation valid during a certain period of time," provided one gives a proper meaning to the individual aspects of this definition. Two essential accompanying aspects of the fashion which are of prime consideration for the economy are:

1. its inherent creation of change—but this is also often overlooked.
2. the imposed standardization of creating the type of need. Let us imagine a certain type of need independent of fashion, the time of such an object in use would probably be longer, the diversity of such individual consumer goods would most likely be greater. Each fashion always causes a multitude of people to standardize their demand as well as they were compelled to change at an earlier stage than an individual consumer would deem necessary—would he have had an independent isolated choice. Both: uniformity and change are relative expressions. For example, at which point in time does the latter turn "traditional costumes" into "fashion," such timing is difficult to determine. It may be said that each change of fashion which results in a shift of need over the time-span of one generation may be "fashion." However, such a differentiation in defining is less important than the comparable aspects of a change of the type of needs over various time-spans. This leads us to the question if, indeed, only the presence is responsible for introducing "fashion" to take its place in history. And what would justify this context when describing the evolution of a modern economy that "fashion" is defined as part of the process of innovation?

No doubt "fashion" does not solely appear in the nineteenth century: we will have to place *its origin*, if at all, at a much earlier time. Actually I would not go as far as Julius Lessing who sees the "spirit of fashion" active constantly throughout all centuries: disapproving attitudes of newly introduced fashion wear, found in moralizing literature as far back as to the founding fathers of the Church, can not necessarily be considered as an existence of "fashion" in the modern sense. But undoubtedly we encounter true fashion in Italian cities already in the fifteenth century[9] and during the sixteenth and seventeenth century, fashion madness expanded considerably to the north.[10] During the renaissance Venice and Florence had imposed dress code fashion for men as well as luxury laws for women. In Naples, for example, where no fashion by-laws existed, the moralists claimed without joking that no differentiation could be made between nobility and commoners. Also, they complained about the very rapid change of fashion and the foolish admiration of everything coming from France whereas it was often originally Italian fashion only returned by the French (Burckhardt).

And the rulers' exquisite time of the ancient regime, the century of Watteau, Boucher, Fragonard, Greuze cannot be imagined other than under the temperamental sceptre of the fashion goddess. If Mercier proclaims at one point[11]

> il est plus difficile à Paris, de fixer l'admiration publique que de la faire naître; on brise impitoyablement l'idole qu'on encensait la veille et dès qu'on s'aperçoit qu'un homme ou qu'un parti veut dogmatiser, on rit; et voilà soudain l'homme culbuté et le parti dissous

these words could have been used throughout all of his work as a motto because they signify the essence of everything he told us about old Paris.

And despite all this, one is tempted to declare that the real meaning of fashion only blossomed during the past century, only within one generation, so that only lately the full fashion characteristics left a distinct mark to such a degree which allowed such determining influence on the course of the economy which at this point entirely inspires our interest for fashion. However, what it is that predominantly characterizes *modern fashion* and what fashion in former times either did not have or only of much lesser intensity is the following:

1. the immense *quantity of commonly used items* which it includes. This diversity is produced by the increased expansion of production of goods in general. It is incredible what is required today for example for the perfection of feminine cosmetic or what is required for a cavalier; and the more useless the object the more fashionable it becomes. What the dandy employs, if in full outfit, besides all his "gadgets" other than the complete clothing he wears, fills a neatly packed small suitcase. The diversity of these "fashion articles" will still increase because new categories of fashionable consumer goods are constantly added. Just recently the following clothing articles were given fashionable design status: underwear, ties, hats, i.e., straw hats, boots, umbrellas, etc.;
2. the *absolute common acceptance of fashion* which only took place in our time. Though in the renaissance, despite the upcoming influence from France, the diversity of fashion even in some Italian cities still continued to evolve[12] and continued more or less up to the nineteenth century, the consistency of the type of needs remained restricted to a certain social class. It is the pattern of our times that fashion spreads with the intensity

of expanding gas in no time completely in all areas of modern culture. Today, the trend toward equality is widespread, not hindered by any regional or rank barriers. At last

3. the *rapid speed in the change of fashion* becomes also a characteristic sign for fashion in our times. What we have analyzed as a change of fashion over past centuries has always only been a shift in the types of need determined over the years. Today it is not uncommon, for example, that women's fashion changes within the same season four to five times. And if we believe to detect a certain "fashion" with a lasting life span over a number of years, we are highly astonished and talk about it when it refers to fashion of clothing—until such a lasting design becomes part of our "traditional fashion" e.g., men's tuxedos. However, also in this case the lasting life span only refers to the archetype: fashion continuously experiments and varies with details. Who, for instance, would not be able to recognize the two- or three-year-old tuxedo through the difference in cut and material?

> Like a naughty child that will not stop pestering, fashion is driven; tugging, moving, modifying and reversing, stretching, shortening, tacking, threading, creasing, ruffling, whirling, inflating, whisking, flattering, brushing, curling, puffing up, in short it is devilish work, every inch a showpiece but also rigid overpowering, without imagination, identical, similar to a formal tutor of Spanish Court customs as she dictates in a cool manner followed by absolute agitation; or acts like a wild bumble bee or a disgruntled aunt, like a group of wild teenagers and their pedantic supervisor, all this combined.[13]

What exactly is it why all these characteristic traits of fashion have become so dominant in our time, which preferably labels itself as time of enlightenment? This question has of course been asked often and has been answered just as often but I must confess that I am not fully satisfied with any attempted explanation. I am not referring to the characteristics or fashion in general. Simmel's and Vischer's research is of such quality that hardly anything new could be added. The basic thoughts of both authors that fashion "displays a special way of life, where one tries to find a compromise between the tendency of social equality and individual different stimulants" (Simmel) is certainly a correct interpretation of the psychological peculiarity in fashionable behavior. But I refer to those theories where intensive progression of fashion in our times evolves and penetrates all social life of today, especially modern fashion with the above mentioned temperament. They all make a distinct artificial and doctrinaire impression: Vischer for example sees the strong expression of fashion in our time as the result of a strong concentration reflecting on the train of thoughts of the eighteenth century, grounded and molded into our conscious. On first glance one is aware that the author does not have a realistic perception of the way and manner "fashion" works nowadays, and also not of the driving forces mainly being responsible for its creation. It appears to me, however, that the exact knowledge of these processes only leads us to trace the peculiar circumstances of fashion as it is developed in our time, giving us the means to properly answer the raised questions.

In order to interpret such an extraordinary *complicated relationship at work in the creation of fashion*, I select a certain branch where fashion plays a dominant role: i.e., women's fashion. I will simply mention how fashion tends to evolve within this development.[14]

Let us begin with the *Breslauer Damenmäntel-Konfektionshaus,* a ladies' coat store which we will enter during the Whit week in 1900. We will notice the sales departments stocked with jackets and coats needed for the spring and summer of 1900 which final destination is not of our concern here. We also find huge wholesale warehouses stocked with garments to be worn in the winter 1900/1901. These are presently only sample collections for the traveling sales agents setting up their orders all over the province, the same fashion collections to be taken by the group of salesmen to their customers outside of Breslau the week after Whit Sunday. These coats and jackets are of a certain fashion: the fashion of the following winter. How was this created? We could use the words *through inbreeding*: Designers of the *Breslauer Haus* have made sketches and patterns of winter clothes, linking them with the existing summer fashion, which are then manufactured: upon approval. But predominantly borrowed ideas are represented by rows of garments in our local stores: most of the displayed pieces are according to Berlin models which the owner of the store had bought a few weeks earlier in the Capital's leading fashion house, the *Mannheimer & Co.* Our journey to the roots of fashion leads us to Berlin: what kind of intuition had created the Berlin collection samples? Again in part by means of individual design: a larger and more skilled staff of designers employed by Berlin's fashion stores has created a new winter fashion by changing and modifying the proposed summer patterns and previous winter patterns from 1899/1900—everything depends on these changes: for example if the winter clothing of the coming season has copied the opened slit-type sleeve of the summer fashion of 1900—quite impractical and purely for the sake of it—this part of summer fashion becomes a winter farce. However, even the Berlin collections which are the leaders for German provinces have only some uniquely own creations. Foreign models have also considerably influenced the development. This time, models from Paris, which Berlin salesmen have bought in Paris during the winter of 1899/1900. Paris has numerous stores dealing exclusively with designer clothes and distribution of such sample creations, the so-called *maisons d'échantillonneurs*. Where do these houses get their fashion from? These too are not own creations, they reflect a predominantly strong creative influence. These reflections of such "echantillonneurs" finally are the famous tailors of the glittery or less glittery and glamorous world in Paris radiating fashion in all directions. They are the ones that create the original fashion, in our example the winter fashion 1900/1901 for *Leitomischel* and *Krotoschin* in spring, summer, and fall of 1899.

This is a study on its own, a very original and interesting chapter: "The Genesis of Paris Fashion" some parts of which I may repeat here.[15]

The great masters of dressmaking are world renowned as a club of their own: the "grands couturiers," the "tapissiers des femmes," as they like to call themselves and which Michelet is said to have called them: "pour un tailleur, qui sent modèlle et recifie la nature je donnerais trois sculpteurs classiques." They are not few in number. Even the leading houses can be counted almost by the dozen, among which the most prestigious are Rouff and Lafferière, Pingat and Worth, lately above all Doeuillet and Doucet. These very top are almost autonomous in "creating" fashion; rarely do they make use of an "inspiration" of the "vendeurs d'idées," the "dessinateurs de figurines," of which twelve exist in Paris and who sell for hard cash. They follow their client's instructions seldom and only as an exception.

In fact this is only their medium, the instrument they use. Above all, the dominant stars and next in line the heroes on stage—in spring 1899 for example Me Bartet as Francillon, presently Réjane, who is Doucet's *Mannequin*—serve to "promote" most of the creations of the mentioned masters. However, because the spell of the *demi-mondaine* over Paris naturally is not as great in the winter as it is during the nicer periods of the year, the actual creative fashion seasons occur in spring and fall: highlights are the *firis* in the *salons*, the *concours hippique*, the races in Auteuil and above all the Grand Prix in Longchamps during the spring, and lately also the Grand Prix in the fall. If the new fashion becomes a success, the *mondaine* soon follows the *demi-mondaine* and a continuous process as previously described can go on 1½ to 2 years later until it also reaches the small border villages near Russia.

We mentioned: the European-American fashion is the very own creation of Paris tailors. This is only correct to a certain extent: it only refers to the style "*fasson*" of garments. Let's keep in mind that our master must compose his creation with the help of practical fabrics, he needs silk and wool, velvet and fur, laces and frills, borders of all kinds, buttons and buckles, feathers and flowers, in short an unlimited array of ready-made articles which are already a common supply by the time they reach the *couturier*, which, therefore, *already must be established as being fashionable.* Without doubt the "creative" tailor has also an influence on fashionable items in all branches where such items serve his creations. On the whole, however, he uses the fabrics and accessories as supplied to him by different industries for his creations. In our discussion regarding fashion we have again reached a further aspect: we must consider the creation of fashion in the supplementary industries of accessories for tailors.

And again we enter the designer offices who serve the manufacturers when they draw "samples" and "models" for items such as fabrics, borders, draping, produced by the factories and assembled in sample collections to be presented to the clients (in this case not the consumer but another manufacturer or wholesaler or retailer). Whoever cannot afford an in-house designer subscribes to such new "designs." In Paris the textile branch maintains speciality stores for such sample productions, where large weavers at home and abroad can cover their requirements of new ideas and designs for every season in exchange of lump sum payments. Some branches of certain industries had such sample collections of the new fashion approved by a collective vote of salesmen.

The "chambre syndicale de fleurs et des plumes" issues a color chart as a standard guideline for all flower and feather goods annually. This in turn is influenced by the silk ribbon sample charts sent out for viewing by the silk ribbon manufacturers of Lyon and can be bought at a price of three Marks everywhere.

This results in a net of interdependent business relations between several branches of a certain industry in accordance with this slightly schematic description. In fact this is still an endlessly complicated process where fashion is revitalized and redistributed. Even if it is in theory and in a larger perspective correct that the general development of women's fashion accessories, i.e., the fabric and button fashion was created in the winter of 1898/99 by the French industry for dresses and coats later worn in the eastern province of Germany during the winter 1900/1901, one must consider that this straight line of development is crossed by numerous tendencies of different directions: because German or other tailors and stylists copy the French fashion from the original without using the tedious mechanisms of inter-mediation on which we based our description; that designs and sample collections were distributed earlier in the textile industry than their finished garments. They therefore can create their own fashion because they assist in distributing throughout the numerous fashion magazines and fashion journals the new fashion already at the moment of their creation, partially spreading fashion out throughout the world at its embryo stage. The informants want to have heard, e.g., as written in the *Confectionär* on June 1, 1899,

> that the master couturiers of Worth and Pingat have withdrawn their support of a tighter sleeve for coats and paletots of the fall season....Redfern will create fall models made of two types of fabric...At Franck in Rue Auber they intend to imitate a carp's pattern....Doucet will try with the promotion of the M^{me}Rejane to market the Empire-dress line again, etc. etc.

Finally it remains to be considered that when a foreign duchess or ambassador's wife brings her design, acquired from a famous Paris "dessinateur de figurines," to her tailor in Vienna, London, or St. Petersburg for sewing, he borrows the bright inspirations of taste from the center of creation. Occasionally one can also reckon with an own creation at events such as the Ascot race or Vienna Derby. At least it is possible that during such happenings a new English or Vienna fashion trend is born and may take off all over Europe and America, for once not beginning in Paris.

All this can be applied to the one—indeed most important—

province of the fashion empire. For all the rest other often deviating rules apply. For instance, the center of the creation of gentlemen's fashion comes from the milieu of the Prince of Wales, who's rules of hat forms and tie colors reach out far beyond the two borders of India. Shoes and boots are particularly capricious in regard to fashion. Since Vienna's influence receded, they often obtain their guidelines from America and one could state that this fashion is revived in a more abstract sense: often only by mediation of professional magazines and fashion journals, without interference (in the actual sense) of actual liveliness of such feet. Sometimes even this triggers a special fashion. For instance the Molière shoe-creation became popular soon after the actress Otero walked along the beaches of Ostende in 1899, etc.

I would think that what has been mentioned so far is sufficient to draw conclusions about the subject we are dealing with. A determining fact drawn from the study of the processes of fashion creation is the observation that consumer participation remains restricted to a minimum; the driving force behind the creation of modern fashion is in fact the venture capitalist. The performance of the Prince of Wales or a Paris actress can be attributed as supportive mediators.

All aspects of modern fashion, some of which we have mentioned already, therefore can be explained from the characteristics of a capitalistic cycle within the economy: a task which now can be solved without any difficulty.

A businessman, be it a producer or salesman, is driven by competition to always offer his customers the newest or he runs the risk of losing them. If half a dozen of garment factories compete in selling to a small town clothing store it appears absolutely unthinkable that all are not at a level of the latest fashion trend. The fabric mill offering a city tailor a design outdated by just a few months or the cotton factory not offering the fashion accessories bazaar the latest products would be eliminated from the start. Business, therefore, always strives to be up-to-date—*at the very least*, to always have the newest sample collections and the latest designer display copies. This explains the wide spread generalization of fashion. A large number of business categories are determined to *at least* outbid competition with alluring novelties enticing the customer to make a purchase. In a capitalistic market such a competition builds up the second tendency of modern fashion: the tendency of a fast turnover.

An atmosphere of feverish creativity is established wherever the producer is at work generating his own "latest creation," e.g., when a clothing manufacturer or a textile factory employ their own designers, especially those stores that only exist in order to supply novelties to others. One squeezes water out of a stone, racks his brains, how to come up with something "new" over and again—and this is of prime importance—in order to be marketed successfully. At this point I will repeat a report of a situation of the textile industry which reflects the mood of all branches of businesses and highlights the situation. In the issue dated May 11, 1899 of the *Confectionär* it reads that reviewing sample collections (for spring 1900) has begun:

> This expensive and difficult section of our production causes us more headaches from season to season. The question: which samples to choose from? is easily asked but hard to be answered. New products, new articles, new designs are to be marketed. Years ago this was easy for producers and designers when this topic was not as worn out and demand was more favorable. But now, where enormous efforts have been made everywhere and are still made, where over the past years already almost everything has been shown and offered, where each form of embellishment, be it leaves or flowers or ornaments, diagonal, long stripes and traverse pattern in every possible direction has been exploited, each combination and each patch has been tried out and applied, and each type of yarn has been used in all possible seam types and combinations, it becomes difficult for manufacturers, chief designers, collection managers and technical designers, it is often a substantial headache: assembling a new collection. Only a few years ago it was sufficient if the technical designers presented contrasting materials, at the most with some 'Rhine Gold' ornamental stripes. You would choose from a number of patterns of satin bases, repp-crême and some simple creations and would order some 'Rhine Gold' borders and some bereavement crêpes and the designer's collection would be completed. If something new came up, and that was at the time not very complicated, not much extra work was done over a period of one or more seasons including the *now totally vanished follow-up collection*, except...(it follows a list of stereotype samples). All these articles had been selected continuously and successfully.

Under such conditions it is easily understandable that manufacturers are highly pleased if an opportunity for "novelties" opens up or expands from somewhere else, in other words, if such article becomes more susceptible to fashion than before. A report (*Confectionär* of 13 July 1899) of the tie making branch reads:

> It cannot be overlooked that tie makers are given an ever increasing tolerance in

> their selection of fabrics....Former shades considered as bad taste are slowly looked upon as flattering. The more varied the color scale the more interesting and advantageous business becomes for the manufacturer and the retailer 'detailleur' because under such conditions *more frequently a radical change of genre* can occur which was out of question under former circumstances. Fashion has moved to the confection field of men's ties and sets all concerned factors in bustling motion.

Some other conditions within the social environment must be met to actually have an effect on the change of fashion from increasing competition amongst the businesses. As is presently the case, it could be possible that one competitor has an advantage over the other by offering better quality or lower prices of a product which is similar in style and material. Why this change through the transition of fashion? Firstly because more likely a fictitious advantage is created where a realistic one is no longer sustainable. It might well be still easier to make something different than better or cheaper. Additionally one may consider that an inclination of buying is enhanced if the newly advertised product has minor variations compared with the earlier one: an article is replaced because it is no longer "modern" despite the fact that it has not been worn out: Storch's well known "opinionated consumption." Last not least this identifies and takes into account the mood of the today's people, who, as a consequence of their inner restlessness, also increasingly enjoy change. But the decisive determining factor has not yet been brought up; which is the following: one of the main lures of our business managers is to make goods more marketable by giving them an appearance of greater elegance and that these items above all appeal to a consumer of a socially higher level in society—lending a certain prestige. It is the ultimate pride of the servant to wear the same brand of shirts the rich nobleman wears, of the maid to wear the same jacket as her mistress, the butcher's wife to possess the same velvet couch as the privy councilor, etc. A trait, obviously as old as the existence of social differences, an aspiration which could never before be met as perfectly as in our time, where technical advancements know no barriers for the *contrefaçon*, where the most expensive fabrics, the most complicated style could be imitated for one-tenth of its original price by mass production. Furthermore one may consider the enormous fast speed with which any new fashion reaches the attention of Messieurs *Toutlemonde*: by means of newspapers, fashion journals, but also due to increased traveling, etc.

The local clothing store owner complained: a few years ago, whenever a saleswoman arrived in the village with her new sample collection and began to unpack her suitcase that a crowd of astonishing admirers gathered around this foreign lady and exclamations of *oh's!* were expressed by the onlookers. Now you hear: "but excuse me...I recently read in my journal about the latest fashion, which is entirely missing here—as it appears to me—in your collection, dear Sir!..." And barely has the fashionable style become popular, the ladies' long paletot caught the attention within the circles of the beauties of Ostrowo, the clothing industry delivers exactly the same for 30 Marks which recently could not be bought below 80 Marks. A stylish summer shirt for men barely had been discovered with great effort, one which not every shopper could wear: the not starched, colorful shirts with attached cufflinks because they were too expensive, then already next summer those same colored shirts enhanced with soft inserts are available at a price of 1 Mark per piece, etc. This creates a true *steeple-chase* for new forms and materials. A peculiar characteristic of fashion is that it loses its value the moment it is a duplication of inferior quality. This forces a perpetual general distribution of a novelty to those levels of the general population which feel somewhat better to constantly keep on looking for changing their required articles. It initiates a wild chase with increasing speed as production and transportation improve, constantly searching for new forms. When a new fashion has barely entered the upper society, it depreciates by the fact that the lower society adopts it as well; an uninterrupted circle of a permanent revolution of taste, consumption, and production.

The modern large department stores, i.e., *les grands magasins de nouveautés* play an important role in this process of understanding the inner nature of modern "fashion madness." One of their preferred tactics is to place an order of a huge quantity of a particular fabric or other fashion article with the manufacturer right after the first peak of demand had reached and surpassed the top circles of the rich and those wanting to look rich. Thus making it possible to buy at a lower price and to use it as a door crasher passing it on at cost: the consequences are that ladies who wish to dress à la mode or furnish their household accordingly and who do not possess enough money but wish to imitate the top ten thousands of society now eagerly use the opportunity to buy *en masse* the *dernière nouvauté* in the *Bon Marché* or Louvre. Naturally, these goods are not bought at all by the "better" high society.

With this last train of thoughts we already surpassed the theme that this chapter was dedicated to: the change or transformation of consumption—and already moved to the next subject which will deal with the interpretation of new forms or a reformation of ways of supply.

We will leave this charming chapter of "madness à la mode" and the manner in which it presently plays its droll role with the impression that our explanations have clearly shown, the relations existing between the fashion phenomenon and the structure of our economy. One needs not to fear of being accused of exaggerating if one states: fashion is the favored child of capitalism. It stems from the latter inner characteristics and expresses its uniqueness unlike any other phenomenon of our social life in our time.

Notes

1. Cf. *Fachberichte aus dem Gebiete der schweizerischen Gewerbe*, 1896, p. 120.
2. It cannot be doubted by an attentive observer that this development is only at its beginning. It will receive a tremendous support to the extent of an expansion of co-operative economic activities. Lately this idea was supported by a brilliant as well as an energetic calculating promoter, Lily Braun; see her writings *Hauswirtschaft und Sozialdemokratie* [*Home Economy and Social Democracy*], 1901.
3. A vivid description of a change of taste in relation to clothing in a small west Prussian village (Löbau), is found in U. IV. 195 f. 201. The influence of "fashion" in this process of unity is mentioned on page 1701 and others.
4. Complaint brought forward in the Upper House in France, 1597, that the British "remplissent le royaume de leurs vieux chapeaux, bottes et savates qu'ils font porter à pleins vaisseaux en Picardie et en Normandie." G. D'Avenel, *Le mécanisme de la vie moderne*, 1896, p. 32.
5. *Jahrbuch deutscher Städte* 9. 253.
6. Compare the writings discussing the history of fashion and historical costumes: Falke, *Die deutsche Trachten- und Modenwelt. Ein Beitrag zur deutschen Kulturgeschichte* [*The German Costumes and Fashion World—An Essay of German Cultural History*], 1858; Weiss, *Kostümkunde* [*Costume History*]; J. Lessing, *Der Modeteufel. und viele andere* [*Fashion Madness and many others*]. An entertaining popular written story about fashion (clothing) written by R. Schulze, a chapter of *Die Modenarrheiten* [*Fashion Madness*], 1868, 1868.
7. Compare, e.g., G. Simmel, *Zur Psychologie der Mode in der "Zeit"* [*Psychology of Fashion in the "Zeit"*], 12 Oct. 1895 .

8. F.T. Vischer has dedicated one of his most amusing writings to our subject: *Mode und Cynismus*, 1st ed., 1878; 3rd ed., 1888.
9. Compare J. Burckhardt, *Cultur der Renaissance* [*Culture of Renaissance*], 3rd ed., vol. 2 (1878), 111 and *passim*.
10. Literature is more often concerned with "Madness of Fashion": Compare, e.g., L. Hartmann, *Der à la mode-Teufel*, 1675 (cited from Lessing); or certain parts in Horneck, *Oesterreich über Alles, wenn es nur will*, 1684, p. 18.
11. Mercier, *Tableau de Paris 2*, 1783, 75.
12. J. Burckhardt, *a.a.O.*, 113.
13. Vischer, *a.a.O.,* 52.
14. The following description originates primarily from own experience and the discussions with industrialists and wholesalers of several branches. The only part used from existing literature is the work of Coffignon, *Les Coulisses de la Mode* (ca. 1888), which inspired me. However, it is written in a sketchy feuilletonistic style. Also many of the trade journals offer rich material about individual subjects which however need to be updated in a scientific way, each branch has half a dozen or more of these journals, namely Austrian, French, and American. Very explicit is the German journal of the *Confectionär* which is published two times weekly per season with issues with 64 glossy pages. The description mentioned in the text has been verified according to the previous annual issues of the *Confectionär.*
15. Apart from the already mentioned writings also compare: G. Worth, *La couture et la confection des vètements* und *Circulaire* No. 14 *Series A des Musée social* (30 June 1897): "L'industrie de la couture et de la confection à Paris."

IV

The Interaction of Economy, Technology, and Politics

10

The Influence of Technical Inventions

Is it possible in picture to one's mind that peculiar economic animal, the modern commercial man, without reference to the technical inventions and improvements of the last five centuries, particularly those that have facilitated production and transport? We think not. But what is meant by technical improvements? In the widest sense, any applied knowledge to achieve a given end; in the narrower sense, the utilization of instruments either for manufacturing goods or for moving from place to place commodities, persons, or news.

Such being the case, are we justified in placing technical inventions among the social factors that have helped to mold the capitalist spirit? Surely technical inventions are due to individual knowledge. That criticism is just; but it must be remembered that the first condition for the growth of technical knowledge is an organized social system. Another objection must also be met. We talk of the effects of technical inventions on the capitalist spirit. But may it not be asserted that technical inventions are themselves the offspring of the capitalist spirit? How, then, can they be looked upon as its generator?

In the first place, every technical invention is not necessarily due to capitalist enterprise. Many advances in technical science are due to pure accident, and even those that are sought after often take on a shape least expected. But suppose that indeed every mechanical invention be due to the influence of the capitalist spirit, would not each invention, in its turn, help to shape the capitalist spirit in its further growth? We see this over and over again: cause and effect combine as influences in its development.

The effects on the capitalist spirit exercised by technical improvements may be of two kinds, those that are direct, which we shall call primary, and those that are indirect, or secondary.

The very existence of an invention is due to enterprise. Inherently, therefore, all inventions exercise a primary influence on capitalism. Carry your mind back to 1484, before the discovery of the nautical astrolabe. No ship could venture on the ocean, for it had no means of directing its course aright. Overseas voyages were therefore impossible. But as soon as this difficulty was overcome, think what opportunities were opened out to enterprising spirits.

Take another instance. Before the water-pump was invented in the sixteenth century, a limit was set to mining, seeing that man could not control the water in mines. But when it became possible to extend the working of old mines and to open any number of new ones, what an impetus must have been given to capitalists, who had only been waiting for their opportunity. Indeed, we can see how in the sixteenth century the gradual introduction of the water-pump into mines was followed by the participation of moneyed men in mining; in other words, how the mining industry was placed on a capitalist basis.

The same process manifests itself from century to century. Every invention that renders production on a large scale possible, and makes the process of manufacture more roundabout, results in the stirring up of latent powers of enterprise. Inventions give the conditions necessary for capitalist undertakings, but they also force their pace. The more complex and extended production and transport become, the more capitalist spirits are tempted to master the new conditions. "Undertakers to the fore" is the cry whenever a new invention is patented. Consequently, technical advance acts as a selective force among those who are engaged in economic activities; it trains the capitalist undertaker, from whom more and more is expected, the more the latest inventions make it necessary to have a more complex organization if the best results of technical science are to be attained.

We may go so far as to regard it as a law, certainly applicable to modern inventions, that the work of the capitalist undertaker in modern times goes on increasing. For every new mechanical appliance means the use of a greater number of instruments of production; means also, in the great majority of cases, the lengthening of the processes of production.

Look at our big industries of today—those which manufacture tools for production; which make machinery and the materials for machines. Undertaking on the largest possible scale is called for in these branches of manufacture—machine-making, iron-founding, coal-mining. It is obvious that those countries which, by reason of their natural resources, are best fitted for the growth of industries of this kind, are also splendid nurseries of the capitalist spirit. Accordingly, the coal and iron fields of Germany, England, and America have not been without influence on the expansion of modern enterprise. The same holds good for those countries that are blessed with an abundant water supply. Directly the water can be utilized as a motive power, say to generate electricity, an army of undertakers will rush to the spot. Incidentally, it is apparent why the capitalist spirit takes on different aspects in different countries. But certain it is that if any land is rich in coal and iron it will possess a more developed capitalism than its less favored neighbors.

One other fact must not be lost sight of. Technical improvements in our day have developed beyond the dreams of man. They have liberated applied science from the organized, living forces of nature, so that it can now utilize the energy which the sun has stored up deep down in the earth. Applied science no longer looks to men of flesh and blood or to the fields and woods for aid in making progress; it relies on dead matter and mechanical power for its achievement. What is the result? Technical improvements know no bounds; they make possible what was inconceivable before; they pile mountain upon mountain and create the universe anew.

We cannot here enter into a consideration of the reasons why technical improvements in modern times have achieved these marvelous things.[1] It must suffice merely to draw attention to the results, with which, indeed, every man is more or less acquainted. But the important fact is the bearing of these boundless possibilities on the growth of the capitalist spirit. Obviously they must have been a most potent factor in its development. The limitless expansion of capitalist enterprise today can be explained only by reference to the undreamed-of possibilities of technical science. You would not have the hustle and the hurry and the scurry of a modern capitalist undertaking if technical science were not able to perform marvels. In order to master this giant, man in his economic activities had to have recourse to organization, and the desire to hold him in complete control kindled a fire in the breasts of our big captains of industry that is consuming them, and with them the rest of us.

Nor must we forget the many-sidedness of technical knowledge. Every day produces something new, and so creates the need for a new form of organization. That only expands the possibilities of the capitalist spirit. Take a small illustration. In one industry, technical knowledge remains at a standstill for a decade or so, and you go on employing the same methods in your factory year after year. In another, technical science revolutionizes the processes of manufacture every few years, and if you are to keep pace with them you must introduce more modern organization. Often enough the new organization demands the foundation of an entirely new enterprise, and so technical improvements may be responsible for the setting up of a new factory or the starting of a new business. In many cases the enterprise owes its origin to the younger and more sanguine brother of the capitalist spirit—speculation. Hence, we may say that technical improvements are often responsible for speculative activity. Look at the history of the last few centuries and you will find that in the wake of epoch-making inventions, or in a period when inventions were particularly numerous, speculation became exceedingly active. Take the case of that wonderful age towards the end of the seventeenth century, to which I have already referred more than once, when speculation was for the first time at fever heat. But technical inventions were also very numerous; and indeed it was no less an age of projecting than one of inventing. Inventions were just beginning to appear, and therefore even those of minor importance were able to produce speculation on a large scale. Later on and more particularly in our own time, technical improvements became so commonplace that only the very important ones had sufficient magnetic power to call forth new enterprises. But their effects were all the more powerful. I need only mention by way of illustration two remarkable periods of speculation in the nineteenth century, one about the middle, in connection with railways, and the other towards the end of it, when there were numerous inventions for utilizing electricity.

All this goes to show that as technical knowledge advances it influences the will-power of modern man in his economic activities. But it does more. It also influences, nay, often enough revolutionizes, his thoughts.

To begin with, it gives that thought a goal and a purpose; which is another way of saying that it stirs and develops rationalism in him; and rational thinking, as we know, is an element of the capitalist spirit. The influence of technical improvements on the growth of economic rationalism in every age has already been noticed by many writers. Every new invention, as one authority puts it,[2] brings man into contact with reality, and by so doing crushes the traditional habits in his character, which, as we have noted above, are rooted deep in his being. So long as the inventions appear at rare intervals, their power to influence man's natural conservatism will not be great. It will be merely, as it were, a scratch on the surface, and before long all trace of it will have vanished. But as soon as inventions come thick and fast, as has been the case since the opening of the modern era, then their effect is more lasting. Constant changes in technical processes cannot but influence the state of mind of those concerned with them. But when the changes are themselves due, as is the case with inventions in our own day, to organized scientific thinking, their influence on the psychology of men is even stronger and more lasting.

All earlier technical advances,[3] remarkable though they were, were empirical in character; they sprang from the personal experience of generations of masters, handed down from one man to another. Those engaged in an industry knew all the "tricks of the trade," and contented themselves with them. The experience which had accumulated in the past was preserved for the future.

But from the seventeenth century onward natural science began to make its influence felt in supplanting the gathered experience of ages as the soil from which inventions sprang up. Henceforth new methods came to be used, not because one man who had acquired them by way of experience showed the way, but because anyone interested could learn the underlying technical laws and be assured of success if he conformed to them. Before, men worked according to rule of thumb; now they looked to laws, the explanation and application of which was the work of rational thinking.

The contrast between the old and new methods of work is paralleled by that between domestic handicrafts and industries on a capitalist basis; and the parallel is by no means accidental. In either case it is a contrast between empiricism and rationalism, or rule-of-thumb and scientific knowledge. Now, when in two such closely related spheres as technical knowledge and economic activities there is so great a similarity in development as that noted above, the inference is surely not far-fetched that the one has had an influence on the other. We may say, then, that economic rationalism owes much of its growth and expansion to technical rationalism.

As a matter of fact, we are not altogether without evidence on this point. Do we not all know that nowadays every business is organized in accordance with the demands of technical science? And does not every director of a business constantly study the technical side of the processes of production? The employment of technical specialists in business, as we have already noted (p. 143), is only in accordance with the demands of economic rationalism. All in all, the needs of technical science call for the very highest economic organization

Thought in economic activities, then, becomes more definite and conscious, in other words, more rational; and modern technical science has tended to make it so. But it has also helped to make it more exact and punctual, by providing the necessary machinery for measuring quantities, more especially for measuring time.

Clocks have played a very important part in the mental history of the business man. Pendulum clocks are said to have been invented in the tenth century; while the first clock worked by wheels was that made by Heinrich von Wick, in Paris, in 1364, for King Charles V. During the fourteenth century, nearly all the large towns in Italy had clocks that could strike twenty-four hours.[4] Watches were first invented by Peter Henlein in 1510. Writing about them in 1511, John Cocläus says, "He made small clocks of iron, which contained many wheels; they indicated and struck forty hours, and could be carried in the bosom or the purse."[5] In 1690, second hands were introduced by John Floyer as a more exact means of examining the pulse-beat—an instance, by the way, of an invention not due to economic needs. Now, the exact measurement of time became possible only when the necessary instruments were available, just as exact calculations in terms of money became possible only when technical progress was able to provide a reliable currency.

Punctual business likewise owes much to the gradual perfection of technical processes. Exact calculations as to the delivery of goods presuppose a reliable system of production; and it is not too much to say that modern means of transport have made modern commerce into a sort of huge automatic machine. Calculations of all kinds, therefore, were to a large extent made possible by technical progress. So was the hustle of the modern business man. Would all this haste be conceivable without railways, telegraphs, and telephones? There are, of course, other reasons also for the breathlessness of modern business, as we shall see; but ultimately it is due to technical progress, which intensifies it and makes it universal.

Technical progress can also be held accountable for the particular way in which the modern business man looks at the world. Everything for him is purely quantitative. No doubt this is due largely to the habit of appraising all things in terms of money. But it is not to be forgotten that what specially characterizes modern science is the same tendency of laying stress on quantity to the neglect of quality. The words of Kant are significant. Only when you can express any natural phenomenon by a mathematical formula are you entitled to speak of a law of nature.

Here, too, it would seem that we have alighted on a parallel development, that between the capitalist spirit of today and the scientific spirit as seen in technical advancement. The parallelism might be carried a good deal further.[6] But it would not be easy to show, in a general way, the influence of scientific on economic thought, and therefore I will not attempt it in this place. I want rather to direct the reader's observation to another psychological phenomenon, wherein once more we may see the interdependence of the capitalist spirit and the progress of technology.

Is it not a fact that the centers of interest in life today are very different from what they used to be? The cause of the change may be traced to the mighty progress in technical science, and its effect on the mental outlook of modern man must be admitted to be stupendous. That interest in problems of technical science is today very much to the fore can be easily understood. The remarkable achievements in the field of applied science have appealed to people's inquisitive faculty, have drawn all eyes on to themselves, and have given our age its cause for pride. And no wonder, when it is recalled that technical progress is the one sphere where we may fearlessly reckon up our gains and losses! The crowd, which always worships success, is quite naturally enthusiastic about those spheres of thought where our greatest achievements have been won, the more so as they are so easy of appreciation. It cannot be gainsaid that most people today (and this is specially true of our youth) are more interested in the progress of wireless telegraphy and aviation than in the problem of original sin or the Sorrows of Werther.

Nor is this all. Technical progress must also be held responsible for another characteristic of our age—that we value material things far too highly. We have grown rich quickly; we have come to regard peace as a certainty; and technical progress has shielded us from dread plagues and cholera. Is it surprising, then, that all idealistic tendencies have been pushed into the background by man's lower instincts—undisturbed enjoyment of pleasures and the craving for creature comforts? We are like a herd of cattle peacefully grazing in the meadow.

The overestimation of material things has had this result on the capitalist undertakers, that it has spurred him on to obtain the means of becoming rich. In other words, it has stirred up his acquisitiveness. The pursuit of the dollars is not so imaginary as some millionaire philosophers, writing from their high tower of princely wealth, would have us believe. On the contrary, it is one of the mightiest motive powers in our modern economy; and the intense greed of gain, generated as we have just observed, in part at least, by the progress of technical science, is one element in the composition of the soul of the modern business man. That this profit-chasing is now bereft of any shame that attached to it of old; that we no longer think it dishonorable for any one to engage in dollar-hunting; that we mix freely with people of whom we know that to make money is their sole aim in life—all this has only tended to cultivate this aspect of the capitalist spirit still more, and the impetus came from the new trend of things produced by advances in technical knowledge.

Another effect of our keen appreciation of technical improvements and our overvaluation of their results has been to intensify the love of profit in the capitalist undertaker in yet another way. It has heightened his interest in the technical side of business and manufacture. We have already noted it as a characteristic of modern economic activities that man is constantly making things, almost senselessly increasing them;

and that the only explanation of the phenomenon (if, indeed, there is an explanation at all) is to be found in a certain childish pleasure in technical perfection. And can we conceive of such delight except in a technical age? Can we conceive it possible, except in such an age, that an undertaker should think it of any consequence whether or not he makes ever so many machines or electric lamps or advertisement posters or airplanes? How can we explain his satisfaction in the mere production of these things, except that a sort of enthusiasm for producing is a driving power within him?

This enthusiasm for mere producing is akin to the zeal for "progress" which fills the soul of many an undertaker, and is responsible in America for the childish smugness of the intellectual life of the country. Every traveler cannot help noticing it. You associate it with children, with colonials, with those devoted to technical progress. For if the senseless idea of "progress" means anything, it means undreamed-of possibilities in the realm of technical science. You cannot say that Kant stands for progress as compared with Plato, or Bentham as compared with Buddha. But you can most certainly say so when you compare the steam-engine of today with that of Watt's!

The transvaluation of values in modern times is almost apparent in the habit of regarding the means to any end as the end itself. Here again, no doubt, money is to blame. But not money alone, for the responsibility is shared by technical science. Technical progress has brought it about that we care far too much to note how a thing is made and how it works, no matter whether it serves a noble end or not. The means (machinery), say, for controlling a whole transport system, or producing a newspaper, are now so wonderful that they take our breath away, and engage our interest to such an extent that we no longer think of the purpose they were intended to serve. We are astounded at the sight of the latest sample of a linotype machine, forgetting all the while that it is printing some journalistic "rag" or other. We feel a shudder down our backs as we watch a flying-machine ascend into the air, but never once do we realize that its only purpose for the present is to add an exciting item to a music-hall program, or, at best, to enrich a few mechanics. And so on in all things. Here, at any rate, is one explanation of the meaningless transvaluation of values in modern life and the futility of capitalist endeavor.

One other point. We have already seen that the bourgeois spirit of our age is utterly careless of man's fate. We noted how man is no longer the central fact of economic activities and economic thought. It is only the procedure that matters—production, transport, price formation. In a word, *Fiat productio et pereat homo*. How are we to account for this tendency, if not by tracing it to the changes which technical progress has brought about? Technology has liberated the work of production from the control of man. Before, we needed the living organism to regulate production; we now direct it by mechanical means.

The natural world, with its fullness of life, has been shattered to atoms; on its ruins an artificial world of dead matter has been erected by human ingenuity. And this is true for the economic sphere as for that of technical science. Technical improvements have had the effect of changing the face of the globe, and our whole view of the universe has changed in consequence. The more technical science tended to make man of less and less importance in the process of production, the more he was thrown into the background, not only so far as economic activities were concerned, but also in the whole sphere of human thought and action.

There are numerous indirect influences exercised by technical progress on the growth of the capitalist spirit, by the creation of circumstances favorable for its development. I propose to deal with two such cases; the reader will easily think of others.

In the preceding chapter we saw how the abundance of the gold and silver mines gave an impetus, in the sixteenth and seventeenth centuries, to the rise of feverish speculation. But we must not forget that the extraction of the precious metals was only made possible by advances in technical knowledge. Indeed, we may go so far as to assert that without technical science America might never have been settled. But I am thinking rather of the epoch-making improvements in mining, by the aid of which Europe was able to enjoy an abundance of silver in the sixteenth century. I recall such inventions as the pumping-engine, or the still more important process of extracting the silver from the ore by the aid of quicksilver—the amalgam process—which dates from about 1557. Once that was known, it was possible, at no great cost, to extract the pure silver on the rugged slopes of the Cordilleras, where it was found; and the new process so cheapened the expenses of production that silver-mining became exceedingly profitable.

This is one illustration of the indirect effects of technical progress on the growth of capitalism. The other that I have in mind made possible the rapid growth of population in the nineteenth century. This was due not so much to an increase in the actual number of births as rather to a decrease in the number of deaths. And was not this decrease due to two causes, both the results of advances in technical knowledge? The one was improved hygienic methods, better precautions against epidemics, and the progress of applied medicine; the other was a more perfected manufacturing and transport system, which enabled more people to be fed, and so to be kept alive. Now, the increase in population had, in its turn, consequences for the development of the capitalist spirit. On the one hand, a growing population necessarily leads to emigration; on the other hand, it expands capitalist enterprise to its utmost capacity. With the effects on capitalism of emigration we have already dealt. As for the expansion of enterprise, is it not obvious that the more people there are in a country, the greater must competition be? With a large population there is an increasing necessity for individuals to be economically active. With a large population it becomes more and more difficult merely to live on your income, merely to be a gentleman at large. The members of a numerous family look very differently on the need of earning their livings than do the members of a small one.

Where the children are many, the parents' fortune is necessarily divided into smaller shares than when the children are few. In the first case, therefore, there is greater call than in the second for the children to engage in some occupation, if they are to remain on the social level of their parents. An increasing population very soon creates a definite attitude of parents towards the economic independence of their children. Parents are more concerned with putting their children to a profitable trade than with leaving them sufficient to live upon without having to work.

The increased growth of the population in the nineteenth century, due chiefly to biological or social causes, has varied in different countries; and the variations will not be unconnected with the greater or smaller intensity of the capitalist spirit in each.

The Influence of Pre-Capitalist Callings

The last set of influences on the capitalist spirit that I shall deal with are the most obvious. A little reflection will show that there were some callings in the pre-capitalist period which were training grounds of capitalism.

First and foremost we must mention trade and commerce, where the seeds of capitalism took root quite early. Trade necessarily taught men the habit of thinking in quantities. The producer in the pre-capitalist age, whether a peasant or craftsman, was dominated, as we have seen, by the idea of quality; the trader, on the other hand, cared less for the quality of his wares, principally because he stood in no personal relation to them. Peasant and craftsman alike had a keen personal interest in the commodities they made; the articles were, in a sense, a part of themselves, an expression of their individuality. The trader was differently situated; his interest in his merchandise was purely objective. He knew little of the travail and care expended on the making of commodities; they reached him in their final form ready for sale, and he was able to look at them from one point of view only—that of their value in exchange. Now, value is represented by a quantity; accordingly, we see a second reason for this quantitative interest. The trader thinks in terms of money, and in the money value all conceptions of quality melt away. In face of this, may it not be said that the trader's calling, like the capitalist's generally, is concerned with money only; that all his thought is influenced by questions of money; and that therefore he must of necessity be a calculator? Of course, in the early stages of trade the calculations were of a primitive kind. But primitive or not, it was calculation, and the trader's calling provided the necessary opportunities for its development.

This holds good of commerce as a whole, and though its various branches and kinds influenced the soul of man in somewhat varying degrees, the direction in every case was towards capitalism.

Look at foreign commerce, the traffic that extends beyond the borders of the state. Its significance for capitalism is much akin to that of the emigration of peoples, for, like the latter, it tends to create a rational outlook on life and rational action. Is not the merchant forced to adapt himself to strange manners and customs? Does he not strive to choose the right place and to adopt the best methods for his activities?

One powerful aid to rationalist thinking is an acquaintance with foreign tongues; and the knowledge of languages comes easily from international trade. All these results of foreign commerce may arise when a central establishment appoints agents in foreign parts. The agents soon take on a more rational life, and before long infect their principals, to whom they send reports, and with whom, often enough, they come into personal contact. The disintegrating influence of commerce on a system of life dominated by tradition became stronger still when branches of one family of traders scattered themselves in all directions. The effect in such cases was the same as that produced by emigration on a large scale. The best instance of such a policy is furnished by Jewish trading families with whom it was almost a maxim to distribute themselves in different commercial centres.[7]

But the Jews did not stand alone in this policy; many a Christian family did likewise. There were Albertis, for example, at the dawn of the fifteenth century, in Italy, England, Flanders, Spain, France, Catalonia, Rhodes, and Barbary.[8]

Nor was this all. Foreign commerce aided the growth of the capitalist spirit by cultivating commercial morality, a specifically capitalist virtue. No doubt religious teaching gave a solid foundation to the confidence of traders in one another. As in so many cases, therefore, we see once more that an element of the capitalist spirit owes its appearance to more than one contributory influence. In this instance it is ethical teaching and business interest. Gustav Freytag was perfectly right when he observed[9]

> that the merchant cannot carry on his calling without a tremendous amount of confidence in others; both in those he himself employs and knows and those who are strangers to him; both in Christians and in heathens. Honesty is a necessity of commercial intercourse, and even if too great a confidence results in loss, nevertheless commercial credit is one of the bases of human intercourse.

The more frequent the intercourse the surer confidence becomes. In the process of time the trader realizes that it is not to his interest to be dishonest. He may lose his customers; he may have to waste a good deal of his time; and the ensuing loss would in all probability hardly compensate him for his ill-gotten profits. It is only natural, therefore, to find a gradual development of commercial morality; and the go-ahead grocers of the fifteenth no less than those of the eighteenth century knew from practical experience that honesty was the best policy. The realization of the soundness of this maxim as making for self-interest must have slowly gained ground with the expansion of foreign trade; and when teachers of morality gave it their support it only sank deeper into men's consciousness.

One other difference is to be noted, that between inland and overseas trade. The latter continues for a long time to have a dash of adventurous freebooting about it. Overseas trade therefore produced the dare-devil merchant who will take risks. Inland trade, on the other hand, rather lays stress on bargaining and calculating, and produced the careful merchant who cautiously balances gains and losses, and guards himself by amply-worded contracts. Inland woolen trade made the Florentines into the clever merchants they were. Indeed, inland trade (as a rule), rather than bold, enterprising overseas trade, cultivated the bourgeois virtues. That is why I cannot conceive of a book on holy economy appearing in the fifteenth century anywhere else than in the center of the woolen trade. Consider further the classical types of successful traders, the Florentines, the Scotch, and the Jews. None of them adventured on the sea; it was not in their blood to do so. From the very first they were inland traders.

A very special rôle in the history of the capitalist spirit was played by money-lending. We have already brought to the notice of our readers that the worldly-wise and energy-loving Schoolmen of the later Middle Ages regarded money-lending as an activity hostile to capitalism—and rightly so; and that they condemned it as sinful. Nevertheless, money-lending had a very wholesome influence on certain tendencies in the capitalist system. Because I look at the problem from another point of view than did St. Antonine of Florence, I can account for the fact that one reason why the Jews were so eminently prepared for capitalism was that they had been money-lenders from the days of Solomon, while in the Middle Ages it was a calling which they practically monopolized. I am convinced that my view on the subject is correct. Money-lending was one of the wellsprings of the capitalist spirit, much more so than trade, especially in an age when production was on a natural basis and quality a prime factor in it. And why? Money-lending knows nothing of quality; its all-embracing concern is with quantities only. In money-lending everything depends on contract, the substance of which relates to what service is to be rendered, and how much payment for it to be made; to expectation and delivery. Money-lending as such has nothing to do with producing for consumption; it does not call for any use of technical appliances; it is an intellectual economic procedure, no more and no less. Indeed, we can scarcely talk of economic activity in reference to money-lending, for there is no physical exertion entailed; and as it is only an intellectual process, its success alone has any meaning. All in all, money-lending is a most fruitful field for the development of the calculating spirit; we can conceive of the money-lender as sitting at his desk with pencil and paper making calculations all day long. Money-lending enables you to earn money without having to work in the sweat of your brow; enables you to make other people work for you, and that without any recourse to force.

What the professional money-lender lacks is, as Antonine saw long ago, the spirit of enterprise. He won't take risks. But should a money-lender, nevertheless, be able to adventure much, he may easily turn into a capitalist undertaker on a large scale. Specific commercial activities are closely intertwined with lending and borrowing. It is easy to see, therefore, that money-lending may develop into capitalist money-dealing—that is to say, into banking; or it may grow into capitalist production—as in the case of the "clothiers." Florence was the center of the woolen trade no less than of banking.

But Florence was more than that. To appreciate why the city on the Arno became the citadel of early capitalism we must recall that it was *par excellence* the city of guilds and of guild influence. An historic accident, the quarrel of the imperialists with the anti-imperial party, brought the guilds some share in the government of the town as early as the twelfth century. "The craft guilds were paid heavily for the support they lent the Emperor, and the Podestà and the councilors were in reality dependent on the new social class that had risen to power."[10] In 1193, the foundation was laid for the democratic development of the city state.

My point, hinted at above, is that the guild influence in the history of Florence was in part responsible for the early rise and growth of capitalism there. It may seem paradoxical to say so, seeing that the guild system is the mortal enemy of capitalism. It is true, nevertheless. A very powerful element in the capitalist spirit hails from the guild-halls. Think of the bourgeois virtues, and more especially of holy economy.

Where was economy more at home than in the guild-hall? The practice was taught by the guilds because necessity forced it on them. The guild members, if they were not to endanger their existence, had to be careful of the pennies, had to live soberly, work hard, be pure, and what not. All these were called Christian virtues, and Christian they certainly were. Their cultivation, without any pressure from without, was a good thing; it spoke well for the self-discipline of those who practiced them. But the grocer or the weaver had them forced upon him by his society; willy-nilly he was brought to the point of view that to get into debt and to waste time in pleasure-seeking or love affairs would surely bring him to beggary. Consequently, the guild members everywhere became "respectable citizens" by force of habit. Long before the Reformation in England, we are told by a writer whose judgment is reliable,[11] long before the Puritan spirit was abroad in the land, "the gaiety of the towns was already sobered by the pressure of business." It was the same in Scotland,[12] where the guilds also narrowed the life of the countryside. Your real yeoman was much like a squire who lives and lets live. But the craftsman in the town declined, his life-blood dried up, his outlook was drab; in a word, he became the ancestor of the "respectable citizen"—the bourgeois.

This bourgeois spirit became part and parcel of the capitalist spirit, and even people who could afford to live in a free-and-easy fashion made industry and frugality their ideals. Many reasons will explain this phenomenon. The morality of the philosophers and the Church was one force that made towards the end. Another was a kind of self-righteousness born of jealousy.

It has been asserted[13] that the whole of modern civilization is marked by this self-righteous jealousy, which, as everybody knows, Nietzsche made responsible for the substitution of aristocratic values by that of crowd morality. I believe that something of the same spirit played a part in the history of capitalism. Does it not adequately explain the raising of lower middle-class principles, born as they were of sheer necessity, into general and highly valued ideals of life? What were simply bourgeois virtues became great human virtues. And who preached them? Middle-class men, generally those who had sunk from the upper class, who looked with jealous eyes at the conduct of their superiors, damned this conduct as sinful, and taught the wickedness of the seigniorial life, though deep down in their hearts they admired and desired it. Study carefully the family records of Alberti and say whether this self-righteous jealousy is not their keynote. I have already quoted passages in which the hatred of the "signori," from whose circles Alberti was excluded, is comic, not to say childish. There are very many such. And in every case the condemnation of the aristocratic way of life, of its hunting, its immorality, its nepotism, ends with pharisaic praise of the writer's own middle-class ideals. There is no doubt that commercial interests, the precepts of philosophy, and the advice of the confessional all contributed to the establishment of a middle-class view of life. But the burning words of scorn that Alberti has for the "signori" whenever he begins to talk about them show that his experience of them must have been pretty unpleasant. But they also show that perhaps the strongest force that made him cling to his middle-class outlook on life was this spirit of self-righteous jealousy.

Throughout all ages this has been the stoutest prop of bourgeois morality. Every respectable citizen, even in our own day, proclaims that the grapes are sour. It is his comfort.

But to return to the guilds. Whenever and wherever these organizations rose to power, so much so that eventually they "called the tune" of the policy of their community, the result always was that their ideals became dominant and universally prized, despite the fact that they first arose merely from the pressure of necessity and that the necessity was made into a virtue. In such cases the guild spirit became the generally accepted one. In Florence we have the best illustration of the tendency. As early as the fifteenth century Florence was just soaked in the bourgeois spirit, while other cities, say Venice, for example, retained their seigniorial mode of life for a much longer space of time.

Notes

1. Cf. W. Sombart. *Die deutsche Volkswirtschaft im 19ten Jahrhundert*, 3rd ed. 1913, ch. 8.
2. A. Vierkandt. *Die Stetigkeit im Kulturwandel*, (1908), p. 109.
3. For a detailed study of the point see W. Sombart. *Die deutsche Volkswirtschaft im 19ten Jahrhundert*. p. 136.
4. L. Muratori. *Scriptores rerum italicarum*. vol. 12. p. 1011 (for Milan); vol. 18, p. 172 (for Bologna, 1356).

5. L. Darmstaedter and R. du Bois-Reymond, *Vier tausend Jahre Pionierarbeit in den exacten Wissenschaften* (1904), p. 24.
6. W. Sombart, *Die deutsche Volkswirtschaft im 19ten Jahrhundert*, p. 139.
7. W. Sombart, *The Jews and Modern Capitalism*, p. 170.
8. Alberti, *I libri della Famiglia* (G. Mancini ed.), Florence 1908, p. 256.
9. G. Freytag, *Bilder aus der deutschen Vergangenheit*, vol. 2, p. 228.
10. Davidsohn, *Geschichte von Florenz*, (1896), vol. 1. p. 601.
11. Mrs. Richard Green, *Town Life in the Fifteenth Century* (1894), vol. 1, p. 152; vol. 2, p. 156.
12. P. Hume Brown, *Scotland in the Time of Queen Mary* (1904), p. 163.
13. Max Scheler, *Über Ressentiment und moralisches Werturteil* (1912), a brilliant essay.

11

The Economic Life of the Future

I.

Predicting the future is always a precarious matter. And it seems to be particularly dangerous in the field of economic and social history. It is above all the cleverest who have been the most thoroughly mistaken.

As evidence of how mistaken important thinkers can be when they seek to anticipate future developments, I offer only three examples:

Alexandre Tocqueville prophesied of the United States of America in the year 1840: "The great stocks of wealth are disappearing, the number of small fortunes is increasing" ("Les grandes richesses disparaissent, le nombre des petites fortunes s'accroît"; *De la démocratie en Amérique*, II:3, p. 176). The same author expresses in the same place the opinion that revolutions will disappear, as will wars and much else.

Gustav Schmoller's posthumous work, whose preface was written on 1 October 1918 by Frau von Schmoller, closes with the words:

> Already today we can say that the monarchy—together with its organs—and the workers present the most active political powers in Germany; against whom the old parties and the remaining classes may well represent the majority, but also the satiated, more inert elements of the state. And whoever believes that the strongest forces in a state maintain themselves will not miss the mark if he prophesies: as

> liberalism once came together for common reforms with the German monarchy, its officialdom and military...so too, one day, will socialism (*Die soziale Frage* [*The Social Question*], 1918, p. 648).

Karl Marx prophesied: (1) the progressive impoverishment of the wage-labourers; (2) the general economic concentration together with the downfall of the artisan and farming classes; (3) the catastrophic breakdown of capitalism.

None of all this has come to pass.

But perhaps these great minds were so disgracefully mistaken precisely because they were so great—and for that reason so in love with their opinion. Perhaps also, however, because they were such ardent politicians, so convinced of their practical ideas, that they did not know how to differentiate between that which they wanted to happen and that which has some prospect of occurring. Distinguishing between these two poles, of course, is the very first condition which must be fulfilled if one wishes to predict the probable development of the future. And then one must be content to draw, in vaguest outline, only the most general trends. It is particularly important, however, to show the different possibilities which emerge from proven facts, and between which the future can then choose; above all, also—and this can be done with considerable certainty—to establish which possible future developments are *out of the question.*

II.

It can be said with some assurance of a good number of opinions regarding the future development of economic life: that they are *wrong.*

1. All those opinions are mistaken which predict the future supremacy of *one* economic system. That would contradict both all current experience and the very nature of economic development. We observe that in the course of history, the number of economic modes prevalent at one time always increases. Economic life develops ever more richly. As in a fugue, a new voice enters, and the previous voices go on sounding. Thus the European Middle Ages already had village economy, manorial economy, and handicraft guilds side by side; then capitalism appeared—but sustenance economy, village economy, and guilds lasted. These economic systems were joined by all the different modes of economic endeavor which I have outlined in the two preceding chapters. And

unquestionably all these economic types will now exist side by side in the economic life of the future: (1) capitalism; (2) cooperatives; (3) public ownership; (4) sustenance economy; (5) handicrafts; (6) farming economy. They will transform themselves inwardly. They will alter their relative proportions. But they will be there; as I will establish still more exactly in the following.

2. All those opinions are mistaken which expect a violent upset of the existing economic constitution and a sudden change of the bases of economic life. This opinion too misjudges the nature of economic development, which always proceeds in the form of a gradual, "organic" reshaping of existing conditions. A new economy "grows," like a plant, or an animal. Forcible interventions may well destroy, but they build nothing. All previous history confirms the accuracy of this observation. If further proof were necessary, the course of economic development in Soviet Russia has produced it.
3. All those opinions are mistaken which count on a speedy regression of economic life back towards precapitalist economic modes. Such a regression will not occur because the interests are too powerful in the conservation of an economy built on the achievements of modern technology: The necessity of nourishing a certain mass of people! Delight in capitalism! Delight in technology!

It is also not to be expected that the material conditions which made this modern development possible will undergo so thorough a change that a more primitive type of economy would become *necessary*. Here I mean, for example, a decline of technical resources which could possibly reduce society to a guild-based economy.

Once, when I was discussing the prospects for the future with *Max Weber*, we raised the question: when would the witches' sabbath which mankind has been celebrating in the capitalist countries since the beginning of the nineteenth century be likely to end? He replied: "When the last tonne of ore is smelted with the last tonne of coal."

This moment will now arrive in a relatively short time. Of course there are still considerable reserves of coal. According to the generally accepted calculations of Frech (*Über Ergiebigkeit und voraussichtliche Erschöpfung der Steinkohlenlager* [*On the productivity and probable exhaustion of the hard coal-beds*], 1901), if coal continues to be extracted at the current rate, the coal deposits will be exhausted in:

150	years in America
200	" in central France, Bohemia, Saxony, northern England;
300	" in the rest of England;
4–500	" in northern France and Saarbrücken;
1000	" in Upper Silesia.

The iron ore deposits, however, will come to an end sooner. According to surveys organized on the occasion of the International Congress of Geologists in the year 1910 (*The Iron Ore Resources of the World*), the known reserves on earth total about 22 billion tonnes (of which 12 are found in Europe and 9.8 in America), from which some 10 billion tonnes of iron can be extracted. If the rate of yield remains the same, these deposits would be worked out in approximately 60 years.

Max Weber's opinion, however—as some will say, "unfortunately"; as others will say, "fortunately"—is incorrect. For our technical resources are by no means exhausted with the end of the coal and iron age; certainly not in terms of the *generation of power*.

If we leave aside petroleum, the supply of which will likewise soon be exhausted, then the following inexhaustible power sources are at mankind's disposal:

1. energy from hydraulic power, which (according to *Wiener*) can deliver 100 million hp;
2. energy from the tides, which technology will unquestionably allow us to take advantage of successfully;
3. energy from the sun's rays, which are already being utilized.

In 1902 a solar power machine was erected on an ostrich farm near Los Angeles. Similar solar engines exist in California and Peru. The technology to make use of solar energy was then perfected by Shuman, who with £300,000 founded the Sun Power Co. (Eastern Hemisphere) Ltd., and who in 1912 in Meadi, Egypt, 15 km south of Cairo, erected a large solar power plant, which waters 200 ha of cotton-growing land. This concern is today already "profitable" wherever 1 tonne of coal costs more than 10 Marks (in Egypt, Peru, Chile, and South Africa, 60–70 Marks are the rule). A calculation of Hanns Günther, in his book *Taten der Technik* (Deeds of technology; Vol. I, 1923, p. 161), comes to the following result: below latitude 20° north each square meter of horizontal earth's surface receives 1.4 million thermal units (calories) annually from the sun's rays, that is to say: every 4 m^2 receives the equivalent of 1 hp. At 100% net efficiency, therefore, in one square kilometer 250,000 hp can be produced. Modern steam-engines need about 4 tonnes of coal for the production of one hp/year. Transformed completely into mechanical energy, then, the 1300 million tonnes of coal mined in 1920 deliver 325 million hp/years. To replace this amount of power by means of solar energy, approximately 13,000 km^2 are therefore necessary: about one-third of the area of Switzerland. The Sahara Desert, however, covers an expanse of 6,000,000 km^2.

If solar energy becomes the source of power, the prime industrial sites are: Mexico, Chile, Peru, South Africa, northern Africa, Afghanistan, Tibet, northern India, Australia. This displacement of industrial sites would be thoroughly in accordance with the transition which will be considered below—the passage of capitalism from the white to the colored races.

In the meantime, to be sure, considerable obstacles still hinder the use of these tremendous sources of power: the net efficiency at present is not 100%, but 0.25% in the Meadi installations (according to Wiener), while the industrious flora, by means of chlorophyll, utilizes 0.5 to 2% of the sun's energy. But what is impossible for modern technology! It will overcome these difficulties as well, and Wilhelm Ostwald's prediction (*Energetische Grundlagen der Kulturwissenschaft* [*Energetic bases of cultural science*; 1909], 47) will certainly come true:

> A later goal of our progress will be...to examine the direct utilization of solar energy, whereby the earth will be covered with machines which accomplish this; and in their shade men will lead a more comfortable existence.

For a summary of the present status of the study of "substitute" power see A. Lübke, *Die sterbende Kohle* (*The dying coal*; 1925), 343ff., 375ff., 418ff.

For a while it appeared that one might hope (or fear) that the technical age would come to an end not because of a lack of power, but more probably because of *lack of materials*. Today we know that this hope (fear) too was unfounded. In recent times material sources have

been discovered which can be described as practically inexhaustible.
These are:

1. scrap, particularly scrap iron, although naturally this material too will ultimately run out at some point; then, however,
2. the supply of aluminum found in aluminum oxide;
3. the quantities of nitrogen in the air.

III.

If we now ask what, in reality, will be the probable formation of the economic life of the future, then we may regard it as a practically certain fact that *the capitalist economic system* will for a long time to come dominate important branches of economic life: all those branches, I think, which are still in the throes of the technical revolution, those in which the enterprises are faced with varied tasks, and those which produce specialty items.

That capitalism in the future will also undergo great transformations, within and without, is surely obvious after our experiences during the age of high capitalism and in the period since the beginning of the World War.

These changes, which I already anticipated in my introduction, will consist primarily of the following:

1. capitalism will lose its dominance;
2. capitalism will have to put up with ever more restraints and interventions on the part of the public authorities: its purely naturalistic mode of existence will, as I put it, assert itself increasingly by means of normative ideas;
3. capitalism will transform itself inwardly further in the direction which we could already perceive in the age of high capitalism. That is to say: it will become calmer, more staid, more reasonable, as befits its increasing age. The main reasons for this change lie in the following:

    a) the driving forces will lose some of their dynamism; the economic subjects will "fatten" and lose their initiative; the "Faustian impulse" will disappear:

        ...once mighty, grand indeed,
        Now, wary-wise, it moves with measured speed.

This assumption indeed is founded only on a proof by induction: we observe, as I have shown in my *Bourgeois* [*The Quintessence of Capitalism*], that up to now all the nations of Europe which once held the leadership in economic life have traveled the same path of degeneration through loss of initiative, either in the form of feudalization or in the form of comfortable decline: the Italians, the Spaniards, the Dutch, finally the English. Who could still recognize in the Englishman of today the traits that *Bagehot* praised, at the beginning of the 1870s, in the introduction to his *Lombard Street*: Only the Englishman, he opines, has "the propensity to variation." "All sudden trades come to England." The Englishmen are "specially quick in comparison with their neighbours on the continent at seizing on novel mercantile opportunities"(!). "England has a special machinery for getting into trade new men, who will be content with low prices and this machinery will probable secure her success, for no other country is soon likely to rival it effectually."

These are the same characteristics which were attributed only a lifetime later *precisely to the Germans in contrast to the English*. Should the German and the American, or perhaps the Jew, represent an exception and preserve their "Faustian impulse" to the end of their days? It is not very probable.

It is moreover the case that

b) the development of economic life to ever greater stability, of business concerns to ever more ponderous machinery, of market relationships to ever greater interdependence—these developments constrict the room for entrepreneurial daring ever more; and that

c) the latitude for capitalistic nature—which is always, as we know, equivalent to an urge to expansion—is also reduced by the fact that the population will unquestionably grow increasingly slowly. Earlier, I showed that the birthrate in the West European countries and among the Anglo-Saxon population in many parts of America has been in continual decline for a lifetime now, and that the decrease in population has temporarily been halted only through a still larger decrease in mortality. However, because the rapid development of economic life in the age of high capitalism, as we have seen, is for the most part to be attributed to the unprecedented increase in population, the obvious conclusion is that the rate must slow down if the population ceases to increase, or even decreases in number.

All this hinges on the supposition that capitalism remains, as it has up to now, an affair of the white race. That can now change, however, and probably will change. There is much to be said for the assumption that the future will belong no longer to the white race, but rather to the colored races. They have been treated long enough as mere economic objects and have absorbed enough of European nature to free themselves from the guardianship of the white race. No doubt they will have also their own capitalism. But the capitalism of the Chinese, the Malays and the Negroes is no longer "modern capitalism" as I have outlined it in this work. It will be a construct which will carry some traits of European-American capitalism; in its essentials, however, it will be entirely different from our capitalism, since it rests on completely different bases. One must always keep in mind, however, that such phenomena of civilization as modern capitalism, no less than the cultures of people, are also historic individuals, who appear but once in history. Indeed, that is the basic idea which has guided me in the writing of this work.

IV.

Besides capitalism, in the economic life of the future ever more room will be taken up by all those economic systems which are somehow based on *planned economy*. So we can designate in summary those modern economic types in which the principle of working to satisfy needs again takes precedence over the principle of working for profit. Their spirit will be marked by an ever more prominent cultivation of rationalism, while at the same time pursuit of profit and individualism, which in concert with rationalism had formed the capitalistic spirit, pass away. The technology on which they rest will take over the achievements of the modern technologies, but it must shed their revolutionary character for reasons which I will examine presently. The form of these new economic systems will keep a number of traits of capitalism; in particular its large-scale character and the depersonalization which constitutes the essence of the modern organization. In this respect all forms of planned economy will be alike, while in addition to these, different economic forms will develop side by side. All the developments that we have already seen take place beside this one in the age of high capitalism will also survive in the future economy and will gain in significance: cooperatives, publicly-owned corporations, organizations combining public and private ownership.

This planned economy will be among them: the *will* of a great many classes with an interest in this economic form will see to it: the will of the workers, as of all relatively poor consumers who want to free themselves from the fetters of capitalism. Whether to their benefit or to their detriment is of no matter. Their will exists, and it will form a sufficiently strong driving force in the economic life of the future. Their organization and their growing influence on state and local administration will see to this.

But more important than their will is this: that the possibility of shaping economic life along either cooperative or publicly-owned lines will also unquestionably become ever greater in the future. One of the few insights of economic science which is both well-founded and experimentally confirmed in its accuracy is the finding that a planned economy, that is to say a large-scale industrial economy without capitalistic leadership, is only possible under conditions—but reliably so under those conditions—where demand is stabilized and the technology of production has progressed beyond its revolutionary initial stage, where distribution and production move in familiar paths, where therefore there is no more need for particular "entrepreneurial" activity. That which *Adam Smith* once distinguished as the sphere of activity of the joint-stock company: the industry "of which all the operations are capable of being reduced to what is called routine or to such a uniformity of method as admits of little or no variation"; those areas of economic life are the ones that today appear to us ripe for nationalization, urbanization, or organization on a cooperative basis. To express it in a picture: shaping the economy "according to plan" means bottling it. Further, however, it is necessary that it be fully worked out beforehand. It is now beyond doubt, however, that the development of a growing part of economic life moves in the direction of this fully developed condition, and that the field of activity of planned industrial economy will thus spread ever more.

> The spirit has gone to the devil,
> The phlegm alone remains;

thus Goethe and Schiller, in their own way, performed the appropriate chemical analysis in their *Xenien*.

V.

We will now, however, gradually have to get used to the thought that the difference between a stabilized and regulated capitalism and a mechanized and streamlined socialism is not very large, and that for the fate of people and their culture it is thus practically *of no consequence whether* the economy is shaped in *capitalist or socialist* fashion. What matters is the following: the mode of operation is in both cases the same; in both cases the entire economy rests on the basis of depersonalization. One may ask, however, how a large cooperatively-owned and a capitalist department store, a Communist and a capitalist blast furnace, a municipally-run and a capitalist streetcar differ from each other. And one will find nothing essential. Perhaps that the "consciousness" of the worker is different here from there. But the shaping of all the working conditions is here and there the same. The working hours depend not on good will, but on the national economic need. The amount of payment is likewise as good as independent of the economic constitution. For we now also know that the profit from capital, divided among the workers, brings no essential increase in wages. And all these things are secondary, moreover, compared with the mode of operation enforced by the operation's organization and by the state of the technology. Ultimately, indeed, only this last is of importance, whether a person spends his existence behind the plow or before the Bessemer converter, in the small shop or in the large department store, in the sailboat or in the boiler-room of a gigantic steamer.

And therefore we are not at all so very interested in whether the formation of the economic life of the future will be capitalist or socialist, whether people will be roasted or boiled, but—to continue the metaphor—whether in the future there will still be possibilities, to escape unroasted and unboiled. That is to say: whether in the economy of the future there will still be room for those economic systems which are *neither* capitalistic *nor* socialist, by which I mean room for sustenance economy, handicraft, farming economy. Here are the two opposed worlds: soul and mind. Here the fate of mankind will be decided: whether the most important element of human action, economic activity, shall belong to the sphere of the soul or the sphere of the mind.

I attempt in the following section to assemble the few reasonably sure predictions that can be made regarding the future of the three economic systems which belong to the sphere of the soul.

VI.

The fate of the *sustenance economy* depends essentially on the fate of the farming economy, about which I will speak further below (under VIII).

Outside the farming economy, the sustenance economy still plays a role today only in individual private households. As long as these survive, so too remnants of the sustenance economy continue to exist. On the future of the private household I dare pass no judgment. The successes which the one-kitchen house movement has hitherto enjoyed in the European countries do not allow us to conclude that a large majority of the population is inclined in the near future to dispense with their private consumption economy. Here much will depend on the development of housing. If there is a tendency to small houses, then household industry, and thereby sustenance production as well, will win more room. The groups of allotment gardens in the metropolises serve as evidence that in some—by no means in all—people there exists a powerful longing for control of their own domesticity. A garden, a coop, and a larder now always belong to this arrangement. And where there are these three accessories, then is room once more for an increase in sustenance production.

A part of the sustenance economy will probably also be carried out in the future in charitable contexts.

VII.

The attempt has repeatedly been made to distinguish those areas of economic life in which (industrial) *handicraft* should have a secure existence in the future. The following have been described as such areas (*Schönberg*): (1) the applied arts, (2) personal services, (3) localized trade, (4) repair work. My account has already proven that the monopoly ascribed to handicraft in these areas has failed even to survive into the age of high capitalism. The assumption that these activities were fundamentally guaranteed to the workman only arose due to a confusion between manual labor and handicraft. In the first two areas this is evident: because artistic work and personal service cannot be performed *by machine*, the hasty conclusion has been drawn that—therefore—only handicraft could be considered for them. Without considering that a large-scale business organization is possible in the most varied economic systems: capitalistic, cooperative, public-owned, also without the utilization of machinery. I have already indicated that the applied arts above all have been snatched already in the present from the realm of handicraft. And nothing stands in the way of thinking that in the future, hair care will be carried out in large cooperative or municipal concerns. But localized trade and even repair work are also not areas which would have to remain *fundamentally* guaranteed to handicraft.

On the other hand, it must be conceded that in certain spheres of activity, such as the two last-named, the competition is made considerably easier for handicraft; and so, as we have seen, handicraft has survived to a greater extent in these spheres. There is no foreseeable reason, however, why this should change in the future. This could happen only if a doctrinaire government were to forbid private concerns, including the workshops, altogether. Given the strong interest which wide sections of the population have invested in handicraft, however, this is not likely. Even the strict Soviet regime has had to readmit handicraft. So it can be counted on, then, that in the foreseeable future industrial handicraft will survive in its present condition, which, as we have seen, is still quite considerable.

The above mentioned is equally true for the remaining branches of handicraft. The professional shopkeeper, above all, will exercise his welcome function in all economic constitutions and continue—in defiance of all department stores and cooperatives—with undiminished vitality.

VIII.

If in the economy of the future the artisan class will just maintain the modest place which it holds today, so too the *farming community* will presumably increase still further in extent and significance. The peripheral farming community will grow stronger because it will free itself from the bondage in which West European capitalism has held it. The West and Central European farming community, however, will first develop quite thoroughly. The "internal colonization" will progress. The share of agriculture in economic life as a whole will increase considerably, since only thereby will the overpopulated areas of our continent be able to stay alive after a fashion. For it can no longer be doubted that a regression of the European tumor is necessary to keep the organism alive. If the capitalism of the colored races begins to develop, it means an end to the exploitative position of Europe. Such deformations as the English national economy, in which the agricultural population had dwindled to 8%, will then no longer be possible. The nations must again develop their own agrarian bases on which their national economy can rest securely, and that will occur by no other means—given the prevailing democratic trends—than through increase in the farming community. The agrarian reform program of Lloyd George will be exemplary for all those European countries in which agriculture had been too much neglected.

That the farmer of the future will not be the same as he is today, we may conclude from the changes which a large part of the farming community has already learned during the age of high capitalism. The "modernizing" and, on a larger scale, rationalizing process will make progress. At the end of this development stands the American farmer with his telephone, Ford auto, and bank account, whose wife wears silk stockings. The farmer of the stripe of Andreas Höfer or the peasant of Büttner or Jörn Uhl is (unfortunately! some will say, and fortunately! others) gone forever. Nevertheless, however, the farming community will always form an area of economic life in which the soul can develop, because it can never be fully conquered either by capitalism or by socialism. Its internal essence protects it against such a conquest.

Never can the spirit which dominates the farming community become a purely capitalistic one, because the autocracy of the pursuit of profit is impossible. Impossible, since an agricultural concern is never appraised only from the point of view of profitability: love of the agricultural profession, affection for the soil, aspirations to independence and autonomy, hunger for land, family tradition and other completely irrational motives are as decisive as the purely economic motive. Where these prevail, however, it is much more the principle of satisfying needs which conducts them than the pure profit principle. *Chayanov's* observations in this regard in his book *Die Lehre von der bäuerlichen Wirtschaft* (The doctrine of the rural economy; 1923) are well worth reading.

We must also always remain mindful that agriculture is the only work that can be pursued for its own sake, that therefore does not need to be a necessary means to an end. This holds true for rural holdings, but even more so for estate farming, which likewise can never be completely suffused by the capitalistic spirit. One can pursue agriculture for agriculture's sake, or acquire property for the sake of delight in property; which obviously is not the case for a business concern, a blast furnace, or a sulphuric acid factory.

But even if the individual farmer (and farmers in general) wanted to devote himself completely to the capitalistic spirit out of personal enthusiasm, he could never successfully turn his holding into a purely capitalistic enterprise, because complete depersonalization of the process is not possible in the field of agriculture. I have already produced some evidence of this (see Chapter 53, section I).[#] Here I add a few more examples:

1. Agricultural operation rebels against the system of management, because neither the organization of the operation itself nor the individual work can be fully standardized.

   Thus, piecework is much less easily applicable in the realm of agriculture than elsewhere, above all because the individual work cannot be subject to quality control. Even the harvesting cannot be controlled, let alone the tilling; whose result is visible only much later, without one knowing whether a bad result is to be attributed to the work or to the weather. All agricultural processes, however, are only to a slight extent reducible to set patterns and so capable of standardization. They must thus be individualized. It has been correctly observed that the less agricultural work is executed according to rules set up beforehand, the greater is the success.

   In the course of organizing the undertaking, however, the farmer must always select the correct option from countless possibilities which differ from case to case within the operation. "The theory of agricultural management can only set up certain general points of view and guidelines; their application to the actual organization must be left to the judgement, indeed to the feeling of the individual farmer" (*Schiff*). This is above all because external natural processes, and their influence on the growth of plants and animals, can never be exactly foreseen. Therefore decisions

[#] Sombart refers to his *Der Moderne Kapitalismus*.

must be arrived at and carried out, arrangements made and altered, from moment to moment. Consider, for instance, bringing in the harvest!

2. The agricultural operation allows no fully implemented system of accounting, since the books cannot be balanced in purely financial terms: because of the widespread trade by means of barter, because the business concern is linked with the household affairs, because the different branches of the operation are entwined into each other. *Walther Schiff* has dealt with this problem energetically and has illuminated it in essential points. The agricultural operation cannot be totally subject to calculation, mainly for the following reasons:
    a) The agricultural operation forms a community in terms of using materials: raw materials, subsidiary materials, waste products, which are produced in one branch of the operation, are utilized productively in another: stable manure, straw, forage crops.
    b) The agricultural operation forms a community in terms of using equipment and supplies: most of the means of production (tools, machines, buildings, draft animals), the workers, and the land itself serve different crops successively or simultaneously during the year.
    c) The agricultural operation forms a community in terms of using agricultural land: the expenses distribute themselves across a series of economic periods—the profit from one crop in one year is determined in part through the crop grown in the preceding year; yet at the same time this year's crop also influences the next year's profit (loc. cit., p. 460f.).

3) The agricultural operation is not suited to the introduction of a complete system of instruments or machines, sufficient reasons for which I have already produced elsewhere: see Chapter 51, section II.[#]

The position that agricultural activity is barred to a thorough depersonalization, as I have developed here, is expressed in slightly different words by our best agriculturist, *Friedrich Aereboe*; who in his *Allgemeine landwirtschaftliche Betriebslehre* (General theory of agricultural management; 3. Ed., p. 219/20) emphatically summarizes the result of his investigations as follows:

> A progressive industrialization of the whole national economy might very well take the processing of farm products increasingly out of the hands of agriculture, but the agricultural production itself can never be industrialized. Agriculture always remains the last area of the national economy which can resist a far-reaching division of labour and concentration of labour, while at a high stage of development it tends to combine labour forces on a cooperative basis.

[#] The reference is again to *Der Moderne Kapitalismus.*

IX.

It is in such variegated terms that I see the economic life of the future. The old ways remain, the old ways undergo changes, new ways arise. And the whole process of reorganization takes place quite gradually, "organically" we are in the habit of saying, as a plant or an animal grows. Without any disasters (apart from the severe wear and tear which will accompany the shrinking of Western Europe), without sudden interruption (save as a result of violent interventions), without any dramatic momentum. No doubt that is a much more boring view than, for example, the view represented by *Marx*. How exciting it is to read Chapter 23 of the first volume of his *Das Kapital*! It may be regrettable, from the artistic point of view, that development takes place so very differently in reality from *Marx's* assumption in his work. But if we are to proceed scientifically we must now resign ourselves to this. I said this already at the beginning, and I repeat it here in conclusion. The right opinion is usually more boring than the wrong one. Yet we must express it, if our task exists therein:

Vitam impendere vero.

12

Why is there no Socialism in the United States?

Capitalism in the United States

The United States of America is capitalism's land of promise. All conditions needed for its complete and pure development were first fulfilled here. In no other country and among no other people was capitalism favored with circumstances that permitted it to develop to the most advanced state.

In no other country is it possible to accumulate capital so rapidly. There are several reasons for this. The United States is rich in precious metals: North America produces a third of all the silver and a quarter of all the gold in the world. It is rich in fertile soils: the Mississippi Plain comprises about five times as much of the best humus soil as do the black earth districts of southern Russia and Hungary together. It is rich in abundant deposits of useful minerals that today give three times as much output as any European deposits. As a result of these characteristics and by virtue of the developed state of its man-made technology, America is more suited than any other country to provide capitalism with the means for conquering the world. The United States now produces almost as much pig iron as all other countries in the world put together—in 1905, 23 million tons as against 29.5 million tons produced by the rest of the world. The United States is more suited than any other country for capitalist expansion. The Mississippi Plain is ideally positioned for economically viable agriculture and for the unlimited growth of transportation: it is an area of 3.8 million square kilometers, therefore approximately seven times the size of the German Empire,* without any barrier to communication and, by way of a bonus, it is already provided with several natural means of transportation. On the Atlantic coast there are fifty-five good harbors that have waited thousands of years for capitalist exploitation. The United States therefore has a vast market area, and compared with America a European state is scarcely more than a medieval city and its dependent territory. The striving after endless expansion, so fundamental to every capitalist economy, can be freely fulfilled for the first time in these North American expanses that stretch far beyond where the eye can see. Such striving found itself constantly checked within the restrictive confines of Europe, and doctrines of free trade and trade agreements could always only be poor substitutes for it. One can truly say that if one wanted to construct the ideal country for the development of capitalism on the lines required by this economic system, such a country could take on the dimensions and particular characteristics only of the United States.

And what of the people? Men have been molded for centuries as if in a task of conscious preparation, and the most recent generations of them were appointed to pave the way for capitalism's invasion of the virgin terrain of America. Finished with Europe, they moved over to the New World with the will to carve themselves a new life based on principles of pure reason. They had left all remnants of their European character behind in their former homes, together with all superfluous romanticism and sentimentality. They had left everything of their feudal artisan existence, as well as all sense of traditionalism, and had taken across with them only what was necessary and of service to the development of a capitalist economy, namely a powerful, unremitting energy and an ideology that turned activity in the pursuit of capitalist aims into a duty, as if it were a response to a command from God to

---

* *Ed.*—In 1906 the German Empire extended from Alsace-Lorraine in the west to East Prussia in the east and included a large part of what is now Poland. The Empire then comprised 208,830 square miles.

the faithful. Max Weber has demonstrated in our journal* the close connections that exist between the postulates of the puritan Protestant ethic and the requirements of a rational capitalist economy. Furthermore, as a resource to those leading the implementation of this new economic system came wage laborers from a population apparently also made in order to develop capitalism to the most advanced form. For centuries labor was scarce and therefore expensive, which compelled employers to devise its most rational utilization and thereby fully to control how their businesses came to be organized. It compelled them also to think systematically of making labor superfluous by means of "labor-saving machinery." Thus began a drive towards the highest technological perfection, something that was never able to happen to the same degree in a country with an old civilization. Following that, when the most advanced forms of economic and technological organization had been created, endless multitudes of people poured in, who could increasingly be used only as resource material in the service of capitalist interests, as the possibilities of existence outside the capitalist nexus were reduced. It is known that during recent decades at least half-a-million people have entered the United States each year and that the number of arrivals has risen to three-quarters of a million or more in many years.

In fact, nowhere on earth have the economic system and the essence of capitalism reached as full a development as in North America.

Nowhere else is acquisitiveness as clearly seen as it is there, nor are the desire for gain and the making of money for its own sake so exclusively the be-all and end-all of every economic activity. Every minute of life is filled with this striving, and only death ends the insatiable yearning for profit. Making a living from anything other than capitalism is as good as unknown in the United States, and an economic rationalism of a purity unknown in any European country serves this desire for gain. Capitalism presses forward remorselessly, even when its path is strewn with corpses. The data that provide us with

---

* *Ed.*—Max Weber's essay, *Die protestantische Ethik und der Geist des Kapitalismus*, a later version of which was translated into English by Talcott Parsons as *The Protestant Ethic and the Spirit of Capitalism*, new ed. (New York, 1958), was first published in the *Archiv für Sozialwissenschaft und Sozialpolitik*, XX-XXI (1904–5). The present work of Sombart's also first appeared in Volume XXI of the same journal; see Preface to the Original German Edition, p. vii. Max Weber and Werner Sombart were both associated with the *Archiv* in editorial capacities.

information on the extent of railway accidents in the United States are merely symbolic of this. The [New York] *Evening Post* has calculated that from 1898 to 1900 the number of people killed on the American railways was 21,847, which is equal to the number of Englishmen killed in the Boer War during the same period, including those who died of illnesses in military hospitals.* In 1903 the number of people killed on the American railways was 11,006, while in Austria in the same year it was 172. If one standardizes these figures per hundred kilometers and per million passengers, one finds that accidents happened in America at a rate of 3.4 per hundred kilometers, as opposed to 0.86 in Austria, and that they happened at a rate of 19 per million passengers in America, compared with one of 0.99 per million passengers in Austria.† This economic and industrial system and its

* *Ed.*—The figure given actually covers accidents in the three years from 1 July 1897 to 30 June 1900. Sombart has apparently taken his reference to the account in the *New York Evening Post* from John Graham Brooks, *The Social Unrest: Studies in Labor and Socialist Movements* (New York, 1903) 210. See also, for example, U.S. Department of Commerce, Bureau of the Census, *Historical Statistics of the United States; From Colonial Times to 1957* (Washington, D.C., 1960) 437. The same *Evening Post* reference has been used in Otto L. Bettman, *The Good Old Days—They Were Terrible!* (New York, 1974) 71.

† The figures used in the standardisation calculations are those of Philippovich. [In the several volumes and editions of his major work, *Grundriß der Politischen Oekonomie* [*Outline of Political Economy*], the economist Eugen von Philippovich (1858–1917) sometimes uses data on changes in the length of railway track in different countries as a measure of the growth of productive capital. These are the data to which Sombart is referring here. Philippovich's work apparently contains nothing on railway accidents *per se* or on the number of passengers carried. The Editor has some misgivings about the total accuracy of the American data. It is unclear why Sombart explicitly says 1903 as being the year to which these data refer, for till 1916 the Statistical Reports of the Interstate Commerce Commission, which are the primary sources for American railway-accident data, reported for years ending 30 June. In the year ending 30 June 1903, 9840 people were reported as having been killed on American railways; see, for example, *Historical Statistics*, 437. (In the following twelve months the figure was 10,046, and Sombart's figure of 11,006 cannot be located in any of the standard sources.)

In calculating the accident rate per length of track, Sombart has apparently used length-of-track data referring to 1902, or, if referring to some other year, an arithmetic error or misprint occurs in his text. There were 202,472 miles (325,821 kilometers) of 'first' railway track owned by railway companies in the continental United States in 1902 (ibid., 429). However, the same source gives the figure of 1903 as 207,977 miles (334,711 kilometers). In calculating the accident rate per million passengers carried Sombart has apparently used as his base the number of passengers carried in the year ending 30 June 1900, which was 576,831,000; however, the figure for the number carried in the year ending 30 June 1903 is 694,892,000 (ibid., 430). Therefore the recalculated rates of deaths for the year ending 30 June 1903 are 2.94 per hundred kilometers and 14.2 per million passengers carried.—*Ed.*]

accompanying technology are employed relentlessly to guarantee the highest profit. While in Germany we see public indignation when a colliery shuts down one mine or another, year in and year out the management of the American trust determines with great equanimity which enterprises are to be worked and which left idle. In this way capitalism readily creates the economic organization after its own image: this is shown in location of industry, structure of individual businesses, size and shape of factories, organization of trade and commerce, and in co-ordination between production and marketing of goods. When one knows that everything has been deliberately made for a rational purpose, one is obliged to conclude from this that everything has been deliberately made to suit capitalist interests.

The financial rewards of this could not fail to appear. In terms of her capital base—that is, the amount of her capital accumulation—the United States (despite her comparative youth) is today way beyond all other countries. The yardsticks by which one can measure the state of the capitalist surge are the numbers of bank returns. In 1882, 7,304 banks reported to the Comptroller of the Currency, but in 1904 there were 18,844 of them. The banks of 1882 had capital assets of $712,100,000 and those of 1904 had assets of $1,473,904,674. In 1882 bank deposits amounted to $2,785,407,000, and in 1904 they were $10,448,545,990.[1] The total banking power of the United States, made up of capital, surplus profits, deposits, and circulation, is estimated by the same source to be $13,826,000,000, while the corresponding figures for all the other countries in the world taken together are reckoned to amount to only $19,781,000,000.[2] The amount of capital that has flowed into industry alone within the last twenty years should not therefore surprise us. According to the Census, the amounts of capital invested in manufactures in 1880, 1890, and 1900 were as follows:[*]

---

[*] *Ed.*—For the years 1890 and 1900 there are slight discrepancies between the figures that Sombart has given in his text and those in the Census source that he must have consulted. For 1890 the figure should be $6,525,156,486, and for 1900 it should be $9,835,086,909; the latter figure includes information on eighty-five governmental establishments in the District of Columbia, so that comparisons with the figures of earlier Censuses are possible, and it excludes data on Hawaii (which became a Territory of the United States in 1900). See United States Census Office, *Census Reports, Twelfth Census of the United States Taken in the Year 1900*, VII, Manufacturers, Part I, United States by Industries (Washington, D.C., 1902) Table I, p. xlvii.

1880: $2,790,272,606
1890: $6,525,050,759
1900: $9,831,486,500

It is known also that the United States is the country where the model of the Marxist theory of development is being most precisely fulfilled, since the concentration of capital has reached the stage (as described in the famous penultimate chapter of *Capital*) at which the final cataclysm of the capitalist world is near at hand.* The most recent statistics on the number and size of the trusts give the following striking picture.[3]

There are seven 'greater' industrial trusts into which have been combined 1,528 concerns that were formerly independent of each other. The capital concentrated in them amounts to $2,662,700,000. The largest of these seven giants is the United States Steel Corporation with nominal capital assets of $1,370,000,000, and the second largest is the Consolidated Tobacco Co. with only $502,900,000. These are followed by 298 'lesser' industrial trusts that control 3,426 plants and together have at their disposal capital assets in excess of $4,055,000,000. Thirteen industrial trusts with 334 plants and $528,000,000 in capital assets are at present in the process of being formed, so that the total number of industrial trusts amounts to 318, with 5,288 plants and $7,246,000,000 in capital assets. To these should be added 111 of the 'greater' franchise trusts (such as telephone, telegraph, gas, electricity, and street-car operations) with 1,336 individual subsidiaries and $3,735,000,000 in capital. And now comes the *pièce de résistance*: the group of the large railroad concerns. There are six of these, of whom none comprises less than a thousand million dollars. Together they have at their disposal over $9,017,000,000, and they control 790 subsidiaries. Finally, we have yet to mention the "independent" railroad companies with capital assets of $380,000,000.

If one adds together all these giant combinations, within which by far the largest part of American economic life is included, one arrives at the enormous total of 8,664 'controlled' subsidiaries and $20,379,000,000 in capital assets. Just think! Eighty-five thousand

* *Ed.*—Sombart's reference is to *Capital*, Vol. I, Part VIII, Chapter 23, "Historical Tendency of Capitalistic Accumulation."

million marks concentrated in the hands of a few capitalists!*

Perhaps one may best recognize how dominant the capitalist system is by examining the American social structure, which no longer contains any feature of non-capitalist origin. Nowhere do we meet residues of the pre-capitalist classes whose presence in greater or lesser degree gives every European society a characteristic feature. There is no feudal aristocracy, and instead the capitalist magnates have the field to themselves. The time that Marx could foresee only in his imagination when he wrote *Capital* has already arrived in the United States. Here the "eminent spinners," the "extensive sausage makers," and the "influential shoe black dealers," as well as the railway barons, force the people to pay them homage. James Bryce has written:

> When the master of one of the greatest Western lines travels towards the Pacific on his palace car, his journey is like a royal progress. Governors of States and Territories bow before him; legislatures receive him in solemn session; cities and towns seek to propitiate him, for has he not the means of making or marring a city's fortunes?[4]

There is no half nor wholly feudal peasantry or class of artisans. In their place is a versatile group of farmers and a handful of petty capitalist entrepreneurs in trade and industry. Both of these classes have been heavily tarred with the capitalist brush. They are both led on by a search for profit, as they build up their businesses rationally and with due regard for economy. Also, the organization of this entire labor force into jobs following the dictates of present-day capitalism lets the occupational sectors at the center of the capitalist nexus predominate more as the years go by. Today agriculture, even in a country that is still half a colony, makes up a smaller part of the occupational structure than in Germany, and the proportion in trade and transportation, which is now considerably larger than in Germany, is increasing quickly. From 1880 to 1900 the proportion of the gainfully employed population in agricultural pursuits in the United States fell from 44.3 to 35.7 percent (as compared with 36.12 percent in Germany), and the proportion of persons engaged in trade and transportation rose from 10.8 to 16.4 percent (as compared with 11.39 percent in Germany).*

---

* *Ed.*—The exchange rate at the time Sombart was writing was 4.20 marks for 1 American dollar.

* *Ed.*—Sombart has taken the American data from United States Census Office, *Occupations at*

At the same time the entire life-style of the people increasingly adopted a manner suited to capitalism.

Today the United States is already—and I repeat, despite its youth—a country of cities, or more exactly, a country of large cities.[†] I do not mean this only in the numerical sense, although the statistics also make the extent of its urbanization clearly recognizable. Actually, calculating for the country as a whole, the urban proportion of the population today is not quite as great as in Germany: for example, in 1900, 41.2 percent lived in places of over 2,500 inhabitants in the United States, as against 54.3 percent living in places of over 2,000 inhabitants in Germany. However, this is not the complete picture. First, the proportion of the population of the United States living in large cities of over 100,000 inhabitants is already greater today than anywhere else in the world, with the exception of England. At 18.7 percent it approaches a fifth of the entire population. Second, the shifting of the population towards the cities is taking place at a rapid pace; between 1890 and 1900 the urban portion of the population rose from 29.2 to 41.2 percent, as mentioned above. Third, the low total number is explained by the numerical domination of the South, where there are relatively few towns. If one considers only the Eastern states of the country, one finds there only 31.8 percent of the population living in rural areas, as against 35.8 percent in large cities of over 100,000 inhabitants.[‡] However, when I say that the United States is a land of

---

the Twelfth Census (Washington, D.C., 1904), Table XXI, p. lxxxvi. Sombart's data on the occupational distributions between different sectors of the German economy cannot be reconciled fully with those given in official sources. The most recent data available to Sombart when he was writing would have pertained to 1895. According to German Empire, Kaiserliches Statistisches Amt, *Statistisches Jahrbuch für das Deutsche Reich, 1904 [Statistical Yearbook for the German Empire, 1904*], xxv (Berlin, 1904) 13, 36.19 (not 36.12) percent of the employed population in 1895 were principally engaged in agriculture, horticulture, animal-breeding, forestry or fishing, while 10.21 (not 11.39) percent were engaged in trade and transportation (including the running of inns and public houses).

† *Ed.*—The Verbal distinction in German is between *Stadt* and *Großstadt*. Since 1887 official international statistical practice had recognized several categories of city according to the criterion of size. Sombart's use of the word *Stadt* embraces all categories, but a *Großstadt* necessarily had more than 100,000 inhabitants.

‡ All numerical data for which no special source is named are taken from the Census. [—*Ed.* Sombart has clearly taken some of his data on American urbanisation from United States Census Office, *Twelfth Census*, I, Population, Part I, Table XXIX, p. lxxxiii. However, some of his figures do not totally agree with those given in other standard sources, and in one respect Sombart is seriously misleading because he has failed to realize that a new Census definition of 'urban'

cities, I mean it in a deeper and inner sense that particularly expresses why I am relating urbanism and capitalism. I mean it in the sense of a type of settlement that differs from spontaneous growth, rests on a purely rational basis, is defined from purely quantitative perspective and represents as it were the deeper meaning of the word 'urban.' Only in the most infrequent cases does the European city fully incorporate this idea. The latter has mostly grown spontaneously, and yet it is basically only an enlarged village, the essence of which is reflected in its appearance. What has Nuremberg in common with Chicago? Nothing, except the superficial characteristic that in both places many people relying for their sustenance on supplies from outside live concentrated next to one another. In matters of the spirit there is no resemblance. The former is a village-like, spontaneous formation, while the latter is a real city artificially set up according to principles of rationality, in which (as Tönnies would say) all traces of *Gemeinschaft* have been extinguished and pure *Gesellschaft* has been established. However, if in old Europe the city takes after the countryside (or rather has done till now) and has brought the character of the latter to itself, in the United States, on the contrary, the flat countryside is basically only an urban settlement that lacks cities. The same rational intelligence that created the box-like cities has gone out across

---

was introduced into some of the analyses of the 1900 Census.

> In the reports of 1880, 1890, and 1900 Censuses, the urban population was variously defined as the population living in places of 4000 inhabitants or more, or 8000 inhabitants or more. The first publication in which the population of places having 2500 inhabitants or more was officially designated as urban was the *Supplementary Analysis of the Twelfth Census (1900)* (*Historical Statistics*, 2).

United States, Department of Commerce and labor, *Statistical Abstract of the United States, 1911*, XXXIV (Washington, D.C., 1912) 54, says that the urban population in 1900, namely "that residing in cities and other incorporated places of 2,500 inhabitants or more, including New England towns of that population," was 40.5 (not 41.2) percent of the whole, and, if the Eastern states that Sombart mentions correspond to the New England and Middle Atlantic geographic divisions, their rural population in 1900 was 30.9 (not 31.8) percent.

The so-called change in the urban population from 29.2 to 41.2 (or perhaps 40.5) percent confuses two definitions of the urban population; the first incorporates the 8000 minimum and the second the 2,500 minimum. Between 1890 and 1900 the percentage of the population living in places of 8,000 or more changed from 29.2 to 33.1 percent (*Twelfth Census*, I, Table XXIX, p. lxxxiii). In the same period thcentage living in places of 2,500 or more changed from 36.1 to 40.5 percent (*Statistical Abstract, 1911*) 54. All these figures pertain to all states and territories in the contiguous continental United States.]

the countryside with a surveyor's chain, and following a single uniform plan, has divided this entire enormous area into exactly equal squares. From the first moment on this could not but rule out any idea of natural and spontaneous settlement.

Nor, for that matter, does the United States lack the feature that has always been conspicuous in the structure of a society resting on capitalist foundations—namely, the tremendous contrasts between wealth and poverty. The United States does not have any exact statistics on income and wealth, but we do possess several attempts to estimate the distribution of wealth which, though not to be regarded as perfect statements, may none the less lay claim to some value since they have been undertaken conscientiously and with regard for all available material.[5] According to these sources, out of total private wealth which was estimated at sixty billion dollars in 1890,[*] thirty-three billion, or 54.8 percent, was in the hands of 125,000 families, who represented 1 percent of all families, while 6,250,000 families (50 percent) were without property.

At the present time the ultimate distribution of total wealth may still be taking shape, but it may be said indisputably that the absolute contrasts between poor and rich are nowhere in the world anything like as great as they are in the United States. Above all, this is because the rich over there are so very much richer than the same group in Germany. In America there are certainly more people who own 1,000,000,000 marks than there are people owning 100,000,000 marks in Germany. Anyone who has ever been in Newport, the Baiae of New York,[†] will have picked up the impression that in America having a million is commonplace. There is certainly no other place in the world where the princely palace of the very grandest style is so obviously the standard type of residence, while anyone who has wandered once through Tiffany's department store in New York will always sense something akin to the odor of poverty in even the most splendid luxury businesses of large European cities. Because Tiffany's also has branches in Paris and London,[6] it can serve excellently for drawing

---

[*] *Ed.*—This is $60,000,000,000. An American or continental billion equals a thousand millions.

[†] *Ed.*—Sombart is referring to Newport, Rhode Island. Baiae was a luxury watering-place in the imperial Roman period situated near Cumae on the Bay of Naples. It was a favourite of the poet, Horace. Only ruins of the Roman establishment now remain.

comparisons between the extravagance and therefore the wealth of the top four hundred families in the three countries concerned. The managers of the New York head office told me that most of the merchandise they offer for sale in New York comes from Europe, where it is made specially for Tiffany's of New York. However, it is completely out of the question that a store in Europe—even Tiffany's own branches in Paris and London—would stock merchandise at prices such as it would fetch in New York. Only in New York are the dearest items said to be brought in for the woman shopper.

On the other hand, the misery of the slums in the large American cities finds its real equal only in the East end of London. Robert Hunter's book, *Poverty*, recently appeared and, although this is not up to the quality of Engels' *The Condition of the Working Class* (despite what Florence Kelley has stated in a review),[7] it is none the less excellently suited to fulfill the purpose that it sets itself—which is to throw light into the depths of the misery in America's large cities. The author has lived for years as a settlement worker in the most infamous quarters of various large industrial cities, he has therefore gained his own impressions, and also he knows how best to give life to the rich literary and statistical material on which he has drawn. He estimates now that the number of people in the United States living below the poverty line, that is, those who are underfed, are poorly clothed or badly housed, totals in times of average prosperity ten million, of whom four million are public paupers. In 1897 over two million people in new York may have received relief.[8] In times of economic expansion, as in 1903, 14 percent of the population of that city lives in distress, and in bad times, as in 1897, the figure is 20 percent. From this it may therefore be estimated that, if one also counts the deserving poor, the number living in poverty in New York and in other large cities would seldom—so the author thinks—fall below 25 percent. In Manhattan, the main part of New York, in the notably prosperous year of 1903, 60,463 families (14 percent of the total) were evicted from their homes. One in every ten persons who die in New York is buried at public expense in Potter's Field.*

---

* *Ed.*—Potter's Field is an American term for a burial ground for paupers or unknown persons, so called after a burial place for strangers in Jerusalem. The Gospel According to St. Matthew, Chapter 27, Verse 7, states: "And they [the chief priests] book counsel, and bought with them

Finally, however, there is yet another infallible sign of the highly developed state of capitalism in the United States; this is the distinctiveness of its national character.

Does the American national character show features that are found universally throughout the entire country? One might doubt it in view of the enormity of the area the country covers, and people who set themselves up as so-called experts on American conditions warn against saying that there is something common to everyone in the country. They say that the differences are as great as those between the individual peoples of Europe and that the American nation really inhabits a continent and not a single country. This wisdom is only superficial. It is true that everything which concerns the character of the countryside is extraordinarily varied in the United States. On the other hand, all institutional matters and in particular the character of the people display a quite startling uniformity. This has been established often enough by real experts, such as Bryce and others, and to anybody who comes into contact with American life and who has the opportunity to look under the surface it must stand out as a special characteristic of the nation. Bryce has convincingly set forth the reasons for this striking conformity in all public institutions in the various individual states of the Union, but what is the source of the homogeneity of the American national character? Or should we not look for an explanation of it, but satisfy ourselves with hypothesizing an idiosyncratic 'American spirit' that dropped out of the blue on to this chosen people for no particular reason and contrary to principles of social causation? We shall be all the less ready to accept this when we cannot really believe in the uniqueness of that exquisite "American spirit."* On closer inspection, we think that we recognize it as an old

---

[the thirty pieces of silver accepted and subsequently returned by Judas Iscariot] the potter's field, to bury strangers in." An idea of what being buried in Potter's Field in New York meant at the turn of the century can be gained from the fate of one of the heroine's lovers in Theodore Dreiser's novel, *Sister Carrie*, which was first published in 1900: "A slow black boat setting forth from the pier at Twenty-seventh Street upon its weekly errand bore, with many others, his nameless body to the Potter's Field."

* *Ed.*—The preceding remarks are almost certainly directed against Hugo Münsterberg, author of *The Americans*, translated by Edwin B. Holt (New York, 1904); this book, originally written in German, was widely read in the period when Sombart was writing. Münsterberg argues that American political life is characterised by "the spirit of self-direction," economic life by "the spirit of self-initiative," intellectual life by "the spirit of self-perfection," and social life by "the

acquaintance who is so familiar to us on Lombard Street or in Berlin West.* Over in America, however, this acquaintance has grown into a purer type and is of more imposing dimensions. We realize that we must seek its source in particular environmental circumstances, as these developed first in Europe and later, but more fully, in America. At the same time we shall thereby explain its uniformity.

However, anybody who examines closely the peculiarities of the American national character must see that its particularly distinctive features have their roots in the capitalist organization of economic life. I want to try to make this credible.

Without doubt and as often recognized, life in a capitalist milieu accustoms the mind to reduce all transactions in the sphere of economic life to money or to para-economic relationships, as is a requisite of this type of economic organization; that is, one takes monetary value as the criterion of measurement, particularly in the evaluation of things and of people. It is evident that, when conduct of this kind becomes adopted and continues for generations, sensitivity for merely qualitatively determined value must gradually diminish. As far as objects are concerned, feeling is lost for anything that is merely beautiful or perfectly formed—that is, for anything which is specifically artistic and which cannot be defined, measured or weighed in quantitative terms. When evaluating things Americans demand that they be either functional and pleasant (as implied by the word 'comfort'), or obviously expensive. Their taste for things of material value is borne out by the fact that all décor in the United States is overdone; this applies to everything from ladies' clothes to the reception areas of a fashionable hotel. If the amount of money that something costs is not immediately evident, then, without more ado, one includes the numerical money-value in one's allusions to the valued object. 'Have you seen the $50,000 Rembrandt in Mr. X's house yet?' is an often heard question. Or, in a newspaper report, 'This morning Carnegie's $500,000 yacht arrived in the harbor from such and such a place.' Among human beings it is natural that one's financial property and income should form the basis of how one is evaluated. Feeling for the unmeasureable uniqueness of personality and for the essence of the indi-

---

spirit of self-assertion."

* *Ed.*—These are references to the financial district of London and Berlin respectively.

vidual disappears.

However, one cannot now overlook the fact that this habit of destroying all qualities by relating them to their measurable monetary value also influences judgments of value in situations where—with the best intentions—it is no longer possible to apply the monetary standard. This habit cannot but evoke a high regard for quantity as such, as an attitude of mind that is encountered in the very center of the American soul. The perspicacious Bryce calls this "a tendency to mistake size for greatness"; there is admiration for every large quantity that can be gauged or measured, whether it be the number of inhabitants of a city, the number of parcels transported, the speed of railway trains, the height of a monument, the width of a river, the frequency of suicides, or whatever. Some people have wanted to explain this "craze for size," which is so characteristic of modern Americans, by means of the sheer size of their country, but why then do the Chinese or the Mongolians from the uplands of Asia not have the same characteristic? Why did the Red Indians not have it, even though they lived on the same vast continent? I put forward the view that, wherever ideas of size develop among such primitive peoples, those ideas have a comical character. They are based on the endlessness of the starry sky, on the boundlessness of the steppe, and what distinguishes them is precisely the fact that they cannot be quantified. The estimation of size in terms of numbers has been able to take root in man's heart only through the medium of money as employed by capitalism (not through money itself, as Simmel erroneously believes.)* The huge dimensions of the American continent have certainly encouraged this characteristic, but the feeling for numbers had first of all to be awaked before it was possible to transform geographical ideas into sizes comprehensible in numerical terms.

Anyone who has been accustomed to value only the quantity of a phenomenon will be inclined to compare two phenomena with each other in order to measure one against the other and thus to attribute to the bigger one the higher value. If one of two phenomena becomes the

---

* *Ed.*—Sombart is referring to Georg Simmel's *Philosophie des Geldes* [*Philosophy of Money*] (Leipzig, 1900). See also Simmel's "The Metropolis and Mental Life," in *Cities and Society: The Revised Reader in Urban Sociology*, ed. Paul K. Hatt and Albert J. Reiss, Jr. (New York, 1957) pp. 635–46.

bigger one during a certain period of time, we call that being successful. Unfortunately the German language cannot express the ideas of both 'size' and 'greatness' in a single word, but the sense of something being big in quantitative terms necessarily goes hand in hand with a high estimation of its success; again, this is a conspicuous feature of the American national character. Being successful, however, means being ahead of others, becoming more, achieving more, and having more than others: in short, of being 'greater.' According to this principle the success that is valued most is that which can be expressed purely in terms of numbers, i.e., the accumulation of riches. Furthermore, even the non-merchant is assessed first of all on the strength of *how much* he has known how to make of his talent. If this test does not result in a satisfactory income, there is no alternative but to take the amount of his fame as the measure of his worth.

The particular emotional reactions being dealt with here are shown perhaps most clearly by the position that the Americans take towards sport. On this subject they are really interested only in the question of who will win. In New York I was present at a mass gathering where a match being fought out as far away as Chicago was transmitted live to the expectant crowd by telegraph as it was going on. The excitement was based only on the tension of wondering which side would win. It is the function of betting to increase this tension: by this the whole activity of sport is again cheerfully reduced to pure cash terms. Can one imagine betting in a Greek stadium? Certainly not. What above all else made everybody happy there was joy both in unquantifiable individual achievement and in personal beauty and strength, and these can be valued just as much in the loser as in the winner. Likewise, would betting be conceivable at a Spanish bull fight? Of course not. However, the women throw their jewelry and the men throw expensive clothes to the torero who knows how to deliver the lethal stroke with elegance and *grandeza*. That is artistic appreciation!

However, the particular character of judgments about value determines how the individual's will operates. If the American prays before the god of Success, he strives to lead a life acceptable to his god.[9] We therefore see in every American—beginning with the paperboy—restlessness, yearning, and compulsion to be way and beyond other people. Neither the enjoyment of life in comfort to the full nor the fine harmony of a personality at peace with itself can be the American's ideal in life; instead, this ideal is constant self-advancement. From this follow haste, restless striving, and ruthless competition in all areas, since, when all individuals are bent on success, each must aim to come ahead of the rest. Thus there begins what one might call a steeplechase, or a search for Good Fortune, as—in somewhat superficial manner—we are wont to express it. However, this steeplechase is different from all other races because the winning-post does not stay still but for ever retreats farther ahead of the advancing runners. We described this striving as restless, but perhaps limitless would be even more appropriate. Any striving after quantities must be limitless because that sort of striving recognizes no limit.

This competitive psychology produces a deep-seated need for freedom of movement. One cannot view one's goal in the face of life and wish to be bound hand and foot. Hence the challenge of *laissez-faire* belongs to those American dogmas and maxims that one cannot help but encounter "when sinking a shaft, so to speak, into an American mind," as Bryce expresses it. However, I should like to explain the general pervasiveness of this basic idea in a slightly different way from Bryce. The aversion from all official supervision from above and from all State intervention, embodied as the "doctrine of non-interference by government with the citizen," certainly originated in a purely doctrinaire, idealistic, and rational spirit among the men of 1776. Yet the modern American now cares only a little for the so-called "exalted principles" of the framers of the constitution, since such principles have no decisive bearing upon his everyday life. If he still clings obstinately to the *laissez-faire* principle, this is because he feels instinctively that this is the only correct guideline for anyone striving for success. The American is really undoctrinaire, and he will readily sacrifice this principle if doing so does not block the path of his advancement. This may be seen from the fact that the same Americans who have written on to their national standard the "unabridged activity of the individual"* sometimes have not the slightest hesitation in limiting in a quite inconsiderate manner the freedom of the individual,[10] or in setting up communist arrangements, the sight of which would make the hair of every liberal Lord Mayor in Germany stand on end.[11]

* *Ed.*—This seems to be a reference to Amendment XIV of the Constitution, which forbids states to "abridge the privileges or immunities of citizens of the United States."

For the average American being successful means first and foremost becoming rich. This explains why that restless striving, which we recognized as an essential part of the American national character, is applied before all else to economic life. In America the best and most energetic people apply themselves to financial careers, whereas in Europe[12] they go into politics. In the mass public an excessive valuation of economic matters develops for the same reason, namely because people believe that in this sphere they can most easily reach the goal for which they strive. By economic matters I mean the capitalist economy whose symbol as it were is the stock certificate that is traded on the Stock Exchange. By participating in speculation on stocks and commodities, the mass public seeks to grab hold of the wheel of fortune where the lucky winnings are found. There is no other country on earth where the public is so involved in the business of speculation as in the United States; there is no country where the population so thoroughly wants to enjoy the fruit of capitalism.[13]

Our observations have now completed a full circle. We started with the subject of capitalism, from which we tried to derive essential elements of the American national character. We see now how the action of this national character itself contributes to the strengthening and development of the capitalist system; thus the unique American spirit is always being reborn from itself, and it is always being transformed into a purer manifestation of the *spiritus capitalisticus purus rectificatus*.

Socialism in the United States

What I have presented in the preceding pages was definitely not intended to describe the American economy (I hope to find the opportunity for this in later studies), and even less was it intended to depict American civilization: furthermore, I never had any intention of giving a full portrayal of the American national character. Of course, much broader foundations would be needed for all those matters. In fact, the only purpose of those lines was to show circumstantial evidence of the existence in the United States of capitalism in an extraordinarily highly developed state. I hope that this is now regarded as having been demonstrated successfully, even if the 'sympathetic reader' has not been ready to follow me on all the digressions.

Quite the contrary, this evidence is merely meant to serve as the starting point for some observations that I want to make on the American proletariat. We know that the position of the wage-laboring class is conditioned by the character of capitalist growth and in particular we have learned both that all social movements have their origin in the situation created by capitalism, and also that modern Socialism is only a response to capitalism. We should therefore obviously start from a consideration of the economic situation if we want to obtain an explanation of the mode of existence of the proletariat in any country. However, this procedure proves itself especially fruitful in the case of the United States. That is to say, in this way we arrive most easily at a clear statement of the problem and are thus saved from the risk of writing without a plan on everything and anything. Let us then proceed.

If, as I have myself always maintained and often stated, modern Socialism follows as a necessary reaction to capitalism, the country with the most advanced capitalist development, namely the United States, would at the same time be the one providing the classic case of Socialism, and its working class would be supporters of the most radical of Socialist movements. However, one hears just the opposite of this asserted from all sides and in all sorts of tones (of complaint if by Socialists, of exultation if spoken by their opponents); it is said that there is absolutely no Socialism among the American working class and that those who in America pass as Socialists are a few broken-down Germans without any following. In fact, an assertion of this kind cannot fail to awaken our most active interest, for here at last is a country with no Socialism, despite its having the most advanced capitalist development. The doctrine of the inevitable Socialist future is refuted by the facts. For the social theorist as well as for the social legislator nothing can be more important than to get to the root of this phenomenon.

To begin with, we must ask whether the statement that there is *no* Socialism in the United States, especially no *American* Socialism, is actually correct. Now, if taken as absolutely as that, it is undoubtedly false.

First of all, there is one or, more precisely, there are two social-democratic parties, in the sense understood throughout continental Europe, that are by no means supported only by Germans. At the Unity Convention of the Socialist Party at Indianapolis in 1901 only

25 of 124 delegates, i.e., about 20 percent, were foreign-born.* At the last Presidential election this party achieved 403,338 votes,† to which are to be added perhaps 50,000 votes for the Socialist Labor Party. Thus, in the United States in 1904 there were about as many social-democratic votes cast as in Germany in 1878‡ or as were cast for the Freisinnige Vereinigung [Liberal Alliance] and the Anti-Semites together in the last election for the Reichstag.§ However, this figure of the Socialist votes in America undoubtedly represents a minimum of the workers with Socialist sympathies, the reasons for which will be given later. Contrary to the situation in Germany, the number of such workers is considerably greater than the votes cast in elections.

What cannot be denied, however, is that the assertion that the American working class does not embrace Socialism is largely true.

This is the primary significance of the election statistics just quoted.

---

* *Ed.*—Sombart has taken these data from Morris Hillquit, *History of Socialism in the United States* (New York 1903); they are to be found on p. 309 of the 5th edition of the book, published in 1910.

† *Ed.*—Many of the vote-totals given by Sombart at various places throughout the book invariably differ slightly from those given in several modern standard sources such as, for example, *The New York Times Encyclopedic Almanac*, 1971 (New York, 1970) 140–3. The size of these discrepancies is always inconsequential.

‡ *Ed.*—The year 1878 saw the passage of the so-called Socialist Law, which made propaganda activities by the Sozialistische Arbeiterpartei Deutschlands [Socialist Workers' Party of Germany] illegal until 1890. In the Reichstag elections of 30 July 1878 the Party polled 437,100 votes, nearly 8 percent of the total number cast nationally. (Sozialistische Arbeiterpartei Deutschlands was the official name of German Social Democracy from 1875 to 1891, when it became the Sozialdemokratische Partei Deutschlands [Social Democratic Party of Germany].)

§ *Ed.*—When Sombart was writing this work, the Freisinnige Vereinigung was a liberal-left group in German politics; it was formed when the Deutschfreisinnige Partei [German Liberal Party] split in two in 1893 after an internal difference on military policy, the other party emerging from the split being the Freisinnige Volkspartei [Liberal People's Party]. In the Reichstag elections of 16 June 1903 the Freisinnige Vereinigung received 243,200 votes, 2.6 percent of the total vote.

By 1906 the Anti-Semites had evolved into basically two groups, the Christlichsoziale Partei [Christian Social Party] and the Wirtschaftliche Vereinigung [Economic Alliance]. The former was the parent anti-Semitic party in German politics, having been founded in 1878, while the latter was an amalgamation of various political groups that had originally split from the Christlichsoziale Partei in 1889 and 1890, had united and divided from each other during the 1890s, only to unite with other small groups into the Wirtschaftliche Vereinigung in 1903. In the 1903 elections the Anti-Semites received 244,500 votes altogether, 2.6 percent of the total vote. At the same election the Sozialdemokratische Partei Deutschlands received 3,010,800 votes, 31.7 percent of the total cast.

One may add considerably to these figures in order to obtain the actual number of Socialists, but even so one will still be dealing with a disappearing minority. The votes cast for the Socialist Presidential candidate in 1904 amount to about 2.5 percent of the total number of votes, and moreover that is the result of only the most recent election. In the 1900 election the Socialist Party achieved only 98,417 votes. Added to this is the fact that these Socialist votes are by no means stable. They fluctuate quite considerably from one year to another, as is evident from the following examples. Votes cast for certain candidacies of the Socialist Party are shown in Table I.*

I shall also try later to give an explanation for the quite remarkable phenomenon of the unpredictable rising and falling of these election figures. For the time being it need only be pointed out, in order to show on what weak foundations the Socialist Party in the United States rests at the moment, even where it has already gained ground.

However, the conclusion suggested by the election figures is now confirmed as being correct by a series of indubitable supporting facts.

The assertion with which we began therefore gains credibility: namely, the broad cross-section of the American proletariat, and precisely those holding an instrumental orientation both among the wage laborers and in particular among the skilled workers, do not embrace Socialism, nor do the most important of their leaders, who (among the more renowned leaders of the national unions) are the great majority. However, this too is to be taken with a grain of salt.

---

* *Ed.*—Several editorial comments upon the data in Table I are in order. One or two of the declines from previously higher vote-totals, e.g., in Chicago and New York, are clearly due, at least in part, to the usual decline in turnout in off-year elections. The decline in the absolute size of the Socialist vote in Texas between 1902 and 1904 is due largely to the fact that the state restricted suffrage by adopting a poll tax by constitutional amendment in 1902, which would have substantially influenced turnout for the first time in 1904. However, there had been a steady decline in turnout in Texas elections since the Populist peak of 1896; see V. O. Key, Jr., Southern Politics in State and Nation (New York, 1949) 534–5. In a later passage Sombart discusses the case of Colorado between 1902 and 1904.

The Southern states of Alabama and Texas still produced far from negligible support for the People's party, even in the period under review. In the South there was a certain mutual substitutability between the People's Party and the Socialist Party, and this worked to the disadvantage of the latter in the period being considered. In 1900 the People's Party's Presidential candidacy won 2.6 percent of the vote in Alabama and 5.1 percent in Texas; in 1904 the respective percentages were 4.6 and 3.4 percent.

TABLE 1

Votes cast for and percentages of the vote received by various candidacies of the Socialist Party of America (sometimes called the Social Democratic Party) in selected states and cities from 1900 to 1905[a]

	1900 (President)	1902 (Governor)	1903 (Treasurer)	1904 (President)	1905
Alabama	928 (0.6)	2,313 (2.4)	—	853 (0.8)	—
Colorado	684 (0.3)	7,431 (4.0)	—	4,304 (1.8)	—
Massachusetts	9,716 (2.3)	33,629 (8.4)	—	13,604 (3.1)	—
Pennsylvania	4,831 (0.4)	21,910 (2.0)	13,245 (1.6)	21,863 (1.8)	—
Texas	1,846 (0.4)	3,513 (1.0)	—	2,791 (1.2)	—
City of Chicago	—	—	—	44,331[b]	23,323[c]
Greater New York[d]	—	—	—	24,600 (3.8)	12,000[c]

Table Notes

a. *Ed.*—The percentages of the vote received by the Socialist Party candidates and the designations of the offices concerned have been added by the Editor after consultation with data on election results given in The World Almanac and Encyclopedia, 1902–5 (New York, 1902–5). In some cases there are slight, but usually insignificant, discrepancies between Sombart's vote-totals and those of the Almanac. Sombart himself must have taken several results in this selection from the Almanac. Most of the others almost certainly were taken from a compilation by A.M. Simons called 'The Socialist Outlook' in International Socialist Review, v (1904–5) 203–17.

Whether Sombart has been particularly fair in his selection of examples for this table might be a subject for considerable debate. With the possible exception of Massachusetts none of the states chosen had or came to have any great reputation for Socialist strength. On the other hand, Illinois cast 6.4 percent of its Presidential votes for the Socialist candidate in 1904. In Milwaukee County, part of which is conterminous with the City of Milwaukee, the Socialist Presidential percentage was 26.0 percent in 1904.

b. *Ed.*—Neither the relevant issue of the Almanac nor the compilation in the International Socialist Review gives results for the City of Chicago only, but in 1904 the Socialist Presidential candidate received a total of 47,743 votes in the whole of Cook County, where Chicago is located; this is 16.9 percent of Cook County's Presidential vote in 1904.

c. *Ed.*—Because access to appropriate sources could not be secured, it was not possible to calculate the percentages of the total vote represented by the 1905 totals nor to ascertain the offices for which these votes were cast, although in each case it was probably for the Mayoralty.

d. The vote-totals for Greater New York have been rounded to the nearest hundred.

Not embracing Socialism does not mean that, like the old English pure trade-unionists, they are disposed to free-trade and free-market principles [*manchesterlich*] and abhor all State intervention or State-socialist reforms.* Today the vast majority of organized workers and their leaders rather favor 'political action', that is, an autonomous workers' politics. Among the demands that the American Federation of Labor[14] wants to be made law are the following:

3. the introduction of a legal work-day of not more than eight hours;
8. the municipal ownership of street-cars, water-works, and gas and electric plants;
9. the nationalization of telegraphs, telephones, railroads, and *mines* [Sombart's emphasis—*Ed.*]; and
10. the abolition of the monopoly system of landholding, and the substitution therefore of a title of occupancy and use only.[15]

This program does indeed mean a serious shaking of the "foundations of our existing social order." It also raises the question of the sense in which I then feel that those asserting that the American working class does not embrace Socialism are right. If I did not fear causing misunderstandings by employing the recently much used and admittedly somewhat ambiguous word, I should answer that the American worker does not embrace the 'spirit' of Socialism as we now understand it in continental Europe, which is essentially

---

* *Ed.*—Sombart clearly assumes some kind of rank-ordered scale of trade-union radicalism. Least radical are the "old English pure trade-unionists" with their *manchesterlich* principles, who abhor State intervention and State Socialism. Somewhat more radical is the pragmatic or instrumental trade-unionism of most American trade unions (and also of the "older English unions," Sombart says later (Introduction, Note 51)—very confusingly in view of his other characterisation of earlier English unionism). At the radical end of the scale are those trade unions that are trying in some way to promote Socialism.

Subsequent historical scholarship casts probable doubt on the accuracy of some of Sombart's classifying. His inconsistency regarding the older English trade unions has been noted. The attribution to the older English trade-unionists of an adherence to *manchesterlich* principles stems from the classic work of Sydney and Beatrice Webb, *The History of Trade Unionism, 1666–1890* (London, 1894). However, this view has been under revision since at least 1937. The seminal articles on the subject are G.D.H. Cole, "Some Notes on British Trade Unionism in the Third Quarter of the Nineteenth Century," in *International Review for Social History*, II, Leiden, (1937) I–23, and R.V. Clements, "British Trade Unions and Popular Political Economy, 1850–1875," in *Economic History Review*, 2nd Series, XIV (1961) 93–104; see also A.E. Musson, *British Trade Unions, 1800–1875* (London, 1972) 54.

Socialism with a Marxist character. However, I prefer to explain in detail what I mean.

1. One feels that the American worker (a phrase still being used as a short form for the 'modal' American worker whose views are dominant in the bulk of the working class and among its leaders) is not on the whole dissatisfied with the present condition of things. On the contrary, he feels that he is well, cheerful and in high spirits—as do all Americans.[16] He has a most rosy and optimistic conception of the world. Live and let live is his basic maxim. As a result, the base of all those feelings and moods upon which a European worker builds his class consciousness is removed: envy, embitterment, and hatred against all those who have more and who live extravagantly.

2. There is expressed in the worker, as in all Americans, a boundless optimism, which comes out as a belief in the mission and greatness of his country, a belief that often has a religious tinge. The Americans think themselves to be God's chosen people, the famous "salt of the earth."* As he so often does, Bryce hits the nail on the head when he says:

> Pessimism is the luxury of a handful; optimism is the private delight, as well as public profession, of nine hundred and ninety-nine out of every thousand, for nowhere does the individual associate himself more constantly and directly with the greatness of his country.[17]

This means, however, that the American worker identifies himself with the present American State. He stands up for the Star-Spangled Banner. He is "patriotically" inclined, as it would be expressed in the German sense. The disintegrative force that leads to class separation, class opposition, class hatred, and class conflict (i.e., the dissension that was characterized above) is weaker in America than in Europe, while the integrative force that both compels the affirmation of the national political community and of the State and that also brings out patriotism is stronger. Among American workers one therefore finds none of the opposition to the State that is to be found in continental-European Socialism. I think that John Mitchell, the well-known leader

* *Ed.*—This phrase is from the Sermon on the Mount; it is to be found in The Gospel According to St Matthew, Chapter 5, Verse 13.

of the miners, expresses the view of the vast majority of American workers today when he says:

> The unions who do oppose the militia fail to recognize that they, as unionists, are a part of the State,...vested with the right of determining in part the policy of the State. The trade union movement in this country can make progress only by identifying itself with the State.[18]

It does not need to be emphasized here that Mitchell (who I suppose is most representative of the "average worker," of the type standing midway between the extremes) already sees it to be necessary to make concessions to the existence of class consciousness and to the beginning of class antithesis, nor that he has therefore already been reproached by more conservative social legislators for preaching among the workers a "narrow and exclusive solidarity."[19] We are not yet concerned with the issue of establishing "developmental trends" (which will be the major subject of exposition in later sections), but rather with gaining a picture of the situation that mirrors as faithfully as possible the present *status quo*.

3. The American worker is not opposed to the capitalist economic system as such, either intellectually or emotionally. Again I should like to quote what Mitchell says on this point. The passages in his book in which he calls the standpoint of the trade unions towards capitalism purely opportunist run as follows:[20]

> Trade unionism is not irrevocably committed to the maintenance of the wage system, nor is it irrevocably committed to its abolition. It demands the constant improvement of the condition of the workingmen, if possible, by the maintenance of the present wage system, if not possible, by its ultimate abolition.

Mitchell's personal conviction, however, is that this "abolition" does not necessarily need to come about, for "the history of trade unionism in the past seems to indicate that by the aid of the State and by the concerted efforts of workingmen, a vast and wide-spread amelioration of their condition can take place under the present system of wages."

Other noted workers' leaders positively emphasize the community of interests of capital and labor. One such leader has said that "they are partners and should divide the results of industry in good faith and in good feeling," that if "laborers in their madness destroy capital such is the work of ignorance and evil passions," and that the future will again produce the full harmony between capital and labor that is now only temporarily disturbed.[21]

However, I believe that the relationship between the American worker and capitalism is even more intimate than is expressed by these manifestations of friendship and demonstrations of respect. I believe that emotionally the American worker has a share in capitalism; I believe that he loves it. Anyway, he devotes his entire body and soul to it. If there is anywhere in America where the restless striving after profit, the complete fruition of the commercial drive, and the passion for business are indigenous, it is in the worker, who wants to earn as much as his strength will allow, and to be as unrestrained as possible. Hence, only rarely do we hear complaints about the lack of adequate protection against dangers at work; instead, the American worker is ready to go along with these dangers, if protective arrangements might diminish his earnings. We therefore encounter restrictions of output and disputes about piece-work or technical innovations much more rarely than in England, for example. I shall demonstrate still more exactly but in a different context that the American worker puts much more into his work and accomplishes more than his European counterpart. However, the greater intensity put into his labor by the American worker is only the extension of his fundamentally capitalist disposition.

Young Edward J. Gainor, a member of the Executive Committee of the National Association of Letter Carriers, certainly speaks from the heart as far as the great majority of the members of his class are concerned, when—in a lecture on "The Government as Employer"—he expresses his principled aversion to workers being public officials; in doing so, he introduces the following reasons for not favoring the situation of the public official:

1. the public official has no prospect of achieving a "social position" by his own labor, in other words, of managing to become rich;
2. after attainment of the maximum wage or salary, no further increase of efficiency occurs, for in the absence of recognition for his success only an idiot will exert himself more than is strictly necessary;
3. the public official is more restricted as to how he can organize his private life; and

4. the public official is barred from a political career, described by Gainor as an "avenue of human endeavor that offers great attractions for all ambitious Americans."[22]

The particular way in which the working class is organized provides the best evidence that the outlook which we come across in the foregoing and similar statements really is that of the bulk of the American working class, which is ruled by the spirit of business.

As is generally known, four different groups or types of workers' organizations exist today in the United States. Of these, one—the Knights of Labor*—has only a past. The heyday of this organization, which was more related to a guild of freemasons than to a modern trade union, was in the middle of the 1880s. For reasons that are not pursued here, the membership of the Knights of Labor rose from 52,000 in 1883 to 703,000 in 1886, only to drop to almost half the latter figure in 1888. As already stated, the Knights were not a trade union in the modern sense; they did not encourage unions within particular sectors of the economy and they abhorred the strike and similar measures. Today they are on their last legs.

Another group of workers' associations has at best only a future. This is made up of those Socialist-inclined trade unions of the West that are united in the American Labor Union.† Their membership is still small. They represent an oppositional minority and we are not therefore considering them at this point.

A third group has neither a past nor a future, and is also insignificant in the present. This is the Socialist Trade and Labor Alliance, which was founded by Daniel De Leon in 1895 and 1896 in opposition to the trade unions.‡

---

* *Ed.*—The Knights of Labor were first organized as a secret society in Philadelphia in 1869 under the title of the Noble Order of Knights of Labor. The society's membership increased during the 1870s, and its officers made public its existence in 1878. A series of reverses in 1886 led to a rapid loss of membership, partly by desertion into the ranks of the newly formed American Federation of Labor. The Knights were led by Terence V. Powderly from 1879 to 1893.

† *Ed.*—The American Labor Union assumed this title in 1902 when the Western Labor Union, a confederation of trade unions in the Rocky Mountain states and territories that had been founded in 1898, was persuaded by Eugene V. Debs to seek national support and therefore altered its name for this purpose. The American Labor Union recognized the political role of the Socialist Party, and in 1905 it also had delegates present at the founding meeting of the Industrial Workers of the World.

‡ *Ed.*—The Socialist Trade and Labor Alliance was founded by De Leon in opposition to the

Finally, the fourth group, by far the most significant and the only one needing to be considered at present, is made up of trade unions united in the American Federation of Labor. The number of organized workers finding their place in the American Federation of Labor has risen enormously during the last ten years. In 1896 membership was 272,315 and in 1900 it was 548,321, and in 1904 it was 1,676,200, which is more than four-fifths of all organized workers in America.

The character of the trade unions bound together in such a large association is not, of course, homogeneous. Since workers with Socialist opinions who belong to the Socialist Party also participate in the trade-union cause with great eagerness and since a large number of organizations dominated by them are also affiliated to the American Federation of Labor, purely social-democratic viewpoints have a chance to be heard at the annual conventions, as well as ultra-conservative ones on the other side. None the less, as I have already pointed out, the leadership of the Federation lies in non-Socialist hands and the great majority of unions united within it favor the distinctly American viewpoint about the position of the wage laborer that I have sketched above.[23] This specifically American spirit is therefore reflected in their politics.[24] They rely on a purely business approach and this leads them to protect the interests of the occupational groups whom they represent by remaining exclusive and by seeking monopolies, without much regard for the proletarian class as a whole and with even less regard for the underclass of unskilled workers.[25] Consequently, they have a strong tendency to guild-like isolation[26] and so produce what is essentially a vertical structuring of the proletariat, the union of which into a single closed class acting for itself is naturally retarded. This politics of business finds its purest expression in the combinations of the monopolistic trade union and the monopolistic employer in the so-called "Alliances," which are organizations aimed

---

American Federation of Labor and, more particularly, to the Knights of Labor, which De Leon and his supporters had previously joined in an attempt to capture its leadership. The Alliance began after De Leon's formal secession from the Knights of Labor, and it was an auxiliary to his political base, the Socialist Labor Party. By 1898 the Alliance had effectively failed and in 1905 its remnants merged with the Industrial Workers of the World.

Daniel De Leon (1852–1914) was born in Curaçao, was a lecturer in Latin-American diplomacy at Columbia University from 1883 to 1885, and joined the Socialist Labor Party in 1890. He was a part of its leadership from 1891 till his death.

at the common exploitation of the public through a union of the employers and workers of a particular sector of the economy. One can describe these sorts of trade unions as capitalist and can contrast them with the Socialist trade unions; the former are carved from the same wood as capitalism itself and, in both their inclinations and their effects, they are directed to the maintenance and strengthening of the capitalist economic system, rather than to its overthrow. The politics of the Socialist trade unions are also tailored to success in the present, but at the same time they do not lose sight of the proletarian class-movement against capitalism.

Enough has been said to establish that the heart of the American trade-union movement has a capitalist character. "Trade unionism is the business method of effecting the betterment of the wage earner under the highly organized conditions of the modern industrial world."* "Collective bargaining is a business matter." In such statements made by those best acquainted with the American trade-union movement is that movement's spirit unambiguously expressed.

Finally, the attitude of the leading trade-unionists to the efforts of the bourgeois social reformers that have been apparent for some years in the United States shows that the former really do want to lead a hard struggle "for the betterment of the wage earner," but without thereby intending to forsake the capitalist economic system. The very different spirit of the American working class, in comparison with European or at least continental-European workers, shows itself here. American workers feel that they are very much in opposition to the employers as far as the establishment of working conditions is concerned, but they are none the less ready to stand shoulder to shoulder with those members of the bourgeoisie who want to support them in their fight. Furthermore, workers' representatives dine freely and frequently with those employers who are willing to come to an understanding with their workers on the basis of equal rights. Among American workers there is no consciousness of opposition specific to proletarian Socialism which characterizes the great majority of

* *Ed.*—Although Sombart does not say so, this quotation is from Tucker, in *MLB*, No. 33, 239. Sombart has already called this writer a "more conservative social legislator." In its context the statement reads more as the author's belief in what the trade unions should see as their major task in order to assist workers to upward social mobility rather than as a description of what is necessarily the reality.

German workers. Let us say that the relationship of Germany to America is therefore as follows. In Germany it is the minority, and certainly not the élite of the working class, that seeks contact with bourgeois social reformers—say in the Gesellschaft für Soziale Reform [Society for Social Reform]*—while the great majority of organized workers remain in unremitting class conflict with all bourgeois so-called 'friends.' In America the reverse is true. The leading trade-unionists (and behind them undoubtedly stand the élite of the organized working class) commune with non-partisan social reformers and with reformist employers in the National Civic Federation,[27] which roughly corresponds to our Gesellschaft für Soziale Reform, and it is only a small fraction that stands resentfully on the side, whereas in Germany it is the majority.

In this sense one is therefore justified in saying that there is no Socialism in America.

From the theoretical as well as the practical point of view, the interesting problem that follows from this conclusion may now be formulated like this: the United States is the country with the most advanced capitalist development, so that its economic structure represents our future. What Marx correctly stated about England in 1867, we may now apply to America. *De te fabula narratur, Europa* [About you, Europe, is the story being told],† when we are reporting about conditions in America, at least as far as capitalist development is concerned. The country representing our own future now has a basically non-Socialist working class. Does this phenomenon therefore represent our

---

* *Ed.*—The Gesellschaft für Soziale Reform was founded in 1901 as the German section of the International Association for Labor Legislation. It was dedicated to promoting the interests of the "socially endangered and economically weak classes." Its published reports and findings did have some influence on German social policy, especially before 1914.

† *Ed.*—This Latin sentence was not used by Sombart fortuitously. It had been used by Marx, without "*Europa*," in his preface to the first German edition of *Capital*, when he was trying to convince his German readers of the relevance to them of his book, despite the fact that most of his examples were English ones:

> However, in case the German reader should self-righteously shrug his shoulders at the conditions of English industrial and agricultural workers or should take solace himself by believing optimistically that things are not nearly as bad in Germany, I must call out to him: *De te fabula narratur*!

See Karl Marx and Friedrich Engels, *Werke* [*Works*] (Berlin, 1964) Vol. 23, 12.

future *too*? Were we wrong to regard the rise of Socialism as a necessary phenomenon in the wake of capitalism? The answer to these questions demands an examination of the reasons that have led to the distinctive mode of thought of the American worker. Our conception of the nature of scientific method prevents us from being satisfied in explaining this by reference to a specifically "American spirit." Instead we shall seek to trace the reasons for its existence by making it our business to establish first of all the conditions of life peculiar to the American proletariat—as viewed from a historical, a political, an economic, and more generally, a social perspective. Once we have understood those conditions and have succeeded in using them to explain the disposition of the American worker, a further question faces us. On what substructure do these conditions of life rest? Is this substructure to be regarded as permanently established, and will it support for ever the structure that is rising on it today; or does it threaten to totter, and along with it the superstructure? To state the matter plainly: are the conditions of the American worker lasting and permanent—either as being specifically American or as lying in the general direction of capitalist development—or are those conditions linked to postulates that are subject to alteration? If the latter is the case, will the alteration be such that the conditions of life turn out to be the same as or similar to those in Europe (which have already produced Socialism), so that the ground in America will be prepared for Socialism? Stated more generally, is there a tendency towards unity in the modern social movement, or must we deal with movements taking different forms in different countries? If there is a tendency towards unity, is this in the direction of Socialism or away from it? Will the future social structures of Europe and America turn out the same or different? Is America or Europe the 'land of the future'?

Notes

1. United States, Fifty-Eighth Congress, House of Representatives, *Forty-second Annual Report of the Comptroller of the Currency, 1904* (Washington, D.C., 1904) 151–2.
2. Ibid., 142.
3. John Moody, *The Truth About the Trusts: A Description and Analysis of the American Trust Movement* (New York, 1904). This book is very useful because it compiles some extremely valuable material from such primary sources as

prospectuses, business reports, balance sheets, and so on. [The book was reprinted and re-issued in 1968—*Ed.*]

4. James Bryce, *The American Commonwealth*, 2nd ed. (London, 1889), 2 vols, II 531.
5. See Charles B. Spahr, *An Essay on the Present Distribution of Wealth in the United States* (New York, 1896) 56, as well as books, *Social Unrest*, 163, and Robert Hunter, *Poverty* (New York, 1904) 21–7, 44. [The 1900 edition of Spahr's book was reprinted and re-issued in 1970. Hunter's book has also been reprinted and re-issued as *Poverty: Social Conscience in the Progressive Era*, ed. Peter d'A. Jones (New York, 1965).—*Ed.*]
6. Of course, a working-class city like Berlin or Vienna is totally out of place in discussions of businesses of this kind.
7. It lacks the broad theoretical sweep that has made Engels' book a landmark in the development of the social sciences. [Florence Kelley's review to which Sombart refers appeared in *American Journal of Sociology*, X (1905) 555–6. Florence Kelley (1859–1932) had been General Secretary of the National Consumers' League since 1899 and was an Associate Editor of *Charities*. She had translated Engels' *The Condition of the Working Class in England* into English.—Ed.]
8. This figure is based on official research by the New York State Board of Charities. There are probably many cases of duplication. Otherwise it really would be dreadful.
9. *In Our Benevolent Feudalism* (New York, 1902) 159–60, W. J. Ghent writes:

> With all ranks and conditions Success becomes the great god; and as though there were not already priests and votaries enough for his proper worship, a special class of publications has recently arisen, which serve as his vowed and consecrated ministers. These teach to the devout but unsophisticated followers of the great god the particular means best adapted to win his grace; how his frown may be averted; or, if his anger is kindled, by what penances and other rites he is to be propitiated. They chant the praises and recite the life-incidents of those who have been most conspicuously blessed and to all the rest of mankind they shout, "Follow our counsel, and some day you shall be even like unto these."

10. We would never let some of these things happen in our so-called autocratically governed Germany. One thinks of the legal impediment in the U.S.A. to the partaking of alcohol.
11. For example, the free supply of all educational materials to all children in the New York public-school system.
12. This is even more true of the Romance-speaking countries and of England than it is of Germany. In Germany, as I have tried to show elsewhere, conditions analogous to those in America predominate in this respect, even though they grew from quite different roots.
13. Nobody has recognized this more clearly than James Bryce; see *American Commonwealth*, II 534–5, 540. I cannot stop myself from reproducing the appropriate passages because, when Bryce sees such things, they are expressed as clear as day.

> In the United States a much larger part of the population, including professional men as well as business men, seem conversant with the subject,

> and there are times when the whole community, not merely city people but also store keepers in country towns, even farmers, even domestic servants, interest themselves actively in share speculations... In many country towns there are small offices, commonly called 'bucket shops', to which farmers and tradesmen resort to effect their purchases and sales in the great stock markets of New York... But go where you will in the Union, ... you feel bonds, stocks and shares in the atmosphere all around you. *Te viente die*—they begin the day with the newspaper at breakfast: they end it with the chat over the nocturnal cigar... The habit of speculation is now a part of their character, and it increases that constitutional excitability and high nervous tension of which they are proud.

14. This is the representative body of the great mass of American trade unions and is led by the conservative Mr. Gompers; up to nine-tenths of its Executive Council is made up of anti-Socialist trade-union leaders. [Samuel Gompers (1850–1924) was President of the American Federation of Labor from its formal founding in 1886 to his death, with the exception of 1895, when he was defeated for the Presidency.—*Ed.*]
15. The political programme was accepted in this form at the annual convention of the American Federation of Labor in 1894; the eighth and ninth planks were accepted unanimously. At the next year's convention a resolution was then passed which stated that the Federation has no political programme as such, since what had been proposed on an advisory basis in the previous year had admittedly been accepted in all its individual points, but not as a whole. The Federation had therefore established only "legislative demands." This alters nothing as far as we are concerned.
16. Those knowing the worker's psyche well speak of an "air of contentment and enthusiastic cheerfulness"; this phrase was written by Professor William G. Sumner and is quoted in Ghent, *Our Benevolent Feudalism*, 122–3. [Actually, Ghent's precise quotation from Summer is: "'An air of contentment and enthusiastic cheerfulness... characterizes our *society* [Editor's emphasis],' writes Professor William G. Sumner, of Yale, in a recent number of *The Independent*." Moreover, Ghent himself was highly critical of Sumner's description; see *Our Benevolent Feudalism*, 174. Kipnis describes Ghent as a member of the Center faction of the Socialist Party in the latter years of the Party's history; see Ira Kipnis, *The American Socialist Movement, 1897–1912* (New York, 1952) 204.—*Ed.*]
17. Bryce, *American Commonwealth*, II 334.
18. John Mitchell, *Organized Labor: Its Problems, Purposes and Ideals and the Present and Future of American Wage Earners* (Philadelphia, 1903) 219. [John Mitchell (1870–1919) was President of the United Mine Workers of America from 1898 until his forced retirement at the hands of miners of bituminous coal in 1907.—*Ed.*]
19. See William Jewett Tucker (President of Dartmouth College, Hanover, New Hampshire), "Labor and Education," in *Massachusetts Labor Bulletin*, No. 33 (Sep. 1904) 237–42.
20. Mitchell, *Organized Labor*, 415.
21. From a speech by the young Secretary-Treasurer of the Minnesota Federation of Labor, W.E. McEwen, entitled "The Future Relations of Labor and Capital," in *Public Policy, Employers and Employes: Full Text of the Addresses Before the*

National Convention of Employers and Employes, with Portraits of the Authors, Held at Minneapolis, Minnesota, September 22–25, 1902 (Chicago, 1903) 247–56. [William Edward McEwen (1874–1933) was Secretary-Treasurer of the Minnesota State Federation of Labor from 1896 to his voluntary resignation in 1914. During most of his period as Secretary-Treasurer he was also editor of *The Labor World*, which was published in Duluth, Minnesota, and he took up full-time duties as its editor after his resignation. He served as Postmaster in Duluth from 1904 to 1908.—*Ed.*]

The reader can find a thorough assessment and exact statement of all the relevant literature in a review that I have given as "Quellen und Literatur zum Studium der Arbeiterfrage und des Sozialismus in den Vereinigten Staaten von America (1902–1904)" ["Sources and Literature in the Study of the Worker Question and Socialism in the United States of America (1902–1904)"], *in Archiv für Sozialwissenschaft und Sozialpolitik*, XX (1905), 633–703.

22. Edward J. Gainor, 'The Government as Employer', in *Public Policy, Employers and Employes*, 100–5. [Edward J. Gainor (1870–1947) was elected to the Executive Committee of the National Association of Letter Carriers in 1901, was elected National Vice-president of the Association in 1905, became President in 1914 and remained in this position till 1941. He was Eighth Vice-President of the American Federation of Labor from 1934 and 1943.—*Ed.*]
23. This is true, even if their strength is not reflected in the composition of the Federation's Executive Council.
24. Or, perhaps it would be better to speak of a specifically Anglo-Saxon spirit, for, as far as I can see, the bulk of American unions are essentially indistinguishable in their behaviour from the older English unions.
25. Numerous unions levy high entry fees, which amount to as much as $50 (210M); this is the sum levied on foreigners and others by the Granite Cutters' International Association of America and the American Flint Glass Workers' Union. Most unions limit the number of apprentices. [The first statement is apparently a serious misrepresentation by Sombart. The constitution of the Granite Cutters' International Association of America that was in force in 1906 states:

> Sec. 62. The initiation fee for apprentices presenting themselves at the first regular meeting of the branch after the expiration of their term of apprenticeship, shall be $3. If application is not made as herein stated, they shall be governed by the following section.
>
> Sec. 63. The initiation fee for all others shall be as follows: For an applicant who has served his apprenticeship in North America, but who has never worked in the vicinity of any branches or districts, shall be $10. Applicants from countries outside of our jurisdiction who present a good standing card or certificate paid up to within three months of application, showing membership in an organization of our craft, shall pay $10. Applicants other than those covered by the above provisions of this section, shall pay $25.... Applicants who have worked in opposition to our Association, to be admitted to membership for $50, excepting that in extreme cases the fee to be $75.00.

Monthly dues to this Association in 1906 were $1.00 per month.

Similarly, in Article XVII of the constitution of the American Flint Glass Workers' Union, as revised and adopted by the Union's thirty-second session in 1909, it is stated:

> Sec. 2. A foreigner applying for admission to membership shall be given a trial at work, and must prove his qualifications for membership before being admitted.
>
> Sec. 3. If a foreigner proves his eligibility and presents a union card from an old country organization, he shall be admitted to membership without his name being submitted to the trade and his initiation fee shall be three dollars.
>
> Sec. 4. If a foreigner applying for admission does not hold a union card, his name shall be submitted to the trade, and he shall pay an initiation fee of ten dollars.

The only mention of $50.00 is as a fine to be levied on individual branches who misrepresent the number of votes cast at their meetings. The same Article states:

> Sec. 7. That any Local casting more votes than those present at the meeting, and voting, shall be fined $50.00 and their votes shall not be counted.

It did not prove possible to consult the version of the Constitution actually in effect at the slightly earlier time to which Sombart is referring, but it seems highly improbable that any reductions of initiation fees of the size that would necessarily be involved here were introduced in the 1909 version.—*Ed.*]

26. In America today jurisdictional or demarcation disputes between individual unions actually form the major subject of interest in trade-union circles. In the time of the guilds the individual guilds probably quarrelled with each other much less than do individual trade unions today, since technical innovations were not so frequent in that peaceful period.
27. The National Civic Federation (NCF) was founded for the purposes of bringing employers and workers into personal contact, in order thereby to moderate their differences and, in particular, of intervening as a mediator in strikes. The Executive Committee consists of three parts: there are fifteen employers; there ar fifteen non-partisan members drawn 'from the public'; however, over half are out-and-out capitalists, and in this section belong, among others, Andrew Carnegie, Grover Cleveland, Oscar S. Straus, the Seligman bankers, and James Speyer: finally, there are sixteen workers' representatives, among whom Samuel Gompers and John Mitchell are foremost. The official organ of the NCF engages in the particular sport of reproducing in every issue the photographs of some renowned trade-union leaders next to those of the big employers. [The National Civic Federation grew out of conferences on arbitration and conciliation held in Chicago in 1900 under the auspices of the Chicago Civic Federation. It assumed the title of National Civic Federation in 1901. Andrew Carnegie (1835–1919) was a millionaire steel magnate; Grover Cleveland (1837–1908) was twenty-second and twenty-fourth President of the United States and from 1905 had been majority stockholder in a life insurance company; Oscar S. Straus (1850–1926) was a lawyer who was ex-Minister to Turkey and had been a member of the Court of Arbitration at The Hague since 1902; only one of several Seligman bankers was, in fact, a member of the Federation's Executive Committee—he was Isaac N. Seligman (1856–1917) of the bankers, J. & W. Seligman & Co.; and James Speyer (1861–1941) was also a banker.

    In fact, a few years after Sombart wrote these words the National Civic Federation became a serious source of contention within the American Federation of

Labor between its conservative leadership and their radical opponents. The Civic Federation had the support of the majority of the leaders of labor, but in 1910 the Socialists in John Mitchell's union, the United Mine Workers, forced him to decide which of the two he wanted to belong to. Mitchell chose his union and resigned as head of the Trade Agreements Department of the National Civic Federation. At the American Federation of Labor's 1911 Convention Socialist delegates fought hard to force a severance of ties between the union movement and the Civic Federation; although their motion was defeated by 11,851 votes to 4,924, their 29 percent of this vote shows that Socialists became a far from insignificant minority within the American Federation of Labor. (See Philip Taft, *The A. F. of L. in the Time of Gompers* (New York, 1970) 225–32, and for the standard history of the National Civic Federation see Marguerite Green, *The National Civic Federation and the American Labor Movement, 1900–1925* (Washington, D. C., 1956).)—*Ed.*]

13

Socialism and the Social Movement

The Meaning of Socialism and the Social Movement[#]

Socialism, in the meaning of the word here adopted, is the intellectual embodiment of the modern Social Movement. That, in its turn, is the conception of all the attempts at emancipation on the part of the proletariat—one of the social classes of our time. In order fully to understand the subject under discussion it will be necessary to form a true notion of what is meant by a social class in general, and in particular of the social class which is of special interest to us here.

By the term "social class," then, I understand a social group, the individuals of which are the representatives of some economic system. In using the words "economic system" I mean a given economic order, or an economic condition of things, which is characterized by one or more prominent economic principles. Any economic order is, in my view, the sum-total of all legal and moral ideas which regulate production and distribution for the time being; and economic principles is the name I give to that chain of motives which influence economic activities of individuals. This will become clearer when we apply these abstract ideas to concrete conditions of the present day.

The idea of social classes and the principles underlying them first

[#] This section is taken from the Introduction to *Socialism and the Social Movement* (first published 1909).

arose in France. In France the events of the great revolution, and perhaps to a greater degree those of the restoration and of the July revolution, served as an object lesson to historians, showing them the component parts of modern society. The writings of Guizot, Mignet, and Louis Blanc already contain all that we know today of the origin and characteristics of social classes. Their presentation of the subject has been adopted by writers of other countries, and the Germans still follow, even to the technical terms, along the lines laid down by the great French historians and their German disciples, of whom the most influential were Lorenz von Stein and Karl Marx. Four classes are thus distinguished in modern society:

1. The nobility and gentry, or feudal party, which corresponds roughly to the feudal aristocracy and which in Germany is called the Junker party. These are the representatives of a feudal system of land holding or, in other words, of a patriarchal manorial system.
2. The lower middle class, which I have characterized as the class of manual labourers in the broadest sense, stands for a system of industry organized on traditional lines and much like the guild system in the Middle Ages.
3. The bourgeoisie or middle class *par excellence*, which is the representative of the capitalist system; and the opposite pole to it, the antithesis of the bourgeoisie:
4. The proletariat.*

Our concern is with the last two classes, more especially with the fourth. We must therefore attempt to make ourselves more fully acquainted with them.

But first, in order to give a clearer idea of what is meant by a social class, let me show briefly the differences and the similarities that exist between the social class and other social groups, for which, indeed, the former is often mistaken. The social class may cover part of the same ground as a division into callings or into grades of wealth, but it does not cover entirely the whole of that ground. A shoemaker may be

---

* *Ed.*—Sombart is fond of making fine distinctions, and therefore it is that he separates the middle class into two sections. It is, perhaps, useful to distinguish people whom he places in his second class, the class called by the French *petite bourgeoisie*, from those who form the bulk of the middle class or bourgeoisie proper. He considers these divisions at great length in his *Modern Capitalism*.

at one and the same time a member of the lower middle class (in his capacity as manual labourer), of the proletariat (in his capacity as wage earner) and of the bourgeoisie (in his capacity as manufacturer of boots and shoes). Again, a country gentleman may be as rich as a banker, a small independent manual labourer may be as poor as a member of the proletariat, yet they belong respectively to different social classes. And even where calling and grade of wealth are the same, it does not necessarily follow that two people will belong to one class. A locksmith of the lower middle class, working independently, may be just as wealthy as a minder in a machine factory, who gets a weekly wage.

The greatest impediment to the clear comprehension of the term "social class" is that it is confounded with "political party." A party and a class are by no means identical. A political party comes into being through some chance circumstance. It is held together by some idea sprung from the historical conditions of the day, which acts as a motive power. Often, too, a party continues to exist for no other reason than that it has been existing. The original idea which goes to form a party may be just as much national, religious, constitutional, or humanitarian, as economic. It is true that often enough there is an inner relationship between political party and social class, yet stress must be laid on the fact that as often there is no connection whatever between the two.

It is possible, and indeed it is not infrequently the case, that the same political principles (e.g., the demand for full political freedom) are in the programme of different classes (e.g., of the bourgeoisie and of the proletariat). The same applies to religious conceptions. For example, the nobility and gentry, the lower middle class, and often also the bourgeoisie all stand for orthodoxy. Moreover, it is by no means exceptional for a political party to include members of different social classes. One need but recall the Centre Party and the National Liberals in Germany in the eighteen-seventies, or the two great parties in England and in the United States. In the same way, a social class may contain members of different political parties. In Germany, the reactionary lower middle class is represented by the Centre Party and the Conservatives; the proletariat (i.e., the wage-earners) by the Centre and the Social Democratic Party. In the course of our considerations we shall see how important for the trend of the social movement in any country is the relationship which exists between the political parties and the social classes.

The object of these pages, then, is to describe the Social Movement of our age—the efforts, that is, at emancipation on the part of that social class which we have termed the proletariat, and which we have characterized for the present as the opposite pole to the middle class. The middle class in its turn we described as the representative of the capitalist system. The real nature of both classes will therefore be understood only when we have made ourselves acquainted with the economic organization of society which is dominant in our day. But we shall only be able to touch upon one or two of its underlying principles.

Capitalism is based on the private ownership of all commodities, and therefore also of those which are required for production—raw material, machinery, factories, land. Historic development has brought it about that production in these days is on a large scale; that is to say, it is carried on by the combination of many labourers under uniform direction. Thus, a thousand men are united to work a mine or a machine-factory, and hundreds to spin or weave in some big establishment. But the same development has also brought it about that those who work together in this way have not the same rights with regard to the means of production. Some own these means of production, and therefore become the directing factors in the work of production, and also owners of the commodities produced. The others, who form the great mass of the workers, are shut out from the possession of the means of production. Hence it follows that, in order to live, they are forced to put their labour power (their only possession) at the disposal of those who do possess the means of production, in return for a money payment. This comes about by way of a wage contract, wherein the labourer, who possesses naught but his labour, agrees with the owner of the means of production, who is on that account the director of production, to undertake to render a certain amount of work in return for a certain amount of pay. When we bear in mind that all production depends on the combination of labour and the material means of production, then the capitalist system of production differs in the first instance from other systems in that the two factors of production are represented by two separate groups, which must meet and combine if a useful product is to ensue. In this the capitalist system differs from, let us say, the craft organization of industry, where the labourers were at the same time the owners of the means of production. But it differs likewise from slavery (where there was also a separation between two social groups) in that in the capitalist system the combination of the two groups comes about by free contract in what is known as the wages contrast.

The capitalist organization of society is characterized by the race for profit and by a peculiar form of mental activity in individuals which I call "economic rationalism." All economic activities are at bottom directed towards the increase of the money which is put into production, or, in technical language, towards the profitable investment of capital. To this end, all the thoughts of the capitalists or owners of the means of production, or of agents paid by them, are occupied day and night in an almost feverish restlessness in order to bring about the most practical and rational shaping of economic and technical processes.

The social class which stands for the interests of the capitalist system is the bourgeoisie, or middle class. It is made up, in the first place, of capitalist employers, and in the second, of a large number of people whose interests are similar to those of the capitalist employers. I am thinking of the following elements: (1) All those who are economically independent (or who would like to be so), and are intent on profit-making, and who, moreover, desire a free legal system favorable to profitmaking. That would include many shopkeepers, property-owners, agents, stock-jobbers and so on, and also the more modern of peasant proprietors. (2) All those who are not economically independent, but are associated with the capitalist employer in his activities, mostly as his representatives; and, as a rule, they participate in his economic success. That would include paid directors of companies, managers, foremen in large businesses and people like them. I have calculated that in Germany there are of people of this kind, who, of course, belong to the bourgeoisie, some 2 1/4 to 2 1/2 millions, i.e., about 3 to 5 per cent of the population.

The class at the opposite pole to this—the one cannot be thought of without the other—I have called the proletariat,—the social class with which we are concerned here. In order to get a true conception of this class we must free ourselves from the picture of a ragged crowd which the term brought to mind before we read Karl Marx. The term "proletariat" is now used in a technical sense to describe that portion of the population which is in the service of capitalist employers in return for wages, and elements akin to them. The word in this meaning is taken from French writers, and was introduced into Germany by Lorenz von Stein in 1842.

Now who are these modern proletarians? How is their position distinguished? What is the goal of their attempts at emancipation, which we call the Social Movement?

The free wage-earners form the bulk of this class—all such persons as are employed in capitalist undertakings, leaving out, of course, those mentioned above as belonging to the bourgeoisie because their interests are bound up with the capitalist system. I have attempted to fix their number for Germany, and conclude that it must be at most some seventeen millions, i.e., about a third of the population. When, in 1847, Marx said: "The proletarian movement is the independent movement of the frightfully large majority for their own interests," it was, perhaps, even for those days and for the whole of western Europe, a "frightfully large" exaggeration, at least when the term "proletariat" was taken in a narrow sense. But the picture becomes entirely different when to the true proletariat, to the full-bloods, are added the innumerable half-bloods—the poorest class of the population, *il popolino*— and also those amongst small farmers and mechanics who live the life of the proletariat, as well as the lowest grade among officials, such as those in the Post Office. When the meaning of the term is thus extended, it includes, for Germany, the whole of the so-called lower or working classes, numbering some thirty-five millions, or over two-thirds of the population. This is not the "frightfully large" majority of the population, but it is certainly very large. In other countries where production is based on the capitalist system, the conditions are no different.

Of the nature of the proletariat I can give only one or two hints here. From these it will be seen what influence the condition of this social class has on the movement of which its members are the agents. I deal with the whole subject fully in my work, *Das Proletariat*, which was published in 1906.

I have already pointed out that in order to get a true conception of the proletariat we must give up the idea of a ragged crowd. Indeed, the life of the proletarian is not always intolerable. Absolute distress is in no way a special characteristic of the class, though, to be sure, there are within it innumerable instances of want. But few proletarians are as badly off as the Russian peasant, or the Chinese coolie, or the Irish tenant, none of whom belong to the proletariat. Many a wage-earner, even in Europe, earns more than a University teacher, and in America the average income of this class falls not much below the maximum salary of an extraordinary professor* in Prussia.

And so, when we see the proletariat moving in order to emancipate itself, when we see that the movement is accompanied by feelings of hate, envy, or revolt, the cause of all this cannot be actual want.

It is probably much more the contrast which the worker observes between his own hard lot and the wealth of many who belong to the class of capitalist employers, wealth which, in his view, he has produced. For it is *he* who toils and moils in their service. This contrast is daily brought to his notice not only when he sees how lavishly wealth demeans itself (the serf in the Middle Ages saw that too), but chiefly because he sees it created afresh daily, because the owners rise to power before his very eyes. On this point Frederick Albert Lange rightly lays stress when he says:

> The feeling of envy never quite vanishes when the poor live beside the rich. It may become blunted in a condition of things which remain long stable. But where there are constant changes, and where the prevailing differences are brought more and more to the front, the feeling of envy becomes very strong. In addition to this (objective) uncertainty of all possession in this age of ours which the proletarian observes, there is the (from the point of view of the proletariat, subjective) uncertainty of the conditions of his existence—the fact that he is not sure today whether he will continue to be able to earn his living to-morrow. For a depression befalling the whole of the economic activities of our time may lead to much unemployment, and so increase the ranks of the hungry.

These constant changes bring home their position to the working classes. The spread of education and intelligence, to which town life contributes no small share, enables them to think about the changes, and about the cause also of the contrast between their own position on the part of the wage-earners. The secret reason is no other than this:

---

* *Ed.*—There are in Germany three stages through which a man generally passes to become a full University professor. He begins by being Privatdocent, when the University gives him a licence to teach, but no salary. The second stage is that of Professor-Extraordinary, and carries a salary with it. Then comes the Ordinary Professor, who, of course, receives a higher salary, and also has a voice in the government of the University.

that all the peculiarities of their life have their root not in any natural, unchangeable conditions, but in the special conditions of social organization, in the peculiar form of the prevailing economic system. "No man can put forth any special claim in the face of Nature, but in Society want at once becomes an injustice either to this social class or to that" (Hegel). Here we have the foundations on which a social movement can arise, for here we have something which may be attacked, viz. the existing social order.

As this criticism of the social order becomes keener, and as dissatisfaction and the wish for better things become stronger, another consideration naturally appears which weighs heavily on the proletariat—they feel their dependence on their masters. This is no longer a legal dependence, as it was in the days of slavery; but it is no less complete. It shows itself in the fact that the worker must look to the capitalist employer for employment, or he must starve. Hence, the complete subordination of the worker to the orders of the employer. Sometimes this subordination is colored by medieval ideas, as when the factory owner regards himself as a kind of patriarch to "his people," and intermeddles in their private affairs. Sometimes, too, the same feeling is exercised in the sphere of politics, when the capitalist class uses its influence to lessen the share of the proletariat in the activities of the State and in the work of government.

These, then, are the causes responsible for the proletarian criticism of the existing social order. But we must look to yet other aspects of the life of the wage-earning class if we are fully to account for the prevailing ideas which are to be found in all the attempts of the proletariat at emancipation. On the one hand, we have the tendency to communist organization of life; and on the other, the tendency to aggregation.

The latter follows immediately from the conglomeration of similarly situated wage-earners side by side, who have no other bond than that of their common work in the service of a capitalist employer; who are like so many grains of sand in a heap, and seldom form a united body outside the factory, except, perhaps, at public meetings. That which capitalism brings together to one spot in the large towns and centers of industry is but a shapeless mass of individuals, who have broken entirely with the past, who have become loosened from all old common bonds—from home, from village, from family—and who commence the new life without any of the ideals of the old. They cling only to the companions whose fate is like their own; who, as individuals, are of no value, and, like themselves, have no longer any tradition to look back upon. The two join hands; they become comrades; and in this way a crowd of comrades is formed, which is distinguished above all else, not by the special qualities of the individual, and not by a common tradition, but by the fact that it is an aggregation of units. Never in all history have so many individuals combined to form a united movement; never in all history was the solid phalanx of the masses so plainly the characteristic of a movement as in that of the proletariat. On all sides is heard the "onward march of the huge labour battalions," with which Lassalle tried to frighten his opponents. To picture the Social Movement of our day to the mind's eye we must imagine a huge wave of humanity, from which scarcely one individual stands out, covering the dry land to the distant horizon. Psychologically, this means that the individual becomes conscious of the enormous power which the masses may wield. The feeling of the modern proletarian as he recalls the fact that he is a member of his class is akin to that which in bygone times filled the breast of the man who belonged to the nobility, to an honored clan, to a great city or to a conquering State, and it is with pride that he declares his allegiance: *Proletarius sum.*

Side by side with this dissolution of all qualitative, or individually colored, differences into the quantitative mass, and having influences in another direction, is the development of modern technical knowledge. Only when we know the special characteristics of this knowledge shall we be able to understand important aspects of the proletarian movement, more especially the tendency to communism.

The socialization of the process of production (by which I mean the increasing specialization and the greater necessity for co-operation in labor) has brought it about that each single commodity is no longer the product of the individual worker, but the result of the combined efforts of many. Formerly the shoemaker who made a pair of shoes was the sole maker of the article in question. The workman in a modern shoe factory, who has only to exercise himself in part of the production of a pair of shoes, has lost all personal relationship to the article as a whole. The process of production in the case of each single commodity is one on communist lines; and so it is an easy matter for the single workmen who combine to produce it to think of the communist organization of the whole of production. In the same way it is easy for the worker, especially if he lives in a city, to think of a common communist basis of consumption, seeing that his surroundings all point in that direction.

The single house, in which purely individualistic tendencies most easily unite, loses all its charm for the poor who live in large common tenements. They feel more and more at home in public places of entertainment, where they can satisfy their intellectual and material wants far better than in their homes. Trade-Union centers, public libraries, concert halls, cafés become new homes for the masses of our large cities. As public buildings, parks, squares, and museums are developed and extended, they are more and more used by the proletariat, especially as the attractions of their individual or family life tend to grow less. Indeed, the family itself breaks up because of the long hours of toil, either in the daytime or at night, outside the home, because of women having to work, and children to begin to work early in life in order to add to the family exchequer. Thus the proletariat is forced by outside influences to forsake their individual interests and merge them in those of the mass.

But to make our view of the modern Social Movement complete we must have regard to the general conditions of our age, amid which this movement is taking place. Here, too, we shall have to content ourselves with a few general remarks. Our age is characterized above all by an intensity of life such as I cannot conceive of any other age. Modern society simply pulsates with life. Much of this is due to the new means of communication which capitalism has created for us. The possibility of arranging business matters in a few hours, despite long distances, by means of the telegraph, or telephone, or newspapers; the possibility of carrying huge masses from place to place by means of the modern methods of transport has brought about a condition of things where a combination of large masses of people is a very simple matter indeed, and has produced within us a feeling, unknown to our grandfathers, of the smallness of space, especially in our large cities where great masses of people move about with ease. At the same time knowledge has increased among the masses, and with knowledge has come demands.

This intensity of life is accompanied by what may be called the nervousness of our time—the restlessness, the haste, the uncertainty of all forms of life. Because of our peculiar economic conditions, this restlessness has made its way into all branches not only of economic, but also of social activity. The age of free competition has brought competition into all walks of life; every one strives to outvie his neighbor, no one rejoices in his portion, and contemplation and its peacefulness are gone for ever.

One other point must be noticed. I mean the revolutionary spirit which is abroad in our time, changing and recasting values in all directions. Everything is in flux—economic activities, science, art, morals, religion; all conceptions are in such an unsettled state that we are beginning to believe there is nothing fixed and everlasting. And here we have one of the most important facts for the explanation of modern social movements. It explains two things. First of all, it accounts for that destructive criticism of all that is established which finds no grain of good anywhere, which throws all former beliefs into the dust-heap and goes to market with new ones. This critical state of mind was already developed in the bourgeoisie; it has been applied to politics, morals, religion and art. The proletariat is only adopting it and applying it to economic and social institutions.

Secondly, the revolutionary spirit above mentioned makes possible the fanatic belief that any wished-for state of things may be achieved. When so much has changed, when such wonders in which no one ever dared to believe have come about before our very eyes, why should there not be more? Why should not all that can be wished for come about? In this way the revolutionary present becomes the feeder of the social Utopia of the future. Edison and Siemens are the spiritual fathers of Bellamy and Bebel.

Here, then, we have the elements out of which Socialism and the Social Movement are built up in our day. We have seen what the starting-point is: the capitalist economic system with the class relationship that exists between the bourgeoisie and the proletariat. We have seen that to this relationship may be traced the origins of discontent and the longing for new conditions, the growth of a will in the proletarian masses, and the wish for emancipation. We have seen the conditions in which the proletarian class live, and from these conditions we have noted not only that there is a tendency to revolt against things as they are, but also the direction in which this revolt is moving (the ideal of a communist organization of society, economically and socially, in which the interests of the masses shall receive their fair share of attention). I use the term proletariat to denote an independent social class striving for this economic system, which, since it has not yet arrived, is an ideal of the future—the economic system which, for the sake of simplicity, we call the Socialist system.

"Socialism and the Social Movement" is but the realization, or attempts at the realization, of this future social state, which shall be more in accord with the needs of the proletariat.

Socialism seeks to bring this end about in the world of ideas, and the Social Movement in the sphere of practical politics.

All theoretical attempts to show the proletariat the goal of its efforts, to call upon it to take up the struggle, to organize the struggle, to show it the way along which it must march if it is to succeed—all this is what we understand by modern Socialism. And all practical attempts actually to carry out these ideas we call the Social Movement. Socialism and the Social Movement, therefore, are but two sides of the same phenomenon. Their relation to each other is that of thought and deed, of soul and body.

Our purpose in this book will be to show the growth of this two-sided phenomenon from its very beginning, and to discover the so-called laws of its development. We shall do so impartially, taking no sides in the march of facts before our eyes. We shall observe it all as a botanist observes a plant or a physician an illness—only as an interesting case.

Our aim is thus clearly marked out, and so we shall not attempt to weave into our study all sorts of useless side-issues. We shall keep strictly to the task before us. We shall not include in our considerations all the Socialist theories which have at any time arisen, nor all the Socialist theories of our own day. Only those shall be noticed that have come to have some practical value; that is to say, those which have had some influence on the social changes with which we are concerned. Accordingly, it is not our province to notice Rodbertus any more than to concern ourselves with Carl Marlo or Düring or any number of others.

In the same way it is no concern of ours to pay any attention to movements for improving existing conditions which in these days are often spoken of as "social." I have been blamed for leaving these out of my survey. It has been suggested, for example, that I should have included the Land Reform Movement. I beg to differ. This book has a definite idea in view, and it must be limited to all that bears on the idea, and to nothing else. I might as well have included the Anti-Vaccination Movement, or the Food Reform Movement, or that of the Abolitionists, or of the Housing Reformers, or indeed of any other group of reformers. All these, however, are beyond my scope here. Only those movements which are brought about by the proletariat are of interest to us in this book, and even not all of these, but only such as attempt to replace the Capitalist by the Socialist organization of society. All other Proletarian Movements, which aim at improving the condition of the working classes within the prevailing capitalist order, will be noticed only in so far as they touch, or support, that other great Social Movement.

What I mean by this will become clearer as we go along.

Conclusion#

Let us review the course we have traversed in these pages.

We saw that as a result of the Social and Economic Revolution brought about by Capitalism during the last hundred years or so, a spirit of unrest has filled the minds and hearts of many, and has found its expression in a desire for a new social order and for the liberation of mankind from the bonds of Capitalism. Socialist ideas came into existence. We saw how the proletariat, the class that was oppressed, accepted the ideas with open arms, and how the modern Social Movement then grew up.

It may be asked, have all the attempts at ameliorating the conditions of life ended merely in a great movement of the masses? Has it all resulted in a restless, continued, progressive motion, like some never-ending process? It would seem that our age is in reality characterized in this way; it would seem that Socialism is imitating Capitalism in its restlessness, only that in Socialism the ends are ideal and not material.

But I do not intend to follow up this train of thought. It would lead us too far afield. Perhaps I shall deal with this most important question as to the value of Socialism in the world's development on another occasion. Here I shall only make one or two remarks concerning the

This section is taken from the Conclusion to *Socialism and the Social Movement.*

embodiment of Socialism, concerning the Social Movement, which we have already examined in its various aspects.

I believe that any one looking dispassionately at the movement must come to the conclusion that it was inevitable. Just as the mountain torrent after a rainstorm must rush down from the highest peaks into the valley below, in accordance with nature's unchangeable laws, so, too, the Social Movement could not but march onward. It is a point of the utmost importance to recognize that the movement is one of those great historical processes that happen in the world; to recognize

> that we are all in the midst of one of those powerful movements in the world's history that change human conditions and make their influence felt on States. To want to deny their influence is as absurd as it is foolish to try and combat them with powerless weapons (Lorenz von Stein).

There are still people who imagine that the Social Movement is the work of a few wicked agitators; or that in Germany Social Democracy was called into being by Bismarck's policy. Such views of necessity lead to the conclusion that there must be some magic formula, or a course of action of some kind, that will kill the movement. What a misconception! What ignorance of the real character of the Social Movement! I hope that my consideration of the subject has made it perfectly clear that the Social Movement was an historical necessity.

One would have thought that the recognition of the fact that the Social Movement is inevitable would have had some influence on the practical policy of the ruling classes of today. One would have expected them to perceive that force is unable to sweep away a movement which is brought about by the course of events in history; that if you dam a stream, it does not return to its source, but rather overflows its banks and devastates the country round. But this lesson seems not to have been learned yet. The measures adopted in some countries to prevent the people from participating in political life, the means taken to hinder the growth of the constitution along democratic lines, appear nothing less than ridiculous. The pressure of the steam is not lessened when you close up the ventilators!

But we shall have to recognize even more than that the movement was inevitable. We shall have to accustom ourselves to the thought that the movement has taken the only form possible—that it could not be otherwise than socialistic in its tendencies, and that it could adopt no other means than the class war for their realization. To show this necessity was one of the objects of this book.

It is clear that attempts at the realization of socialist ends by means of the class war will continue to be made in the near future. There can be little doubt, therefore, that the civilization of the future will be shaped by it. We shall thus do well to consider class war a little more in detail, and to ask, What has it in store for us? What duties will it put upon us?

To begin with, we must get as clear a notion as possible of what is meant by class war. We have already spoken of it more than once in these pages; but it is so important that a repetition will perhaps be useful, especially as there are still people to be found in whose souls the word strikes terror. But even where the term is not quite so horrifying, it is still wrongly understood by very many.

Class war is not identical with civil war, as some people would imagine. It does not call up the picture of bloody street fights behind barricades; it has nothing to do with murderous attempts on life; it does not have recourse to dynamite or petroleum. Such a distorted view is probably the result of confusing political with social struggles. Political struggles need not necessarily become civil wars, though history has shown that they have done so in many cases, especially under absolute governments. But in countries with liberal or democratic constitutions civil war is not easily conceivable.

As a matter of fact, the class war has but little in common with political struggles. This is the case even when the latter adopt violent measures, as in Russia today. The political movement in Russia is only very loosely connected with the proletarian class war. It is engineered by a mixed multitude, and its aims are to bring about a constitution which all classes of society demand.

But the socialist movement of the proletariat is striving, as we have seen, for something very different. The movement desires a new social order, desires to replace Capitalism by Socialism. And this, we repeat, can expect nothing from violent political revolutions. Let us assume that all civilized countries had a democratic constitution like that of the United States or Switzerland. The proletariat would still have to carry out its programme, namely, to socialize the prevailing capitalist system. Every one must see that violent political action would be of little use. Class war must still remain. Stripped of all accretions, and looked at in its simplest form, it can mean in our own age nothing else but the attempt to safeguard the interests of the proletariat in politics and in economic and social life. Every election where the Socialists have a candidate, every co-operative society with the set purpose of helping the proletariat, every real trade-union is a form of the class war, no more and no less than when the landholding class supports high duties on corn, or when a congress of skilled workers demands the institution of a certificate showing fitness, or when a chamber of commerce petitions for favourable stock-exchange legislation.

Once the old conception of the class war is given up, the belief that was current, that the proletariat are drilling their ranks for a great last blow, must also vanish. There is, of course, no such intention. There is no need for any last blow. The class war goes forward quietly, step by step. As a matter of fact, every effort at social reform or social amelioration is a stage further on the way to the goal. And if Social Democrats are somewhat suspicious of social reforms, it is due partly to their feeling that these are only patchwork which will hinder, rather than help forward, the progress of society towards Socialism; and partly to the belief that these reforms may so improve the position of the working classes that they will become satisfied and lose all desire for the class war. I hold that such an eventuality will never come about. The working classes will never again be satisfied. The better off they are, the more will their demands grow. Such is the nature of the modern man!

But the opposition of Social Democrats to social reform is anything but wise. After all, war of whatever kind has some justification only when it improves the conditions of life in one way or another. But is it fair to sacrifice the well-being of the present generation for the sake of the happiness which it is dreamed will be the lot of future generations? Surely the present also has claims. To improve the lives of those of our own generation is surely as great a duty as that of preparing a better future. Every real improvement in the condition of the working classes is an end in itself. If one sorrow is lessened, and one tear dried, as good a piece of work is accomplished as building up the foundations of a future where there shall be no sorrow and no tears. The popular leaders must see to it that the living are helped; they must look at the present and not always be thinking only of the future. No one will deny that it is a fine thing to inspire the masses with enthusiasm; no one will deny that struggle in itself may be useful. But let us not forget that mankind requires more than this for life; and that to make it possible for men to live lives worthy of humanity is no small achievement.

The duty of the Social Democratic leaders, then, is to support every social reform which tends to ameliorate the lives of the masses, no matter from what quarter it comes, and at the same time to keep their eyes fixed on their final goal. If they do this they will have a practical policy that will be free from the danger of opportunism. Not Socialism *or* Social Reform but Socialism *and* Social Reform will be the policy of the leaders if they are wise.

Bound up with this is the important question which the Social Democratic leaders will have to face: What should be their relation to the non-socialist parties?

Only the old-fashioned conception of the class war could lead to the belief that the proletariat must be in opposition to all other elements of the population. One can understand that a small sect in its early days should wish to remain apart. Small sects usually do. It is important that their member should profess the faith in all its purity, and should be enthusiastic in the cause. Contact with the outside world, and with stronger bodies, has the danger of weakening both the faith and the enthusiasm, and is therefore suicidal. But when a party has increased enormously, the danger appears to be insignificant.

One would have thought that the Socialist movement had reached such a stage of development as to be free from fear of harmful influences from without, and that it would not object, therefore, to unite with other parliamentary parties in case of need. Experience has proved that a combination of Social Democrats with non-socialist groups has in no way endangered the idea of the class war and the socialist goal. Of course, such a combination pre-supposes the rejection of such antiquated ideas as that of "the great day," or "the Dictatorship of the Proletariat," or of "violent revolution." At the same time, it is necessary to be fully conscious of the real value and importance of one's own party. For if, on the one hand, the policy of a party of standing apart is a sign of weakness, it may be due, on the other hand, to an over-estimation of strength. I believe that the Social Democrats in Germany are suffering from this form of conceit. The enormous number of votes cast in their favour at the elections has led them to believe that they have an extraordinary influence in Parliament. But, as a matter of fact, in actual practice their influence is not very large. It is, of course, impossible to judge of the socialist movement in any country merely by the number of socialist votes. If it were possible, we should have to admit that the movement in Germany is stronger than anywhere else. But I believe that quite the contrary is the case. I believe that nowhere in civilized countries has it a weaker position than in Germany, despite its three million votes. Jaurès made this quite clear at the Amsterdam Congress, when he said—

> Europe and the world are oppressed at the present moment by something which is weakening the guarantee of peace, lessening the chances of the realization of political liberty, and hindering the progress of Socialism and of the working classes; in a word, it is a stumbling-block to all political and social progress all over the world. I am thinking not of the compromises made by the French Socialists with the democratic parties in order to help forward freedom and progress and peace. No. It is the political weakness of the German Social Democratic party that is in my mind. (Expressions of surprise on all sides.)
>
> At the Dresden Congress, which was held after the great political victory when three million votes were registered for the party, we expected that you would adopt some definite policy, some course of action. You cried out joyfully in your newspapers, 'The Empire is ours. Ours is the world!' My friends, you were mistaken. The Empire is not yet yours. Why, you are not even certain whether the International Socialist Congress will be allowed to take place in your capital!

There is little doubt that the powerlessness of the German Social Democratic party is due to an exaggerated notion of its strength, and the tendency to gloss over real weakness by fine phrases. Moreover, it has shown itself incapable of combining with other parties in order to bring about certain reforms which were sorely needed.

But we must remember that in all countries (with, perhaps, the exception of Australia) Socialism is today, and will continue to be in the near future, the faith of only a small minority. It would be a good thing if the leaders of the movement took this thought to heart.

One other fact has been ascribed to class war by those who hold antiquated ideas of it. They say that class war meant not human love but human hate. I do not think that is correct. I believe that in the class war it is quite possible to think of our common humanity, and of that which unites all men in one family, as well as of the things which separate them in the social struggle.

The agents in the struggle are men, with the same joys and the same sorrows, for whom God and the world, birth and death, youth and age, love and friendship, fidelity and treachery, health and sickness, all mean the same to those on the one side as on the other, and the social struggle, when all is said, is but a small affair compared with these things.

> See! we hate, we struggle, we are separated by different views and feelings,
> But your hair, like mine, is showing locks of grey.

It is quite possible to respect the man in one's opponent. Have we not all been able to do so in our own experience?

For the class that is striving to restore the old humanistic ideal of humanity, this ought to be an accepted principle. How can it be otherwise? Is it conceivable that the proletariat should hate a portion of their fellow-men until they obtain the power in the State, and then all at once turn their hate into love? Is it possible to be enthusiastic for the idea of a common humanity, and at the same time hate three-fourths of humanity because they hold different political views, or have different economic interests? It is true that the average Socialist in many (not all) countries is an embittered, morose individual, who gives one the impression that he hates all the world. But his appearance and his feelings are not due to the class war. That war can, and ought to be, carried on with clean, and not poisoned, weapons. How much is sinned in this respect on both sides! To speak slightly of one's opponent, or to ascribe low motives to his actions, is hardly necessary, and does not in the least strengthen one's own position. Nay, any one who adopts a policy of war and of struggle, who regards war and struggle as having been the means of bringing about all that has occurred in history, ought to find no difficulty in fighting fairly, and respecting the motives of his opponent, believing that they are just as disinterested as his own.

And why? Because such a man looks on conflict and struggle as being natural, just as much as the thunderstorm is natural. Only he who regards war as something artificial, brought about by wicked men, will think that the motives of his opponents are wicked. But once a man realizes that the class war is inevitable, that it must come from the very nature of social life, that it is nothing but the opposition of two differing opinions, each with its own outlook on life, he will perceive that his opponent is fighting from as good impulses as his own. And so he will be able to respect the man in him. He will not despise or mock him; he will fight him fairly and squarely.

Let us learn this lesson from England, where the opposing forces fight like gentlemen. I trust that this will be the case soon on the Continent also, for a fair fight shows a truer conception of what class war means.

The Germans, more than others, need to learn the lesson which Lassalle taught:

> To treat an opponent fairly and justly is the first duty of a man, and the working classes more than others should specially lay it to heart.

Then, and only then, will the higher feelings in the human breast have the upper hand over man's passions, and the class war will bring not destruction, but the blessings of civilization. Then, and only then, will it be true to say that "war is the father of all things," and therefore also of those that are good.

Index of Names

Subject Index